Illuminating Counsel

Illuminating Counsel

How the Least Holy Books of the Hebrew Bible
Explore Life's Most Important Issues

JONATHAN TERAM

WIPF *&* STOCK · Eugene, Oregon

ILLUMINATING COUNSEL
How the Least Holy Books of the Hebrew Bible Explore Life's Most Important Issues

Copyright © 2021 Jonathan Teram. All rights reserved. Except for brief quotations in critical publications or reviews, no part of this book may be reproduced in any manner without prior written permission from the publisher. Write: Permissions, Wipf and Stock Publishers, 199 W. 8th Ave., Suite 3, Eugene, OR 97401.

Wipf & Stock
An Imprint of Wipf and Stock Publishers
199 W. 8th Ave., Suite 3
Eugene, OR 97401

www.wipfandstock.com

PAPERBACK ISBN: 978-1-5326-7238-5
HARDCOVER ISBN: 978-1-5326-7245-3
EBOOK ISBN: 978-1-5326-7252-1

12/16/20

Unless otherwise indicated, all Scripture quotations are from The ESV® Bible (The Holy Bible, English Standard Version®), copyright © 2001 by Crossway, a publishing ministry of Good News Publishers. Used by permission. All rights reserved.

Inspired by my students

Dedicated to my Aunt Jaynee

Who is this that darkens counsel by words without knowledge? —Job 38:2

Contents

Preface | ix

1. The Writings | 1
2. Why the Least Holy Books are So Stupendous | 20
3. A Very Brief Taste of the Wonders of Biblical Hebrew Poetry | 28
4. A Very Brief Overview of the Psalms | 36
5. Songs without Music (Psalms) | 41
6. The Pursuit of Wisdom (Proverbs) | 69
7. Darkening and Illuminating Counsel (Job) | 99
8. A Celebration of Kindness (Ruth) | 132
9. The Power of Love (The Song of Songs) | 154
10. Eat, Drink, and Rejoice (Ecclesiastes) | 181
11. No Sorrow Like Her Sorrow (Lamentations) | 204
12. The Brave Hidden Jew (Esther) | 221
13. The Wise Jew Who Refused to Hide (Daniel) | 241
14. Returning Home (Ezra-Nehemiah) | 261
15. Ending with a New Beginning (Chronicles) | 286

Epilogue | 298

Acknowledgments | 301
Bibliography | 303
Subject Index | 309
Ancient Document Index | 317

Preface

DR. JOEL WILLITTS WAS kind to offer me a course which a more seasoned professor, who was on sabbatical, usually teaches. I had a choice. I could either teach the Prophets or the Writings. At first, I thought I'd be better suited for the Prophets since my master's thesis was on Isaiah (published under the title *You are Israel.*)[1] However, upon reflection I realized the Writings are more diverse and more palatable to a modern audience than the Prophets. So I chose to teach the Writings. The official name of the course was "Old Testament Poetry and Wisdom Literature." Teaching this course was one of the best experiences of my life.

Sadly, I will not get to teach it again for some time. The bittersweetness of this reality created in me a desire to write. I turned the course into the book you are now reading.

My first book, whatever its merits, was written for advanced students of the Bible, which means it's unreadable for the vast majority of people. I wanted to write a book that almost anyone can read. That's why this book is written in a more relaxed literary style and contains personal anecdotes. I simply inform the reader what the Bible says and how the books of the Bible relate to each other and how they relate to all of life.

This book is intended for students who are not quite novices of the Bible, but not intermediate either. I do think, though, that novices and intermediate students can get something from it. Were I to teach the course again, I would use this book to create a "flipped" class where the book is the lecture and the class-time is a discussion. But I hope anyone interested in the Bible would read it. Despite it's length, I'm fairly confident it flows well.

I wrote this book for Jews, Christians, and anyone else interested in the Bible, whether religious or not. I unabashedly state the Hebrew Bible is Jewish through and through. For this reason, I use BCE for dating, rather than BC. I don't mean any offense to Christians. If you want, you can interpret BCE to mean "Before [the] Christian Era."

On the other hand, I risk offending Jews because I break Jewish law by sometimes referring to God by his name, "Yahweh." "Yahweh" is translated "the LORD" in most English translations, following the Jewish practice of substituting the Hebrew

---

1. Full title: *You Are Israel: How Isaiah Uses Genesis as a Means of Identity Formation.*

word *adonai* for the four-letter name of God, which can be represented by the English letters YHWH. I think in some cases, though, using the name of God as it appears in the Hebrew text makes the Bible easier to understand.

No book is the final word on the Bible. I'm sure I don't say anything that hasn't been said before. It's also likely that I made historical and interpretive errors. Please factcheck me and look up the sources I cite.

I am nothing if not passionate about the Hebrew Bible. I hope my passion will be evident in the pages that follow. If I can get people interested in the Hebrew Bible, I will have accomplished my task.

1

The Writings

"MANY GREAT TEACHINGS HAVE been given to us through the Law and the Prophets and the others books[1] that followed them, and for these we should praise Israel for instruction and wisdom."[2] So said the grandson of one Yeshua ben Sira in the early second century BCE. This book you are reading is about those "other books." My contention is that those books are some of the most life-changing pieces of literature ever written. They are as relevant to people living today as they were to people living millennia ago. They are as relevant to the committed nonreligious as they are to the religious.[3]

But how we read those books matters. If you read them individually, separate from each other, you'll be moved, inspired, and challenged, for each book stands on its own and is unique. But if you wish to *really* plunge the depths of sublimity; if you *really* want to learn what it means to be human, to struggle with your mortality, to go through death's dark valley and come out on the other side, to confront your pain and in so doing find healing, then I contend those books must be read together, not separately. They must be read as an anthology.

But if you open a Bible, you will most likely *not* find those books together as an anthology. Some of them will be grouped together but the rest will be scattered amongst the other books of the Bible. Why is this the case? To answer that, we need to understand a few elementary aspects of the order of the Bible's books.

It's a peculiar thing that the Bible is the sacred text of two religions, namely Judaism and Christianity. Yet that statement needs to be qualified. For Christians, the Bible is divided into two "testaments"—the Old Testament and the New Testament.

---

1. The NRSV translates the Greek phrase as "others" and has a footnote that says "other books." Orlinky argues it should be translated "other books." See Orlinky, "Some Terms," 483–90.

2. NRSV.

3. I'm interpreting the "other books" to refer to the Ketuvim, or "Writings." This is a matter of controversy. My interpretation is more literary than dogmatic. See Lim, *The Formation of the Jewish Canon*, 101–2.

These titles are a rather strange translation of the phrases "old covenant" and "new covenant."[4] The "old covenant" refers to the covenant God made with Israel at Sinai (Exod 19–24). The "new covenant," prophesied by the prophet Jeremiah in Jer 31:31–34, refers to the covenant ratified by Jesus (Luke 22:20). Basically, the "old covenant" is Judaism and the "new covenant" is Christianity. But this is not what is meant by the titles "Old Testament" and "New Testament." The Old Testament refers to the collection of thirty-nine Hebrew books.[5] The New Testament—twenty-seven books written in Greek—contains the four gospels, the book of Acts (a sequel to the gospel of Luke), Paul's letters, the "general" (or "catholic") letters including the letter to the Hebrews, and the Johannine writings.

The part of the Bible that Judaism and Christianity share is the Old Testament. However, Judaism and Christianity have very different interpretations of the Old Testament. They have even arranged the books of their text differently, with a different order of books and with different categorizations. As Rabbi Jonathan Sacks has said (only half facetiously), the Jewish Bible and the Christian Bible are "two completely different books that happen to contain the same words."[6]

Historically, Christians have not been as comfortable with the Old Testament as with the New Testament, despite affirming unequivocally that the Old Testament is Holy Scripture (that is, the authoritative "word of God"). A professed Christian in the early second century named Marcion of Sinope argued the god of the Old Testament was different (and worse) than the god of the New Testament. Marcion thus denied the Old Testament was Scripture. He's actually the first person to develop a New Testament canon—a much shorter canon than the one we have now and one which was stripped of quotations from the Old Testament. The church condemned Marcion as a heretic, but the church's defense of the Old Testament was strikingly anti-Jewish.[7] It seems that, for the church, the Old Testament was about two things: First, the Old Testament foretold Jesus. The prophecies were proofs that Christianity's view of Jesus is correct—that Jesus is the Messiah, the Son of God. Second, the Old Testament was basically the story of the rejection of the Jewish people as the "chosen nation." The Old Testament's commandments were deemed inferior to the "law of Christ."[8] These points were emphasized with ever increasing ferocity by Christian leaders whenever Christians began wandering into synagogues to observe Jewish holidays. This view of the Old Testament is part of a theological doctrine known as *supersessionism*. Supersessionism means that Judaism and Jews have been replaced by Christianity and the church. From there it's not a large leap to say the New Testament *as a book* is superior to the Old Testament, even while affirming that both Testaments are "God's word."

4. "Covenant" in Latin is *testamentum*.

5. In Judaism there are twenty-four books. This will be explained below.

6. Rabbi Sacks, "A Tale of Two Women."

7. Gager, *The Origins of Anti-Semitism*, loc. 2974.

8. See, for example, Justin Martyr, *Dialogue with Trypho*, ch. IX.

The Writings

The title "Old Testament" doesn't help. It could well be that the title unconsciously prejudices Christians against the Old Testament. After all, who wants an *old* car when they can have a brand new one? This is the attitude many Christians have had of the Old Testament, and one that many Christians still have. There's a sense in which the New Testament is viewed as an upgrade. There's a deep-seated feeling that the Old Testament has value but it's not relevant to the Christian life.

This problem has been tackled by numerous Old Testament scholars. I recommend the books *Do We Need the New Testament?: Letting the Old Testament Speak for Itself* by John Goldingay, and *The Old Testament Is Dying: A Diagnosis and Recommended Treatment* by Brent Strawn. I approach the problem from my own perspective. My goal is modest. I want people to appreciate, if nothing else, the literary and philosophical aspects of the Old Testament. It will be shown that part of appreciating the Old Testament involves appreciating the Jewish people as a *living* people with a deep and rich heritage. The view that the Old Testament is the story of the rejection of the Jews must be abandoned. My concern is that the title "Old Testament" makes these goals a little more difficult to achieve than they otherwise would be.

The title "Old Testament" originates from 2 Cor 3:14. In that letter, Paul speaks of the "old covenant" not as the covenant God made with Israel at Sinai (although that's never totally out of view), but as a collection of books that Jews read on the Sabbath—i.e., the Hebrew Bible, or at least part of it. However, most of the time the New Testament (including Paul's letters) calls the Old Testament simply "the Scriptures" (1 Cor 15:3). The Old Testament was the only Bible the primitive church knew. Christianity actually existed before one word of the New Testament had been written.

Modern scholars have sought a replacement for the term "Old Testament." Goldingay,[9] like John L. McLaughlin,[10] refers to it as the "First Covenant." This phrase comes from the book of Hebrews (8:7; 9:1; 9:15; 9:18), though Hebrews is referring to the Sinaitic covenant rather than the collection of Hebrew books. The moniker "First Covenant" won't work for Jews (I'll explain why below) but "First Covenant" is refreshing because it doesn't connote the Hebrew Bible as something passé. McLaughlin deems "First Covenant" to be a preferable title to "Hebrew Bible" because naming the different parts of the Bible after their language would lead us to refer to the New Testament as the "Greek Bible," which would not be an adequate descriptor and one which few would want to use anyway.[11] Unfortunately, at this point it seems nigh impossible to break the convention of using the title "Old Testament." We shall therefore embrace the title and use it to refer only to the Christian arrangement of the Hebrew books.

---

9. Goldingay, *Do We Need the New Testament?*, loc. 78–95. Goldingay's translation of the Hebrew Bible is called *The First Testament*.

10. McLaughlin, *The Ancient Near East*, loc. 46.

11. McLaughlin, *The Ancient Near East*, loc. 52. McLaughlin also notes that calling the "First Testament" the "Hebrew Bible" fails to recognize that parts of Daniel and Ezra are written in Aramaic.

THE OLD TESTAMENT

The Old Testament's order of books comes from the Septuagint as found in early Christian codices. The Septuagint is the Greek translation of the Hebrew Bible. It's the very first translation of the Hebrew Bible and dates back to around the mid- to early third century BCE.[12] The word itself means "seventy," thusly named because of the tradition that seventy-two translators translated it separately and yet identically.[13] Hence it's abbreviated "LXX."

The Old Testament's order, the way we have it today, is slightly different than the Septuagint's. The biggest difference is that the Septuagint contains a series of books called the Apocrypha. The Apocrypha is an anthology of Jewish books which were written between the completion of the Old Testament and before the start of the New Testament. Hence, it's part of what's called the "Intertestamental" literature. The Catholic Church and the Orthodox Church consider the Apocrypha to be Scripture; Judaism and Protestantism do not.[14] In the Septuagint, the books of the Apocrypha are scattered throughout. In some Catholic and Orthodox Bibles, the books of the Apocrypha are collected and placed at the end of the Old Testament, as an appendix.[15] For our purposes, we will take up the order of the Protestant Old Testament since that is the lowest common denominator of Judaism and Christianity.

The Old Testament is divided into four sections:

- The Law (or Pentateuch)
- The History Books
- The Wisdom (or Poetical) Books
- The Prophets

"Pentateuch" is a Greek word which means "Five Scrolls." (This should not be confused with a Hebrew phrase which we will use frequently in this book and which means the same thing but refers to different books.) The Pentateuch is also known as the "Five Books of Moses" because of the tradition that Moses is their author. The books of the Pentateuch are:

- Genesis
- Exodus
- Leviticus

12. Initially, the Septuagint consisted of just the Torah but by the first century the entire Hebrew Bible had been translated.

13. The source for this tradition is the *Letter of Aristeas*.

14. Emanuel Tov believes it's possible that the Qumran community—the community of the Dead Sea Scrolls—accepted some books of the Apocrypha as Scripture. see https://youtu.be/hD5Tez5xZe0.

15. The apocryphal section of the Catholic/Orthodox Bible is referred to as the "deuterocanonical books."

The Writings

- Numbers
- Deuteronomy

"Genesis" means "beginning" and is aptly named since the book deals with the creation of the world and the origin of Israel. "Exodus" means "exit." Exodus is about the deliverance of Israel from slavery in Egypt and the aforementioned covenant God makes with Israel at Mount Sinai. This is where God gives Israel the law. The commandments are scattered throughout the books of Exodus, Leviticus (named thus because it refers to the things pertaining to the tribe of Levi, which was a priestly tribe), Numbers (the book contains two censuses), and Deuteronomy. Deuteronomy is a Greek word which means "second law." It's a bad translation of the Hebrew words *mishneh torah*, which in context means "copy of the law" (Deut 17:18).

The History Books tell the story of the rise, fall, and restoration of Israel. These books are:

- Joshua
- Judges
- Ruth
- 1 Samuel
- 2 Samuel
- 1 Kings
- 2 Kings
- 1 Chronicles
- 2 Chronicles
- Ezra
- Nehemiah
- Esther

Joshua is about Israel's conquest of the so-called "promised land," i.e., the land of Canaan. Judges is about the turbulent period of Israel's history before the formation of the monarchy. First and Second Samuel are about the rise of the monarchy and the covenant God makes with David—that David's dynasty will be eternal. First and Second Kings are about the fall of the monarchy. The monarchy is divided during the reign of Rehoboam son of Solomon. The Assyrian Empire destroys the northern kingdom. More than a century later, the Babylonian Empire destroys the southern kingdom. Many of the survivors of the southern kingdom are taken to Babylon. This is referred to as the "exile." First and Second Chronicles are a rewrite of 1 and 2 Samuel and 1 and 2 Kings. Ezra, Nehemiah, and Esther take place after the exile. Hence, those books are referred to as "post-exilic."

The third section of the Old Testament is the Wisdom Books, sometimes called the Poetical Books. These books are:

- Job
- Psalms
- Proverbs
- Ecclesiastes
- The Song of Solomon (or The Song of Songs)[16]

Job is about a righteous man who suffered immensely. He and his friends argue with each other about God, justice, and the nature of suffering. The psalms are the lyrics of religious songs. Almost half of them are attributed to David. The book of Psalms, also known as the Psalter, is often referred to as "Israel's hymnal." Proverbs is the first book attributed to Solomon and is written from the perspective of a father imparting wisdom and the love of wisdom to his son. Ecclesiastes, also a Solomonic book,[17] is a quasi-philosophical reflection on life and the pursuit of happiness. Ecclesiastes is the only book in this category that is mostly written in prose. And the Song of Solomon—the third and final Solomonic book—is a collection of erotic poetry. (Yes, you read that correctly!)

It's probable that Job heads the list because Job seems to take place in a pre-Israelite time period. Psalms is associated with David. Proverbs, Ecclesiastes, and the Song of Solomon are all associated with David's son, Solomon. The arrangement of the Wisdom Books, therefore, is in some sense chronological.

The fourth section, the Prophets, consists of the following books:

- Isaiah
- Jeremiah
- Lamentations
- Ezekiel
- Daniel
- Hosea
- Joel
- Amos
- Obadiah
- Jonah
- Micah

16. Sometimes the Song of Songs is referred to as "Canticles."

17. Although this will be qualified in a later chapter.

The Writings

- Nahum

- Habakkuk

- Zephaniah

- Haggai

- Zechariah

- Malachi

The Prophets are divided into two sections: The Major Prophets and the Minor Prophets. The Major Prophets are Isaiah, Jeremiah, Ezekiel. Daniel can also be placed in this category, as well as Lamentations even though Lamentations is not a book of prophecy. Lamentations' full name is "The Lamentations of Jeremiah." Thus Jeremiah and Lamentations are connected in the Old Testament. The twelve remaining books are called the Minor Prophets. The designations "major" and "minor" refer to the size of the books, not the importance of the prophets themselves. The book of Isaiah is sixty-six chapters long; the book of Habakkuk is three chapters long. Hence, Isaiah is a "major" prophet and Habakkuk is a "minor" prophet.[18]

To recap, here is the entire Old Testament:

Pentateuch	History	Wisdom	Prophets
Genesis	Joshua	Job	Isaiah
Exodus	Judges	Psalms	Jeremiah
Leviticus	Ruth	Proverbs	Lamentations
Numbers	1 Samuel	Ecclesiastes	Ezekiel
Deuteronomy	2 Samuel	The Song of Songs	Daniel
	1 Kings		Hosea
	2 Kings		Joel
	1 Chronicles		Amos
	2 Chronicles		Obadiah
	Ezra		Jonah
	Nehemiah		Micah

18. Daniel's categorization is a bit dubious since Daniel has only twelve chapters and Hosea has fourteen chapters.

Pentateuch	History	Wisdom	Prophets
	Esther		Nahum
			Habakkuk
			Zephaniah
			Haggai
			Zechariah
			Malachi

THE TANAKH

Judaism does not refer to the Hebrew Bible as the "Old Testament." That title only makes sense if one acknowledges the New Testament as sacred literature. The same goes for the title "First Testament." If Judaism called it the "first," it would be acknowledging a second. If Judaism acknowledged such a thing, Judaism would not be Judaism. Therefore, whenever people refer to the Hebrew Bible as the "Old Testament," they're betraying a Christian bias, even if unknowingly or innocently. This isn't necessarily bad, but we should be cognizant of such things.

Jews call the Old Testament the *Tanakh*. Tanakh is an acronym. The T stands for *Torah*. The N stands for *Nevi'im*. The K stands for *Ketuvim*. *Torah* is often translated "law" but it literally means "teaching" or "instruction." *Nevi'im* means "prophets." *Ketuvim* means "writings." The Ketuvim is also sometimes called the *Hagiographa*, which is a Greek word that means "sacred writings."

Whereas the Old Testament is divided into four sections, the Tanakh is divided into three sections: the Torah, the Prophets, and the Writings. Behind this threefold division is the belief that each section is not of equal holiness. The Torah is the holiest part of the Tanakh, for the Torah represents God's word spoken from God directly to Israel. This is indicated in the text itself where it says the law was "written with the finger of God" (Exod 31:18; Deut 9:10).[19] No other part of the Bible—Old Testament or New Testament—makes that claim. Second Timothy 3:16 says "All scripture is God-breathed," but only the Torah is written in God's own handwriting.

The Prophets also represent God speaking to Israel but, unlike the Torah, God's word comes to Israel indirectly, through human mediators, namely the prophets

---

19. Be sure to compare Exod 34:1 with Exod 34:27–28. Does God write or does Moses write? The commandments come from God, but Jewish and Christian tradition both hold that Moses is the author of the Pentateuch.

The Writings

themselves. Hence we see the phrases "the word of the LORD" and "declares the LORD" scattered throughout these books.

The Ketuvim—the Writings—are altogether different. These are considered the least holy books because they represent, not God's word coming down to Israel, but Israel's word going up to God or humans teaching other humans. This is not to say the Ketuvim isn't considered holy. It *is* holy. It's just that it's less holy than the Torah and the Prophets.[20]

The books of the Torah and their order are identical to the Pentateuch although their Hebrew names are different than their Old Testament counterparts. Judaism names books after the first word, or first few words, of the book:

- *Breshit* ("In the Beginning") [Genesis]
- *Shmot* ("Names") [Exodus]
- *Vayikra* ("And He Called") [Leviticus]
- *Bamidbar* ("In the Desert") [Numbers]
- *Dvarim* ("Words") [Deuteronomy]

Yet whereas the Torah and Pentateuch are identical, the Prophets section of the Tanakh is different than the Old Testament's Prophets section. In the Tanakh, the books of the Prophets are:

- Joshua
- Judges
- Samuel (1 and 2)
- Kings (1 and 2)
- Isaiah
- Jeremiah
- Ezekiel
- *Trei Asar* (Hosea, Joel, Amos, Obadiah, Jonah, Micah, Nahum, Habakkuk, Zephaniah, Haggai, Zechariah, Malachi)

Notice the "Prophets" section in the Tanakh contains some of the Old Testament's History books. Modern scholars refer to the Prophets' history books as the "Deuteronomistic History" because of their perceived linguistic and theological connections to Deuteronomy. Judaism refers to these books as the "Former Prophets." Notice that 1 and 2 Samuel are one book and 1 and 2 Kings are one book.[21] The prophetic books proper—those books named after their respective prophet—are referred to as the

---

20. Sarna, *On the Book of Psalms*, 3.

21. This is the case with the LXX as well.

Illuminating Counsel

"Latter Prophets." Judaism does not divide the Latter Prophets into the categories of major and minor.[22] Rather, the Latter Prophets consists of Isaiah, Jeremiah, Ezekiel, and *Trei Asar*—Aramaic for "The Twelve." In the Tanakh, the twelve "minor prophets" are considered one book.

Whereas the order of the books of the Torah have always been fixed, locked, and without dispute, this is not the case with the books of the Prophets. There's a passage from the section of the Babylonian Talmud[23] called *Baba Batra* which discusses the Torah, Prophets, and Writings. The text states that the Prophets are Joshua, Judges, Samuel, Kings, Jeremiah, Ezekiel, Isaiah, and the Twelve. The order of the Twelve is not fully discussed except to explain why Hosea is the first of the Twelve despite not being the first chronologically.[24] But then the text discusses why Jeremiah and Ezekiel precede Isaiah even though chronologically Isaiah the prophet preceded Jeremiah and Ezekiel.[25] The explanation is lovely. Jeremiah ends with the destruction of Jerusalem and Ezekiel begins with the destruction of Jerusalem. Ezekiel ends with consolation and Isaiah is all about consolation.[26] This creates a nice pattern: destruction to destruction, consolation to consolation. But for some reason this order didn't stick. Every printed version of the Tanakh has Isaiah preceding Jeremiah and Ezekiel.

That leaves us with the third section of the Tanakh—the Ketuvim, or "Writings"—the subject of this book. But here we encounter a couple of problems. The order of the books of the Ketuvim is the least firmly established of the three sections of the Tanakh. Look again at the words of Yeshua ben Sira's grandson, quoted at the beginning of this chapter. The Law and the Prophets are clearly named. We can therefore assume that they were fixed and locked by the early second century BCE. The third section, however, he calls "the other books." A little later he refers to them as "the other books of our ancestors" and "the rest of the books." The lack of an official title suggests that what Baba Batra calls the Ketuvim, or the Writings, was fluid and not fixed early on. The Ketuvim was the last part of the Tanakh to be canonized. Even after the Ketuvim was established, some Jews thought some of the books of the Ketuvim should not be in the Bible.

---

22. These terms are widely accepted today among Jews and Christians but the first use of "Minor Prophets" comes from the Christian theologian Augustine, who lived in the late fourth and early fifth centuries.

23. The Talmud is a collection of Jewish writings. It consists of a the Mishnah (Jewish authoritative traditions) and a commentary on the Mishnah. It is from the fifth century CE. It is the second most important collection of writing in Judaism next to the Tanakh.

24. Canonical order—that is, the order the books appear in the Bible—is not necessarily the same as chronological order.

25. Isaiah son of Amoz was a prophet from the eighth century BCE. Jeremiah and Ezekiel were prophets from the sixth century BCE.

26. *Baba Batra* 14b–15a.

The Writings

The canonicity of the books of the Ketuvim is not disputed in Baba Batra. However, Baba Batra provides an order of the books which has, for some reason, been abandoned. According to Baba Batra, the order is:

- Ruth
- Psalms [*Tehillim* in Hebrew, which means "Praises"]
- Job
- Proverbs
- Ecclesiastes [*Kohelet* in Hebrew]
- The Song of Songs
- Lamentations [*Eikha* in Hebrew, which means "How" or "Alas"]
- Daniel
- Esther
- Ezra-Nehemiah
- Chronicles (1 and 2) [*Divrei Hayamim* in Hebrew, which means "The Matters of the Days"]

Baba Batra doesn't explain this order except for the priority of Ruth. According to Jewish tradition, Job lived during the time of Moses. One would think, then, that because Job precedes the other books of the Ketuvim chronologically, Job should be at the top of the list. But Job is about suffering and suffering is deemed to be an unsuitable subject for the beginning the Ketuvim. Ruth is about suffering too, of course, but Ruth's suffering leads to redemption, specifically the Davidic dynasty. This is why Ruth is Baba Batra's first book of the Ketuvim.

But the great medieval codices—the Aleppo Codex and the Leningrad Codex[27]—arrange the Ketuvim differently. Here's their order:

- Chronicles (1 and 2)
- Psalms
- Job
- Proverbs
- Ruth
- The Song of Songs
- Ecclesiastes
- Lamentations

---

27. The Leningrad Codex is our oldest completed version of the Hebrew Bible. It is based on the Aleppo Codex but the Aleppo Codex is now missing the Torah.

11

Illuminating Counsel

- Esther

- Daniel

- Ezra-Nehemiah

This order has not stuck completely either, though printed editions of the Tanakh are closer to this order than to Baba Batra's. The biggest difference is that the Ketuvim in the medieval codices begins with Chronicles. It's now accepted in Judaism, following Baba Batra, that Chronicles is the very last book of the Ketuvim, and hence of the Tanakh. Yet there are still variations with the books of the Ketuvim in modern editions. *Biblia Hebraica Struttgartensia*—this is the scholarly edition of the Tanakh[28]—presents the order of the Ketuvim as follows:

- Psalms

- Job

- Proverbs

- Ruth

- The Song of Songs

- Ecclesiastes

- Lamentations

- Esther

- Daniel

- Ezra-Nehemiah

- Chronicles (1 and 2)

Other printed editions have a slight variation on that order:

- Psalms

- Proverbs

- Job

- The Song of Songs

- Ruth

- Lamentations

- Ecclesiastes

- Esther

- Daniel

---

28. BHS contains scholarly notes regarding textual variants from other manuscripts aside from the Leningrad Codex.

The Writings

- Ezra-Nehemiah

- Chronicles (1 and 2)

Sometimes Proverbs precedes Job. Sometimes the Song of Songs precedes Ruth. Sometimes Lamentations precedes Ecclesiastes.

What's clear is that the Ketuvim, as we now have it, has three subdivisions. The first subdivision is called the Poetical Books in English and *Sifrei Emet* in Hebrew. Sifrei Emet means "Books of Truth." The books of Sifrei Emet are Psalms, Proverbs, and Job. The reason these books are called Sifrei Emet is because *emet* is an acronym created by the first letter (in Hebrew) of Psalms, Proverbs, and Job read backwards.

The books of Sifrei Emet are also considerably larger than the rest of the books of the Ketuvim, Chronicles being the exception. It seems like a clever and stylistic move to begin the Ketuvim with the larger books. Doing so gives the shorter books some breathing room, if you will.

The second section of the Ketuvim is called *Hamesh Megillot*, which means "Five Scrolls."[29] These "scrolls" are Ruth, the Song of Songs, Ecclesiastes, Lamentations, and Esther. These books are grouped together (contra the Baba Batra order) for liturgical reasons. Each of these books is read on a Jewish holiday:

- Ruth is read on *Shavuot*—the "Festival of Weeks" ("Pentecost" in Greek)

- The Song of Songs is read on *Pesach*—"Passover," also called the "Festival of Unleavened Bread"

- Ecclesiastes is read on *Sukkot*—the "Festival of Booths"

- Lamentations is read on *Tisha B'Av*—the ninth day of the Hebrew month of Av

- Esther is read on *Purim*—(this word means "lots," as in the things you cast)

The holiday on which the the Song of Songs is read—Passover—precedes the holiday on which Ruth is read—Shavuot. Passover is in the early spring. Shavuot is precisely five weeks after Passover (hence the reason it's called "Weeks," or "Pentecost," which means "fifty" in Greek). The holiday on which Lamentations is read—Tisha B'Av—is in late summer and the holiday on which Ecclesiastes is read—Sukkot—is in autumn. This is why many orders of the Ketuvim, contra the Leningrad Codex, have the Song of Songs before Ruth, and Lamentations before Ecclesiastes.

Why are these books read on these holidays? With Esther, the answer is self-evident. The events of Esther are the basis for Purim; Purim's institution is recorded in Esth 9:20–32. This is the only holiday of the five that is explicitly mentioned in these books.

The reading of Lamentations on the ninth of Av makes sense if one knows what the ninth of Av is about. The ninth of Av is the anniversary of the destruction of the

---

29. Again, not to be confused with the Pentateuch, which means the same thing.

Jewish temple (both temples, actually). The destruction of the temple is the subject of Lamentations.

But what about the other three scrolls? There are two connections between Passover and the Song of Songs. First, Judaism interpreted the Song of Songs as an allegory of God's love for Israel and vice versa. The love story of God and Israel began with the exodus from Egypt—the very thing Passover commemorates. Second, Passover is always in the spring. The Jewish calendar, which is based on the lunar cycle, has fewer days than the Gregorian calendar. That means that with each passing year, Passover gets pushed back into winter. This is why the Jewish leap year adds an entire month. Passover cannot be in any season other than spring. The Song of Songs takes place in spring (Song 2:11). Therefore, the Song of Songs takes place during the time of Passover.

Passover, Shavuot, and Sukkot each have agricultural significance. Passover marks the beginning of the barley harvest. Shavuot, also called the "Festival of Firstfruits," marks the end of the barley harvest and the beginning of the wheat harvest. The period of time between Passover and Shavuot is referred to as the "counting of the *omer*" (see Lev 23:15–16). (An "*omer*" is a measure of barley.) Ruth takes place during the counting of the omer—the days leading up to Shavuot (Ruth 1:22).

Shavuot is not assigned any historical significance in the Torah. This sets it apart from Passover, which commemorates the exodus from Egypt, and Sukkot, which commemorates the wandering in the wilderness. Jewish tradition, therefore, added an historical significance to Shavuot. Shavuot commemorates the giving of the Torah on Mount Sinai. (The timeframe actually works if you look closely at Exod 19:1.) This is another connection with Ruth, since Ruth emphasizes the Torah's benefits to society.

Sukkot is the most joyous holiday of the year. Also called the "Festival of Ingathering," it's an autumn holiday marking the end of the harvest (Lev 23:39–43; Deut 16:13–15). It's the forerunner of the American Thanksgiving. But Ecclesiastes seems like one of the most depressing books of the Bible. If that's the case, maybe Ecclesiastes being read on Sukkot is meant to somber us up a little. It's a reality check. Every day is not a party!

But what if Ecclesiastes is read on Sukkot precisely because as Sukkot is a holiday of joy, so too Ecclesiastes is a book of joy, contrary to the popular perception of the book? I will argue that viewing Ecclesiastes as a book of misery is wrongheaded.

Holiday	Time Period	Book
Passover	March–April	The Song of Songs
Shavuot	June–July	Ruth
Tisha B'Av	July–August	Lamentations

The Writings

Holiday	Time Period	Book
Sukkot	September-October	Ecclesiastes
Purim	February-March	Esther

That leaves us with the third and final subsection of the Ketuvim. This section is called the "Other Books." Certainly that's not the most creative title imaginable! These books are Daniel, Ezra-Nehemiah, and Chronicles. Here we can once again note the irony that two religions share the same text and yet have different interpretations of it. The interpretations are so different that Judaism and Christianity do not even count the books the same. Ask a biblically literate Christian and he will tell you there are thirty-nine books in the Old Testament. But there are twenty-four books in the Tanakh. How can that be? In Judaism, 1 and 2 Samuel are one book, 1 and 2 Kings are one book, 1 and 2 Chronicles are one book, Ezra and Nehemiah are one book, and the twelve minor prophets are one book. Hence, twenty-four books, not thirty-nine.

IS THE KETUVIM LOGICAL?

At first blush it seems the Ketuvim reflects the Old Testament's "Wisdom Books." All five of the Wisdom Books are in the Ketuvim.[30] Notice also that Baba Batra's order of those five books is the same as the Old Testament's. The Ketuvim, however, contains more than the Wisdom Books. In the Old Testament, Ruth is placed in the History Books. That placement is perfectly reasonable. Ruth is telling a story which functions as a bridge between the period of the Judges (within which Ruth takes place) and the period of the monarchy (which begins in the subsequent book, 1 Samuel). There is even evidence that some ancient sages viewed Judges and Ruth as one book.[31] Yet in the Tanakh, Ruth is removed from the History Books and placed in the back, in the Writings. Ruth is also a book written entirely in prose. The Ketuvim is not a collection of poetry.

Lamentations follows Jeremiah in the Old Testament and, like Judges and Ruth, some thought of Jeremiah and Lamentations as one book.[32] Lamentations' placement in the Prophets of the Old Testament is logical because tradition has it that Jeremiah is the author of Lamentations. While authorial traditions can sometimes be outlandish, the tradition of Jeremiah as author of Lamentations is plausible.[33] Jeremiah composed

---

30. The Wisdom Books should really be thought of as Proverbs, Job, and Ecclesiastes. There are a few psalms in the Psalter about wisdom but the Psalter at large is not a wisdom book. I don't consider the Song of Songs to be a wisdom book either.

31. Lim, *The Formation of the Jewish Canon*, 39–41.

32. Lim, *The Formation of the Jewish Canon*, 39–41.

33. Wright, *The Message of Lamentations*, 27.

lamentations (with a lowercase L) when Josiah died (2 Chr 25:35). Jeremiah also witnessed the destruction of Jerusalem—the subject of the book of Lamentations. Consider, then, the effect of the Old Testament order: the reader reads this very tumultuous prophetic book in which the prophet pleads with the king not to rebel against Babylon. The king fails to listen to the weeping prophet and thus the nation, the holy city, and the temple suffer the consequences. Then the reader reads Lamentations which, in this context, functions as a dirge. The reader pauses to contemplate the magnitude of what had just transpired. Put another way, first the reader reads how Jerusalem died (Jeremiah); then the reader attends Jerusalem's funeral (Lamentations). This effect is totally lost in the Tanakh, for the Tanakh separates Lamentations from Jeremiah and sticks it behind Ecclesiastes.

Esther, like Ruth, is part of the History Books section of the Old Testament. Once again we must admit that that placement is perfectly reasonable. Like Ruth, Esther tells a story which is set within an historical context (in Esther's case, the Persian Empire). But, like Ruth, Judaism considers Esther part of the Ketuvim.

The Old Testament's placement of Daniel is also logical. Daniel clearly seems to be a prophet. He receives revelation from God—dreams and visions and their interpretations—and he is set within an historical context which situates him quite nicely after Ezekiel (although technically Daniel is brought to Babylon before Ezekiel). Daniel is also one of those rare books in the Old Testament to mention another prophet—in his case, Jeremiah (Dan 9:2).[34] Judaism, however, does not consider Daniel a prophet. That's why, in the Tanakh, Daniel is consigned to the back of the Bible.

Truly the most confounding thing, even more than the placement of Daniel, is that Ezra-Nehemiah and Chronicles are in the Ketuvim. Maybe we can argue Daniel is not a prophet—*maybe*—but Ezra-Nehemiah and Chronicles are so clearly history books, which is precisely why the Old Testament has them in the History section.[35] Chronicles is a re-telling of Samuel and Kings from a post-exilic perspective. Ezra-Nehemiah is about the return of the Jews from exile and the restoration of the nation (the temple, the law, and Jerusalem). If one reads the Old Testament, one can read the entire history of Israel in one fell swoop—one long fell swoop, yes, but one fell swoop nonetheless! That's not possible in the Tanakh. Not only does the Tanakh stick these history books in the Ketuvim with the likes of Psalms and Proverbs, it also changes their order. Chronologically, the events of Chronicles precede Ezra-Nehemiah. In fact, Ezra-Nehemiah is a perfect sequel to Chronicles because it picks up exactly where Chronicles leaves off. Chronicles ends with the decree of Cyrus allowing the Jews to return to their homeland. Ezra-Nehemiah begins with the decree of Cyrus. The Tanakh, however, has Chronicles *after* Ezra-Nehemiah.[36] That hardly seems like a climactic finale to the Bible!

34. Jeremiah mentions Micah in Jer 26:18.

35. Remember there is no history section in the Tanakh.

36. Again, this is not the order of the medieval manuscripts.

The Writings

What is Chronicles doing in the Ketuvim anyway? If Kings is in the Prophets, why is Chronicles in the Writings? Did the sages who arranged the order of the Tanakh stick it in the back, making it the caboose of the Bible, because they didn't know what to do with it? True, the Leningrad Codex has Chronicles as the first book of the Ketuvim, but apparently no one thought Chronicles should be anywhere else other than the Ketuvim. At any rate, it certainly seems the Old Testament's order is far more logical than the Tanakh's order.

Ketuvim Books	Old Testament Section
Psalms	Wisdom
Proverbs	Wisdom
Job	Wisdom
Ruth	History
Song of Songs	Wisdom
Ecclesiastes	Wisdom
Lamentations	Prophets
Esther	History
Daniel	Prophets
Ezra-Nehemiah	History
Chronicles	History

And yet, the apparent illogic of the Tanakh's order is its advantage! Because it's counterintuitive, it causes us to think about issues we wouldn't think about when reading the Old Testament. For example, by placing Chronicles in the Ketuvim, and at the end of the Ketuvim at that, we're asking questions about Chronicles which, frankly, most readers of the Old Testament never ask. (Most readers of the Bible tend to ignore Chronicles anyway!) The Tanakh also enables us to see connections between books which we would not see in the Old Testament. Take Proverbs and Job, for example. Whether Job precedes Proverbs or the other way around doesn't matter. They are adjacent in Tanakh but not in the Old Testament. Grouping them together causes them to dialogue with each other which creates an immensely enlightening read because they seem to be discussing the same issue from different perspectives.

Separating Ruth from Judges breaks up the nice chronology in the Old Testament, but it also creates a new dynamic. Ruth's chemistry is different in the Ketuvim than it is in the History Books of the Old Testament. In the Ketuvim, Ruth is now dialoguing with books which seem, at first blush, completely unrelated. The reader of the Ketuvim, therefore, views Ruth differently than the reader of the Old Testament. Fresh questions come to mind. Is there a connection between Ruth and Psalms? Between Ruth and Proverbs? Between Ruth and Job? What about the Song of Songs? Does reading the Song of Songs together with Ruth cause us to make a connection between the two lovers in the Song and Ruth and Boaz? The same is true with Lamentations. There's no doubt Lamentations is a good fit between Jeremiah and Ezekiel, but Lamentations amongst the Wisdom Books works so well on so many levels. For one thing, we are invited to make connections between Lamentations and Psalms, Lamentations and Proverbs, Lamentations and Job, and so on. Moreover, in the Prophets, Lamentations (which is only five chapters long) is squished between two giant books. In the Ketuvim, Lamentations is in its own weight class, so to speak.

What about the connections between Esther and Daniel? In the Old Testament, Esther and Daniel are separated by the Wisdom Books. In the Tanakh, they're on the same team and are adjacent to each other. Since Daniel bears striking similarities to Joseph, reading Esther with Daniel causes us to see Esther's similarities to Joseph.[37] Then we read on to Ezra-Nehemiah. In the Old Testament, Daniel is separate from Ezra-Nehemiah but in the Tanakh they're grouped together. The reader of the Tanakh realizes that Esther, Daniel, Ezra-Nehemiah all feature a type of protagonist which Yoram Hazony calls the "court Jew"—that is, a Jew living in exile who rises to prominence in the gentile king's court.[38] Daniel's similarities to Joseph remind us that Joseph is the first such figure in the Bible. We also realize that Moses bears similarities to Joseph, for Moses, too, is a court Jew. And then we realize that Esther bears striking similarities to Moses. Thus the Ketuvim reaches back to the Torah and creates a fascinating chain of biblical characters: Joseph, Moses, Esther, Mordecai (the male protagonist in Esther), Daniel, Ezra, and Nehemiah. The issues involved with these "court Jews" are not just of immense importance in the Bible, but are also tremendously relevant to the Jewish people—both ancient Jews as well as contemporary Jews.

It may seem that Daniel's placement in the Ketuvim is bad for Daniel—that Daniel is more prominent and more likely to be read when it's in the Prophets. Indeed, I always felt that Christians focus on Daniel more than Jews do, though, if true, there may be other reasons for that. But the powerful literary chain of the "court Jew" theme shows us that Daniel works perfectly in the Ketuvim. Moreover, like Ruth and Lamentations, Daniel is now dialoguing with Ketuvim books. The connections between Daniel and the Wisdom Books are intriguing!

37. Joseph is a character in the book of Genesis. See Gen 37–50.

38. Hazony, *God and Politics in Esther*, 83–90.

The Writings

And the questions regarding Chronicles will not go away. What does Chronicles have to do with any of the other books of the Ketuvim? Why does Chronicles come after Ezra-Nehemiah? Why does the Tanakh, in its settled form, end with Chronicles? We will attempt to answer these questions throughout the course of this book.

We can't say one order is better than another. However, I think we *can* say the arrangement of books is not value neutral.[39] Here is the order of the books of the Tanakh with its categories; this is the order of the Ketuvim which I will take up in this book:

Torah (Law)	Nevi'im (Prophets)	Ketuvim (Writings)
Genesis	Joshua	Psalms
Exodus	Judges	Proverbs
Leviticus	Samuel	Job
Numbers	Kings	Ruth
Deuteronomy	Isaiah	The Song of Songs
	Jeremiah	Ecclesiastes
	Ezekiel	Lamentations
	Trei Asar	Esther
		Daniel
		Ezra-Nehemiah
		Chronicles

Books of Truth	The Five Scrolls	The Other Books
Psalms	Ruth	Daniel
Proverbs	The Song of Songs	Ezra-Nehemiah
Job	Ecclesiastes	Chronicles
	Lamentations	
	Esther	

39. See Goswell, "The Canonical Position(s)," 129.

2

Why the Least Holy Books are So Stupendous

ONE OF MY FAVORITE pieces of music is Rachmaninoff's second piano concerto. As is typical of concerti, Rachmaninoff's second piano concerto contains three movements. The first movement is dark, containing moments of repose and fiery unrest. The second movement is tranquil and emotively contemplative. My friend Damion says it reminds him of morning. I tend to think of a quiet starry night when I listen. The third movement is triumphant. It's fast-paced, loud, and more joyous than the previous material.

The Tanakh is like a concerto. It contains three movements: the Torah (the Law), the Nevi-im (the Prophets), and Ketuvim (the Writings). The Ketuvim is the finale of the Tankah. It's also the most variegated of the three movements. The Torah contains narratives and laws. The Nevi'im contains historiography and prophecy. But the Ketuvim contains religious songs, proverbs, poetic discourses, narratives, love songs, lectures, court tales, apocalyptic visions, as well as historiography.

But the Ketuvim itself can be likened to a concerto, for, as we said, the Ketuvim contains three movements: the Books of Truth, the Five Scrolls, and the Other Books.

The Books of Truth begin with passion. We're struck by the emotional turbulence of Psalms. Proverbs is the exact opposite. Proverbs is as cerebral as Psalms is emotional. Job, though, takes us in a much darker direction in which we have to deal with the problem of suffering.

The themes of the Five Scrolls are no less deep but they are packaged in short books. I would be very happy if all I had were the Five Scrolls to read over and over again on a deserted island.

The third movement, as we mentioned, is the most confounding of all because, at first blush, it doesn't seem to fit with the rest of the Ketuvim. As we shall see, it actually fits beautifully.

Daniel is a bridge from the Five Scrolls to the Other Books. Thematically, the first half of Daniel is like Esther. The second half of Daniel, though, fits with Ezra-Nehemiah. Daniel begins at the beginning of the exile but ends in the post-exilic period.

20

Why the Least Holy Books are So Stupendous

Since Deuteronomy (at least), through the Deuteronomistic History, through the Prophets, the issue of Israel's exile has been drummed into the reader's head. Most of the tension derives from the build up to the exile—Israel's continuous breaking of the covenant. Then it finally happens. We get both the historical account of the destruction of the kingdoms (Israel and Judah) as well as the prophetic perspective of those events. But Ezra-Nehemiah is about the *restoration* of Israel.

Now think about how the order of the books makes an impact. In the Old Testament, we get Deuteronomy followed by the History Books telling us of the rise and fall and restoration of Israel. We take a break from all that with the Wisdom Books but then we're thrust backward in time with the Prophets. Although at least three of the prophets are post-exilic (Haggai, Zechariah, Malachi),[1] they don't feel like they arrive at a satisfying conclusion. Indeed, the Old Testament ends with the word "destruction" (Mal 4:6 [3:26])!

The Old Testament's order makes it a perfect "Part I" ending with a "To Be Continued . . ." Malachi promises to send Elijah before the "Lord" comes to his temple. The New Testament functions as a sequel. The beginning of the New Testament's first book, Matthew, contains a bridge between the Old and the New. All four of the New Testament's Gospels present John the Baptist as the fulfillment of Malachi's prophecy to send Elijah to prepare the way for Jesus, the Lord (Mal 4:5 [3:25]).[2] I'm simplifying here, but that's the gist of it.

What people don't realize, however, is that the Tanakh *does* have a conclusive ending, narratively speaking. The Tanakh is about how Israel entered the land, how Israel was expelled from the land, and how Israel *returned* to the land. For the Tanakh to end with the restoration of Israel is a very insightful and powerful move. In the Tanakh, the restoration of the Jewish people is not buried amidst much larger books as it is in the Old Testament. It may not be emphasized as much as the downfall, but the restoration is the third movement, the finale of the the third movement, the very last thing the reader of the Hebrew Bible reads. Thus the restoration of Israel makes a greater impact in the Tanakh than it does in the Old Testament.

SUFFERING

Suffering is at the heart of each of the books of the Ketuvim:

- *Psalms*. A third of the psalms are laments. Psalms gives us insight into the heart and mind of those who are going through physical, emotional, and spiritual turmoil due to persecution, disease, loneliness, and guilt.

---

1. I suspect the book of Joel is post-exilic but its time period is not explicitly stated.

2. In John 1:21, John the Baptist denies being Elijah. But John presents John the Baptist as the forerunner of Jesus. Be sure to see Matt 11:14; Luke 1:17; John 1:23; and compare Mark 1:6 with 2 Kgs 1:8.

- *Proverbs.* Suffering is the thing the writer is cautioning the reader to avoid. If we're not careful, if we act foolishly, we will end up in poverty or even dead.

- *Job.* His name is virtually synonymous with suffering. Job loses his children, his wealth, and his health.

- *Ruth.* Naomi loses her husband and her two sons. Her name means "sweetness" but she prefers to be called "Mara"—"bitterness"—because, she says, God has made her life bitter. Note the connection between Ruth and Job. Both deal with the greatest loss of all—the loss of children—as well as God's role as the source of human suffering.

- *The Song of Songs.* The woman in the Song is assaulted by the keepers of the city. It's implied that this assault is sexual in nature. The key verse of the Song mentions death, which shows us that the shadow of death is not out of view even in the exuberance of young love and the rebirth of spring.

- *Ecclesiastes.* The primary speaker finds that every avenue of life he pursues leads to misery. He explicitly says he hated life (Eccl 2:17). Death, too, overshadows everything. What do we gain out of life? How can we gain anything out of life when death conquers all so thoroughly and swiftly?

- *Lamentations.* This is about the destruction of Jerusalem and it describes hellacious atrocities. The thought of starvation being so severe that mothers are eating their children is beyond horrific.

- *Esther.* An antisemite comes up with a plot to annihilate the Jews from the face of the earth. Yes, we should be reminded of the Holocaust!

- *Daniel.* Daniel and his friends are taken captive to Babylon. On more than one occasion, they are sentenced to death. The end of Daniel focuses on an existential crisis facing the Jewish people.

- *Ezra-Nehemiah.* Although this book is about restoration, the small Jewish community in their land face many obstacles to rebuilding. They also have to deal with the pain of guilt—both past and present.

- *Chronicles.* This is the history of the fall of the Israelite monarchy.

What's fascinating is that each of these books presents a different response to suffering. Here's how I summarize their respective responses:

Books	Response to Suffering
Psalms	Prayer
Proverbs	Wisdom

Why the Least Holy Books are So Stupendous

Books	Response to Suffering
Job	Humility
Ruth	Kindness
The Song of Songs	Love
Ecclesiastes	Joy
Lamentations	Lamentation
Esther	Courage
Daniel	Faithfulness
Ezra-Nehemiah	Persistence
Chronicles	Worship

Psalms is essentially about prayer. The psalms *are* prayers. No matter what anyone goes through in life, prayer is a means of expressing our emotions. Through prayer, we praise God, complain to God, and thank God.

The main message of Proverbs is that the pursuit of wisdom is the greatest of all pursuits and will lead to a life which flourishes. Wisdom is our greatest weapon against death.

The book of Job reminds us that human wisdom is severely limited. When suffering occurs, we should recognize that we cannot fully comprehend its cosmic causes. Suffering cannot be an excuse to become arrogant. Humility, therefore, is necessary for one to be truly wise.

The key Hebrew word in Ruth is *hesed*, which essentially means "kindness." The characters show immense kindness to each other despite their suffering. The key Hebrew word in the Song of Songs—not because of its frequency but because of its placement within the book—is *ahav*, which means "love." Love is the lovers' fortress where they are sheltered from suffering. And the key Hebrew word in Ecclesiastes is—shockingly?—*simcha*, which means "joy." Despite the frustrations of life, we can choose to rejoice.

While Lamentations does not use the word "lament" (it's not called "Lamentations" in Hebrew),[3] it seems clear that Zion's response to the atrocity she has experienced is to sing of her sorrows. In Esther, the key moment is when Esther has to risk

---

3. The book of Lamentations is called *Eikha* in Hebrew, which literally means the "How" or the "Alas." *Eikha* is the first word in the book.

her life to save her people. Esther, therefore, promotes the virtue of *courage* when confronted with crisis.

Daniel and his friends show us the meaning of faithfulness to God. They maintain their integrity and their identity despite attacks on their lives.

Ezra-Nehemiah reminds us how to overcome obstacles. We must be persistent despite what others say or do. Move onward and forward, one foot in front of the other. Ezra-Nehemiah shows us the meaning of persistence.

Chronicles is not merely a history of the fall of the monarchy. Its message is that there's forgiveness and redemption for those who have sinned and suffered. Worship is the response to God's healing.

There are two important points to take from this. First, *explaining* suffering is less important than *responding* to suffering. I write this as the entire world is quarantining because of the coronavirus. It reminds me of the words of Gandalf in *The Lord of the Rings*. Frodo says, "I wish it need not have happened in my time." Gandalf responds, "So do I . . . and so do all who live to see such times. But that is not for them to decide. All we have to decide is what to do with the time that is given us."[4]

Viktor Frankl was a psychoanalyst and a prisoner in Auschwitz. In his book, *Man's Search for Meaning*, he writes about how in the midst of misery in the "camp" ("camp" sounds too nice a descriptor for Auschwitz), Frankl began to think of his wife with fondness. Unbeknownst to him, his wife had been killed. Nevertheless, the thought of her took him to another place. Frankl says this:

> A thought transfixed me: for the first time in my life I saw the truth as it is set into song by so many poets, proclaimed as the final wisdom by so many thinkers. The truth—that love is the ultimate and the highest goal to which man can aspire. Then I grasped the meaning of the greatest secret that human poetry and human thought and belief have to impart: The salvation of man is through love and in love. I understood how a man who has nothing left in this world still may know bliss, be it only for a brief moment, in the contemplation of his beloved. In a position of utter desolation, when man cannot express himself in positive action, when his only achievement may consist in enduring his sufferings in the right way—an honorable way—in such a position man can, through loving contemplation of the image he carries of his beloved, achieve fulfillment. For the first time in my life I was able to understand the meaning of the words, "The angels are lost in perpetual contemplation of an infinite glory."[5]

Mel Gibson illustrated this concept in *Braveheart*. At the end, just before William Wallace is about to be beheaded after being tortured, he sees the apparition of his late wife. Her lovely visage brings a smile to his face in the last moment of his life. It's about the power of the mind to transcend suffering. We are not helpless even if we feel we

4. Tolkien, *The Lord of the Rings*, 51.

5. Frankl, *Man's Search for Meaning*, 37.

are. We may not be able to change our situation, but we can change ourselves. There are things even the worst tragedies cannot take from us.

The second point is that there's not one single response to suffering that serves as a one-size-fits-all. In the Ketuvim, love is only one possible response to suffering. Proverbs would argue that love without wisdom is fruitless. Yet wisdom is not the immediate remedy for personified Zion in Lamentations whose children have been massacred. For her, the immediate response to pain is to lament. The brilliance of the Ketuvim is that its ideas reflect the complexities of life. It will not allow us to settle with easy solutions to difficult problems.

THE FEMININE

Despite Proverbs being a very masculine book, almost entirely from a male point of view, there's a feminine aspect in the book which is very striking. Proverbs is about wisdom and wisdom in Proverbs is personified as a woman. Proverbs ends with a description of an idealistic woman. Job wipes the slate clean as far as that's concerned. The only woman who speaks in Job—Mrs. Job—is nameless and is a temptress of sorts (a common biblical trope). She also has only one line of dialogue. But Ruth changes everything. The beginning of Ruth makes us think that this is a typical biblical story about a man, but we quickly learn that it's about two women. As a result, Ruth features women speaking to each other more than any other book of the Bible.[6] The masculine nature of Proverbs and Job, while acknowledging the significance of women, tends to portray women in "black and white" terms.[7] Women are either wisdom or folly, good or evil, faithful or adulterous. When we enter the Five Scrolls, we see that that portrayal changes. The portrayal of the feminine becomes more sophisticated and three-dimensional as the Ketuvim progresses.

In the Five Scrolls, if we place Ruth as the first book of the five, we end up having the only books of the Bible named after women bracketing the set. The Song of Songs is also extraordinarily feminine. It begins with a woman speaking. It ends with a woman speaking. The woman's voice in the Song is also more prominent than the man's. The woman of the Song is the only woman in the Bible to describe herself as beautiful. The Bible has no problem telling us when a woman is attractive.[8] Yet in those cases it's always the narrator who tells us this. The women of the Bible are far too modest. The woman in the Song of Songs, however, boldly declares, "I am beautiful" (Song 1:5).[9] Lamentations is also quite feminine in nature, for it features a feminine personification of Zion, much the way Proverbs features a feminine personification of wisdom. The Five Scrolls are immensely, strangely, and wondrously feminine.

6. Tull, *Esther and Ruth*, loc. 1064.

7. See Camp, "Woman Wisdom."

8. The Bible also describes men as attractive. See, for example, 2 Sam 14:25.

9. Weems, *What Matters Most*, 32.

Except for Ecclesiastes! Ecclesiastes is hyper-masculine. Ecclesiastes 7:26–28 sounds like the speaker had his heart broken and stomped on by more than one woman! The masculine nature of Ecclesiastes, right in the middle of the Five Scrolls (at least according to the order I'm taking up here), draws attention to the feminine character of the other four books. In turn, the feminine character of the other four books causes Ecclesiastes to stand out.

Ruth and Esther are inversions of each other. Ruth is about a non-Jew who becomes a Jew and marries a Jew. Esther is about a Jew who, in effect, becomes a non-Jew and marries a non-Jew. Both women perform actions which are among the most consequential actions of any character in the Bible. Likewise, the Song of Songs and Lamentations are inversions of each other. The Song of Songs is about a woman in love. Lamentations is about a woman who is "like a widow" and abandoned.

SUBVERSIONS

There's a delightful book by Judy Klitsner which opened my eyes to a beautiful and intriguing aspect of the Tanakh. The book is called *Subversive Sequels: How Biblical Stories Mine and Undermine Each Other*. Her book made me realize that many people have the wrong idea about how the Tanakh expresses Truth (with a capital T). Perhaps this misunderstanding is due to the fact that people are reading a Jewish book without Jewish lenses. It seems many people think that the Tanakh simply declares truths in the form of dogmas. This assumption is understandable in light of the commandments of the Torah (dogmas certainly have their place), but it's ultimately only partially true, especially when we consider the Ketuvim. The Tanakh argues with itself. It does not speak in one voice from one perspective.[10] The philosophy of the Tanakh is that Truth can only be ascertained through debate and diversity of thought.

One of the best professors I ever had was my Shakespeare professor. He also taught a course on the Bible which I regret not taking. However, he did reference the Bible frequently in the Shakespeare class. I vividly remember my professor saying the meaning of life according to the Bible is to wrestle with God. I wish I asked him why he thought that or what that even means, but after spending the last sixteen years thinking about it, I think I now understand. It's a remarkable thing that Jacob's alias—the namesake of the "chosen nation"—is "Israel," which means "the one who wrestles with God" (Gen 32:28). The Bible means this in a positive sense. To *not* wrestle with God is to accept the world as it is. It's to say that murder, rape, disease, and poverty are God's will and we must not resist them. To wrestle with God means that we are, in effect, partnering with God to create a better world. Therefore, it should hardly be surprising that the Tanakh features a lot of arguing with itself.

10. Brueggemann, *Theology of the Old Testament*, 317. Brueggemann refers to the subversive voices as Israel's "countertestimony."

Why the Least Holy Books are So Stupendous

When we look at the books of the Ketuvim, we see that these books are not only connected, not only presenting different responses to suffering, but are also subverting other books and theologies of the Tanakh. They even subvert each other! The case of Proverbs and Job is the most straightforward example of this. Proverbs states that suffering is self-inflicted. If you do what is wise and right, you will flourish. If you act foolishly, you will suffer. As we will discuss later, this is actually the dominant strand of thinking in the Tanakh and its champion is Deuteronomy. This perspective is also the subject of the opening psalm—the very first thing we read in the Ketuvim. Job, however, says, "Not so fast!" Job presents a righteous man whose suffering is *not* caused by any human action. Proverbs is true, but it's not the whole truth.

Ruth, too, is subversive and, like Job, Ruth's sparring partner is Deuteronomy. Deuteronomy 23:3–6 bars Moabites from the assembly of Israel up to the tenth generation. Ruth is about a Moabite who becomes the great-grandmother of King David. How can Deuteronomy and Ruth be reconciled? Judaism found a loophole. Since Deuteronomy uses the masculine form of the word "Moabite," the prohibition applies only to men and therefore doesn't apply to Ruth.[11] Clever! Even so, it's a bit too lawyerish for my taste. Deuteronomy forbids Moabites from entering the assembly of the Lord because the Moabites didn't give food and water to the Israelites when they were hungry. The book of Ruth is about Israelites who move to Moab because of a famine and marry into a Moabite family. They stay in Moab for ten years. The implication is that the Moabites *do* give food and water to this Jewish family. Can we resist thinking that Ruth is softening the prohibition of Deuteronomy?

The Song of Songs is also a very subversive little book. It subverts at least two passages in the Bible. Song 7:10 subverts Gen 3:16's description of marital inequality. Song 8:10 subverts the polygamy of Solomon as described in 1 Kgs 11:3.

And Ecclesiastes is probably the most subversive book of the Tanakh. Ecclesiastes subverts Proverbs' most important truth-claims. Ecclesiastes is so subversive it even subverts itself!

Again, this should be viewed as wondrous, not something disturbing or, far worse, a barrier to faith. There's no "theory of everything" in the Tanakh. The Tanakh contains a myriad of ideas which must be held together, even if they're in tension with each other.[12] Nothing is completely true alone. The whole truth is found only when we recognize the diversity within the unity.

11. Sacks, *Ceremony and Celebration*, 310–11.

12. For a New Testament application of the same principle, see Snodgrass, *Between Two Truths*.

3

A Very Brief Taste of the Wonders of Biblical Hebrew Poetry

THE BIBLE AS LITERATURE

WE'RE LIVING IN A very unpoetic age. Most people don't read poetry, let alone write it. It's nigh impossible to get a book of poetry published. As for our lyrics, we've gone from "Some Enchanted Evening" to "Break Up with Your Girlfriend, I'm Bored."

The Tanakh, therefore, is at a disadvantage. Truly, the Tanakh is a literary phenomenon. Not only did the Tanakh pioneer and develop the third-person prose narrative,[1] it's also saturated with poetry. There's much more poetry in the Tanakh than there is in the New Testament. But if people don't read poetry, how will they appreciate the literary artistry of the Tanakh? The Tanakh, then, is not unlike classical music; it's become an acquired taste.

But that's not the full extent of the problem. The Bible has become the most divisive of all books because it's a religious text. More than that, it's the foundational religious text for the dominant religion in the West, which means it's viewed as particularly controversial. No one today has a problem with public schools teaching Greek mythology, but the Bible is basically forbidden. The result of this is that large segments of the population know more about Zeus and Mount Olympus than Moses and Mount Sinai.

Let me mention my Shakespeare professor again. I remember when he told the class the story of David and Bathsheba. Somehow that story related to whatever play we were studying. He made the story come alive for us. I knew the story very well and yet I was hanging on every word he said, eager to find out what happens next.

My professor's knowledge and passion for the Bible confounded me. Was he religious? Most religious people I know wouldn't say that David was trying to "save his

---

1. Alter, *The Art of Biblical Narrative*, 27. "It is peculiar, and culturally significant, that among ancient peoples, only Israel should have chosen to cast its sacred national traditions in prose."

28

own personal ass" (however true that may be)! But if he wasn't religious, why was he so interested in the Bible? (Back then I didn't know that many of the most prominent Bible scholars are nonbelievers.) So I decided to ask him about it. But I thought it would be too invasive to explicitly ask him if he was religious. Instead, I asked him if he views the Bible as literature. In my twenty-two-year-old mind, if one views the Bible as literature, it means that one does *not* view the Bible as the authoritative "word of God." His answer revealed my bias and lack of understanding. He looked at me somewhat incredulously and said, "Of course I view the Bible as literature! That's what it is!" He's absolutely right. The Bible *is* literature. The reader is certainly free to read it as *more* than literature (i.e., as the authoritative word of God), but the reader is not free to read it as something *other* than literature. You can view the Bible as literature or you can view the Bible as sacred literature, but either way, the Bible is literature!

Yet viewing the Bible as something other than literature is precisely what many people in our society have done. Because the Bible is viewed as something distinct from literature, the religious community has not been eager to learn how literary scholars would analyze it, and literary scholars have not shown much of an interest in analyzing it.[2] I contend both groups need each other. The insights of literary scholars are invaluable to biblical scholarship. And not only the insights of literary scholars; actors are needed too. This is because we obviously don't have tone of voice in the Bible. Tone of voice can affect interpretation immensely. Actors can show the rest of us different ways of portraying different characters. Most readers of the Bible have probably not even thought of how ambiguous certain lines of dialogue in the Bible are. Literary theorists and actors dialogue with each other when it comes to analyzing Shakespeare. I know the Bible is not a play (plays were a Greek thing, not a Jewish thing!), but I don't see why it's different in principle. The religious community needs the insights of literary theorists, actors, psychologists, philosophers, lawyers, and many more people besides. And on the other side of the equation, the secular community learns about Zeus and Hamlet, but knows precious little of the brilliant narratives of Genesis and the magnificent poetry of Job.

In this book I hope to do my part to introduce people to the Bible. Those who are most resistant to reading the Bible might be surprised how much they'll love it. Their lives might even be changed as result of reading it.

POETIC FEATURES AND DEVICES

Let's go back to Yeshua ben Sira's grandson for a moment. The grandfather wrote a book in Hebrew. The grandson translated it into Greek and added a prologue. In the prologue he wrote this:

---

2. Robert Alter, Adele Berlin, and Meir Sternberg have written extensively on the literary aspects of the Bible. Their works have changed the face of biblical scholarship. See also Harold Bloom's *The Book of J*. Bloom was a professor of literature at Yale University.

Illuminating Counsel

> You are invited therefore to read [my grandfather's book] with goodwill and attention, and to be indulgent in cases where, despite our diligent labor in translating, we may seem to have rendered some phrases imperfectly. For what was originally expressed in Hebrew does not have exactly the same sense when translated into another language. Not only this book, but even the Law itself, the Prophecies, and the rest of the books differ not a little when read in the original.[3]

Amen! It's very tempting for the modern reader to forget that the Bible was not written in English (or whatever translation the reader happens to be reading). Translations are invaluable but something is always lost in translation. There's a famous quote: "Reading a poem in translation is like kissing your sweetheart through a veil." We will also do well to remember the Italian phrase: *Traduttore, traditore!* "The translator is a traitor!"

I make my students read Aviya Kushner's *The Grammar of God: A Journey Into the Words and Worlds of the Bible*. It's remarkable how a book about grammar can be so moving. Kushner shows how the Bible reads differently in Hebrew than it does in English. I believe her book is essential reading for any beginning student of the Bible. I certainly prefer it to a dry-as-burnt-toast textbook.

Since Hebrew is so different than English, it should not be surprising that biblical Hebrew poetry works quite differently than English poetry. One of the beauties of biblical Hebrew is that, though its vocabulary is sorely limited, especially compared to English, it also needs far fewer words to express itself. Thus Hebrew words are often pregnant with meaning and can carry quite a punch. This also allows for a more economical and minimalistic literary style, both in poetry and in prose.[4]

Biblical Hebrew poetry does not use rhyme as a literary device. When rhymes do occur, they're usually incidental. These incidental rhymes are caused by suffixes which are attached to verbs and nouns. Let me try to illustrate this. In English, if I talk about what belongs to me, I would use the word "my." I would speak of my hat, my scarf, and my gloves. In biblical Hebrew, each of those phrases would be one word. They would be expressed as the hat-of-me, the scarf-of-me, and the gloves-of-me. It might therefore seem like each of those phrases/words rhyme (all ending in "me"), but that's just how Hebrew expresses itself.

A good example of incidental rhyme is found in Ps 3. I will transliterate the Hebrew knowing that you, dear reader, may not be able to pronounce the words correctly. Don't be intimidated by the language. Even if you don't know the proper pronunciation, my point will be sufficiently illustrated. The first line of Ps 3 after the superscription (I'll explain what that means later) is this:

---

3. NRSV.

4. Linafelt, *The Hebrew Bible as Literature*, 9–10.

30

A Very Brief Taste of the Wonders of Biblical Hebrew Poetry

> *Ma-rabu tsarai;*
>> *rabim kamim alai.*

Notice: *tsarai* rhymes with *alai*, but the reason they rhyme is because the *ai* (pronounced like the English word "eye") is the possessive plural. *Tzarai* means "tormentors of me" or "my tormentors." *Alai* means "against me." You may have also noticed that *rabim* and *kamim* rhyme. This, too, is incidental. The *im* suffix is the non-possessive masculine plural form.

Having said that, sometimes biblical poets will choose words that rhyme because biblical Hebrew is meant to be read aloud and the poets were very much concerned with how the words sound and how they flow. For example, Prov 31:29 says, "Many women have done excellently . . ." That's the translation of these Hebrew words: *Rabot banot asu hayil . . . Banot* literally means "daughters." The more typical Hebrew word for "women" is *nashim. Nashim* is one of those anomalous words—a feminine word that has a masculine plural ending. Which sounds better to you: *rabot nashim asu hayil* or *rabot banot asu hayil*? Clearly the latter. The poet chose the word *banot* ("daughters") because the feminine ending of *banot* (*ot*) matches the feminine ending of *rabot.*

But that sort of rhyming is the exception, not the rule. The key feature of Hebrew poetry is not the rhyming of words but the rhyming of *thoughts*.[5] This is known as "parallelism." But let me back up for a moment. Whether poetry or prose, each verse of the Hebrew Bible is usually divided into two parts, though these parts are not necessarily symmetrical. Sometimes there are three versets[6] in a sentence. We see this in the very first sentence of the very first psalm. But even when there are three versets, there's still one pause, thus dividing the line into two. We can think of this pause as a comma or a semicolon. I prefer to think of it with a musical term: a half-cadence. The cadence occurs at the end of a musical phrase where the harmony goes to the tonic, or the I [one] chord. The half-cadence occurs at the halfway point and usually ends on the dominant, or the V [five] chord. You've heard that a thousand times in songs even if you don't know what it is. Biblical Hebrew lines are conceived musically in that way. The parallelisms work with the twofold division of the lines.

There are basically four kinds of parallelism. The first kind is called *synonymous parallelism*. How do synonymous parallelisms work? Imagine you're a poet. You have your first line: "Save, O LORD, for the godly one is gone." Pretty grim, but a real concern, no doubt! But now what? What should the next line be? Where should you go

---

5. Alter, *The Art of Biblical Poetry*, loc. 249–61. Alter criticizes the definition of parallelism as "thought-rhymes." However, I am describing parallelism this way while qualifying it with Alter's view that parallelism does not merely restate the previous verset but rather intensifies it.

6. Alter uses the word "verset" to describe half, or part, of a line of poetry. Alter prefers using the word "verset" over the more tradition German word *hemistich* or the word colon/cola. *The Art of Biblical Poetry*, loc. 249.

Illuminating Counsel

from there? Synonymous parallelism repeats the sentiment but states it in a different way. The repetition either intensifies the original thought or clarifies it:[7]

> Save, O LORD, for the godly one is gone,
>> *for the faithful have vanished from among the children of man.*" (Ps 12:1)

Notice: "godly one" (which is one word in Hebrew) is synonymously paralleled with "the faithful." Also "gone" is paralleled (and intensified) with "vanished from among the children of man."

The second kind of parallelism is called *antithetical parallelism*. If synonymous parallelism's second line restates the first line, antithetical parallelism's second line is the *opposite* of the first line. So imagine making a statement about God's rescuing activity: "For you save a humble people . . ." Now, to make an antithetical parallelism you would state something opposite to that, something like this:

> For you save a humble people,
>> *but the haughty eyes you bring down.* (Ps 18:27)

Notice: "humble people" is antithetically paralleled with "haughty eyes." "Save" is antithetically paralleled with "bring down."

The third kind of parallelism is called *synthetic parallelism*. This, I think, is thusly named because we don't know what else to call it. The second line is neither synonymous nor antithetical to the first line. Rather, it tells us something new. Again, imagine you're a poet. You come up with a nice opening line: "The eyes of all look to you . . ." Now, don't restate that line and don't say the opposite of it. Rather, give us a logical followup to it:

> The eyes of all look to you,
>> *and you give them their food in due season.* (Ps 145:15)

The fourth kind of parallelism is called *climactic parallelism*. Ryken says in climactic parallelism "the second line repeats part of the first line and then adds to it."[8] Let's say your first line is, "Ascribe to the LORD, O families of the peoples . . ." Your second line, then, will begin with the phrase "Ascribe to the LORD." What shall the "families of the peoples" ascribe to the LORD?

> Ascribe to the LORD, O families of the peoples,
>> *ascribe to the LORD glory and strength!* (Ps 96:7)

We mustn't presume, however, that parallelism is the only poetic device in biblical Hebrew poetry. It's prominent—yes—but there's plenty of poetry in the Bible that is not written in parallelisms. There's also prose in the Bible that contains parallelisms. Parallelism doesn't make something poetic any more than rhyming makes something

---

7. Alter, *The Art of Biblical Poetry*, loc. 362.

8. Ryken, *Sweeter Than Honey, Richer Than Gold*, loc. 956.

A Very Brief Taste of the Wonders of Biblical Hebrew Poetry

poetic. What makes something poetic is rhythmic verses rather than full sentences combined with a stylized and rich use of language: the use of metaphors, similes, wordplays, and a myriad of other devices. Poetry uses words in an artistic way in order to convey ideas and feelings that cannot be adequately expressed in prose. Poetry is to prose what singing is to speaking.

Let's look at an example:

> In you, O LORD, do I take refuge;
> > let me never be put to shame;
> > in your righteousness deliver me!
> Incline your ear to me;
> > rescue me speedily!
> Be a rock and a refuge for me,
> > a strong fortress to save me!
> For you are my rock and my fortress;
> > and for your name's sake you lead me and guide me;
> you take me out of the net they have hidden for me,
> > for you are my refuge.
> Into your hand I commit my spirit;
> > you have redeemed me, O LORD, faithful God. (Ps 31:1–5 [2–6])

Notice this is written in *verse* rather than full sentences. We should give the editors of modern translations of the Bible credit for arranging the text in this way, helping the reader to immediately recognize that she is reading poetry rather than prose. The ancient and medieval manuscripts do not differentiate between the two.

Notice that the first couplet and last couplet match. They both say the psalmist is placing himself "in" or "into" God's care. Notice also that God's name—"the LORD" (literally Yahweh)—appears in the first verset and the last verset. This is called an *inclusio*. An *inclusio* is a word or phrase or thought that appears in the beginning and end of a passage.

Notice also the psalmist's use of metaphors. God is his "rock" and "fortress." The psalmist is in a "net" but God is his "refuge." These are common metaphors in the psalms.

God is anthropomorphized. God—an invisible entity—is given human body parts. The psalmist asks God to incline his "ear" to him and the psalmist commits his spirit into God's "hand." Christians will recognize that Jesus quotes this text as he was about to die (Luke 23:46).

The psalmist uses synonyms, some of which are lost in translation. "Be a rock (*tsur*) of refuge for me . . . for you are my rock (*sal'i*) and my fortress." Also, the first word translated "refuge" ("In you, O LORD, do I take *refuge*") is a different Hebrew word than the second word translated "refuge" ("Be a rock of *refuge*"). The latter "refuge" more literally means "strength." The vocabulary in biblical poetry is far more extensive than the vocabulary in biblical prose. The psalmist prays that God will "deliver" him, "rescue" him, and "save" him.

33

The psalmist uses repetition. The word "fortress" (*metsuda*) is used twice. The aforementioned word "strength" which is translated "refuge" (*ma'oz*) is used twice. The Hebrew pronoun *atah*, which means "you," is used twice ("For *you* are my rock and my refuge . . . for *you* are my refuge").

Then there's the assonance (words with similar sounds). The words translated "lead me" and "guide me" sound similar to each other (*tanheni u'tnahaleni*).[9] The TS sound is prominent. "In your righteousness"—*b'tsidkat'kha*. "Rescue me"—*hatsileni*. "Rock of strength"—*l'tsur ma'oz*. "A strong fortress"—*metsudot*. "You take me out"—*totsi'eni*.

All of these devices are magnified as the psalm progresses. The psalmist continues with the anthropomorphisms and emphasis of body parts. He makes numerous wordplays with the TS sound. "Rock," as we noted, is *tsur*. The psalmist also uses the words *tsar* ("distress"), *tsarar* ("adversaries"), *matsor* ("besieged"), and *notser* ("preserves").[10] He continues to use synonyms, especially for the words "refuge" and "strength." He continues to use repetition, especially with the words "deliver" and "save."

This is just a sample of a treasure trove of poetic devices in the Ketuvim. Many books have been written about biblical Hebrew poetry. I highly recommend Robert Alter's *The Art of Biblical Poetry*, which is a companion piece to his seminal *The Art of Biblical Narrative*. If you have less time, you can read David L. Peterson's *Interpreting Biblical Poetry* or Leland Ryken's *Sweeter Than Honey, Richer Than Gold: A Guided Study of Biblical Poetry*. For a concise summation of the poetic devices in the psalms, I recommend Benjamin Segal's *A New Psalm: The Psalms as Literature*.[11]

When putting together my class on the Ketuvim, I decided to have my students compose a psalm. Their psalm was to be in English, of course, but they had to use the Tanakh's poetic devices. Parallelisms were required. After that, they had to use at least four other poetic devices of their choosing, as listed by Segal. They then had to analyze and interpret their psalm. Out of respect for my nonreligious students, I told them the psalm didn't have to be a proper psalm. It could be about their pet goldfish for all I cared. The point of the assessment was the poetic devices, not the subject matter. I realized the only way to truly understand the Bible's poetry is not to be tested on it but to use it in the creative process; to think like a biblical poet.

What surprised me most was not how good the students' poetry was or even how well they utilized the poetic devices. What surprised me most was how much, by their own admission, they loved the assignment. One student said it was the best assignment she had all semester—and she had many good ones, including analyzing Brahms' fourth symphony. Brahms' fourth symphony is one of the greatest masterpieces of music ever composed, so what she said was a big compliment indeed! Another surprise was how poignant and personal these poems were. The student who

9. Psalm 31:3[4] bears similarities to the famous Ps 23.

10. Segal, *A New Psalm*, 140–44.

11. Segal, *A New Psalm*, xxiv–xxviii.

A Very Brief Taste of the Wonders of Biblical Hebrew Poetry

studied Brahms had recently attended the funeral of a child. Inspired by that, she wrote her psalm from the perspective of Bathsheba losing her baby (2 Sam 12).

I hope that studying the Bible, particularly the Ketuvim, will inspire people to be creative. I hope reading the Bible's thrilling epic narratives will inspire people to write their own stories. I hope reading the Bible's exquisite poetry will inspire people to write their own poetry. And it wouldn't hurt if reading the Bible inspired people to experience the joys of learning another language.

4

A Very Brief Overview of the Psalms

ARRANGEMENT AND GENRES

THERE IS ONE BOOK of Psalms but there are five books of psalms within the one book of Psalms. Confusing, I know! This is why I like using the word *Psalter*. The Psalter refers to the entirety of the psalms. There is one Psalter but five books within the one Psalter. All our printed Bibles have these divisions:

- Book I: Pss 1–41
- Book II: Pss 42–72
- Book III: Pss 73–89
- Book IV: Pss 90–106
- Book V: Pss 107–50

Nancy deClaissé-Walford has an interesting thesis regarding how each of these five books works together. She argues the Psalter tells Israel's story from David to the exile and back. The overall theology of the Psalms, according to her, is the kingship of God. Her article is a must-read for any student of this literature.[1]

Form criticism is an important part of the study of the Psalter. You mustn't think "criticism" in this sense means that the psalms are being criticized. They're not being criticized; they're being *analyzed*. Form criticism seeks to understand how the psalms functioned in their historical and theological contexts by grouping them into genres. This work was pioneered by a German scholar named Hermann Gunkel in his book, *Psalms—A Form-Critical Introduction*.

Generally, the Psalms break down into five genres:

---

1. deClaissé-Walford, "The Canonical Shape of the Psalms," in Ballard and Tucker, *Introduction to Wisdom Literature*, 93–110.

A Very Brief Overview of the Psalms

- Praise Hymn
- Thanksgiving
- Lament
- Wisdom/Torah
- Zion/Royal

The praise hymns are general praises to God whereas the thanksgivings are praises given due to more specific circumstances. A praise hymn will praise God for creating and sustaining the world. A thanksgiving will praise God for rescuing the psalmist from distress. Laments are complaints and expressions of distress and sadness. Both the thanksgivings and the laments come in an individual voice and a communal voice.

The laments have two sub-genres: the penitential psalms and the imprecatory psalms. Penitential psalms are confessions of sin. There are seven of them, as identified by a Christian theologian from antiquity named Cassiodorus.[2] Seven out of 150 is not a lot. While guilt and forgiveness are central issues in Christianity, most psalms don't deal with this theme. Rather, the psalms are much more focused on an innocent figure being hunted by his enemies. It makes some sense, then, that there would be imprecatory psalms, which are psalms that curse enemies. These psalms are the most difficult for modern readers, especially for Christians, because they seem antithetical to Christianity's teaching to "love your enemies" (Matt 5:44). I think many Christians love the psalms but are also confounded by them.

Wisdom/Torah psalms pertain to how we should live. Torah and wisdom are basically interchangeable concepts. I will say more about this when we discuss Proverbs.

Zion/royal psalms are either about Jerusalem, the Davidic king, or God's kingship. Some of these psalms are particularly important in Christianity due to their messianic overtones.

Walter Brueggemann has a different yet complimentary way of classifying the psalms. He breaks the psalms into three categories:

- Psalms of Orientation
- Psalms of Disorientation
- Psalms of Reorientation[3]

There are some psalms which celebrate being in a relationship with God (Orientation). Then there are psalms which complain about some kind of distress (Disorientation). When that distress is overcome, the psalmist celebrates a reunion with God (Reorientation).

---

2. Psalms 6, 32, 38, 51, 102, 130, 143.

3. Brueggemann, *Spirituality of Psalms*, loc. 132–47.

Illuminating Counsel

These categories are compelling because they can be applied to the entire Bible. The Bible itself breaks down into three movements: God creates, humans mess up, God redeems. God makes a covenant with Israel, Israel breaks the covenant with God, God renews the covenant with Israel. Orientation, disorientation, reorientation. Indeed, all of life seems to fit within that pattern, though we are constantly sliding from disorientation to reorientation and back. In life, we don't "arrive" anywhere until we die.

Less well-known than Brueggemann's classification is Erich Fromm's. Fromm divides the psalms into four categories:

- One-Mood Psalms
- Dynamic Psalms
- Hymnic Psalms
- Messianic Psalms[4]

We've already noted the hymns and the royals (messianic). The "One-Mood" and "Dynamic" classifications are interesting. One-mood psalms are like a piece of music which doesn't modulate to a different key. Fromm cites Ps 23 as an example. But other psalms have more than one mood. These are the dynamic psalms. Psalm 27 is one of the best examples of a dynamic psalm. We will look at that psalm in some detail shortly. Segal speaks of psalms like Ps 27 as psalms which utilize a poetic device called "contradictory sections."[5]

The abrupt changes in mood within the dynamic psalms have caused some scholars to posit more than one author. The theory is that psalms like Ps 27 were originally two psalms. Many years after they were composed, an editor sewed them together, so to speak. This is called *source criticism*. It's the attempt to find the sources within the Bible before the editor got his hands on them. The theory is certainly plausible. There are some psalms which probably were *one* psalm but were *separated* by an editor. Psalm 9 and Ps 10 are an example of that. In the Septuagint (the Greek translation of the Tanakh), Ps 9 and Ps 10 are one psalm. Psalm 9 and Ps 10 are an *acrostic*. An acrostic is a type of poem in which each line begins with a successive letter of the alphabet. Psalm 9 begins with the Hebrew equivalent of A and goes through the alphabet until ending with the Hebrew equivalent of K. Psalm 10 picks up where Ps 9 leaves off. Psalm 10 begins with the Hebrew equivalent of L. Psalm 10 then breaks up the acrostic only to return to it later, ending with the Hebrew equivalents of W, X, Y, Z.[6] So again, it's hardly beyond the realm of possibility that an editor took two psalms and combined them into one. Nevertheless, I take a conservative approach. As a general

4. Fromm, *You Shall Be As Gods*, 203–4.

5. Segal, *A New Psalm*, xxvi.

6. Segal, *A New Psalm*, 42–43. We must note two things about Ps 10. First, it doesn't contain a superscription like most of the other psalms in Book I. But second, Ps 10 has a radically different mood than Ps 9.

A Very Brief Overview of the Psalms

principle, I interpret the dynamic psalms as one psalm until I see strong evidence that they were originally two.[7] More often than not, I see evidence of their unity.

SUPERSCRIPTIONS

Most psalms contain *superscriptions*. These are subheadings which often attribute a psalm to a particular person. Sometimes they place the psalm within an historical context. Seventy-three of the psalms are attributed to David. They will say things like: "A Psalm of David" or even simply "Of David." Thirteen of those seventy-three psalms are placed within a specific event in David's life. Twelve of those thirteen psalms occur in the first two books of psalms (the exception being Ps 142, which is in Book V). Thus the psalms are, by and large, associated with David—"the sweet psalmist of Israel" (2 Sam 23:1). David's song of deliverance in 2 Sam 22 is basically Ps 18. The psalms also reflect David's life and passion. The psalmist is constantly pursued by enemies, as was David, and the psalms express love for God, as did David (compare 2 Sam 6:16 with Ps 149:3). But we mustn't think that all the psalms are associated with David. Twelve psalms are attributed to one Asaph, who was a Levite temple musician. Eleven psalms are attributed to the "sons of Korah." Two psalms are attributed to Solomon.[8]

The superscriptions also contain musical directions, some of which are not translatable. The word "*selah*," which is found throughout the psalms (though not in superscriptions), is believed to be a musical term. Many of the superscriptions begin with the words, "To the choirmaster." The "choirmaster" must have been some kind of an ancient music director. Some superscriptions indicate that the psalm is to be accompanied by stringed instruments. Psalm 5 is to be accompanied by flutes. Some superscriptions indicate that the psalm is to be sung with a particular melody. I love how musical the Bible is!

In all likelihood, the superscriptions were not written by the original psalmist but were added much later by an editor or editors. It's the editor who arranged the psalms in the Psalter. Some people might find that difficult to accept, wanting to believe instead that the only hand on the text was the hand of the writer. But this is both untenable and unnecessary. It's untenable because the psalms sometimes contradict their superscriptions.[9] It's unnecessary because part of the beauty of the Bible is the process of editing that shaped it. The Bible is a collaborative work.

Ironically, those who reject the notion that the superscriptions were written by an editor tend to skip over the superscriptions in public readings of the psalms. This is not the Jewish practice. In Christian Bibles, the superscriptions are in smaller print

---

7. I am in complete agreement with Segal about this. See *A New Psalm*, xxvi.

8. There are psalms which are attributed to individuals we know little to nothing about.

9. The superscription of Ps 51 indicates that David wrote it after he confessed his sin of adultery and murder. This corresponds to 2 Sam 11–12. However, Ps 51:18–19[20–21] seems to be from an exilic perspective.

than the rest of the psalm and the first verse of the psalm begins *after* the superscription. In Jewish Bibles, the superscription is part of the psalm and is always counted as the first verse. This is frustrating because it means that the verse numbers in the English translation of Psalms are usually one number off from the Hebrew. With long superscriptions, such as Ps 51's, the verse numbers are two numbers off. (I will indicate the Hebrew verses in brackets when they differ from the English.) The point, though, is that the Jewish practice is to always begin reading the psalm with the superscription. Thus a Christian would say the first line of Ps 23 is "The Lord is my shepherd." A Jew would say the first line of Ps 23 is *Mizmor l'David*—"A Psalm of David." Just as the work of the editors of a book, magazine, journal, and movie are invaluable, so too the work of the editors of the Bible ought to be read and appreciated.

JOURNEY INTO THE PSALMS

Having said what we needed to say about biblical Hebrew poetry and the categorizations of the psalms (which is very little compared to all that *could* be said), we are now ready to begin our journey into the first book of the Ketuvim. What you will notice is that the psalms are very Jewish and yet remarkably universal. They are Jewish because they were written by Jews, for Jews, and with complete devotion to the God of Israel. They are universal because they express virtually every emotion a person is capable of feeling. I remember having a conversation with my father about the different ways Jews and Christians view the psalms. At the end of the conversation, my father told me his verdict: "The psalms belong to the world." And so they do.

The universality of the psalms is true for every book of the Ketuvim. This is partly why the Ketuvim is so special. It also speaks to the role of Jews in history. Perhaps no other people in the world has been so intentional about being unique. It's remarkable, then, that Jews wrote books that all peoples have related to. It's a reminder that humans are paradoxical. We're all unique and yet we're all the same.

Since there are 150 psalms, all that can be offered in our study is a sampling. I will try to give you a taste of a little of everything—a smorgasbord, if you will—so that you get a sense of what the Psalter is about. This will be my general approach throughout this book, though I can give a more comprehensive treatment of some of the shorter books of the Ketuvim. I write with the hope that you will be inspired to read these wonderful poems and books for yourself and come up with your own thoughts about them.

5

Songs without Music
(Psalms)

IMAGINE YOU'RE THE EDITOR in Chief of the Psalter. You have 150 psalms scattered on your desk. Your job is to arrange them into one volume. Where do you begin? You have praise hymns, thanksgivings, laments, Torah/wisdoms, and Zion/royals. Which genre would you choose to be your leadoff batter?

I ask students this question. Most of them tend to say either a thanksgiving or a lament. I find starting off with a lament to be a bit jarring but I applaud the boldness of it. Starting off with a thanksgiving makes some sense, I suppose. If it were up to me, I would start off with a hymn. We've been told time and time again by preachers that the Psalter was Israel's hymnal. Starting with a hymn seems fitting. It sets the right tone.

The Psalter, though, doesn't begin with a praise hymn, thanksgiving, or lament. It begins with a Torah psalm. But this shouldn't really be a surprise. We've already noted that the Torah is the most important part of the Tanakh. It's no coincidence that the Prophets section begins with mentioning the Torah (Josh 1:7–8) and ends with mentioning the Torah (Mal 4:4 [3:22]). It seems perfectly fitting, then, for the Ketuvim to begin with mentioning the Torah. This aspect of the Bible is a bit obfuscated by the Old Testament, for in the Old Testament Joshua is part of the History Books, not the Prophets. Yet if we keep this emphasis on Torah in mind, the logic of the Ketuvim—particularly the logic of the *ending* of the Ketuvim—will begin to become clear.

TORAH AND WISDOM

The very first verse of the very first psalm, which is the very first line of the Ketuvim, sounds like this in Hebrew: "*Ashrei ha-ish, asher lo halakh ba-atzat reshaim . . .*" Notice

Illuminating Counsel

the assonance. The SH sound has prominence, as does the R sound.[1] Clearly this is meant to be read aloud so that we can hear "the music of the words."[2]

Many English translations translate the first word—*ashrei*—as "blessed." This is not the most accurate meaning of the word. There's a word for "blessed" and it's a very important word, both in the Bible as well as in Judaism. "Blessed" in Hebrew is *barukh*. This word does, indeed, occur in the Psalter in very important places. Sometimes it's translated "praise." But that's not what *ashrei* means. *Ashrei* means "happy."

Ashrei occurs in numerous places in the Psalter. It's not only the first word of the first psalm. It's also the first word in the last line of the second psalm—"*Happy* are those who take refuge in him" (2:12b). It's the first word after the superscription of the last psalm of the first book of Psalms—"*Happy* is the one who considers the poor" (41:1[2]).[3] Don't think for one moment that that's a coincidence. We're beholding the brilliance of the editor.

In between Ps 2 and Ps 41 the word occurs in Ps 32—"*Happy* is the one whose transgressions are forgiven" (32:1[2]). The word has prominence in Ps 84. In fact, Judaism combined Ps 84:4[5]—"*Happy* are those who dwell in your house"—with Ps 145. This is a daily prayer which is called the *Ashrei*. All in all, the word "happy" occurs twenty-six times in the Psalter, which is more than all the other occurrences of that word in the other books of the Tanakh combined.

We can therefore say that *happiness* is a major theme of the Psalter. What's truly fascinating is the thick irony of this theme. While the word "happy" features so prominently in the Psalter, a third of the Psalter consists of laments. The Psalter contains some of the most impassioned expressions of suffering in the Bible. This is a dynamic emotional tension because it reflects the reality of life. How many people are actually "happy"? Is there really such a thing as happiness? The Psalter is ultimately a book of triumphant exuberance, but it takes the entire Psalter—all 150 psalms—to get there. There are no shortcuts to happiness. The road to it is paved with many tears.

Let's now return to Ps 1:

> Happy is the man who does not walk in the counsel of the wicked ones
>> and in the way of sinners does not stand,
>>> and in the seat of scoffers does not sit (Ps 1:1).[4]

How interesting that Ps 1 begins with a negative statement ("who does *not*"). The first step toward happiness is to *not* do bad things. The great insight here is that Ps 1 links happiness with *goodness*. This is quite a contrast to the zeitgeist of contemporary Western culture. Many people intuit that happiness is linked to money or possessions. Certainly how we look matters a great deal, we think. And we want others to love us

---

1. Sarna, *On the Book of Psalms*, 31.
2. I am in debt to Emma Andersen for this phrase.
3. These translations are mine.
4. My translation.

42

Songs without Music

and think highly of us. But according to Ps 1, it's not about what you have, or what others think about you; the key to happiness is your *character*.

The poetry of Ps 1 isn't the height of passion but it is quite clever. Notice the progression of the parallelism: from *walking* to *standing* to *sitting*. Notice, too, the solitary "man" over against the many wicked ones, sinners, and scoffers.[5] The path toward evil is broad, but we have no chance of being happy if we follow it.

The happy person does not bend to peer pressure. He does not follow the crowd. Instead, he "[delights] in the teaching [*torah*] of the LORD" and he "recites his teaching [*torah*] day and night" (Ps 1:2). Imagine that that verse is a hyperlink. Click on it and Ps 19 will open. Psalm 19 expounds on the importance and essentiality of the Torah. It's a dynamic psalm containing three "contradictory sections." The first six verses are about creation, the next five verses are about the Torah, and the last four verses are about prayer. These sections seem unconnected and the transitions seem awkward, but there are threads throughout the psalm that hold the sections together. Let's take a look. I will italicize, bolden, and underline the connections:

> The heavens *declare* the glory of God,
>   and the sky above *proclaims* his handiwork.
> Day to day pours out *speech*,
>   and night to night reveals knowledge.
> There is no *speech*, nor are there *words*,
>   whose *voice* is not heard.
> Their *voice* goes out through all the earth,
>   and their *words* to the end of the world.
> In them he has set a tent for the **sun**,
>   which comes out like a bridegroom leaving his chamber,
>   and, like a strong man, runs its course with joy.
> Its rising is from the end of the heavens,
>   and its circuit to the end of them,
>   and there is nothing hidden from its heat.
>
> The law of the LORD is perfect,
>   reviving the soul;
> the testimony of the LORD is sure,
>   making wise the simple;
> the precepts of the LORD are right,
>   rejoicing the ***heart***;
> the commandment of the LORD is pure,
>   **enlightening** the eyes;
> the fear of the LORD is clean,
>   enduring forever;

5. Segal, *A New Psalm*, 5.

the rules of the LORD are true,
>and righteous altogether.
More to be desired are they than **gold**,
>even much **fine gold**;
sweeter also than **honey**
>and drippings of the honeycomb.

Moreover, by them is your servant warned;
>in keeping them there is great reward.
Who can discern his errors?
>Declare me innocent from <u>hidden</u> faults.
Keep back your servant also from presumptuous sins;
>let them not have dominion over me!
Then I shall be blameless,
>and innocent of great transgression.
Let the *words* of my mouth and the meditation of my **_heart_**
>be acceptable in your sight,
>O LORD, my rock and my redeemer.

This chart will help you see the connections:

	Speech/Words	Sun/Light/Gold	Hidden	Heart
Creation	√	√	√	
Law		√		√
Prayer	√		√	√

Psalm 19 begins with the *speech* of the heavens; it ends with a prayer regarding the *speech* of the psalmist. The creation section emphasizes the role of the **sun**; the Torah section says the Torah **enlightens** and is better than **gold** and **honey**—both of which are a bright golden color, like the sun when it rises and sets. The creation section mentions that nothing is <u>hidden</u> from the sun's heat; the psalmist prays that he will be declared innocent of <u>hidden</u> sins (because nothing can be hidden from God). The creation section says the *words* of the heavens are acceptable; the psalmist prays for his *words* to be acceptable. The Torah section says the Torah makes the **_heart_** rejoice; the psalmist prays the meditation of his **_heart_** will be acceptable.[6] No wonder C. S. Lewis considered Ps 19 to be, not only the greatest psalm, but also one of the greatest poems ever written.[7]

---

6. Segal, *A New Psalm*, loc. 2265.

7. Lewis, *Reflections on the Psalms*, 63.

Songs without Music

But Ps 19 is also like a hyperlink. Click on it and Ps 119 will come up. Psalm 119 is a massive acrostic—the longest psalm and the longest "chapter" in the entire Bible. The longest chapter in the Bible is about the Torah!

Lewis, because of his Protestant background, was stunned by this. How can the psalms sing praises about "law," calling it "sweeter than honey" (Ps 19:10 [11]; 119:103)?[8] To Jews, however, this is no surprise at all. It should tell us that the Protestant perspective, as valuable as it is, is nevertheless not the only perspective from which to read the Bible. It should also tell us that we cannot think of Torah the same way we think of "law." No one—and I mean *no one*—would call the Illinois State Law "sweeter than honey"! But Judaism has always thought of the Torah as God's teachings on life and ethics. "Thou shalt not murder" is a cold, hard commandment, but it also teaches us about the value of life. Likewise, "Thou shalt not commit adultery" teaches us about sexual boundaries. "Thou shalt not steal" teaches us about the value of property. "Thou shalt not bear false witness" teaches us about the value of truth. And so on. The psalms are telling us that we cannot worship God, let alone live, if we do not know *how* to live; if we do not know the principles of right and wrong.

Back to Ps 1—its message is clear: God will cause the righteous to flourish whereas God will crush the wicked. Thus the solitary happy man is "like a tree planted by streams of water that yields its fruit in its season, and its leaf does not whither" (Ps 1:3). The wicked ones, however, are like "chaff" that is blown away. Psalm 1 ends with an antithetical parallelism: "For the LORD knows the way of the righteous, but the way of the wicked will perish" (Ps 1:6).

Psalm 1, therefore, embodies a very important theological idea which is often referred to as the "Retribution Principle." This is the notion that God will punish the wicked and vindicate the righteous. We reap what we sow. This principle will show up again and again in the Ketuvim in important, and perhaps even surprising, ways.

But now let's jump to Ps 73. The first psalm of Book I of the Psalter is a Torah psalm. The first psalm of Book III of the Psalter is a wisdom psalm. Torah and Wisdom are two sides of the same coin because they're both about morality.

The psalmist of Ps 73 states his theme at the outset:

> Truly God is good to Israel,
>> to those who are pure in heart. (Ps 73:1)

This sentiment is the psalmist's theological premise as well as his theological conclusion. Yet he confesses that he nearly doubted this truth:

> But as for me, my feet had almost stumbled,
>> my steps had nearly slipped.
> For I was envious of the arrogant
>> when I saw the prosperity of the wicked. (Ps 73:2–3)

---

8. Lewis, *Reflections on the Psalms*, 54–55.

What's going on here is that Ps 73 is wrestling with the truth expressed in Ps 1. If we take Ps 1 at face value, we are led to think there would not be any reason to envy the wicked. But the psalmist of Ps 73 looks out his window and he doesn't see the righteous flourishing like trees planted beside streams of water and the wicked being blown away like chaff. Rather, he sees the righteous struggling and the wicked possessing *shalom* (the Hebrew word translated "prosperity"). Is Ps 1 too simplistic to be true?

The psalmist then lists all the reasons he envied the wicked. Psalm 1 extolled the virtue of meditating on the Torah day and night. In Ps 73, the psalmist is now disregarding the part of the Torah that says "Thou shalt not covet anything that is thy neighbor's" (Exod 20:17).

But the psalmist told us that his feet had *nearly* slipped. What caused him to regain his footing? Halfway through the psalm he tells us:

> But when I thought how to understand this
>> it seemed to me a wearisome task
> Until I went into the sanctuary of God;
>> then I discerned their end. (Ps 73:16)

What was it about the sanctuary that changed his heart? I cannot help but think of Shakespeare's twenty-ninth sonnet:

> When, in disgrace with fortune and men's eyes,
> I all alone beweep my outcast state,
> And trouble deaf heaven with my bootless cries,
> And look upon myself and curse my fate,
> Wishing me like to one more rich in hope,
> Featured like him, like him with friends possessed,
> Desiring this man's art and that man's scope,
> With what I most enjoy contented least;
> Yet in these thoughts myself almost despising,
> Haply I think on thee, and then my state,
> (Like to the lark at break of day arising
> From sullen earth) sings hymns at heaven's gate;
>> For thy sweet love remembered such wealth brings
>> That then I scorn to change my state with kings.

There seems to me to be a powerful connection between this sonnet and Ps 73. Like our psalm, this sonnet deals with envy. And like our psalm, the speaker has a turning point. His turning point is when he thinks of his friend. Thinking of his friend causes him to come to his senses. He wakes up from his enviousness and sees his own life in an entirely new light. This is precisely what the psalmist describes. As the speaker of the sonnet is woken from his envy by thinking of his friend, the psalmist is woken from his envy by thinking of God. From the beginning of the description of

Songs without Music

the prosperity of the wicked to the entering of the sanctuary, "God" is mentioned only once—in v. 11—and it's actually the wicked who are mentioning God in that verse. This changes after v. 16. From v. 16 to the penultimate verse, everything is addressed to God. The last verse forms an *inclusio* with the first verse. Both the first verse and the last verse use the words "good" and "God." Thus the psalmist comes full circle and ends up affirming Ps 1.

Nothing in the world had changed to make the psalmist affirm God's goodness and Ps 1's Retribution Principle. The only thing that changed was the psalmist's perspective. In the first sixteen verses, we notice he constantly uses the third-person plural: *They* have this. *They* have that. *They* are blessed. And so on. It rings over and over again like a refrain. All he thinks about is *them*. In thinking about *them* he is really thinking about himself, for he compares himself to them, which is the reason for his discontentment. After v. 16, however, we are immersed with the second-person singular: *You* do this. *You* do that. *You* are this. And so on. This is the principle of cognitive therapy. Changing how you think changes how you feel. Thinking about God instead of the wicked cures him of his envy and dramatically changes his disposition. He, in effect, becomes the happy man of Ps 1.

But we also notice that his view of the wicked was filled with hyperbole. Do the wicked really have "no pangs until death" (Ps 73:4)? We can say the psalmist initially had a skewed view of the wicked. He envied them because he thought their lives were better than his. After entering the sanctuary he realizes that that's not the case. However, after v. 16 the psalmist continues to use hyperbole, only this time it's in the other direction. "How [the wicked] are destroyed in a moment, swept away by utter terrors!" (Ps 73:19). If the wicked are destroyed "in a moment," why did he envy them in the first place? Is the second half of the psalm based on empirical evidence or is it based on faith? We must realize it's the nature of poetry to utilize exaggerations. The exaggerations in Ps 73 are meant to paint a picture of God's goodness. They're also pedagogical. Psalm 73 teaches us that envy is destructive. But these exaggerations also cause us to wrestle with the logic of Ps 73; the exaggerations do not allow us to accept Ps 73's logic unconditionally. Psalm 73 is very black and white. Does not reality contain shades grey and plaid?

Next we turn to Ps 90, the first book of Book IV of the Psalter. This, too, is a wisdom psalm. How can anyone think that's a coincidence? Three of the five books of the Psalter begin with Torah/Wisdom psalms because we cannot praise God, or even express our emotions, unless we orient ourselves toward right living. Morality is paramount.

Psalm 90 is very clever in how it unfolds. For one thing, the superscription can cause us to read it as Moses's personal prayer, but the psalm works well even without this added layer. It begins like a praise hymn ("Lord, you have been our refuge in all generations"—Ps 90:1), particularly because it brings up creation ("Before the mountains were brought forth . . . from everlasting to everlasting you are God"—Ps 90:2).

47

However, this is not a praise hymn at all. The psalmist oscillates between truths about God and truths about humanity ("For we are all consumed by your anger; by your wrath we are overwhelmed"—Ps 90:7). The reader soon realizes what's going on. The psalmist is comparing God's eternality ("For a thousand years in your sight are like yesterday when it is past"—Ps 90:4) with humanity's mortality ("The days of our lives are seventy years, or perhaps eighty, if we are strong"—Ps 90:10).

We should keep it tucked in the back of our mind that Ps 90 unequivocally views human mortality as God's punishment of humanity for our collective sins ("Who considers the power of your anger? Your wrath is as great as the fear that is due you"—Ps 90:11; cf. Gen 6:3). The psalms take the Retribution Principle for granted, which is why the psalmists get very upset when God doesn't seem to enforce it. The key verse, however, is v. 12: "So teach us to count our days that we may gain a heart of wisdom." There's no life after death here. There's only existence and nonexistence. The message of Ps 90 is that the best way to fight death is to gain wisdom. Death comes to us all and our time here is very short. We must make sure that we keep that sobering fact in mind and in doing so make the best use of our time. *Wasting time* is the worst thing we can do. This is very close to the thought of Ps 39:4–6 [5–7]:

> LORD, let me know my end,
>> and what is the measure of my days;
>> let me know how fleeting my life is.
> You have made my days a few handbreadths,
>> and my lifetime is as nothing in your sight.
> Surely everyone stands as a mere breath.
>> Surely everyone goes about like a shadow.
> Surely for nothing they are in turmoil;
>> they heap up, and do not know who will gather.

I first paid attention to these words from Ps 39 when I began listening to Brahms. Brahms set the German translation of this text to music in the third movement of his requiem. The music is haunting and perfectly captures the mood of the psalm. These words spooked me the first time I read them. I interpreted the psalmist as saying, "God, tell me the day I'm going to die." But I don't want to know when I will die! I don't want to think about it! The psalmist, though, *wants* this information. Why? Because knowing one's mortality is a key to wisdom. Partly this is because it's foolish to act like our time is unlimited. Cognizance of our mortality also reminds us that we're not God. We cannot be wise so long as we have a "God complex."

LAMENT

The soberness of Ps 39 provides us with a segue to discussing the laments. Indeed, the last five verses of Ps 90 are very lament-esque. This indicates a weakness of form criticism. Psalms do not always break down into neat categorizations.

Take Ps 3, for instance—the first official lament of the Psalter. The psalmist complains about his enemies: "O LORD, many are my foes! Many are rising against me." But the psalmist knows that God is his "shield." The psalmist is, in a sense, bullet proof, just like Abraham (Gen 15:1). And so with confidence he says, "I lie down and sleep; I wake again, for the LORD sustains me" (Ps 3:5[6]). The psalmist calls upon God to deliver him from his enemies and he is very confident this will happen ("Deliverance belongs to the LORD"—Ps 3:8[9]). So how much of a lament is Ps 3? It's a complaint but it has a lot of confidence within it. A tearjerker it is not.

Psalm 6, though, is another story:

> O LORD, do not rebuke me in your anger,
> > or discipline me in your wrath.
> Be gracious to me, O LORD, for I am languishing;
> > O LORD, heal me, for my bones are shaking with terror. (Ps 6:1–2[2–3])

This is an unsettling beginning. What is wrong with this psalmist? It's possible that he's suffering from an illness or injury. This, of course, is attributed to God punishing him for his sins, i.e., the Retribution Principle at work. Later on in the psalm, however, he mentions his enemies ("workers of evil"). Either the "languishing," "healing," and "shaking of the bones" is literal and the enemies are gloating over his ailment, or those terms are all metaphorical. But again, either way, this is all an expression of God's wrath. That's why Ps 6 is considered penitential.

Verse 3 (4 in Hebrew) is heartbreaking:

> My soul is also struck with terror,
> > But you, O LORD—how long?

The psalmist cannot even finish his thought. It's as if he was about to say something to God, something *about* God, perhaps something positive. "But you, O LORD . . . *are my strength and my fortress.*" But those words cannot pass through his lips. His suffering is too great for him to be so confident. He's seemingly in too much pain to be loquacious. All he can say is, "*How long?*" These are the words of someone who is in emotional torment. Though different words are used in Hebrew, the sentiment of Ps 13 is the same:

> How long, O Lord? Will you forget me forever?
> > How long will you hide your face from me?
> How long must I bear pain in my soul,
> > and have sorrow in my heart all day long?
> How long shall my enemy be exalted over me? (Ps 13:1–2)

The laments are not bashful in displaying brute anguish. They hold back nothing. The psalmist is not embarrassed to say: "every night I flood my bed with tears; I drench my couch with my weeping" (Ps 6:6[7]).

The laments are indeed part of the "wrestling with God" tradition. We see that theme in Ps 10:1—"Why, O LORD, do you stand far away? Why do you hide yourself in times of trouble?" Think about how irreverent that sounds! Can you imagine a Christian hymnal daring to speak to God this way? The irony is that Jesus used this language. Jesus quoted the words of Ps 22:1 (22:2 in Hebrew)—"My God, my God, why have you forsaken me?" (Matt 27:46; Mark 15:34). He spoke those words in his native tongue of Aramaic rather than in the psalmist's Hebrew, indicating that he was not coldly quoting Scripture but was making the bitter cry of that psalm an expression of his own anguish.

Once again, however, we see that the laments are not pure lamentations. Psalm 13 ends on a hopeful note, as does Ps 22. These are dynamic psalms. Both of these psalms begin in a minor key and modulate to a major key. Psalm 22 begins with that impassioned cry, but in the middle of the psalm there's a turning point; it's implied that God rescued the psalmist from his enemies. In other words, God had *not* abandoned the psalmist as the psalmist had thought. Psalm 22 actually ends in praise and slides quite beautifully and naturally into Ps 23. That's another brilliant piece of editing, which we'll discuss shortly.

The one lament that is an unequivocal lamentation is Ps 88. It begins with a statement of trust in God but with a hint that the psalmist's prayer is occasioned by trouble:

> O LORD, God of my salvation,
>> when, at night, I cry out in your presence,
> let my prayer come before you;
>> incline your ear to my cry. (Ps 88:1[2])

The psalmist wastes no time telling us why he's praying:

> For my soul is full of troubles,
>> and my life draws near to Sheol.
> I am counted among those who go down to the Pit;
>> I am like those who have no help,
> like those forsaken among the dead,
>> like the slain that lie in the grave,
> like those whom you remember no more,
>> for they are cut off from your hand. (Ps 88:3–5[4–6])

"Sheol" is a Hebrew word which refers to the realm of the dead. It basically means "death." Death is indeed all over this text. He's as close to death as a living person can be. He's a proverbial "goner."

Songs without Music

What is the cause of his suffering? It's unclear but mention of "enemies" is notably lacking. Kathryn Greene-McCreight believes he's suffering from mental illness.[9] Whatever it was, as we've already seen, it's taken for granted that God is the ultimate source of the psalmist's woes:

> You have put me in the depths of the Pit,
> in the regions dark and deep.
> Your wrath lies heavy upon me,
> and you overwhelm me with all your waves.
> You have caused my companions to shun me;
> you have made me a thing of horror to them. (Ps 88:6–8[7–9])

The prominence of "you" is very effective. God is the "God of his salvation" but it is God who has caused him to suffer. This means that God is the only one who can relieve his sufferings. The psalmist tries reasoning with God:

> Do you work wonders for the dead?
> Do the shades rise up to praise you?
> Is your steadfast love declared in the grave,
> or your faithfulness in Abaddon?[10]
> Are your wonders known in the darkness,
> or your saving help in the land of forgetfulness? (Ps 88:10–12[11–13])

We've already mentioned that the psalms do not contain a faith in the afterlife, at least as a place of hope and eternal comfort. This is true for virtually the entire Ketuvim. One of the mistakes Christians make is that they impose the full spectrum of Christian theology onto the psalms. I understand that none of the books of the Bible can be read in complete isolation from the canon, for being placed in the Bible makes them part of a whole. Finding cohesion and unity among the Bible's books is an understandable and worthy endeavor. On the other hand, we simply must, at least at the start, interpret these books on their own terms if we are to interpret them reasonably and honestly. If the hope of the psalms is to "go to heaven," why is the psalmist so upset? Why does the psalmist say death is a "land of forgetfulness" where no one praises God? Say that the psalmist is ignorant of the Christian hope, but do not turn him into a Christian, for he isn't one.

In any event, there's no happy ending in Ps 88:

> O LORD, why do you cast me off?
> Why do you hide your face from me?
> Wretched and close to death from my youth up,
> I suffer your terrors; I am desperate.

---

9. Greene-McCreight, *Darkness Is My Only Companion*, loc. 217–38

10. "Abaddon" is a Hebrew word which basically means "oblivion." It's another word for "death."

Illuminating Counsel

> Your wrath has swept over me;
>> your dreadful assaults destroy me.
> They surround me like a flood all day long;
>> from all sides they close in on me.
> You have caused friend and neighbor to shun me;
>> my companions have become darkness. (Ps 88:14–18[15–19])

The poetry conjures up images of being killed by the sea. It isn't just drowning, though. The sea—God's instrument of death—is beating him down. I do sympathize with Greene-McCreight's perspective. I think we're dealing with physical illness but we cannot leave the psyche out of the picture. The psalmist is desperately lonely. "My companions have become darkness" is a devastating line. This makes me think of someone who has been placed in a dilapidated nursing home and abandoned by her family. It makes me wonder if the psalmist was a leper living in a leper colony. The poet's choice to end the psalm with the word "darkness" leaves the reader with the feeling of hopelessness.

Psalm 88 precedes a communal lament in which the community is suffering from the cognitive dissonance of the destruction of David's dynasty despite the Davidic covenant of 2 Sam 7, which is restated at the outset of the Psalter, in Ps 2. Psalm 89 wrestles with Ps 2 just as Ps 73 wrestles with Ps 1. Thus the placement of Ps 88 next to Ps 89 enables us to interpret the psalmist of Ps 88 as a microcosm of the Kingdom of Judah. I'm fairly sure this was intended by the psalmist, so, once again, we applaud the brilliance of the editor. How the psalms are arranged adds layers of meaning to them.

The only positive aspect to Ps 88 is that the psalmist hasn't given up praying. "Every day I call to you, LORD," he says. "I spread out my hands to you" (Ps 88:9[10]). "But I, O LORD, cry out to you; in the morning my prayer comes before you" (Ps 88:13[14]). Is this his final prayer before giving up on God? Or are we to think he will continue praying until he dies despite only receiving the sound of static as a response? I choose to believe the latter. Here we see the Ketuvim's dealings with suffering. How is a sufferer to respond to pain? Not by pretending it doesn't exist. Psalms' response to suffering is *prayer*.

Psalm 88 shows us the realism of the Ketuvim. Do we imagine the psalmist recovered from his ailment? I have known people stricken with cancer who were prayed for by a great many people. They still died. I reckon the same happened to our suffering psalmist; he succumbed to his illness. That's not the point, though. The psalms are not interested in "proving" the existence of God or the goodness of God by selecting only the pieces of evidence which support those propositions. In giving us a lament which ends with the word "darkness," the psalms are, in a sense, telling us that it's reasonable to lament. Suffering, arguing with God, wresting with God—these things don't make you a bad person. Neither do we need to wear a metaphorical mask to show others how strong our faith is. When things go awry we don't have to fake a smile in the presence of God. Yes, there are times we need to "cowboy up" (if you'll pardon the

expression) and work through our pain, but we cannot do that at the expense of being honest about our pain.

I have a cousin who's a psychologist. While doing research on a paper about the intersection of religion and psychology, I asked her about which therapies she finds most effective. She told me that, for the most part, all therapies have been found equally effective.[11] What brings healing is not a particular type of therapy but the personal connection made by the therapist and the sufferer. The therapist represents humanity. The sufferer feels alienated from humanity. By connecting with the therapist, the sufferer reconnects to the world. It's not a stretch to say that the psalms have the same effect, with God in the role of the therapist. All the sufferers, regardless of the type of suffering they experience, feel alienated from God and the world. That alienation is overcome through prayer. Prayer is not a spell one chants. It's a way of building a relationship with God. It is the relationship that brings healing, even if the prayers are not answered (or at least not answered the way one would want them to be).

Fromm, himself a psychoanalyst, made a tremendously profound point from the instructiveness of the dynamic psalms, like Ps 13 which begins with turmoil but ends with hope. Said Fromm: "The cure of despair is not achieved by encouraging thoughts, not even by feeling part of the despair; it is achieved by the seeming paradox that despair *can be overcome only if it has been fully experienced.*"[12] I first read that about a month after my mother died. While she was sick I felt a kind of emotional nausea. My emotions from her awful decline and imminent death were stirring within me, but I couldn't weep. I wanted to weep so desperately but my eyes stubbornly remained dry. My heart was numb. It was only when she died, and especially at her funeral, that the emotion finally poured out of me. It poured out hard. I cried so intensely that it felt like I would never stop crying. But tears can be a gift. If prayer can induce tears, then prayer is worth it regardless if one's petition is granted or denied.

THANKSGIVING

Psalm 23 is not really a thanksgiving but we cannot survey the Psalter without mentioning the most famous psalm of all. Here it is in the famous and beautiful (though not entirely literally translated) King James Version:

> A Psalm of David.
> The LORD is my shepherd;
>> I shall not want.
> He maketh me to lie down in green pastures:
>> he leadeth me beside the still waters.
> He restoreth my soul:
>> he leadeth me in the paths of righteousness for his name's sake.

11. The exception, she said, is that cognitive therapy is particularly effective with treating anxiety.

12. Fromm, *You Shall Be As Gods*, 238.

Illuminating Counsel

Yea, though I walk through the valley of the shadow of death, I will fear no evil:
for thou art with me; thy rod and thy staff they comfort me.
Thou preparest a table before me in the presence of mine enemies:
thou anointest my head with oil; my cup runneth over.
Surely goodness and mercy shall follow me all the days of my life:
and I will dwell in the house of the LORD for ever. (Ps 23:1–6)

What makes this psalm so special? First, I would say the length is a factor. It's short and therefore easy to memorize. Second, it contains a very powerful and effective use of images. We begin with a metaphor: God is a shepherd and the psalmist is a sheep. If we interpret this with the superscription it becomes particularly meaningful because David was a shepherd (1 Sam 16:11; 17:34–35). The man who shepherded sheep is now shepherded by God. Psalm 23 contains a device called "Opening Verse."[13] In the first line, the poet states his theme. The rest of the poem is a development of said theme. The poet develops it with ever-changing scenery. At least for the first half of the psalm, each line has the sheep in a different setting. First we see the sheep lying down on grass. The image makes us feel peaceful and relaxed. Then we see the sheep led beside "waters of serenity." That's a more literal translation, and a better one, I think, than "still waters." Not that I don't like "still waters." "Still waters" makes me think of the Simon and Garfunkel song "Bridge Over Troubled Water." "Still waters" is the opposite of "troubled waters." But "waters of serenity"—the Hebrew word literally means "rest"—tells us not just about the water but also about the sheep. By being led upon the "waters of serenity," the sheep enters a state of serenity. This, too, affects the reader's mood. It's like the reader is listening to very soothing music. The reader and the sheep are connected. Whatever the sheep feels, the reader also feels. Whatever is true of the sheep is true of the reader.

"He restores my soul"—a translation of two words Hebrew words which literally mean "He returns my life to me"—describes a person who has been through strife but is now replenished. But at this point we must ask if we're still in the metaphor. Are we still talking about sheep or are we now talking about humans? It seems the metaphor has been diluted and the language of the psalm is ambiguous. Being led on the "paths of righteousness" (literally "circuitous paths of righteousness" or perhaps "right circuitous paths") strains the metaphor further. By the time we get to the "valley of the shadow of death" (or "the valley of deep darkness") we have slid out of the metaphor entirely, but the reader doesn't mind this. The transition is so smooth that it feels natural rather than jarring. Then the poet mentions the "rod" and "staff"—all the sudden we're back in the metaphor! Yet the remainder of the psalm abandons the metaphor for good. Not once does it feel like the unity of the psalm has been violated.

The first half of the psalm took us from fields of grass, to waters of serenity, to circuitous paths, to a valley of darkness. The second half of the psalm gives us other

13. Segal, *A New Psalm*, xxvii.

54

Songs without Music

images, albeit ones that are human rather than sheepish. There's a banquet table. The psalmist has a feast while his enemies are looking on from the sidelines. Ointment is poured on his face. This is perhaps equivalent to a spa treatment. A cup is filled to the brim with wine. This is exactly how Jews fill their wine cups on holidays. In restaurants, the glass of wine is always filled halfway. In Jewish homes, the cup is filled to the point that the wine "runneth over." This represents the overflowing of blessings. "I shall not want" is an understatement! The psalmist has much more than he needs.

The KJV makes a mistake by translating the verb in the final verse as "follow" when it really should be translated "pursue." Normally, as we read time and again in the psalms, the enemies pursue the psalmist to try to kill him. But now it's "goodness and mercy" ("kindness" is a better translation than "mercy") that pursues him. Notice the use of God's name in the last line—"And I will live in the house of the LORD [Yahweh] forever." The poet creates an *inclusio*. The only times God's name is used in the psalm are in the first verse and the last verse.

We should also consider the artistic use of grammar. In the first part of the psalm, the psalmist speaks in third-person. He's writing *about* God. That changes right in the middle of the psalm. The poet switches to second-person—"for *you* are with me."[14] That's a tremendously effective transition, especially since the reader is taken away from the greenness of the pastures, the blueness of the waters, and the circuitousness of righteous paths, and brought into the blackness of the valley. The psalmist is in the lowest point (a valley) and he should be in distress, only he isn't. He feels comfort because he has this dynamic relationship with God. The psalm celebrates the joy of having a relationship with God. God takes care of the psalmist. God lies him down, God leads him, God restores him, God comforts him. This is why this psalm has helped soldiers in the trenches and it's why it's read at funerals, both in Jewish and Christian tradition. It's what helped me overcome my fear of flying and my fear of seeing my dear mother languishing in hospital.

And notice, too, the connection between Ps 23 and Ps 22. Psalm 22 begins with the thought that God abandoned the psalmist. Psalm 23 affirms the opposite; God is "with" the psalmist. The words "for you are with me"—three words in Hebrew—are precisely in the middle of the psalm. If we do not count the superscription, there are exactly twenty-six words before "for you are with me" and exactly twenty-six words after "for you are with me."[15] I don't think that's an accident. Each word is very carefully chosen but the psalm never seems mathematical or mechanical. This is brilliant poetry!

Psalm 27 bears similarities to Ps 23, so much so that they make good companions. Reading them adjacently also proves to be enlightening. Psalm 27 also begins with "Opening Verse":

---

14. The change of person is a literary device known as *enallage*.

15. Bazak, "Numerical Devices in Biblical Poetry," 334.

Illuminating Counsel

The LORD is my light and my salvation;
  whom shall I fear?
The LORD is the stronghold of my life;
  of whom shall I be afraid? (Ps 27:1)

From the start we are given a tone of extreme confidence, the same kind of confidence as going through the valley of death's shadow and not being afraid of evil. In Ps 27, the psalmist doesn't fear his enemies who encamp around him. They try to eat him like the ravenous beasts that they are, but they're the ones who end up falling (Ps 27:2). Like Ps 23, the psalmist wants to live in the house of Yahweh all the days of his life; he adds that he wishes to gaze upon the "beauty" of Yahweh (Ps 27:4). As the psalmist of Ps 23 ate and drank in the presence of his enemies, so the psalmist in Ps 27 has his head "lifted up above [his] enemies" and worships God in triumph (Ps 27:6).

But the second half of Ps 27 feels completely different from the first half. All the sudden, the confidence of the psalmist dissipates:

Hear, O LORD, when I cry aloud;
  be gracious to me and answer me!
You have said, "Seek my face."
My heart says to you,
  "Your face, LORD, do I seek."
  Hide not your face from me.
Turn not your servant away in anger,
  O you who have been my help.
Cast me not off; forsake me not,
  O God of my salvation!
For my father and my mother have forsaken me,
  but the LORD will take me in. (Ps 27:7–10)

This sounds like a lament! It's not quite as desperate as Ps 88 or even Ps 6, but compared to the first six verses of Ps 27, it's definitely more a lamentation than anything else. What is truly interesting is that this dynamic psalm is different than most of the other two-mood-ers. Most dynamic psalms start with a lament and end joyously. Psalm 27 moves in the opposite direction. Instead of moving from anxiety to confidence, Ps 27 moves from confidence to anxiety.

Psalm 27's juxtaposition of confidence and anxiety reflects the reality of life. Sometimes our confidence changes from hour to hour. This is not because our faith is weak necessarily. It's because we're human. The heroes of the Tanakh are not angels or saints. They're human beings who, definitionally, are deeply flawed. One minute they're leading God's people; the next minute they're praying to die!

Psalm 30 is a proper thanksgiving psalm. It could be viewed as a companion piece to Ps 6 or even Ps 88. Psalm 30 seems to be about someone who was sick but was then restored to health. The superscription, which actually has two layers in and

56

of itself,[16] makes us think it's about the events of Hanukkah—the rededication of the temple after the successful Maccabean revolt against Antiochus IV in 164 BCE. This is yet another illustration of how the superscriptions don't always fit with their psalms but they nevertheless add an extra layer of meaning to them.

The reason Ps 30 is a particularly good companion to Ps 88 is because they both express the same view of death:

> What profit is there in my death,
>> if I go down to the pit?
> Will the dust praise you?
>> Will it tell of your faithfulness? (Ps 30:9[10], cf. Ps 88:10–12[11–13])

With the absence of an afterlife, death is seemingly invincible and thus the need to be rescued from death is all the more urgent. But God did it! God healed the supplicant:

> You have turned for me my mourning into dancing;
>> you have loosed my sackcloth
>> and clothed me with gladness,
> that my glory may sing your praise and not be silent.
>> O LORD my God, I will give thanks to you forever! (Ps 30:11–12[12–13])

These verses are a magnificent expression of the power of joy. We need to bear them in mind because we will hear their sentiment echoed later in the Ketuvim. We will also see their sentiment subverted.

A student of mine made the observation that Ps 30 can be read backwards. This was probably unintentional on the part of the psalmist but it sort of works due to the cyclical nature of biblical Hebrew poetry. One of the most common literary structures in the Bible is called *chiasmus* or *chiastic structure*. A chiastic structure looks like this:

A
  B
  B
A

Sometimes there's a middle component:

A
  B
    C
  B
A

16. The superscription literally says, "A Psalm [A Song at the Dedication of the House] of David."

Illuminating Counsel

This is what Mark Throntveit calls a "concentric arrangement."[17] The "C" component usually contains the theological point of the passage. Psalm 30 contains such a structure.[18] Observe:

I will extol you, O LORD, for you have drawn me up
    and have not let my foes **rejoice** [Heb: *simcha*] over me.
O LORD my God, I cried to you for help,
    and you have healed me.
O LORD, you have brought up my soul from Sheol;
    you restored me to life from among those who **go down to the pit**.
Sing praises to the LORD, O you his saints,
    and give thanks to his holy name.
For his anger is but for a moment,
    and his **favor** is for a lifetime.
Weeping may tarry for the night,
    but joy comes with the morning.
<u>As for me, I said in my prosperity,</u>
    <u>"I shall never be moved."</u>
By your **favor**, O LORD,
    you made my mountain stand strong;
you hid your face;
    I was dismayed.
To you, O LORD, I cry,
    and to the Lord I plead for mercy:
"What profit is there in my death,
    if I **go down to the pit**?
Will the dust praise you?
    Will it tell of your faithfulness?
Hear, O LORD, and be merciful to me!
    O LORD, be my helper!"
You have turned for me my mourning into dancing;
    you have loosed my sackcloth
    and clothed me with **gladness** [Heb: *simcha*],
that my glory may sing your praise and not be silent.
    O LORD my God, I will give thanks to you forever!

---

17. Throntveit, *Ezra-Nehemiah*, 4–6.
18. Segal, *A New Psalm*, 135–36.

Songs without Music

So look what we have here:

A—rejoice/gladness
   B—go down to the pit
      C—favor
         D—Prosperity
      C—favor
   B—go down to the pit
A—rejoice/gladness

The word "favor" (the C section) is bracketing the line, "As for me, I said in my prosperity, 'I shall never be moved.'" This is the concentric line, labeled D. It arguably means that the psalmist arrogantly thought he was secure. But then God "hid [his] face" from the psalmist and the psalmist became "dismayed." So the psalmist had a "fall" but was subsequently restored. He was humbled as a result. His newfound humility has made him exceedingly grateful to God for his mercy.

The psalms emphasize thanksgiving more than any part of the Bible. Observe:

- ". . . proclaiming thanksgiving aloud and telling all your wonderful deeds." (Ps 26:7)
- "The one who offers thanksgiving as his sacrifice glorifies me; to one who orders his way rightly I will show the salvation of God!" (Ps 50:23)
- "I will praise the name of God with a song; I will magnify him with thanksgiving." (Ps 68:30[31])
- "Let us come into his presence with thanksgiving; let us make a joyful noise to him with songs of praise!" (Ps 95:2)
- "And let them offer sacrifices of thanksgiving, and tell of his deeds in songs of joy!" (Ps 107:22)
- "I will offer to you the sacrifice of thanksgiving and call on the name of the LORD." (Ps 116:17)
- "Sing to the LORD with thanksgiving; make melody to our God on the lyre!" (Ps 147:7)

The superscription of Ps 100 is "A Psalm for Thanksgiving"—

> Make a joyful noise to the LORD, all the earth!
>   Serve the LORD with gladness!
>   Come into his presence with singing!
> Know that the LORD, he is God!
>   It is he who made us, and we are his;
>   we are his people, and the sheep of his pasture.

Enter his gates with thanksgiving,
>and his courts with praise!
>Give thanks to him; bless his name!
For the LORD is good;
>his steadfast love endures forever,
>and his faithfulness to all generations.

The Hebrew word translated "thanksgiving" is *todah.*[19] In modern Hebrew, this word simply means "thank you." A simple word. A simple concept. Infinitely important.

I remember my professor, Jim Bruckner, when teaching on the thanksgiving psalms, told the class that people in contemporary American society don't know how to say "thank you." I was reminded of the time Aunt Jaynee bought clothes for me when I was a teenager. It was an out-of-the-blue gift. I was very grateful because I hated going shopping for clothes (at least at the time). But I never called her to say "thank you." Quite sometime after that—maybe a full year or more—my aunt and I happened to be alone. "You know, you never thanked me for buying you clothes," she said. I felt guilty and tried apologizing with an excuse. She interrupted me and said, "That's why I'll never buy you anything ever again." Ouch. I deserved it entirely, as you know. I'm also glad she said that to me. I'll never forget that sin. Graciously, my aunt did buy me something again—twenty years later. She bought me a coat the week my mother, her sister, died. And yes, I thanked her for it!

I do think we have a problem with gratitude in our culture. We complain so much and yet we have heat, air conditioning, cars, laptops, cell phones, apartments and condos and houses, food of every variety and for every diet. We go on vacations and spend time with friends and family. We have hospitals, doctors, nurses, dentists. When we have a headache we take ibuprofen and it goes away. We have *anesthesia*— imagine surgery, or even having a cavity filled, without it! We have the freedom to criticize the president—the most powerful person in the world. We have the freedom to worship in a church, mosque, synagogue, temple, or not at all. We are the most fortunate people in the history of humanity! That doesn't mean life is easy. Life is often tragic. The psalms know that. But the psalms also know that without gratitude, we have no chance of being happy. The psalms, then, teach us how to say "thank you."

ZION AND ROYAL

I put the royal psalms in the same category as the Zion psalms despite the fact that they contain notable differences. As previously mentioned, the royal psalms are particularly meaningful to Christians because of their messianic overtones. The New Testament applies Ps 2 (a poetic reflection on the Davidic covenant) and Ps 45 (the king's wedding) to Jesus (Acts 4:23–31 and Heb 1:8–9, respectively). While Ps 72 (a prayer

19. Many times, the word that's translated "thanks" in our English translations is the more proper word for "praise."

for the new king) is not explicitly mentioned in the New Testament, many Christians see it as an allusion to Jesus. There are also those royal psalms which speak of Yahweh as king (Pss 93–99, for example).

The Zion psalms, though, are about Israel's love for Jerusalem. These psalms encapsulate a theology which we shall call "Zion Theology." Zion Theology states that Zion-Jerusalem is indestructible because it's God's city, just as the Davidic dynasty was viewed as indestructible because of God's covenant with David (2 Sam 7).

We have a trilogy of Zion psalms in Pss 46, 47, and 48. Psalm 46 is a beloved psalm:

> God is our refuge and strength,
>> a very present help in trouble.
> Therefore we will not fear though the earth gives way,
>> though the mountains be moved into the heart of the sea,
> though its waters roar and foam,
>> though the mountains tremble at its swelling. (Ps 46:1–3[2–4])

These words were permanently planted in my heart when I heard them read at the funeral of a young woman I knew who committed suicide. Her mother—one of the strongest women I've ever known—wailed for a brief moment in the funeral but was otherwise remarkably composed, even telling me about her charity work when I came to console her. Her younger brother and older sister were sad but they seemed to have a peace about them. Her older brother, though, like Jacob, refused to be comforted. He was paralyzed by his grief. I hugged him but he wouldn't hug back. The look of sadness and anger in his face still haunts me when I think about it. There were no words I, or anyone, could speak that would have made anything better for him. That's why we read passages from the psalms at funerals. The words of the psalms succeed when ours fail. "Be still, and know that I am God," says Ps 46:10[11].

But Ps 46 is really about Jerusalem:

> There is a river whose streams make glad the city of God,
>> the holy habitation of the Most High. (Ps 46:4[5])

Jerusalem actually doesn't have a river, unless this is a reference to Hezekiah's water tunnel, which doesn't seem likely. In any case, Jerusalem is besieged by foreign invaders, but because it's the "city of God" any attempt to destroy her will fail:

> God is in the midst of her; she shall not be moved;
>> God will help her when morning dawns.
> The nations rage, the kingdoms totter;
>> he utters his voice, the earth melts.
> The LORD of hosts is with us;
>> the God of Jacob is our fortress. (Ps 46:5–7[6–8])

Illuminating Counsel

Psalm 48 reinforces that message:

For behold, the kings assembled;
    they came on together.
As soon as they saw it, they were astounded;
    they were in panic; they took to flight.
Trembling took hold of them there,
    anguish as of a woman in labor.
By the east wind you shattered
    the ships of Tarshish.
As we have heard, so have we seen
    in the city of the LORD of hosts,
in the city of our God,
    which God will establish forever. (Ps 48:4–8[5–9])

Zion is eternal and the nations who dare to destroy Jerusalem will only reap trouble upon themselves.

The problem, of course, is that Jerusalem *was* destroyed. Does that mean the Zion Theology was a fraud? The most famous of all Zion psalms—Ps 137—is a psalm from the perspective of Jews exiled in Babylon after the Babylonians sacked the royal city:

By the rivers of Babylon—
    there we sat down and there we wept
    when we remembered Zion.
On the willows there
    we hung up our harps.
For there our captors
    asked us for songs,
and our tormentors asked for mirth, saying,
    "Sing us one of the songs of Zion!"
How could we sing the LORD's song
    in a foreign land?
If I forget you, O Jerusalem,
    let my right hand wither!
Let my tongue cling to the roof of my mouth,
    if I do not remember you,
if I do not set Jerusalem
    above my highest joy.
Remember, O Lord, against the Edomites
    the day of Jerusalem's fall,
how they said, "Tear it down! Tear it down!
    Down to its foundations!"

Songs without Music

> O daughter Babylon, you devastator!
>> Happy shall they be who pay you back
>> what you have done to us!
> Happy shall they be who take your little ones
>> and dash them against the rock![20]

The opening phrase—"the rivers of Babylon"—while clearly referring to the Tigris and Euphrates, causes us to think of that aforementioned imagined river. The Jews are no longer being made glad by the streams of the river in the city of God. They're now sitting beside foreign rivers while weeping rivers of tears.

The Babylonians tell them to sing their "songs of Zion" (which the exiles refer to as the "song of the LORD"). What "songs of Zion" are the Babylonians referring to? Psalm 46! Psalm 47! Psalm 48![21] But the only reason the Babylonians want them to sing those songs is so they can mock them. How can the Jews sing their songs proclaiming the eternality of Jerusalem while Jerusalem lay in ruins? Singing those songs would be like pouring salt on a wound, to put it mildly. How could they endure such humiliation? Yet if they do *not* sing their songs of Zion, they will be inclined to forget Zion altogether, which is what they resolved *not* to do in the first line of the psalm. I think it's implied that they do sing their songs. Forgetting Jerusalem is worse than being humiliated.

Psalm 137 is about the love of the Jewish people for Jerusalem. Christians often fail to comprehend this, partly because they're reading a Jewish text from a non-Jewish perspective and partly because Christians tend to "spiritualize" Jerusalem. Yet Ps 137 says Jerusalem is the "highest joy" of the Jewish people. The Jewish love for Jerusalem is not idolatrous or carnal; it's biblical faith. For Jews, Jerusalem and God are inseparable.

The ending of Ps 137, however, makes it one of the most controversial psalms in the Psalter. Whereas Ps 1 and Ps 41 told us such lofty things about what will make us truly happy (meditating on the Torah and helping the poor), Ps 137 says that the "happy" person will be the one who massacres Lady Babylon's children.

This seems like a fitting time to discuss the imprecatory psalms. Psalm 109 is the chief imprecatory psalm. It's the angriest, most vitriolic of them all. The psalmist wishes for his enemy's children to "wander about and beg, seeking food far from the ruins they inhabit" (Ps 109:10), among many other things. The NRSV softens Ps 109 by placing the curses in the mouth of the psalmist's enemy rather than the psalmist. In other words, from the NRSV's perspective, the psalmist is quoting what his enemy is saying about him. But even if that's the case—and I'm doubtful it is—it doesn't solve all our problems because there are other imprecatory psalms where it's clear, beyond dispute, that the psalmist is the one calling down the curses:

20. This is the NRSV.

21. This is a point Jon D. Levenson made. See Gordon College, "Faith Seeking Understanding the Anguish and Joy of Jerusalem," YouTube.

Illuminating Counsel

O God, break the teeth in their mouths;
    tear out the fangs of the young lions, O LORD!
Let them vanish like water that runs away;
    when he aims his arrows, let them be blunted.
Let them be like the snail that dissolves into slime,
    like the stillborn child who never sees the sun.
Sooner than your pots can feel the heat of thorns,
    whether green or ablaze, may he sweep them away. (Ps 58:6–9[7–10])

What are we to make of this?

Walter Brueggemann views the imprecatory psalms positively in the sense that the psalmist is being honest about his feelings.[22] The imprecatory psalms are therapeutic for the psalmist. They are likewise therapeutic for a suffering community that reads them. To excise the imprecatory psalms from the Psalter would stifle the voice of an oppressed community and, inadvertently, deny that oppression is part of the human condition.

Along those lines, another problem with the way we read the imprecatory psalms is that we assume the "enemies" in the psalms are like the annoying people we encounter at the store. Back in the day, when I worked at Kinko's, an angry customer told me I was "braindead" when I told him the truth that Kinko's is not owned by FedEx. (A year later Kinko's was purchased by FedEx and eventually renamed FedEx Office—go figure!) I'd like to think of that guy as an "enemy" but that's not the kind of enemy the psalms are referring to. The "enemies" and "sinners" and "wicked ones" of the psalms are much closer to ISIS or the Nazis than rude customers. I'm not defending calling down curses on people, but I am urging that we contextualize texts properly. The Jewish exiles *wished* that someone would dash the Babylonian babies against the rocks, but that is *literally* what the Babylonians did to the Jews.

Most of the Zion psalms, though, are quite hopeful. The "Songs of Ascents" (Pss 120–34) are almost all associated with Zion. Psalm 121 is one of the most beloved psalms in the Psalter: "I lift my eyes to the hills. From where does my help come? My help comes from the LORD, who made heaven and earth" (Ps 121:1–2). Lifting one's eyes to the hills conjures up the image of pilgrims, or returnees from Babylon, going "up" to Jerusalem[23] to worship at the (new) temple. Psalm 122 is more explicitly about Jerusalem: "I was glad when they said to me, 'Let us go to the house of the LORD!' Our feet have been standing within your gates, O Jerusalem" (Ps 122:1). Psalm 122 contains the famous line, "Pray for the peace of Jerusalem" (Ps 122:6). In Hebrew, the word translated "pray" literally means "ask." The word "ask" is intentionally chosen over "pray" because "ask" creates a gorgeous assonance with the other two words, emphasizing the SH sound, the L sound, and the M sound: *sha'alu shlom Yerushalayim*. In Ps 125, those who trust in God are likened to Mount Zion because Mount

22. Brueggemann, *Praying the Psalms*, 63–64.

23. In the Bible, one always goes "up" to Jerusalem, even if one is traveling south.

Zion is unmovable and inviolable. Does this imply the return from exile vindicates the truthfulness of the Zion Theology? Psalm 132:13–14 says, "For the LORD has chosen Zion; he has desired it for his dwelling place; 'This is my resting place forever.'" But Ps 126 contains a hint of insecurity:

> When the LORD restored the fortunes of Zion,
>   we were like those who dream.
> Then our mouth was filled with laughter,
>   and our tongue with shouts of joy;
> then they said among the nations,
>   "The LORD has done great things for them."
> The LORD has done great things for us;
>   we are glad.
>
> Restore our fortunes, O LORD,
>   like streams in the Negeb!
> Those who sow in tears
>   shall reap with shouts of joy!
> He who goes out weeping,
>   bearing the seed for sowing,
> shall come home with shouts of joy,
>   bringing his sheaves with him. (Ps 126:1–6)

What's curious about this dynamic psalm is that it seems like the second half should precede the first half. The second half is a prayer for Zion to be restored. The first half is an account of that prayer having come to pass. The dream came true! But Ps 126 has it the other way around. The first half seems so secure, so ideal, so perfect. "*When* God restored the fortunes of Zion . . ." It happened! It's done! But since the second half *prays* for Zion's fortunes to be restored ("Restore our fortunes, O LORD"), it seems like reality has not completely aligned with the returnees' expectations. God restored the fortunes of Zion, and yet there is more "restoring" to be done. What matters, though, is that the returnees trust that God will do it. Trusting in God is one of the themes that runs through the entire Psalter regardless of the genre.

PRAISE

The first pure psalm of praise is Ps 8. It contains perhaps the most famous and overt *inclusio* in the Psalter—"O LORD, our Lord, how majestic is your name in all the earth" (Ps 8:1, 9[2, 10])! Yet Ps 8 is not merely about God's kingship. Psalm 8 deals with the role of humanity in God's world. It's a poetic reflection on Gen 1:26–28—the statement that humans are created in the image and likeness of God:

Illuminating Counsel

When I look at your heavens, the work of your fingers,
    the moon and the stars, which you have set in place,
what is man that you are mindful of him,
    and the son of man that you care for him? (Ps 8:3–4[4–5])

Humans have been graced with a lofty position (". . . you have made them a little lower than the heavenly beings and crowned them with glory and honor"). Humans are unique among all of God's creatures. But there's a sense in which humans are not worthy of such an honor. It's untrue that the biblical pre-scientific view of the universe caused the ancient Jews to have a hubristic view of humanity. To the contrary, the notion that humans are God's image-bearers gives humans both humility as well as dignity.

The hymns tend to emphasize creation. For example:

Let all the earth fear the LORD;
    let all the inhabitants of the world stand in awe of him!
For he spoke, and it came to be;
    he commanded, and it stood firm. (Ps 33:8–9)

And this:

The earth is the LORD's and the fullness thereof,
    the world and those who dwell therein,
for he has founded it upon the seas
    and established it upon the rivers. (Ps 24:1–2)

God is the sustainer of all things:

These all look to you,
    to give them their food in due season.
When you give it to them, they gather it up;
    when you open your hand, they are filled with good things. (Ps 104:27–28)

The eyes of all look to you,
    and you give them their food in due season.
You open your hand;
    you satisfy the desire of every living thing. (Ps 145:15–16)

God is also praised because of his love:

Your steadfast love, O LORD, extends to the heavens,
    your faithfulness to the clouds.
Your righteousness is like the mountains of God;
    your judgments are like the great deep;
    man and beast you save, O LORD. (Ps 36:5–6[6–7])

Psalm 104 is perhaps the quintessential praise psalm. It thanks God for nothing except that God is God and God created a wonderful world. Psalm 104 also contains

Songs without Music

the first use of the Hebrew word which is usually transliterated in English as *hallelujah*, which means "praise Yah," or "praise the LORD." This word appears in the Tanakh only in the psalms but it's transliterated into Greek in the New Testament's book of Revelation (see Rev 19:1–6). It's *translated* in the translation of Psalms ("praise the LORD") but *transliterated* in the translation of Revelation ("hallelujah"). Therefore, if not for Revelation, this word would be unknown to the non-Jewish world.

We should also credit George Frideric Handel for the popularity of this word. "Hallelujah" has become a part of our culture because Handel set it to a very famous piece of music in his masterpiece oratorio *Messiah*. The music perfectly encapsulates the power of the word and the joy associated with the hymnic psalms.

We must also note the famous Leonard Cohen song "Hallelujah." Cohen brilliantly explores different aspects of the concept of "hallelujah." Cohen has taken the rollercoaster of emotions found in the Psalter and put them together in his own unique way. Alan Light notes how the word "hallelujah" resonates with people whether they are religious or not.[24] It resonates with people even if they have no clue that it's a Hebrew word and are oblivious to its meaning, which most people probably are. The word *feels* spiritual. Thanks to Psalms, Revelation, Handel, and Cohen this word has elevated countless souls.

"Hallelujah" appears as an *inclusio* in Pss 146–50. These last five psalms are a fitting way to end the Psalter. Surely it's no coincidence that the Psalter ends on such a high note of praise. We began with a Torah psalm and we end with a praise psalm. Just as we began with the thought of a human being happy, so humanity finds its greatest happiness in praising God. The psalms have taken us to the depths of despair and the valley of death's shadow, but we finally arrive at a point of exuberance where all seems right with the world.

Psalm 150, the final psalm, is worthy of special attention:

> Praise the LORD!
> Praise God in his sanctuary;
> > praise him in his mighty heavens!
> Praise him for his mighty deeds;
> > praise him according to his excellent greatness!
> Praise him with trumpet sound;
> > praise him with lute and harp!
> Praise him with tambourine and dance;
> > praise him with strings and pipe!
> Praise him with sounding cymbals;
> > praise him with loud clashing cymbals!
> Let everything that has breath praise the LORD!
> Praise the LORD!

24. Light, *The Holy or the Broken*, 178–85.

This is a simple psalm to analyze. It tells the reader what to do ("Praise God"), why to do it ("for his mighty deeds"), where to do it ("in his sanctuary" and "in his heavens"), and how to do it ("with trumpet sound . . .").[25] All four musical instrument families are mentioned: brass ("trumpet"), strings ("lute and harp"), percussion "(tambourine"), and winds ("pipe").[26] The word "breath" seems particularly significant. Animals have "breath" too. "Breath" reminds us of Gen 2:7. God breathes the "breath of life" into the man's nostrils, thus causing him to be a "living being." In that sense, the book of Psalms creates an *inclusio* with Genesis. The aspiration of the Psalter is that all creatures will put away their idols and worship Yahweh, the Creator.

The word "dance" indicates that the musical instruments mentioned in Ps 150 might not be meant to accompany singing. Singing is conspicuously *not* mentioned in Ps 150. Only instruments and dance are explicitly mentioned. These are non-verbal forms of expression.[27] If this interpretation is correct, how wonderful a thought is that?! The book of Psalms—this book of splendiferous poetry—is telling us that there are some experiences and emotions words cannot describe. There are some thoughts too great for words. Only non-verbal communication—only instrumental music and dance—can express the inexpressible.

25. Limburg, *Psalms for Sojourners*, loc. 753.

26. Brueggemann and Bellinger, *Psalms*, 635.

27. Glazer, *Psalms of the Jewish Liturgy*, loc. 1028–31. Glazner says that Ps 150 reaches "beyond words, and even beyond prayer, to whole-body-praise."

6

The Pursuit of Wisdom
(Proverbs)

STRUCTURE

THE SIX SUPERSCRIPTIONS OF Proverbs form the book's structure:

- "The proverbs of Solomon, son of David, king of Israel" (Prov 1–9)
- "The proverbs of Solomon" (Prov 10:1—22:16)
- "The words of the wise" (Prov 22:17—24:22)
- "The proverbs of Solomon which the men of Hezekiah king of Judah copied" (Prov 25–29)
- "The words of Agur son of Jakeh" (Prov 30)
- "The words of King Lemuel—an oracle that his mother taught him" (Prov 31)

As you can see, Solomon's name has prominence. It makes sense that Psalms precedes Proverbs in the canonical order. Psalms is largely associated with David; Proverbs is largely associated with David's son, Solomon. Proverbs is the first of three Solomonic books, the other two being the Song of Songs and Ecclesiastes.[1]

It's interesting that a section of Proverbs is said to have been redacted by the "men of Hezekiah." Hezekiah is one of the most righteous kings of Judah (2 Kgs 18:5). But we don't know who Agur is. Neither is there any record of a king named Lemuel. We know the names of the kings of Judah. None of them are named Lemuel. Jewish tradition states that Lemuel is actually Solomon.

Proverbs is written entirely in poetry. Proverbs 1–9 are a poetic discourse on the benefits of wisdom. The actual proverbs of the book of Proverbs don't appear until ch. 10. Virtually the entirety of the remainder of the book consists of these proverbs.

1. Psalm 72 and Ps 127 are attributed to Solomon.

Illuminating Counsel

A proverb is a short poetical statement which conveys a general truth.[2] Virtually all the proverbs are couplets which contain parallelisms. The benefits of using proverbs as a pedagogical tool is they're easy to memorize.

The proverbs appear to be arranged randomly but they cover virtually every topic one can think of. F. LaGard Smith arranged the proverbs topically in his *The Daily Bible*.[3] Here's a sampling of his subheadings:

- Concern for Self
- Pride and Humility
- Selfishness
- Jealousy
- Envy
- Greed
- Control of Self
- Rashness
- Temper and Patience
- Drunkenness and Gluttony
- Adultery
- Prostitution
- Appropriate Speech
- Slander and Gossip
- Lying
- Solicitation to Evil
- Violence
- Revenge
- Dissension and Strife
- Meddling
- Accurate Weights
- Boundary Stones
- Bribery
- Justice
- False Witnesses

2. This is a universal definition but I owe the wording to James Bruckner.

3. Smith, *The Daily Bible*, "Topical Contents for the Book of Proverbs," in Appendix.

The Pursuit of Wisdom

- Wealth and Poverty
- Oppression of the Poor
- Industriousness
- Conservation
- Parents and Children
- The Elderly
- Women and Wives
- Kings and Rulers
- Companions
- Reputation
- Courage
- Hope

Proverbs is as comprehensive about human behavior as Psalms is about human emotions.

SOLOMON THE WISE

The superscription of Proverbs beckons us to recall the historical record of Solomon's rule as recorded in the book of Kings.[4] After Solomon secures his throne (1 Kgs 1–2), God comes to him in a dream and says, "Ask what I shall give you" (1 Kgs 3:5). God basically plays the role of a genie, allowing Solomon to have, not three, but one wish. Here's how Solomon responds:

> You have shown great and steadfast love to your servant David my father, because he walked before you in faithfulness, in righteousness, and in uprightness of heart toward you. And you have kept for him this great and steadfast love and have given him a son to sit on his throne this day. And now, O LORD my God, you have made your servant king in place of David my father, although I am but a little child. I do not know how to go out or come in. And your servant is in the midst of your people whom you have chosen, a great people, too many to be numbered or counted for multitude. Give your servant therefore an understanding mind to govern your people, that I may discern between good and evil, for who is able to govern this your great people? (1 Kgs 3:6–9)

Solomon asks for wisdom! What's fascinating about this is that 1 Kgs 1–2 are very violent chapters. Solomon establishes his rule through violence. And yet, in 1 Kgs

---

4. It is also recorded in 2 Chronicles, which is a hint that Chronicles is relevant to the other books of the Ketuvim.

71

Illuminating Counsel

3, Solomon admits he doesn't know what he's doing. It's as if he realizes that violence is not the right way to establish his reign.

God is very impressed with Solomon's answer. Other kings would have asked for longevity, wealth, or the death of their enemies. Since Solomon asked for wisdom instead of those things, God grants Solomon's request and, as a bonus, gives him the lavishness he didn't ask for.

The very next story (1 Kgs 3:16–28) is a test case of Solomon's newly given wisdom. It's the famous tale of the two prostitutes and the splitting of the baby. "[A]ll Israel heard of the judgment that the king had rendered, and they stood in awe of the king, because they perceived that the wisdom of God was in him to do justice" (1 Kgs 3:28).

The text goes on to tell us that Solomon's wisdom was "beyond measure" and his "breadth of mind [was] like the sand on the seashore" (1 Kgs 4:29). His wisdom "surpassed all the wisdom of the east and all the wisdom of Egypt" (1 Kgs 4:30). As a result, peoples from other lands were coming to Jerusalem to hear Solomon expound on life (1 Kgs 4:34). Solomon took the Queen of Sheba's breath away when she experienced his wisdom firsthand (1 Kgs 10:6).

First Kings 4:32 tells us that Solomon "spoke 3,000 proverbs, and his songs were 1,005." The latter number is oddly precise. Why didn't the writer round down to 1,000? In any event, it makes sense that the book of Proverbs is associated with Solomon. His name is virtually synonymous with wisdom.

And yet, the end of Solomon's narrative in 1 Kings is tragic from a biblical perspective. First Kings 11 tells us that Solomon had an exceedingly large harem—seven hundred wives and three hundred concubines. These are mostly foreign women—polytheists—who consequently turn his heart away from God. Solomon becomes an idolater. It's the problem of idolatry which eventually brings down both kingdoms according to the Deuteronomistic history (2 Kgs 17:7–23). The temple of God, which Solomon built, ends up in ruins.

All of this casts a question mark over Solomon's legacy. Should he be remembered positively or negatively? I don't think anyone in the Tanakh has a greater ascent, and thus no one in the Tanakh has a steeper fall. How did a man so wise act so foolishly?

WISDOM

The book of Proverbs has a "statement of purpose." It wants the readers

> To know wisdom and instruction,
>> to understand words of insight,
> to receive instruction in wise dealing,
>> in righteousness, justice, and equity;
> to give prudence to the simple,
>> knowledge and discretion to the youth—
> Let the wise hear and increase in learning,
>> and the one who understands obtain guidance,

The Pursuit of Wisdom

to understand a proverb and a saying,
the words of the wise and their riddles. (Prov 1:2–6)

Clearly the book of Proverbs is about wisdom. Proverbs is one of the Tanakh's three wisdom books, the other two being Job and Ecclesiastes. Excluding those two books, the word "wisdom" appears in Proverbs more than it appears in every other book of the Tanakh combined.

But what is wisdom? Proverbs doesn't really define it. Rather, it groups the word "wisdom" with synonyms. For example, the words "wisdom and instruction" are a *hendiadys*. A "hendiadys" is when two different words are joined together by the word "and" and yet mean the same thing. Therefore, wisdom = instruction. Likewise, knowing "wisdom" is synonymous with knowing "words of insight" and "wise dealings." Knowing "wisdom" is synonymous with gaining "prudence" and "knowledge and discretion" (also a hendiadys). Knowing wisdom is synonymous with understanding "proverbs," "sayings," and "riddles."

We often differentiate "wisdom" from "knowledge." I love the bumper sticker that says, "Knowledge is knowing a tomato is a fruit. Wisdom is knowing not to put it in a fruit salad." Knowledge is information one possesses. Wisdom is the ability to apply that information. A person may have a lot of knowledge but lack wisdom. This is why wisdom is often associated with age. I know elderly people who don't know anything about smart phones and computers and yet, due to their experience, they understand life much better than a young person who can operate a computer like a virtuoso. IQ is not the same as EQ.

Yet, the book of Proverbs uses the words "knowledge" and "wisdom" synonymously. This can be seen when we look at a variation of one of the book's key verses:

The fear of the LORD is the beginning of knowledge;
fools despise wisdom and instruction. (Prov 1:7)

The fear of the LORD is the beginning of wisdom,
and the knowledge of the Holy One is insight. (Prov 9:10)

Notice the words "wisdom" and "knowledge" are interchangeable. Proverbs uses those words in synonymous parallelisms:

For the LORD gives wisdom;
From his mouth come knowledge and understanding. (Prov 2:6)

[F]or wisdom will come into your heart,
and knowledge will be pleasant to your soul. (Prov 2:10)

A scoffer seeks wisdom in vain,
but knowledge is easy for a man of understanding. (Prov 14:6)

We can make two points about this. First, we can say the biblical notion of wisdom is broader than the modern notion of wisdom. For example, in 1 Kgs 4:33–34 we read that Solomon

> spoke of trees, from the cedar that is in Lebanon to the hyssop that grows out of the wall. He spoke also of beasts, and of birds, and of reptiles, and of fish. And people of all nations came to hear the wisdom of Solomon, and from all the kings of the earth, who had heard of his wisdom.

Here, "wisdom" refers to *science*. It's primitive science—yes—but it's science nonetheless. The word "science" comes from the Latin word *scientia*, which means "knowledge." Back in Newton's day, science was called "natural philosophy." "Philosophy" is a Greek word which means "love of wisdom." The book of Proverbs, therefore, is concerned with *education*. Proverbs 25:2 says, "It is the glory of God to conceal things, and the honor of kings to search things out." This implies we have an obligation to explore God's creation in order to learn how the world works. It's a biblical mandate for doing science.

Second, we can say the biblical notion of knowledge is broader than the modern notion of knowledge. In the Bible, knowledge is not just the ABCs and the times table. Knowledge includes *ethics*. This is why Proverbs' "statement of purpose" says that we are to receive instruction in "righteousness, justice, and equity."

In the Bible, wisdom is chiefly concerned with *character*.[5] Everything we do, and how we do it, says something about who we are. Proverbs is about character formation. Wisdom is the knowledge we need to possess in order to live a morally upright life. Wisdom is the knowledge we need to possess in order to help us overcome our self-destructive tendencies. This puts wisdom very close to Torah. This might be a bit simplistic, but essentially wisdom is Torah in the form of proverbs and maxims rather than commandments.[6]

THE GREATEST PURSUIT

Proverbs says, both explicitly and implicitly, that wisdom is the most important and valuable thing a person can possess:

> Get wisdom; get insight;
>> do not forget, and do not turn away from the words of my mouth.
> Do not forsake her, and she will keep you;
>> love her, and she will guard you.

---

5. Koptak, *Proverbs*, 24.

6. For a nuanced view of the relationship of the Torah and Wisdom, see Longman, *The Fear of the Lord is Wisdom*, 12–13. Sacks, though, disagrees. He thinks Wisdom and Torah are "very different." See Sacks, *Ceremony and Celebration*, 118.

The Pursuit of Wisdom

The beginning of wisdom is this: Get wisdom,
and whatever you get, get insight.
Prize her highly, and she will exalt you;
she will honor you if you embrace her.
She will place on your head a graceful garland;
she will bestow on you a beautiful crown. (Prov 4:5–9)

My son, eat honey, for it is good,
and the drippings of the honeycomb are sweet to your taste.
Know that wisdom is such to your soul;
if you find it, there will be a future,
and your hope will not be cut off. (Prov 24:13–14)

The teaching of the wise is a fountain of life,
that one may turn away from the snares of death. (Prov 13:14)

How much better to get wisdom than gold!
To get understanding is to be chosen rather than silver. (Prov 16:16)

Solomon initially embodied this principle like no one else. When he could have asked for wealth, he instead asked for wisdom. Wisdom is more valuable than all the money in the world. What good is money if you don't have the wisdom to use it well? What good is longevity if you repeatedly make foolish decisions? As Ps 90:12 said, wisdom is the greatest weapon against death and suffering.

I'm not sure how many people today think this way. We're tremendously impressed by looks and wealth. I don't hear many people talk about wisdom. Education, yes. College degrees, yes. STEM, yes. Wisdom, not so much.

Love, of course, is highly valued. Love is also extremely important in the Bible, even in Proverbs. Proverbs says, "Hatred stirs up strife, but love covers all offenses" (Prov 10:12). Even so, the Beatles' notion that "all you need is love" is nonsense. Othello described himself as "one who loved not wisely, but too well."[7] He strangled his wife to death out of misplaced jealousy! You need more than love. You need wisdom. Love without wisdom is often destructive. Proverbs says as much in this way:

Desire without knowledge is not good,
and whoever makes haste with his feet misses his way. (Prov 19:2)

Proverbs urges us to be passionate about learning to discern right from wrong. Gaining wisdom is the key to a fulfilling life. I love Prov 4:7—"The beginning of wisdom is this: *to get wisdom!*" The first step to becoming wise is to recognize the value of wisdom.

---

7. Shakespeare, *Othello*, Act V, scene 2.

THE FEAR OF THE LORD

How does one become wise? Proverbs says that wisdom begins with the "fear of the LORD." Psalm 111:10 says exactly the same thing:

> The fear of the LORD is the beginning of wisdom;
>   all those who practice it have a good understanding.

But that begs the question: what is the "fear of the LORD"? Like the word "wisdom," the "fear of the LORD" is not defined exactly. Proverbs speaks of it as a "thing" in and of itself. We're told the simpletons "did not choose the fear of the LORD" (Prov 1:29). But if you seek wisdom "you will understand the fear of the LORD" (Prov 2:5). In Prov 3:7, "fear the LORD" seems to be a way of saying "do good deeds." Proverbs 8:13 says the "fear of the LORD is the hatred of evil." Consequently, the "fear of the LORD prolongs life" (Prov 10:27; cf. 14:27). Proverbs 15:33 contains a quasi-definition: the "fear of the LORD is instruction in wisdom."

Despite being the ultimate good in Proverbs, the phrase is a stumbling block to readers of the Bible. For religious people, the troublesome word is the word "fear." Aren't we commanded to *love* God? How can we love a God whom we're afraid of? "Love" and "fear" seem mutually exclusive. Yet Deuteronomy uses those two words interchangeably. A few verses before Deuteronomy says to "love the LORD your God with all your heart, all your soul, and all your might" (Deut 6:5), it says to "fear the LORD your God, you, and your son and your son's son, by keeping all his statutes and commandments" (Deut 6:2).

We can try to soften the word "fear." In Hebrew, the word translated "fear" can mean "to be afraid of," but it can also mean "revere." Since Hebrew has fewer words than English, Hebrew words often cover a wider range of meaning than English words. "Revere," then, may not be off the mark in many of these verses. I suppose we could say that if one is in good standing with God, one's "fear" is expressed as *reverence*. If one is not in good standing with God, one's "fear" is expressed as *fright*.

Nevertheless, I think "fear of the LORD" is the best translation. "Fear of the LORD" is an idiom and, therefore, needs to be taken as a whole in its context. Longman is correct when he says the "fear of the LORD" basically means *submitting to God.*[8] Proverbs wants the reader to understand that wisdom comes from God. We cannot be wise unless we recognize that we are not the source of wisdom.

But now we have another problem. Whereas religious people might find the word "fear" to be a stumbling block, non-religious people find the word "LORD" to be a stumbling block. The text seems to be saying that nonreligious people are fools simply because they don't believe in God. Dennis Prager says that this verse in Proverbs (and Ps 111:10) is what brought him back to religious faith. It's what made him realize that

---

8. Longman, *The Fear of the Lord is Wisdom*, 12.

The Pursuit of Wisdom

Columbia University was teaching him folly. "No God, no wisdom," he says.[9] Psalms 14:1 and 53:1 say just that: "The fool says in his heart, 'There is no God.'"

Proverbs is certainly not a book of secular wisdom.[10] It frequently uses the name of Israel's god, Yahweh, which is translated "the LORD":

> Many are the plans in the mind of a man,
>> but it is the purpose of the LORD that will stand. (Prov 19:21)

Proverbs also strongly affirms God's providence and the Retribution Principle:

> The eyes of the LORD are in every place,
>> keeping watch on the evil and the good. (Prov 15:3)

> The eyes of the LORD keep watch over knowledge,
>> but he overthrows the words of the traitor. (Prov 22:12)

The irony of all this is that there's evidence Proverbs was influenced by the Egyptian Wisdom tradition.[11] Does the intersection of Jewish and pagan wisdom demonstrate that one can be wise without believing in the existence of Israel's God? Here I will reveal my bias. I'm critical of many aspects of secularism. I think one does not need to be a believer to recognize that the Bible has had a positive influence on our society.[12] I agree with Yoram Hazony—the notion that we can get rid of the Bible and rebuild morality from the ground up is as unrealistic as it is hubristic.[13] On the other hand, I know many foolish religious people and I have learned from a great many nonreligious people. Many religious people fail to realize that they often start with the answers in their thinking rather than follow the evidence wherever it leads. Some religious people not only deny science, but also have irrational interpretations of the Bible ranging from the ridiculous to the truly evil. Neither the religious nor the nonreligious have a monopoly on wisdom. Folly, however, is everywhere. What Proverbs condemns is the notion that one can be wise without learning from, or listening to, others. "The way of the fool is right in his own eyes, but a wise man listens to advice" (Prov 12:15). If a nonbeliever lives by that maxim, the nonbeliever, in a sense, at least partially, possesses the "fear of the LORD." If a believer does not live by that maxim, the believer does *not* possess the "fear of the LORD." The "fear of the LORD" is really about how you live more than what you believe.

---

9. Prager, "How I Found God at Columbia."

10. Longman, *The Fear of the Lord is Wisdom*, 13–14.

11. McLaughlin, *The Ancient Near East*, 40–45.

12. I recommend to you the book *America's Prophet: Moses and the American Story* by Bruce Feiler.

13. Yoram Hazony, "Is the Bible a Work of Philosophy?"

WHO IS WISE?

> Do not reprove a scoffer, or he will hate you;
> reprove a wise man, and he will love you. (Prov 9:8)

This verse is baked in my consciousness because of an email I received from a student a week or two after the semester ended. The student very cautiously and gently rebuked me for something I had said in class early in the semester. Of course, it was obvious that this student was purposely sending this email *after* she had received her grade (which was an A)! In any case, after rebuking me, she said she deemed me to be a wise person. She then quoted Prov 9:8 and admitted that she was "hiding behind the Bible."

I despise being criticized. It feels like being punched in the gut. Sometimes I obsess over the criticism. It reverberates in my mind for days, sometimes weeks. It's also annoying when I excuse other's flaws but they feel the need to nitpick mine.

But I also knew that this student is a good person. If she thought I had done something which was "bad form," as she put it, I knew I needed to self-evaluate. I re-read Prov 9:8 and thought about what it means. I replied to her email, apologized for what I said, and told her to "keep quoting Proverbs."

What an incredible statement Prov 9:8 is! Who is wise? A wise person is *not* someone who doesn't make mistakes! If that were the case, you would never need to reprove a wise person. The difference between a wise person and a scoffer is not that the wise person doesn't make mistakes; it's that the wise person will listen to rebuke whereas the scoffer will not. Even if the criticism is harsh and unfair—and I have been the recipient of some very harsh, even cruel, criticism—there might still be something in it to learn from.[14]

Proverbs, therefore, makes wisdom accessible to all. There's a Jewish saying: "Who is wise? He who learns from all men, as it is said, 'From all my teachers have I gotten understanding'" (Pirkei Avot 4:1, paraphrasing Ps 119:99). We don't have to understand all of life's mysteries to be wise. We don't have to have a PhD to be wise. We don't have to be eighty years old to be wise. All we have to do is be willing to listen and learn. That's something all of us can do—religious and nonreligious alike.

Generally speaking, we're not good at taking criticism. We also tend to resist learning from others, particularly from those who are of a different ideological tribe, so to speak. Christians don't want to learn from Jews. Jews don't want to learn from Christians. Muslims don't want to learn from Hindus. Religious people don't want to learn from atheists. Atheists don't want to learn from religious people. Democrats don't want to learn from Republicans. Republicans don't want to learn from Democrats. I remember feeling this problem after I read a life-changing book. I was surprised and disappointed when I learned that the author is of a different political party than the

---

14. Telushkin, *Words That Hurt, Words That Heal*, 104.

The Pursuit of Wisdom

one I belong to. But truth is truth. I can learn things from people I disagree with. The irony of our time is that more information is accessible to us than at any other time in human history, and yet we seem to be listening to each other less than in previous generations. We do a lot of tweeting, but not a lot of listening.

THE GREATEST VICE AND THE GREATEST VIRTUE

> There is a way that seems right to a man,
>> but its end is the way to death. (Prov 14:12; 16:25)

The "end" refers to the consequences of a given action. We tend to act without thinking about the consequences of our actions. We tend to do what we do because it feels good in the moment.

There's a Jewish story about a boy who goes into a pool and shrieks because the water is cold. He comes out and breathes a sigh of relief when his father wraps him in a blanket. The father tells him that those two sounds—the sound of the shriek and the sound of relief—are all of life. The only question is which sound will come first.[15] Studying is burdensome, but you will be happy when you see your grades. Partying is fun, but you will be miserable when you see your grades.

The person the proverb is describing is one who is "wise in his own eyes." One who is wise in his own eyes does not fear the LORD. Such a person doesn't submit to God, for he believes that he himself is the source of wisdom. He knows best. He's above criticism. The Bible has a word to describe this attitude. It's the word "pride."

Pride, of course, can have a positive connotation. It's the warm feeling you have when you, or your loved ones, accomplish something. What parent doesn't feel tremendous pride when seeing their child graduate college? It would be awful if a parent didn't feel pride in such a situation.

Pride can also refer to self-respect. In that sense, to lose one's pride is to lose one's dignity. A wife who lets her husband berate her, a man who feels like such a failure that he no longer tries to succeed, people who are ashamed of the accidents of their existence—such people have no pride.

But that's *not* what the Bible means by the word "pride." The Bible is all for feeling good about accomplishments and self-respect. In the Bible, "pride" refers to arrogance, conceit, haughtiness, superciliousness, pompousness, grandiosity. A proud person is an arrogant person. A proud person is someone who inflates his own importance. A proud person is someone who thinks of himself as greater than he really is (see Rom 12:3), as greater than others, perhaps even equal to God. C. S. Lewis calls pride "the great sin." "Pride leads to every other vice: it is the complete anti-God state of mind."[16]

---

15. Greenberg, "Easy or Hard?," chabad.org.

16. Lewis, *Mere Christianity*, 110.

Illuminating Counsel

Let's return to Solomon. How can someone so wise act so foolishly? How can someone so wise think that having a harem of one thousand women is a good idea?! Clearly, Solomon didn't consider the "end" of the matter. How can we explain this paradox?

I wonder if Solomon was haunted by his father's legacy. David is mentioned quite often in 1 Kings even though David dies in ch. 2. The text tells us that "Solomon loved the LORD, walking in the statutes of David his father" (1 Kgs 3:3). Solomon mentions David nearly incessantly. Even when others praise Solomon, David's name is mentioned. "Blessed be the LORD this day," says Hiram, "who has given to David a wise son to be over this great people" (1 Kgs 5:7). Solomon builds the temple, but that idea came from David; Solomon was fulfilling his father's dream. Solomon acknowledges this, saying, "For I have risen in place of David my father, and sit on the throne of Israel . . ." (1 Kgs 8:24). Solomon prays to God that God fulfill the promise he made to David—that David's throne will be eternal. God tells Solomon:

> And as for you, if you will walk before me, as David your father walked, with integrity of heart and uprightness, doing according to all that I have commanded you, and keeping my statutes and my rules, then I will establish your royal throne over Israel forever, as I promised David your father, saying, "You shall not lack a man on the throne of Israel." (1 Kgs 9:4–5)

But then we read this:

> For when Solomon was old his wives turned away his heart after other gods, and his heart was not wholly true to the LORD his God, as was the heart of David his father. For Solomon went after Ashtoreth the goddess of the Sidonians, and after Milcom the abomination of the Ammonites. So Solomon did what was evil in the sight of the LORD and did not wholly follow the LORD, as David his father had done. (1 Kgs 11:4–6)

So I can't help but think that the text is comparing Solomon with David. Despite his own tremendous accomplishments, did Solomon feel trapped in the shadow of his father? Solomon fails to live up to his father's legacy. David, for all his faults, never committed idolatry. And, as Rabbi David Wolpe has noted, David's greatest attribute was his willingness to listen to reproach and advice, whether it was from Abigail (1 Sam 25:23–35), from Nathan (2 Sam 12:1–13), from the woman of Tekoa (2 Sam 14:4–21), or even from Joab (2 Sam 19:4–8).[17] By contrast, when God tells Solomon that his son will rule over only the tribe of Judah and that the rest of the tribes of Israel will be ruled by Jeroboam son of Nebat, Solomon (unsuccessfully) orders Jeroboam to be killed (1 Kgs 11:40).

We also cannot ignore Solomon's lavishness. "Solomon ruled over all the kingdoms from the Euphrates to the land of the Philistines and to the border of Egypt. They brought tribute and served Solomon all the days of his life" (1 Kgs 4:21). No

17. Wolpe, *David*, 55–56.

80

The Pursuit of Wisdom

Israelite king had a larger kingdom than Solomon. The text tells us that he had "40,000 stalls of horses for his chariots, and 12,000 horsemen" (1 Kgs 4:26). Solomon built the temple in eleven years, but spent thirteen years building his own house. The text's description of his grandeur is tedious and yet instructive:

> Now the weight of gold that came to Solomon in one year was 666 talents of gold, besides that which came from the explorers and from the business of the merchants, and from all the kings of the west and from the governors of the land. King Solomon made 200 large shields of beaten gold; 600 shekels of gold went into each shield. And he made 300 shields of beaten gold; three minas of gold went into each shield. And the king put them in the House of the Forest of Lebanon. The king also made a great ivory throne and overlaid it with the finest gold. The throne had six steps, and the throne had a round top, and on each side of the seat were armrests and two lions standing beside the armrests, while twelve lions stood there, one on each end of a step on the six steps. The like of it was never made in any kingdom. All King Solomon's drinking vessels were of gold, and all the vessels of the House of the Forest of Lebanon were of pure gold. None were of silver; silver was not considered as anything in the days of Solomon. For the king had a fleet of ships of Tarshish at sea with the fleet of Hiram. Once every three years the fleet of ships of Tarshish used to come bringing gold, silver, ivory, apes, and peacocks. (1 Kgs 10:14–22)

Is it really so hard to see why Solomon fell? He fell, not because he lacked wisdom, but because he lacked *humility*.

Love requires wisdom. But wisdom has its own prerequisite. Wisdom requires humility. Thus says Proverbs:

> When pride comes, then comes disgrace,
> but with the humble is wisdom. (Prov 11:2)

> Everyone who is arrogant in heart is an abomination to the LORD;
> be assured, he will not go unpunished. (Prov 16:5)

> Before destruction a man's heart is haughty,
> but humility comes before honor. (Prov 18:12)

> The reward for humility and fear of the LORD
> is riches and honor and life. (Prov 22:4)

> One's pride will bring him low,
> but he who is lowly in spirit will obtain honor. (Prov 29:23)

This became a life-lesson for me in the days leading up to my graduation from graduate school. I had learned that my university awards a special medallion for the valedictorian. Unlike other schools, though, the valedictorian is not revealed until the

commencement ceremony. The previous year, my friend Mike won the award. His GPA was announced. It was 3.87. My GPA was 3.973. Had I graduated with him, I would have won the award. I figured, then, that I was a shoe-in for it. Mike himself told me that I would probably win it. However, he told me I may have competition from another student—Eric—whom Mike referred to as a "formidable scholar." I knew Eric but never had a class with him. He's a great guy and a fantastic singer but I had no idea that he was so erudite. I began to doubt whether I would win the medallion. A 3.973 is wonderful, but it's not unbeatable. If only I could have gotten a 4.0! Truth be told, the reason I didn't get a 4.0 is because I had returned from school after a long hiatus and I was a bit "rusty." I received an A- in a class called "Research Methods" in my very first semester. I got an A on the final paper but some of my other written assignments were less than excellent and I submitted a major assignment late. I also got an A- on a one-credit Independent Study on the Intertestamental literature. I did far more work than what was required. My final paper was forty-two pages long. Still, quality trumps quantity. I deserved the A-. That was in the summer of my first year. Had I taken those classes in my second year, I think I would have gotten an A in both of them. The point, though, is that it would be awful to lose to a GPA that was just .027 higher than mine!

A few weeks before commencement, academic awards were given. I won two of them—Hebrew and History. My rival won only one. I was later told that it was against the rules for a student to win more than one of these awards. Yet both of my professors refused to back down. This renewed my confidence. How could I not win the medallion?

But then something happened that made me doubt myself again. I knew that the university secretly contacts the valedictorian's family to create a biography of the student which is read by the president of the university at commencement. So I called my father and told him that someone from my university might be calling him. I didn't want my father to give them information about me that might be too embarrassing. But a few days before commencement, when I asked my father if someone had called, he said no. Of course, the university tells the family to keep it a secret, but I know my father and I could tell that he was being truthful. No one had called him. I resolved that Eric, or someone else, must have had a 4.0. Or maybe the university didn't have my father's phone number. He's my only contact. Did they have it or not? Was there still hope that I could win?

I finally realized that I was obsessed with this award. I was shocked by how egotistical, self-centered, and arrogant I was. My thoughts and feelings were contrary to all the things I value. This was the greatest spiritual crisis of my life. I desperately needed advice. The problem was that I was apprehensive about telling people what I was struggling with because I didn't want anyone to think—or to *know*—that I was narcissistic. So I decided to email Mike. He was the only person I could think of who could relate. I was taking a risk in telling him precisely how I felt. He had a good

The Pursuit of Wisdom

impression of me. If he knew how petty I really am, he might not want to be friends with me. Nevertheless, I came clean:

> . . . had I not learned about that medallion which you won, my life would be better right now. I've been obsessing over it in a very unhealthy way. I am actually frightened by how prideful I truly am. It has gotten to the point where I am not excited to graduate and that I cannot think about anything else—though, frankly, I'm disgusted with my attitude and thoughts.

> . . . my own pride is hurting me because I might lose by .02 or .01 of a point. And it's so stupid because I could have gotten an A in both of those classes. History was MUCH more difficult than Research Methods. Therefore, I feel haunted by this.

> . . . Losing is probably better for my soul . . . The lack of joy I feel about graduating is the price I pay for my pride.

To say Mike's response was compassionate is an understatement. What he told me was one of the most important pieces of wisdom I've ever received:

> But, yes, I agree: your pride is stupid. All pride is stupid. We're organic creatures who poop and will die and we fill our lives with things to distract us from these facts and among our favorite distractions are calculable numbers like GPAs or stock prices or "the most toys" by any name. What a load of crap. I wish I could cure myself of stupid mind games like that. I don't think less of you. In fact, I think the ridiculous scrupulosity over your GPA is just about matched by the courage and vulnerability demonstrated in talking about it. We'll call it even.

His email was a godsend. It woke me up from the "dark night of the soul" I was experiencing. I am immensely grateful that he helped me resolve this—that he helped me get over myself *before* my commencement ceremony. I enjoyed my commencement ceremony . . . and I was completely at peace when the recipient's name was read.

Pride *is* stupid. It turns us into losers even when we win. No matter how smart you are, or how good you are at something, there's always someone smarter, faster, and better. To wrap your identity in being the "best" is to set yourself up for failure. This is why pride's cousin is envy.

> A tranquil heart gives life to the flesh,
>> but envy makes the bones rot. (Prov 14:30)

If you become an envious person, you forfeit whatever chance you have of being happy. When I find myself envying others, I tell myself that that's the attitude of a loser. Losers envy others for their success. Winners admire successful people and try to learn from them.

Everyone struggles with pride. There's not a single human being who is incapable of arrogance. The problem is we're blind to it. We notice hubris in others much easier than in ourselves. We're in denial about who and what we are. Lewis said, "If you think you are not conceited, it means you are very conceited indeed."[18]

The Bible views humility as the most important value of all. And what is humility? According to Robert Moore, humility is just two things: "knowing your limitations" and "getting the help you need."[19]

I'm convinced there's no issue in life more important than pride and humility. Lewis said, "Nearly all those evils in the world which people put down to greed and selfishness are really far more the result of Pride."[20] Arrogant people can neither love others nor be wise, because they put themselves above others. Pride is the cause of racism. Pride is at the root of genocide. Pride is why you and I do the ugly things we do. Pride is the reason the world is broken.

The quest for wisdom is not about becoming smart, but about becoming humble. Humble people are wise and wise people are humble. Lord Chesterfield said it best: "In seeking wisdom, thou art wise; in imagining that thou hast attained it—thou art a fool."

WOMAN WISDOM AND WOMAN FOLLY

Proverbs is written from the perspective of a father teaching his son. All of the warnings are from a male point of view. The father repeatedly warns his son of the adulteress (literally the "strange woman") (Prov 2:16). Adultery is a major theme in Proverbs. All of ch. 5, half of ch. 6, and all of ch. 7 are about the temptation to commit adultery. The libido is necessary for the perpetuation of our species, but it also clouds the judgment. Ironically, David had an adulterous affair with Solomon's mother, who was the wife of another man at the time. And, of course, Solomon is known for his absurdly massive harem. Even godly men succumb to sexual temptation.

The male-centric nature of the book of Proverbs puts the onus on the teacher to transpose these warnings so that they are relevant to women.[21] Virtually everything said about men can be applied to women in some way. We're all human.

While the speaker in Proverbs is the father, we should remember that the mother is also present and involved in the character formation of her son. The father tells his son to "forsake not [his] mother's teaching" (Prov 1:8; 6:20).[22] Moreover, the sayings of

18. Lewis, *Mere Christianity*, 114.

19. Moore, *Facing the Dragon*, 71.

20. Lewis, *Mere Christianity*, 110.

21. Koptak, *Proverbs*, 214–15. Koptak quotes Bellis, "Gender and Motives," in Brenner and Fontaine, *Wisdom and Psalms*, 90–91.

22. "Teaching" is the translation of the word *torah*.

The Pursuit of Wisdom

King Lemuel (whoever he was) in Prov 31 are really the teachings of his mother (Prov 31:1). Thus Prov 31 is actually the words of a woman teaching a man.

What's truly remarkable is that the voice of wisdom in Proverbs is actually a feminine voice. Proverbs personifies wisdom and folly as women.

Why are wisdom and folly personified? And why as women? The answer to the second question is rather basic: the Hebrew words for wisdom and folly (*hokhma* and *kesilut*) are feminine. If those concepts are personified, it's only natural that they be personified as women. As to why they are personified at all, the answer, I think, is that it makes the text more interesting and gets the author's point across more effectively.[23] Proverbs wants us to love wisdom (Prov 29:3). This is made easier when wisdom—an abstraction—is personified. Conversely, the voice of folly becomes the voice of temptation calling out to us on a daily basis, urging us towards corruption.

The feminine personifications add a sense of variety to the book. They contrast so beautifully with the father's male voice. The personification of wisdom begins in ch. 1. The father warns his son about a hypothetical gang. The gang calls out for the lad to join, but the father urges his son to resist the call.

> My son, if sinners entice you,
>> do not consent.
> If they say, "Come with us, let us lie in wait for blood;
>> let us ambush the innocent without reason;
> like Sheol let us swallow them alive,
>> and whole, like those who go down to the pit;
> we shall find all precious goods,
>> we shall fill our houses with plunder;
> throw in your lot among us;
>> we will all have one purse"—
> my son, do not walk in the way with them;
>> hold back your foot from their paths,
> for their feet run to evil,
>> and they make haste to shed blood.
> For in vain is a net spread
>> in the sight of any bird,
> but these men lie in wait for their own blood;
>> they set an ambush for their own lives.
> Such are the ways of everyone who is greedy for unjust gain;
>> it takes away the life of its possessors. (Prov 1:10–19)

This is a rhapsody on Ps 1. Don't walk in the counsel of the wicked, or stand in the way of sinners, or sit in the seat of scoffers—no matter how enticing it might seem.

The father then tells the son about wisdom:

---

23. You should know that many scholars believe the personification of wisdom is inspired by Near Eastern writings about the goddess Asherah. See Smith, *The Early History of God*, 94–97.

Illuminating Counsel

Wisdom cries aloud in the street,
  in the markets she raises her voice;
at the head of the noisy streets she cries out;
  at the entrance of the city gates she speaks:
"How long, O simple ones, will you love being simple?
How long will scoffers delight in their scoffing
  and fools hate knowledge?
If you turn at my reproof,
behold, I will pour out my spirit to you;
  I will make my words known to you.
Because I have called and you refused to listen,
  have stretched out my hand and no one has heeded,
because you have ignored all my counsel
  and would have none of my reproof,
I also will laugh at your calamity;
  I will mock when terror strikes you,
when terror strikes you like a storm
  and your calamity comes like a whirlwind,
  when distress and anguish come upon you.
Then they will call upon me, but I will not answer;
  they will seek me diligently but will not find me.
Because they hated knowledge
  and did not choose the fear of the LORD,
would have none of my counsel
  and despised all my reproof,
therefore they shall eat the fruit of their way,
  and have their fill of their own devices.
For the simple are killed by their turning away,
  and the complacency of fools destroys them;
but whoever listens to me will dwell secure
  and will be at ease, without dread of disaster. (Prov 1:20–33)

She seems quite cantankerous! This is because the "simpletons" have failed to listen to her. The simpletons have chosen to walk in the counsel of the wicked, to stand in the way of sinners, and to sit in the seat of scoffers. The simpletons are a negative example for the son. Don't be like them!

The fullest and climactic expression of the personification of wisdom occurs in Prov 8. We can divide that chapter into two sections along with a coda. The first section is Prov 8:1–21. Here wisdom calls out to all humans, especially the simpletons and the fools. What we notice in this discourse is that wisdom is in a better mood than she was in Prov 1. There she was rather perturbed because the simpletons rejected her. Here, though, there seems to be hope that even the fools might listen and change the course of their lives:

The Pursuit of Wisdom

By me kings reign,
    and rulers decree what is just;
by me princes rule,
    and nobles, all who govern justly.
I love those who love me,
    and those who seek me diligently find me.
Riches and honor are with me,
    enduring wealth and righteousness.
My fruit is better than gold, even fine gold,
    and my yield than choice silver.
I walk in the way of righteousness,
    in the paths of justice,
granting an inheritance to those who love me,
    and filling their treasuries. (Prov 8:15–21)

Her call is compelling. What person wouldn't want to heed her?

The second section is Prov 8:22–31. This is about creation. Wisdom tells the reader how she was with God in the beginning:

The LORD possessed me at the beginning of his work,
    the first of his acts of old.
Ages ago I was set up,
    at the first, before the beginning of the earth.
When there were no depths I was brought forth,
    when there were no springs abounding with water.
Before the mountains had been shaped,
    before the hills, I was brought forth,
before he had made the earth with its fields,
    or the first of the dust of the world.
When he established the heavens, I was there;
    when he drew a circle on the face of the deep,
when he made firm the skies above,
    when he established the fountains of the deep,
when he assigned to the sea its limit,
    so that the waters might not transgress his command,
when he marked out the foundations of the earth,
    then I was beside him, like a master workman,
and I was daily his delight,
    rejoicing before him always,
rejoicing in his inhabited world
    and delighting in the children of man.

This text may remind us of Ps 104 but there is a subtle difference. Psalm 104:24 says that God created the world by his wisdom. But this is not the point made in Prov 8:22–31. The point made in Prov 8:22–31 is simply that wisdom was *with* God

when God created the world. Wisdom was a witness. Wisdom testifies to the joy of creation. The Bible tends to have a grim view of human nature but it celebrates human dignity. Wisdom "delighted in the children of man"! It seems the creation of humanity is likened to the birth of a child. This needs to be remembered when we read the book of Job.

Wisdom, therefore, transcends us. She's like our godmother. She saw us when we came out of the womb. She knows more than we do. She has our best interests in mind. We should trust her. This leads us to the coda:

> And now, O sons, listen to me:
>> blessed are those who keep my ways.
> Hear instruction and be wise,
>> and do not neglect it.
> Blessed is the one who listens to me,
>> watching daily at my gates,
>> waiting beside my doors.
> For whoever finds me finds life
>> and obtains favor from the LORD,
> but he who fails to find me injures himself;
>> all who hate me love death. (Prov 8:32–36)

This seems close to Deut 30:11–20. "Choose life." We don't have a choice to be born and we don't have choice about being mortal, yet the Bible holds out life and death as choices. To love wisdom is to choose life. To despise wisdom is to choose death.

Wisdom's call continues into the next chapter:

> To him who lacks sense she says,
> "Come, eat of my bread
>> and drink of the wine I have mixed.
> Leave your simple ways, and live,
>> and walk in the way of insight." (Prov 9:4–6)

It's never too late to become wise. A mentor of mine said, "Our misdeeds have consequences but they are not quicksand." I love that metaphor! We're not defined by our mistakes, but how we learn from our mistakes. The call of wisdom in the book of Proverbs is stern because of its realistic portrait of the consequences of folly, but it's also full of grace.

But wisdom has a competitor. Her arch-nemesis is folly:

> The woman Folly is loud;
>> she is seductive and knows nothing.
> She sits at the door of her house;
>> she takes a seat on the highest places of the town,
> calling to those who pass by,
>> who are going straight on their way,

The Pursuit of Wisdom

"Whoever is simple, let him turn in here!"
    And to him who lacks sense she says,
"Stolen water is sweet,
    and bread eaten in secret is pleasant."
But he does not know that the dead are there,
    that her guests are in the depths of Sheol. (Prov 9:13–18)

There are always two voices calling to us—one good and one evil.[24] I think the postmodern tendency to view binaries as antiquated and simplistic is foolish. No, not everything is "black and white," but most things probably are; we just take them for granted. I find it interesting, though, that while postmodern thinking downplays the reality of evil, the movies and stories people are obsessed with are all about good and evil. Think *Star Wars*, *The Lord of the Rings*, *Harry Potter*, and virtually all superhero movies.[25]

Proverbs, perhaps more than any other book of the Tanakh, deals with the problem of temptation. We seem to be inclined to do things which are harmful to us. Folly seems to come more naturally than prudence. Indeed, we are a self-destructive species. The good news is that, while we can't change our nature, we can control our self-destructive tendencies. There's always a choice. We must reject the voice of folly and listen instead to the voice of wisdom. Of course, that implies that we're able to distinguish the one voice from the other. Both women promise us wonderful things. Both women claim to be on our side. Yet only one of them will cause us to flourish. How do we discern which voice is wisdom's and which is folly's? I think all of the proverbs in the book of Proverbs are meant to help us in that endeavor!

A TASTE OF PROVERBS' WISDOM

It's impossible in our limited space to discuss the breadth of Proverbs' subject matter. Therefore, I'd like to share just a few verses that you may find enlightening.

Enemies

Do not rejoice when your enemy falls,
    and let not your heart be glad when he stumbles,
lest the LORD see it and be displeased,
    and turn away his anger from him. (Prov 24:17–18)

24. Koptak, *Proverbs*, 25–26.

25. Moore, *Facing the Dragon*, 1.

Illuminating Counsel

> If your enemy is hungry, give him bread to eat,
>> and if he is thirsty, give him water to drink,
> for you will heap burning coals on his head,
>> and the LORD will reward you. (Prov 25:21–22)

The latter passage is quoted in the New Testament (Rom 12:20). This is probably where Jesus's notion of "love your enemies" originates from (Matt 5:44).

Animal Welfare

> Whoever is righteous has regard for the life of his beast,
>> but the mercy of the wicked is cruel. (Prov 12:10)

The Bible values the life of animals. We see the same thing in the Torah (Deut 22:6–7; 25:4).

Anxiety

> Anxiety in a man's heart weighs him down,
>> but a good word makes him glad. (Prov 12:25)

As someone who tends to be anxious, this verse speaks to me. A friend of mine, who's a psychologist, teaches her patients to have a right relationship with anxiety. Anxiety is a defense mechanism. It's there for a reason. Like all things, though, we cannot let it run amok.

This verse also reminds us that we have a moral obligation to speak encouraging words to each other. Encouragement is a powerful medicine.

Neighborliness

> Let your foot be seldom in your neighbor's house,
>> lest he have his fill of you and hate you. (Prov 25:17)

It's amazing how nothing has changed in the last three thousand years! You may be a wonderful person, but too much of a good thing is not good—even when the good thing is you!

Anger

> A soft answer turns away wrath,
>> but a harsh word stirs up anger. (Prov 15:1)

The Pursuit of Wisdom

Proverbs has a lot to say about controlling the tongue. We tend to speak foolishly, presumptuously, and harshly. We lie. We gossip. We slander. In Judaism, this is called *Lashon Hara*, which means "the evil tongue." Sadly, the internet, as wonderful as it is, has caused many people to lose their inhibition. People hide behind a username. Twitter is so often a cesspool of hate. People are so angry. Americans hate each other. This is a moral decay in our society.

How should we respond to the "evil tongue"?

> The vexation of a fool is known at once,
>> but the prudent ignores an insult. (Prov 12:16)

Ignoring an insult is not easy. Our tendency is to hit back. But that's why we have these proverbs. They teach us what is prudent. Then there's this:

> Make no friendship with a man given to anger,
>> nor go with a wrathful man,
> lest you learn his ways
>> and entangle yourself in a snare. (Prov 22:24–25)

This tells us two things. First, anger is contagious, as are most vices. Second, you are not obligated to be friends with everyone you meet. It's not unkind to avoid a person who will corrupt your character. Some people are "toxic." As someone said to me, "Be friendly with everyone, but be friends with only a few." Even choosing friends requires wisdom.

Alcohol

> Wine is a mocker, strong drink a brawler,
>> and whoever is led astray by it is not wise. (Prov 20:1)

The Bible is not opposed to drinking alcohol in principle (wine is very important in Judaism), but it *is* opposed to drunkenness, which it views as folly. In the United States, there were nearly eleven thousand drunk driving fatalities in 2017. Alcohol is a drug that changes how people think and behave.

Judgment

> The one who states his case first seems right,
>> until the other comes and examines him. (Prov 18:17)

We've all experienced this. It's what the movie *12 Angry Men* is about. This is why we should never rush to judgment. Being wise requires one to weigh both sides carefully and follow the evidence wherever it leads.

Money

Proverbs has a lot to say about money. It's deeply concerned with injustices done to the poor:

> Whoever oppresses a poor man insults his Maker,
>> but he who is generous to the needy honors him. (Prov 14:31)

This proverb seeks to get us to humanize the poor. God is on their side. To mess with a poor person is to mess with God. We've been warned.

> The fallow ground of the poor would yield much food,
>> but it is swept away through injustice. (Prov 13:23)

This verse is referring to the law of gleaning mentioned in Lev 19:9 and Lev 23:22. We will mention it again when we look at the book of Ruth. The point is that injustice causes poverty. Hence Proverbs urges generosity:

> One gives freely, yet grows all the richer;
>> another withholds what he should give, and only suffers want.
> Whoever brings blessing will be enriched,
>> and one who waters will himself be watered.
> The people curse him who holds back grain,
>> but a blessing is on the head of him who sells it. (Prov 11:24–26)

These verses are summarized by the maxim, "It is more blessed to give than to receive," which is attributed to Jesus in Acts 20:35.

Proverbs also warns about trusting in wealth:

> Whoever trusts in his riches will fall,
>> but the righteous will flourish like a green leaf. (Prov 11:28)

Trusting in one's wealth is a form of arrogance. Trust in wisdom, not wealth:

> Better is a little with the fear of the LORD
>> than great treasure and trouble with it. (Prov 15:16)

> Better is a poor man who walks in his integrity
>> than a rich man who is crooked in his ways. (Prov 28:6)

> A rich man is wise in his own eyes,
>> but a poor man who has understanding will find him out. (Prov 28:11)

Proverbs, however, is not opposed to wealth. It's opposed to folly. Sometimes the pursuit of wealth and the hoarding of wealth is foolish and sinful. But wealth in and of itself is not bad. Moreover, while injustice causes poverty, not all poverty is caused by injustice. Sometimes poverty is the result of foolishness:

The Pursuit of Wisdom

Go to the ant, O sluggard;
  consider her ways, and be wise.
Without having any chief,
  officer, or ruler,
she prepares her bread in summer
  and gathers her food in harvest.
How long will you lie there, O sluggard?
  When will you arise from your sleep?
A little sleep, a little slumber,
  a little folding of the hands to rest,
and poverty will come upon you like a robber,
  and want like an armed man. (Prov 6:6–11)

A slack hand causes poverty,
  but the hand of the diligent makes rich. (Prov 10:4)

In all toil there is profit,
  but mere talk tends only to poverty. (Prov 14:23)

The sluggard does not plow in the autumn;
  he will seek at harvest and have nothing. (Prov 20:4)

Sometimes our financial troubles are no one's fault but our own. If you want to be poor, all you have to do is be lazy and spend more money than you earn. We don't need to wonder what Proverbs would think about our "buy now, pay later" culture. Proverbs 22:7 says "the borrower is slave to the lender."

Maybe Proverbs' teachings on money is best summarized by Agur in Prov 30:7–9:

Two things I ask of you;
  deny them not to me before I die:
Remove far from me falsehood and lying;
  give me neither poverty nor riches;
  feed me with the food that is needful for me,
lest I be full and deny you
  and say, "Who is the LORD?"
or lest I be poor and steal
  and profane the name of my God.

WONDER WOMAN

The last chapter of Proverbs reflects the teachings of King Lemuel's mother, although it's debatable whether her teachings extend beyond v. 9. Even if they don't, there's an interesting connection between Prov 31:2–9 and Prov 31:10–31. While the latter

passage is the one in which I wish to concentrate, looking at the preceding passage will prove to be illuminating. Proverbs 31:2–9 says this:

> What are you doing, my son? What are you doing, son of my womb?
>> What are you doing, son of my vows?
> Do not give your *strength* to women,
>> your ways to those who destroy kings.
> It is not for kings, O Lemuel,
>> it is not for kings to drink wine,
>> or for rulers to take strong drink,
> lest they drink and forget what has been decreed
>> and pervert the rights of all the afflicted.
> Give strong drink to the one who is perishing,
>> and wine to those in bitter distress;
> let them drink and forget their poverty
>> and remember their misery no more.
> Open your mouth for the mute,
>> for the rights of all who are destitute.
> Open your mouth, judge righteously,
>> defend the rights of the poor and needy.

I have emphasized the word "strength." This is the translation of the Hebrew word *hayil*. Lemuel's mother tells him not to give his "strength" to women. This reminds us of Solomon. (It might also remind us of Samson!) First Kings 11:3 says his many wives "turned away his heart." Such is unbecoming of the ruler of a people.

Notice a contradiction in what Lemuel's mother tells him. The king is not to consume alcohol because it will cause him to forget his primary task, which is to defend the "rights of all the afflicted." There's no way to improve on those values. More than two millennia later, we're still trying to foster a society based on liberty and justice for all. But then she tells him that those who are "perishing" and in "bitter distress" *are* to consume alcohol. Alcohol will help them forget their misery. At first blush that might seem like bad advice. Some people should *not* be given alcohol. It will create other problems.

It wasn't until I was trained as a hospice volunteer that I realized what Lemuel's mother is really saying. She's presenting the biblical case for palliative care. When there's no cure, the best one can hope for is the dulling of pain. Palliative care allows one to die gracefully. There's a scene in the movie *The Good, the Bad, and the Ugly* where "Blondie" lets a dying soldier take a few hits on his cigar. It's a touching moment because it's a kindness that seems so simple and yet its effects are profound. He was giving the dying man one last moment of pleasure.

This brings us to Prov 31:10 which is one of the greatest passages of the Ketuvim. Comparing the translations of that verse will cause us to realize that something from the Hebrew is lost in translation:

The Pursuit of Wisdom

- "An excellent wife who can find?" (ESV, NASB)

- "Who can find a virtuous woman?" (KJV)

- "Who can find a virtuous wife?" (NKJV)

- "A wife of noble character who can find?" (NIV)

- "A capable wife who can find?" (NRSV)

- "A good wife who can find?" (RSV)

Clearly there's an ambiguity with the Hebrew word translated "woman" and "wife." That's not the primary issue, though. The issue is the adjective which is describing this woman. The Hebrew phrase contains only two words: *eshet hayil*. *Eshet* means "woman of" or "wife of" ("woman" and "wife" are the same word in Hebrew). What does *hayil* mean? We've already seen this word. Lemuel's mother used it when she told Lemuel not to give his *strength* to women. *Hayil* means "strength"! Notice that the English translations translate *hayil* as an adjective even though *hayil* is technically a noun. *Eshet hayil*, therefore, means "A woman of strength."[26]

The most literal translation is the NRSV's "a capable wife." The other translations are interpreting *hayil* to mean "strength of character." They may be right, of course. My preference, however, is for the reader to come to that realization herself. While the interpretive translations are not wrong when it comes to the "spirit" of the text, they hide from the reader the primary message of the text: this woman is *strong*. She's Wonder Woman! In fact, the 2017 movie *Wonder Woman* is called *Eshet Hayil* in Israel!

"*Eshet hayil*—who can find? She is far more precious than jewels." That sounds like an insult. Is the writer so misogynistic that he (or she?) thinks most women are weaklings? Does the writer think finding a strong woman is like finding a needle in a haystack? Readers are sometimes too quick to assume ill intent on the part of the Bible. Proverbs says the same thing about men: "Many a man proclaims his own steadfast love, but a faithful man who can find?" (Prov 20:6). How many women today would say "amen" to that statement?! Yes, the text is portraying good people—either men or women—as being rare. This is hyperbole, but it's actually a compliment to women. After all, what wife wants her husband to say that she's just one of many? Wouldn't she rather want him to think that she's irreplaceable?

Yet there's something else here. Proverbs had used the word "find" in relation to wisdom. "Blessed is the one who *finds* wisdom" (Prov 3:13). Likewise, we were told that "she is more precious than jewels, and nothing you desire can compare with her" (Prov 3:15). The feminine personification makes that verse ambiguous when taken out of context. Read in the context of Prov 31, the "she" is the *eshet hayil*. The woman of Prov 31 is described the same way the book had described wisdom.[27]

26. Translating the noun as an adjective is legitimate, but I think the idea is emphasized more when the nounal form is retained.

27. Koptak, *Proverbs*, 675.

Illuminating Counsel

Prov 31 Woman	Wisdom
"A woman of strength who can find?" (31:10)	"Blessed is the one who finds wisdom" (3:13)
"She is far more precious than jewels" (31:10)	"She is more precious than jewels" (3:15)
"She does him good, and not harm, all the days of her life" (31:12)	"Do not forsake her, and she will keep you; love her, and she will guard you" (4:6)

With the feminine personification of wisdom so prominent in Prov 1–9, it hardly seems coincidental that Proverbs ends with a picture of this magnificent woman.

> The heart of her husband trusts in her,
>> and he will have no lack of gain.
> She does him good, and not harm,
>> all the days of her life. (Prov 31:11–12)

This reminds us of Prov 4:6—"Do not forsake [wisdom], and she will keep you; love her, and she will guard you."

> She seeks wool and flax,
>> and works with willing hands.
> She is like the ships of the merchant;
>> she brings her food from afar.
> She rises while it is yet night
>> and provides food for her household
>> and portions for her maidens. (Prov 31:13–15)

How industrious she is! She takes care of her own. She is the provider in her family.

> She considers a field and buys it;
>> with the fruit of her hands she plants a vineyard. (Prov 31:16)

She's business savvy too! She earns money for herself and she invests her money. Keep in mind we're dealing with an ancient Middle Eastern text!

> She dresses herself with strength
>> and makes her arms strong. (Prov 31:17)

These words—"strength" and "strong"—are translations of two different words. They're not the translation of *hayil*. The poet is saving *hayil* for the end in order to form an *inclusio*. The point here is that the synonyms emphasize the woman's strength. Her arms are strong because she works hard.

> She perceives that her merchandise is profitable.
>> Her lamp does not go out at night.
> She puts her hands to the distaff,
>> and her hands hold the spindle. (Prov 31:18–19)

The Pursuit of Wisdom

Again, she has her own business. She earns her own money.

> She opens her hand to the poor
>> and reaches out her hands to the needy. (Prov 31:20)

She's not only physically strong, industrious, and business savvy; she's also generous and kind.

> She is not afraid of snow for her household,
>> for all her household are clothed in scarlet.
> She makes bed coverings for herself;
>> her clothing is fine linen and purple.
> Her husband is known in the gates
>> when he sits among the elders of the land.
> She makes linen garments and sells them;
>> she delivers sashes to the merchant.
> Strength and dignity are her clothing,
>> and she laughs at the time to come. (Prov 31:21–25)

"Strength" is another synonym of *hayil*. That she "laughs at the time to come" is just another layer of magnificence on top of an already extraordinary woman. She's not only physically strong, industrious, business savvy, and generous; she's also carefree in the best possible sense. She's happy; a delight to those around her.

> She opens her mouth with wisdom,
>> and the teaching of kindness is on her tongue. (Prov 31:26)

This is an extraordinary line, for it explicitly connects the woman to Prov 1–9. She embodies wisdom. She's the "poster child," if you will, for the book of Proverbs. Moreover, "teaching of kindness" is the translation of *torat-hesed*. It might not be a stretch to say she's joining together the Wisdom tradition and Torah.

> She looks well to the ways of her household
>> and does not eat the bread of idleness.
> Her children rise up and call her blessed;
>> her husband also, and he praises her:
> "Many women have done excellently,
>> but you surpass them all." (Prov 31:27–29)

When I was a child, I didn't wake up in the morning praising my mother. I woke up in the morning and said things like, "Mom, can you make pancakes for breakfast?" Yes, this text is idealized. That's what makes it so challenging.

"Many women have done excellently . . ." The word "excellently" is actually the translation of *hayil*. Finally, the word returns! "Many women have done excellently, but you surpass them all." This tempers the hyperbole of Prov 31:10. There, the implication seemed to be that you were more likely to run into a ruby than a strong woman.

97

Illuminating Counsel

But here, the text admits that many women are strong. Even so, this woman, to her husband and children, is the greatest woman of all.

Few verses of the Bible are more personal to me than this one. When my mother died in 2013, I wanted to put something on her tombstone in Hebrew to honor her. Out of all the verses in the Bible, I'm amazed and grateful this one came to mind. It's hyperbole and that's okay. Greatness is relative. All things being equal, everyone should view their mother as the greatest woman in the world.

> Charm is deceitful, and beauty is vain,
>> but a woman who fears the LORD is to be praised.
> Give her of the fruit of her hands,
>> and let her works praise her in the gates. (Prov 31:30–31)

The word "vain" is the translation of the Hebrew word *hevel*. We will have a lot to say about this word when we look at Ecclesiastes. Notice, though, that the phrase, "fear of the LORD," has returned. In other words, the use of this phrase forms an *inclusio* with Prov 1:7.

This passage is a favorite among women's church groups. There has been push-back on the use of it. It can easily be viewed as a checklist which implies that if women don't have all these qualities, if they're not awake and working at 4 AM, then they're bad Christians. That would miss the point, of course, as the last verse in the book makes clear. The passage is not for women; it's for men. The whole point of it is for men (starting with King Lemuel?) to appreciate the women in their lives. In Jewish homes, husbands chant this passage over their wives, praising them every single Friday night as they welcome in the Sabbath. Might not the world be a better place if husbands praised their wives more often?

7

Darkening and Illuminating Counsel
(Job)

MY SHAKESPEARE PROFESSOR SAID the three greatest works of literature (in any order) are: Shakespeare's *King Lear*, Melville's *Moby Dick*, and the book of Job.

Why did this secular-minded Yale PhD hold the book of Job in such high esteem? Once again, I failed to ask him. Years later I sent him an email asking him to share his thoughts with me. Do you know what he said? . . . He never responded! Perhaps this is for the best. All these years the onus has been on me to figure out what makes the book of Job so great.

Noting the structure of the book will help us navigate our way through it. The book breaks down in the following way:

- The Prologue (Job 1–2)

- Job's Soliloquy (Job 3)

- Theological Discussion: Job vs. The Three Friends (Job 4–27)

- Intermezzo: The Hymn of Wisdom (Job 28)[1]

- Job's Closing Argument (Job 29–31)

- Elihu's Speech (Job 32–37)

- God's Two Speeches (Job 38–41)

- Epilogue (Job 42)

The prologue and epilogue are a narrative, written in prose. The main body of the book consists almost entirely of poetic dialogues and speeches.

---

1. "Intermezzo" is a musical term which refers to an interlude between two larger movements.

THE PROLOGUE

Proverbs ended with an idealized woman. We're now introduced to an idealized man. His name is Job. He "was blameless and upright, one who feared God and turned away from evil" (Job 1:1). No man in the Tanakh is as morally outstanding. The amazing thing is that Job is not an Israelite. He's from the land of Uz, not the land of Israel. He's "the greatest of all the peoples of the east" (Job 1:3). Yet, while Job is not an Israelite, he, along with everyone else in the book, is a monotheist who worships Yahweh, the God of Israel. The characters are Jewish in orientation but not in ethnicity. Why would a Jewish writer write about non-Jewish characters? It's because the themes of the book are universal. Suffering is a universal problem, not just a Jewish problem.[2]

Job has seven sons and three daughters. He functions as a priest of sorts, offering sacrifices on behalf of his children in case they committed unintentional sins. God has rewarded Job handsomely for his rectitude and piety. He has "seven thousand sheep, three thousand camels, five hundred yoke of oxen, five hundred donkeys, and very many servants" (Job 1:2–3). Adjusted for inflation, we could say that Job would be a billionaire if he lived in 2020.

So Job is as righteous and as wealthy as a person can be.

Having established our protagonist, the narrative then shifts to a scene in the heavenly court. The "sons of God" present themselves before Yahweh. Someone called "Satan" is with them.

Who are these "sons of God"? The answer to that question is actually very complicated and could take up the rest of the chapter. Many scholars think the "sons of God" are deities who make up a "divine council."[3] Judaism and Christianity do not accept that view. Judaism and Christianity view the "sons of God" as angels—heavenly beings that are less than deities. Either way, it seems clear that these "sons of God" function as Yahweh's administration.[4] Yahweh is a chief executive and, like all chief executives, he has a cabinet.

Is "Satan" also part of Yahweh's cabinet? Most Christians assume "Satan" is the devil. Unfortunately, Christians are victims of the English translations. Let's make a few observations. First, notice the word "Satan" is capitalized in the translation. Since there are no capital letters in Hebrew, capitalizing the word is entirely the translator's choice. Second, "Satan" is a *transliteration* rather than a translation. The translator is spelling this Hebrew word with English letters rather than telling the reader what it means. Third, there's something in the Hebrew which the translator has left out. The Hebrew contains the definite article. The text literally says "*ha-satan*"—"*the* satan." By

2. Hidabrut—Torah and Judaism, "The Book of Job—Yitzchak Breitowitz."

3. Friedman, *The Exodus*, 181–82. In my book, *You Are Israel*, I state that Gen 1:26 does not refer to the Divine Council. At the time of writing, my understanding of the Divine Council was erroneous. The Divine Council is, in fact, a good explanation for the first person plurality in that verse. To view my error, see Teram, *You Are Israel*, 29.

4. Walton, *Job*, 62–64.

Darkening and Illuminating Counsel

removing the definite article, transliterating rather than translating, and capitalizing the first letter, the translator is presenting the word as a proper name. This is totally wrong. The word denotes a function, not a name.[5] It ought to be translated as "the adversary" or "the accuser." The English translation, then, is dishonest and misleading. *Traduttore, traditore!*

The accuser is not the devil. There is no devil in the book of Job. In fact, there is no devil in the Tanakh. The villain in Gen 3 is a serpent. It's only the New Testament book of Revelation that says the serpent is the devil, whose name is Satan (Rev 12:9). As I will explain below, interpreting the accuser as the devil distorts the meaning of the book of Job.

Rather than a fallen angel who wants to tempt the whole world to rebel against God, the accuser is best understood to be something like God's Attorney General. He's the chief prosecutor, roaming the earth looking for people to prosecute.[6] That doesn't mean he's a heroic figure. The word "satan" has a negative connotation. He's kind of like Senator Joe McCarthy or Javert from *Les Misérables*. He's overzealous and itching to prosecute someone. That's why God says to him, "Have you considered my servant Job, that there is none like him on earth . . . ?" (Job 1:8). This question is hardly random. God's point is that Job is not prosecutable. His character is impeccable.

The prosecutor, however, is not impressed by Job. He asks a key question, something which sets the tone for the entire book: "Does Job fear God for no reason?" (Job 1:9). The prosecutor is implying that Job only acts righteously because he's reaping a reward for his good deeds. God has placed him in the lap of luxury. "But stretch out your hand now, and touch all that he has, and he will curse you to your face" (Job 1:11). Notice the ferocity of the prosecutor's prediction. Job will not merely curse God. He won't curse God behind God's back. He will curse God *to God's face*.

God, in effect, says to the prosecutor, "Care to make it interesting?" The prosecutor accepts the challenge. God and the prosecutor agree to conduct a social experiment. They will ruin Job's life in order to see if Job fears God only for the rewards. The only condition is that Job's person is not touched.

What's the result of this experiment? All that Job has, all that was mentioned in Job 1:2–3, is taken away from him. His ten children are dead. His vast wealth is erased.

Yet Job's response to this tragedy is perfectly pious: "Naked I came from my mother's womb, and naked shall I return there; the LORD gave, and the LORD has taken away; blessed be the name of the LORD" (Job 1:21). The narrator tells us that Job "did not sin or charge God with wrongdoing" (Job 1:22). From this verse comes a religious principle: Don't blame God, no matter how much you suffer. Everything God gives us is on loan. God has the right to take it back. Faith in God must be unconditional.

The Divine Council convenes again. I get the sense that God is feeling pretty good about being proved right. God almost seems to be bragging when he once again

---

5. Hadibrut—Torah and Judaism, "The Book of Job—Rabbi Yitzchak Breitowitz."

6. This is precisely the role of "the satan" in Zech 3.

101

Illuminating Counsel

asks the prosecutor, "Have you considered my servant Job?" God rubs it in: "He still holds fast his integrity, although you incited me against him to destroy him without reason" (Job 2:3). The prosecutor, however, remains unconvinced and hence unwilling to concede. "Skin for skin," he replies. "All that a man has he will give for his life. But stretch out your hand and touch his bone and his flesh, and he will curse you to your face" (Job 2:4–5). The prosecutor says the experiment was not carried out correctly. The only reason Job didn't curse God is because Job himself wasn't harmed. The prosecutor implies that Job is so selfish he will praise God even if his children are killed so long as he himself remains intact. But if his health is taken away, then his true character will come to light. The prosecutor is exceedingly cynical.

God agrees to conduct a second experiment. The only condition is that Job is not to be killed. After all, what's the point of killing him? They're trying to see where Job's breaking point is. How much suffering can Job take before he lets go of his integrity?

"So [the prosecutor] went out from the presence of the LORD and struck Job with loathsome sores from the sole of his foot to the crown of his head" (Job 2:7). The narrator tells us the bare minimum we need to know to ascertain Job's disposition: "Job took a potsherd with which to scrape himself, and sat among the ashes" (Job 2:8). It's a pitiful sight.

Enter Mrs. Job. She's nameless, has only one line of dialogue, and is the only female speaker in the book. Her function is to heighten the drama by tempting Job. She says to him, "Do you still hold fast your integrity?" This is now the second time the word "integrity" has appeared in the book. Clearly Job's integrity is an issue. She thinks his "integrity" is costing him his dignity. She thinks the only way he can retain, or regain, his dignity is if he curses God. "Curse God and die," she says (Job 2:9). Job rebukes her. "You speak as one of the foolish women would speak," he says (Job 2:10). Apparently no amount of pain will cause Job to let go of his integrity. His response to his wife's advice is as idealistic as before: "Shall we receive the good at the hand of God, and not receive the bad?" (Job 2:10). Again, loyalty to God must be unconditional.

As if to make it clearer that God won the wager, the narrator tells us "Job did not sin with his lips" (Job 2:10). But why does the narrator use the word "lips"? Job didn't sin with his *lips*, but did he sin with his *mind*? Perhaps the narrator's intention was merely to say that Job didn't accuse God of wrongdoing. Had the narrator known that his readers might get the impression that Job *did* sin, just in a less overt manner (i.e., not with his lips), he might have gone back and removed the word "lips" from the text. But the word "lips" is there to stay and the text is now in the hands of the interpreters, as with every work of art. But maybe the narrator *purposely* used the word "lips" to lead the readers to such a conclusion. If so, it would be the first hint of a defect in Job's otherwise seemingly pristine character. We shall return to this issue later.

Job's three friends—Eliphaz, Bildad, and Zophar—come to visit him. "And when they saw him from a distance, they did not recognize him. And they raised their voices and wept, and they tore their robes and sprinkled dust on their heads toward heaven"

(Job 2:12). This verse is quite personal to me. My first encounter with death was the loss of my grandmother during my freshman year of college. I visited her in Florida while she was in hospital on her deathbed. My uncle cautioned the family not to weep in front of her—"because she knows," he said. I couldn't handle being in Grandma's room more than ten seconds. Like Job's friends, I couldn't recognize my grandmother. Her hair was thinner than ever before, she couldn't keep her head up, she couldn't speak, she looked more dead than alive. I stepped out of the room and wept for thirty minutes straight. I wept so vociferously that I wasn't sure I would ever stop weeping. Our narrator may not give us many details, but the things he tells us make an impact because we're able to relate them to our own experiences.

"And they sat with him on the ground seven days and seven nights, and no one spoke a word to him, for they saw that his suffering was very great" (Job 2:13). This is very similar to the Jewish way of mourning, which is called "Sitting Shiva." *Shiva* means "seven." The mourners sit on the floor or on low stools in the home for seven days. The comforters visit and bring food. Jewish custom forbids comforters from initiating conversation with the mourners. Why? Because the mourners may not wish to speak to anyone, which is their right. The comforters must be silent until the mourners speak to them. This is precisely what Job's friends do.

What can one say to someone who has lost a child? I don't think that wound ever fully heals. Most attempts to comfort with words would come off as platitudinous and fall flat. The good news is that you don't have to say anything. All you have to do is be present. "Weep with those that weep" (Rom 12:15). Job's friends sitting silently with Job in his pain is one of the most moving and profound examples of comfort in the Bible. Unfortunately, the silence is short-lived.

JOB'S SOLILOQUY

"After this, Job opened his mouth and cursed the day of his birth" (Job 3:1). With that introduction, the text switches from prose to poetry. The expression of grief is intense and the intensity increases as the soliloquy progresses. Job begins by saying:

> Let the day perish on which I was born,
>> and the night that said,
>> "A man is conceived." (Job 3:3)

It's important that we note a small detail. Job refers to the night a "man" was conceived. This is atypical language. Normally it's a *child* or a *son* that is born, not a *man*. We see this in Jer 20:15, where Jeremiah expresses the same sentiment as Job, but Jeremiah says, "Cursed be the man who brought the news to my father, 'A *son* is born to you.'" But Job says, "A *man* is conceived." Moreover, the Hebrew word translated "man" is not the typical word denoting a male adult. The word Job uses is *gever*. This word denotes a *strong* man. Bear this in mind because we'll return to it later.

Illuminating Counsel

Job continues:

> Let that day be darkness!
>> May God above not seek it,
>> nor light shine upon it. (Job 3:4)

This translation isn't wrong but the verse could be translated in a way that conveys all of the nuances of the Hebrew. A more literal translation is: "That day—let there be darkness." The words "let there be darkness" are a translation of two Hebrew words—"*yehi hoshekh*." Reading the text in Hebrew immediately causes us to think of Gen 1:3—the very first thing God says in the Bible: "Let there be light" ("*yehi or*"). Recognizing that Job is echoing Genesis's creation account makes his message crystal clear. He wishes for his birthday to be *uncreated*. God "saw" the light in Gen 1:4, but Job wishes for God *not* to "seek" his birthday. Job does not want God to shine light upon his birthday as when God shined light into the darkness, thereby creating day and night. This is the first of two times God is mentioned in Job 3.

Job continues:

> Let gloom and deep darkness claim it.
>> Let clouds dwell upon it;
>> let the blackness of the day terrify it.
> That night—let thick darkness seize it!
>> Let it not rejoice among the days of the year;
>> let it not come into the number of the months. (Job 3:5–6)

No passage in the Bible emphasizes *darkness* more than Job 3. Notice the use of synonyms: *Gloom. Deep darkness. Blackness. Thick darkness.* "Deep darkness" and "thick darkness" are both one word in Hebrew. "Deep darkness" is the translation of *tsalmavet*. This is the word used in Ps 23:4, which is translated "the shadow of death." To ensure that there will be no light, Job wants his birthday covered with clouds in order to block the sun.

Notice the verbs: *Claim. Dwell. Terrify. Seize.* Job speaks of darkness as if darkness is a foreign army that will sack his birthday to destroy it.

Job's birthday is personified. Job wishes for it to not rejoice among the other days. In fact, he wants the calendar emended so that his birthday will no longer exist.

Job continues:

> Behold, let that night be barren;
>> let no joyful cry enter it.
> Let those curse it who curse the day,
>> who are ready to rouse up Leviathan. (Job 3:7–8)

This is now the third time in four verses Job has mentioned "night." "Night" intensifies the picture of darkness. The word "barren" seems to be multivalent. The night would be barren because, as we shall see, there are no celestial bodies giving forth

104

Darkening and Illuminating Counsel

light. The night would also be barren because Job is not born. It's as if Job wishes for his birthday to be nuked into oblivion. "Leviathan" is like the nuclear bomb which is to obliterate it. We'll talk more about Leviathan later.

Then comes one of my favorite verses in the Bible:

> Let the stars of its dawn, be dark;
>> let it hope for light, but have none,
>> nor see the eyelids of the morning. (Job 3:9)

Job wants his birthday to be so enshrouded in darkness that there won't even be a flicker of light. He wants his birthday to *hope* for light and yet be denied that light. In other words, he doesn't just want his birthday to perish. He wants his birthday to be psychologically *tortured*! A lesser poet would have just said, "Let that day not have light." The poet of Job was a genius.

But why does Job want his birthday to be tortured? Finally, in v. 10, Job reveals his rationale:

> . . . because it did not shut the doors of my mother's womb,
>> nor hide trouble from my eyes.

The poet has saved this explanation for the end of the first section of Job's soliloquy. The literary tension created by the portrait of darkness finally reaches a very satisfying, albeit horrid, resolution. Job wishes he were never born.

Now comes the second part of his soliloquy. This section is marked out by the word *why*:

> Why did I not die at birth,
>> come out from the womb and expire?
> Why did the knees receive me?
>> Or why the breasts, that I should nurse?
> For then I would have lain down and been quiet;
>> I would have slept; then I would have been at rest,
> with kings and counselors of the earth
>> who rebuilt ruins for themselves,
> or with princes who had gold,
>> who filled their houses with silver.
> Or why was I not as a hidden stillborn child,
>> as infants who never see the light?
> There the wicked cease from troubling,
>> and there the weary are at rest.
> There the prisoners are at ease together;
>> they hear not the voice of the taskmaster.
> The small and the great are there,
>> and the slave is free from his master. (Job 3:11–19)

Job romanticizes death. He longs to go where the greatest of his predecessors have gone. Death seems to be something honorable, a great reward for those who have done great things. The use of the word "light" is particularly effective. Job had wished for darkness to envelope his birthday, but instead he became one who "sees the light" (cf. Job 30:26). In the Bible, light is usually positive and darkness is negative. For Job, however, the opposite is true. The light of life is where suffering is present. The darkness of death is where suffering is ended. Death emancipates slaves. Death brings equality between the oppressed and the oppressors. In the words of Hamlet, death is "a consummation devoutly to be wished."

But Job hasn't received what he wished for. Hence he laments:

> Why is light given to him who is in misery,
>   and life to the bitter in soul,
> who long for death, but it comes not,
>   and dig for it more than for hidden treasures,
> who rejoice exceedingly
>   and are glad when they find the grave?
> Why is light given to a man whose way is hidden,
>   whom God has hedged in?
> For my sighing comes instead of my bread,
>   and my groanings are poured out like water.
> For the thing that I fear comes upon me,
>   and what I dread befalls me.
> I am not at ease, nor am I quiet;
>   I have no rest, but trouble comes. (Job 3:20–26)

Why did Job want his birthday to "hope for light" and be denied it? Because Job, like so many other sufferers, hoped for the liberating darkness of death but torturously remained in the oppressive light of life.

God is mentioned for the second and final time in the chapter. God is the one who "hedges in" the sufferer. That is hardly a positive statement. Job gets off the subject of God very quickly, though. It's curious how Job's soliloquy is almost godless. In light of his statements in the prologue, the virtual absence of God in ch. 3 is striking.

Job's worst fear has become a reality. Every parent's worst fear is to lose a child. Job has lost all ten of his children. His final line is marked out by the negative particle:

> I am *not* at ease, *nor* am I quiet;
>   I am *not* at rest, but trouble comes. (Job 3:26)

Job is not merely sad. He's tormented with anxiety.

How many people in the world feel this way right now? How many people in your neighborhood? How many people in your workplace or classroom? Whenever I'm in a room full of people, I always assume there's someone there who has wanted to die at some point in his or her life. Their way is hidden, as Job says. We may not know who

Darkening and Illuminating Counsel

they are, but more people feel this way than we may realize. The world is filled with sadness and despair.

But what about life after death? Eternal life is Christianity's answer to the problem of suffering. "Our present sufferings are not worth comparing with the glory that will be revealed in us," says Paul in Rom 8:18. We "look not to the things that are seen but to the things that are unseen. For the things that are seen are transient, but the things that are unseen are eternal" (2 Cor 4:18). Christians are told to "encourage one another with these words" (1 Thess 4:18).

But there's no thought whatsoever of a hopeful afterlife in the book of Job.[7] When Job talks about the dead being at rest, he's not saying that it's better by far to be with the Lord in heaven than it is to be separated from the Lord on earth (see Phil 1:23). Job is not contrasting temporal life on earth with eternal life in heaven. Job is contrasting *existence* with *nonexistence*. He's saying that suffering can be so severe that it's better to *not* exist than to exist. Hamlet asked, "To be or not to be?" Job resoundingly answers, "Not to be."[8]

The absence of the afterlife in the book of Job raises the question as to how Christians should interpret it. The book of Job is a book of Jewish wisdom. It's not Christian in the same way Romans is. Christians should not let the book of Job alter their theology, but neither should Christians read their theology back into Job. Christians should find a way to interpret Job on its own terms while also maintaining their orthodoxy.

What I think the writer of Job would have us do is wrestle with whether there is hope in *this* life before we jump to the afterlife for hope. Going straight to the afterlife for hope is like taking the easy way out, avoiding the difficult questions of life here and now.

ONE JOB OR TWO?

You may have noticed that Job seems different in chs. 1 and 2 than he does in ch. 3. The Job of the prologue seems very Christian. He doesn't complain (Phil 2:14). He rejoices despite his suffering (Rom 5:3). His attitude is perfectly encapsulated by the great hymn "It Is Well with My Soul." The hymn writer, Horatio Spafford, lost all four of his children at once in an accident at sea while he was at home in Chicago. Only his wife survived. On his way to visit her, he wrote these words:

> When peace like a river attendeth my way,
> > When sorrows like sea billows roll
> Whatever my lot, thou hast taught me to say
> > It is well, it is well, with my soul.

---

7. See, for example, Job 7:9–10.

8. Hamlet's point in his soliloquy is that it's better not to be than to be—it's better to die than to live—because life here is so difficult. But because we don't know what the afterlife is like, we end up choosing life rather than death. It's kind of like the saying: "Better the devil you know [this life] than the devil you don't [the afterlife]." Interestingly, this is *not* the Christian perspective at all!

Illuminating Counsel

But in ch. 3 it is *not* well with Job's soul. The Job of ch. 3, and the remainder of the book, seems much more like a typical sufferer in the Tanakh than one of the apostles in the New Testament. Job complains like the psalmists of the lament psalms. Job wishes for death, as did Moses, Elijah, and Jeremiah.

How can we reconcile the Job of the prologue with the Job of ch. 3?

We could posit different authors. We could say the author of the prologue is not the same person who wrote ch. 3. We could surmise that the prologue was written *after* the rest of the book in order to make the book more pious.

Such emendations, if you will, are not implausible, and many scholars do doubt the unity of the book of Job.[9] However, I can't see how ch. 3 makes sense without *something* preceding it. Chapter 3 is far too abrupt to be the beginning of the book. We need some sort of backstory in order to understand why Job is cursing his birthday.[10]

So often, readers of the Bible read only the prologue and ignore the rest of the book. Thus, the only portrait they see of Job is the pristine one. They then make an exegetical jump from Job 2 to the New Testament, which tells readers to consider trials to be "all joy" (Jas 1:2) and to imitate the "steadfastness of Job" (Jas 5:11). But one cannot understand a forty-two-chapter book if one stops reading at ch. 2.

On the other hand, we cannot dismiss the prologue as if the prologue isn't really part of the book. It's true that some elements in the prologue disappear after ch. 2, but other elements in the prologue return later on, like motifs from one movement of a symphony that are restated in subsequent movements. We must interpret the book of Job as a unitary work of literature because that's how it has come to us.

So, setting aside the possibility of multiple authors, we are left with two options for interpretation. The first option is to accept that the two Jobs have contradictory attitudes. We saw this phenomenon in the Psalter. Contradictions aren't logical, but they're real. The second option is to reinterpret the prologue. Maybe the Job of the prologue is *not* as perfect as he seems. Maybe there's a progression in the prologue that logically leads to the Job of ch. 3 cursing his birthday.

THE THEOLOGICAL DEBATE

Job's friends break their silence.[11] Something Job said has offended them. A theological debate ensues with Job's friends united against him. Eliphaz is the first to speak. He's followed by Bildad and then Zophar. Job responds after each person finishes. This cycle is repeated twice, though on the third round Bildad's speech is very short and

---

9. Alter, *The Art of Biblical Poetry*, loc. 1834.

10. We should note that Job 3 is not structured like a lament psalm. That is why the lament psalms can stand on their own but Job 3 cannot.

11. Notice that, as Job seems perfect in the prologue, so too the friends' response to Job's suffering in the prologue is also seemingly perfect. Both Job and the friends become more imperfect after the prologue.

108

Darkening and Illuminating Counsel

Zophar says nothing. Thus the friends' speeches fizzle out but Job keeps talking. He waxes eloquent about his innocence for three straight chapters.

Job's friends recognize he has suffered immensely but, according to them, that doesn't excuse him from saying things which are untrue.

Eliphaz is very smooth in the way he breaks the silence. He doesn't come out of the gate swinging, as it were. He eases into his complaint: "If one ventures a word with you, will you be impatient? Yet who can keep from speaking?" (Job 4:2). He even compliments Job, knowing that a softer approach is more likely to be effective. "Your words have upheld him who was stumbling," he says, "and you have made firm the feeble knees" (Job 4:4). He has buttered Job up sufficiently to commence a critique. He points out that Job seems "impatient" and "dismayed" (Job 4:5). He acknowledges the "fear [of God]" is Job's "confidence" and his "integrity" is his "hope" (Job 4:6; cf. 1:1; 2:3). But then comes his main point:

> Remember: who that was innocent ever perished?
>> Or where were the upright cut off?
> As I have seen, those who plow iniquity
>> and sow trouble reap the same.
> By the breath of God they perish,
>> and by the blast of his anger they are consumed.
> The roar of the lion, the voice of the fierce lion,
>> the teeth of the young lions are broken.
> The strong lion perishes for lack of prey,
>> and the cubs of the lioness are scattered. (Job 4:7–11)

In other words, Job's suffering is a punishment by God for some sin or sins he had committed. Eliphaz has no evidence of this, of course. He's making an inference. He starts with the premise that the wicked suffer and the righteous flourish. Job is suffering. Therefore, Job has been punished by God for some sort of wickedness.

Eliphaz ends his first discourse with a word of encouragement:

> Behold, happy is the one whom God reproves;
>> therefore despise not the discipline of the Almighty.
> For he wounds, but he binds up;
>> he shatters, but his hands heal.
> He will deliver you from six troubles;
>> in seven no evil shall touch you.
> In famine he will redeem you from death,
>> and in war from the power of the sword.
> You shall be hidden from the lash of the tongue,
>> and shall not fear destruction when it comes.
> At destruction and famine you shall laugh,
>> and shall not fear the beasts of the earth.

Illuminating Counsel

For you shall be in league with the stones of the field,
    and the beasts of the field shall be at peace with you.
You shall know that your tent is at peace,
    and you shall inspect your fold and miss nothing.
You shall know also that your offspring shall be many,
    and your descendants as the grass of the earth.
You shall come to your grave in ripe old age,
    like a sheaf gathered up in its season.
Behold, this we have searched out; it is true.
    Hear, and know it for your good. (Job 5:17–27)

The attentive reader will recognize that Eliphaz is echoing many other biblical texts, particularly texts from Psalms and Proverbs. Notice the similarity between Job 5:18 ("For he wounds, but he binds up; he shatters, but his hands heal") and Ps 147:3 ("He heals the brokenhearted and binds up their wounds"). Likewise, Job 5:17 ("happy is the one whom God reproves; therefore despise not the discipline of the Almighty") is reminiscent of Prov 3:11 ("Do not despise the LORD's discipline or be weary of his reproof . . ."). Theologically, everything Eliphaz says comes from Ps 1. Psalm 1 had established the Retribution Principle. The Retribution Principle is the first thing the reader reads in the Ketuvim. Proverbs followed suit in its own pragmatic way by reminding the reader over and over that foolish actions have negative consequences and wise actions have positive consequences. Psalms and Proverbs get this idea from Deuteronomy:

If you obey the commandments of the LORD your God that I command you today, by loving the LORD your God, by walking in his ways, and by keeping his commandments and his statutes and his rules, then you shall live and multiply, and the LORD your God will bless you in the land that you are entering to take possession of it. But if your heart turns away, and you will not hear, but are drawn away to worship other gods and serve them, I declare to you today, that you shall surely perish. You shall not live long in the land that you are going over the Jordan to enter and possess. (Deut 30:16–18)

The Retribution Principle, expressed here in Deuteronomy, is the theological foundation of the Deuteronomistic History and the Prophets. Notice what Bildad says to Job:

Does God pervert justice?
    Or does the Almighty pervert the right?
If your children have sinned against him,
    he has delivered them into the hand of their transgression.
If you will seek God
    and plead with the Almighty for mercy,
if you are pure and upright,
    surely then he will rouse himself for you
    and restore your rightful habitation.

Darkening and Illuminating Counsel

And though your beginning was small,
    your latter days will be very great. (Job 8:3–7)

Bildad is echoing the prophet Amos, who said, "Seek good and not evil, that you may live; and so the LORD, the God of hosts, will be with you, just as you have said" (Amos 5:14). He assures Job that if he repents, God will grant him mercy. He continues:

Behold, God will not reject a blameless man,
    nor take the hand of evildoers.
He will yet fill your mouth with laughter,
    and your lips with shouting.
Those who hate you will be clothed with shame,
    and the tent of the wicked will be no more. (Job 8:20–22)

That sounds encouraging, yes? Zophar agrees:

If you prepare your heart,
    you will stretch out your hands toward him.
If iniquity is in your hand, put it far away,
    and let not injustice dwell in your tents.
Surely then you will lift up your face without blemish;
    you will be secure and will not fear.
You will forget your misery;
    you will remember it as waters that have passed away.
And your life will be brighter than the noonday;
    its darkness will be like the morning.
And you will feel secure, because there is hope;
    you will look around and take your rest in security.
You will lie down, and none will make you afraid;
    many will court your favor.
But the eyes of the wicked will fail;
    all way of escape will be lost to them,
    and their hope is to breathe their last. (Job 11:13–20)

This is not the way Job sees things. Job maintains his innocence. "I have not denied the words of the Holy One," he says (Job 6:10). He continues:

But now, be pleased to look at me,
    for I will not lie to your face.
Please turn; let no injustice be done.
    Turn now; my vindication is at stake.
Is there any injustice on my tongue?
    Cannot my palate discern the cause of calamity? (Job 6:28–30)

Job doesn't need his friends to tell him why he has suffered. He knows he has not done anything to deserve it. Yes, his suffering is profound:

Illuminating Counsel

My flesh is clothed with worms and dirt;
　　my skin hardens, then breaks out afresh.
My days are swifter than a weaver's shuttle
　　and come to their end without hope. (Job 7:5–6)

But he knows that, however tremendous his suffering is, suffering comes to all people:

Has not man a hard service on earth,
　　and are not his days like the days of a hired hand? (Job 7:1)

Psalm 90 says that the brevity and difficulties of life are due to God punishing humans for their sins. Job doesn't agree. For Job, humans aren't the problem; God is the problem:

What is man, that you make so much of him,
　　and that you set your heart on him,
visit him every morning
　　and test him every moment? (Job 7:17–18)

This is a subversion of Ps 8:4[5].[12] In Ps 8, God's mindfulness of humanity is a blessing. God has elevated humanity to a lofty position humanity doesn't deserve. For Job, God's mindfulness of humanity is a curse. He wants God to leave him, and the rest of us, alone:

How long will you not look away from me,
　　nor leave me alone till I swallow my spit?
If I sin, what do I do to you, you watcher of mankind?
　　Why have you made me your mark?
　　Why have I become a burden to you?
Why do you not pardon my transgression
　　and take away my iniquity?
For now I shall lie in the earth;
　　you will seek me, but I shall not be. (Job 7:19–21)

The psalmists lamented when they thought God turned his face from them. Job laments that God has *not* turned his face from him. Job sounds less like a pious man and more like the late Christopher Hitchens, who viewed God as a celestial dictator.

Job blatantly declares God "destroys both the blameless and the wicked" (Job 9:22). God "mocks at the calamity of the innocent," he says (Job 9:23). Compare that to Bildad's speech in Job 18. Bildad knows only of the suffering of the wicked. There's no room in Bildad's theology for God to intentionally cause the righteous to suffer.

---

12. Fishbane, "Book of Job and Inner-Biblical Discourse," in Perdue and Gilpin, *Voice from the Whirlwind*, 87.

Darkening and Illuminating Counsel

Job not only claims the righteous suffer, he also claims the wicked *prosper*—a proposition explicitly denied by the friends. Job summarizes the friends' position regarding the wicked and then supplies his counterpoint:

> You say, "Swift are they on the face of the waters;
>> their portion is cursed in the land;
>> no treader turns toward their vineyards.
> Drought and heat snatch away the snow waters;
>> so does Sheol those who have sinned.
> The womb forgets them;
>> the worm finds them sweet;
> they are no longer remembered,
>> so wickedness is broken like a tree."
> They wrong the barren, childless woman,
>> and do no good to the widow.
> Yet God prolongs the life of the mighty by his power;
>> they rise up when they despair of life.
> He gives them security, and they are supported,
>> and his eyes are upon their ways.
> They are exalted a little while, and then are gone;
>> they are brought low and gathered up like all others;
>> they are cut off like the heads of grain.
> If it is not so, who will prove me a liar
>> and show that there is nothing in what I say? (Job 24:19–25)

We cannot escape the obvious conclusion: *Job believes God is unjust.* God has not kept the promise of Ps 1. Job wants God to be held accountable. The problem is that God is *God* and Job is merely a human. There's no chance the trial would be fair. Thus Job says: "Though I am in the right, I cannot answer him; I must appeal for mercy to my accuser" (Job 9:15). Job is not willing to give up so easily, though. Job can have his hearing with God if there's an "arbiter" to mediate. Job believes such a person exists and will come to his aid. "I know that my Redeemer lives," he says (Job 19:25). Handel set that passage to beautiful music in *Messiah*, but it actually has nothing to do with the Messiah. It's about Job's arbiter.[13] Job wants his words "engraved in the rock forever" (Job 19:24) so that they will bear witness to him after he has died. His redeemer will "stand upon the earth" (Job 19:25) and Job will, at long last, be vindicated.[14]

The book began with Job being placed on trial. All of the characters in the book—God, the accuser, Job's wife, the friends—have passed judgment on Job. But Job wants the spotlight taken off him and placed onto God. Job is, in effect, saying, "I'm not the one who should be on trial; *God* is the one who should be on trial!"

---

13. Longman, *The Fear of the Lord is Wisdom*, 136.

14. Alter, *The Wisdom Books*, 83–84.

Illuminating Counsel

To be honest, it's hard to argue Job is unreasonable. Are God's actions in the prologue defendable? Did Job deserve to suffer as he did? And please don't defend God by telling me that God was rooting for Job in the wager. If God rooting for me means he's going to take away everything I have and kill my kids, then I'm not sure I want God rooting for me.[15] If that's what God does to those whom he supports, I'd hate to see what he does to his enemies!

One thing is clear: the book of Job issues a direct challenge to the Retribution Principle. The psalmists take it for granted that their illnesses were the consequences of their sins. Proverbs says if you do foolish things, you will pay the price. But here in the book of Job we have a man whom God himself said was blameless and yet was made to suffer as no man in the Bible suffered. Job is subverting Psalms' and Proverbs' understanding of the cause of suffering.

Theodicy is the vindication of God's goodness in light of the existence of suffering. How can a good God allow Job (and the rest of us) to suffer? There are no easy answers. We cannot hide behind our theology. Christians might say Adam and Eve are to blame. Because of their sin, the whole world is cursed. But there's no doctrine of "Original Sin" in Job. We could say "free will" is to blame. God allows us to have free will so that love, which needs to be freely chosen, can exist. This means that, in a world where goodness exists, there will also be evil. Yet, while free will might explain the Holocaust, it doesn't explain cancer. Free will didn't cause Job to become chronically ill. We could say Satan, the devil, is to blame. He "prowls around like a roaring lion, seeking someone to devour" (1 Pet 5:8). But there's no dualism in Job.

What's dualism?

Let's say there's a terrible fire which destroys a church. Where was God? Did God cause the fire? If not, why didn't God stop the fire? Did not God have the power to stop the fire? If he had the power to stop it, and he didn't stop it, how then can we say God is good?

Dualism is the way out of that theological predicament. Dualism inserts the devil into the picture. A dualistic view posits that, because God is good, he did *not* cause the fire. Rather, the devil caused the fire because the devil is evil. Dualism lets God off the hook by blaming the devil for suffering.

This is why the translation of "*ha-satan*" is a major issue. Because of the erroneous translation ("Satan"), many Christians believe the devil is the one who afflicted Job. But that view contradicts everything the book of Job says. God gives "Satan"—the prosecutor—permission to afflict Job. The prosecutor only does what God allows him to do. When Job's livestock die, the man who tells him the bad news doesn't say the devil did it; he says "the fire of God" consumed the livestock (Job 1:16). Job had so eloquently said that God giveth and taketh. He did not say God giveth and the devil taketh. After the prologue, "Satan" is no longer mentioned and is thereby consigned to

---

15. This is the point made by Jim McGuiggan in *Celebrating the Wrath of God*, 95. It's a lovely point, to be sure. The problem is that this point will not satisfy every reader.

irrelevance. Job's friends could have said the devil caused Job to suffer, but they know nothing of a devil. And the very end of the book reminds us of "all the evil that the LORD had brought upon [Job]" (Job 42:11).

Dualism is utterly alien to the book of Job. The buck stops with God.

So why does God cause suffering? Psalms' and Proverbs' answer to that question is the Retribution Principle. The book of Job subverts Psalms and Proverbs. The reader of the book of Job knows the truth. Job didn't deserve what happened to him. What, then, shall we say? Is God unjust?

There's a British TV movie called *God on Trial*, which was inspired by the play *The Trial of God*, by Elie Wiesel. The movie takes place in Auschwitz. A group of Jewish prisoners decide to put God on trial for breaking his covenant with the Jewish people. There's a stirring speech at the end by the one who chooses to prosecute God. He goes through virtually the entire biblical history, highlighting all the acts of violence instigated by God. The prisoners then reach a verdict. *Guilty.* God is found guilty of breach of covenant.

But then the Nazis barge in to take prisoners to the gas chamber. This causes panic among the prisoners. One distraught prisoner turns to the man who prosecuted God and asks him what they should do. The prisoner breaks down and weeps. The prosecutor tells them to pray. He covers his head with his right hand since he doesn't have a yarmulke (a Jewish skullcap), and leads the prisoners in a recitation of Ps 90, which they continue to recite even in the gas chamber as they await their fate.

The power of the film is that it captures the theological tension the religious community has always felt. If dualism is out of the picture, God becomes the source of our suffering. Yet God also remains our only hope. Maybe God has acted unjustly, but we still need God to rescue us.

> Return, O LORD! How long?
>> Have pity on your servants.
> Make us glad for as many days as you have afflicted us,
>> and for as many years as we have seen evil. (Ps 90:13, 15)

IS JOB SELF-RIGHTEOUS?

In ch. 29, Job launches a major defense of his character. Some of the things he says are immensely inspiring. They remind us how awesome goodness truly is. For example, Job says:

> The blessing of him who was about to perish came upon me,
>> and I caused the widow's heart to sing for joy. (Job 29:13)

Illuminating Counsel

Job was so outstanding that, according to him, dying people blessed him, as if blessing Job was their last words. He was so kind to widows that he filled their hearts with joy. When was the last time you caused a widow to sing? Job continues:

> I was eyes to the blind
>> and feet to the lame.
> I was a father to the needy,
>> and I searched out the cause of him whom I did not know. (Job 29:15–16)

How many of us can say the same? The world would be a better place if we were more cognizant of the needs of those less fortunate than ourselves. The world would be a better place if we were more like Job.

Job is also a one-woman man:

> I have made a covenant with my eyes;
>> how then could I gaze at a virgin? (Job 31:1)

Perhaps this statement is all the more extraordinary in light of the fact that his wife may not have been Mrs. Wonderful. Nevertheless, Job swears to his faithfulness:

> If my heart has been enticed toward a woman,
>> and I have lain in wait at my neighbor's door,
> then let my wife grind for another,
>> and let others bow down on her.
> For that would be a heinous crime;
>> that would be an iniquity to be punished by the judges;
> for that would be a fire that consumes as far as Abaddon,
>> and it would burn to the root all my increase. (Job 31:9–12)

How many husbands can say the same? How many husbands secretly look at pornography on the internet? How many husbands secretly text other women?

Job goes on and on about how he has lived his life caring for the underprivileged. Again he swears to it. "Let my shoulder blade fall from my shoulder, and let my arm be broken from its socket," he says, if he did not do all that he said he did for the poor (Job 31:22).

Chapter 31 is like a miniature version of Proverbs. Proverbs cautions the reader to stay away from the adulteress. Proverbs extols the virtues of helping the poor. Job has conformed his life to those teachings. Job is the quintessential wise person.

The contrast between Job's goodness and his suffering causes us to sympathize with him. "But now they laugh at me, men who are younger than I," he says (Job 30:1). People mock him in song (Job 30:9). They spit on him (Job 30:10). God is the one who started this. God initiated Job's suffering. Humans, in their cruelty, have made his suffering even worse (Job 30:11–15). And what does God do in response?

Darkening and Illuminating Counsel

God has cast me into the mire,
  and I have become like dust and ashes.
I cry to you for help and you do not answer me;
  I stand, and you only look at me.
You have turned cruel to me;
  with the might of your hand you persecute me.
You lift me up on the wind; you make me ride on it,
  and you toss me about in the roar of the storm.
For I know that you will bring me to death
  and to the house appointed for all living. (Job 30:19–23)

How can we not feel sorry for Job? The man who helped so many is now abandoned by God and despised by people. Job might even remind Christians of Jesus. "My God, my God, why have you forsaken me" (Ps 22:1)?!

Then Job makes one last plea for vindication:

Oh, that I had one to hear me!
  (Here is my signature! Let the Almighty answer me!)
  Oh, that I had the indictment written by my adversary!
Surely I would carry it on my shoulder;
  I would bind it on me as a crown;
I would give him an account of all my steps;
  like a prince I would approach him.
If my land has cried out against me
  and its furrows have wept together,
if I have eaten its yield without payment
  and made its owners breathe their last,
let thorns grow instead of wheat,
  and foul weeds instead of barley. (Job 31:35–40)

With that, the narrator tells us, "The words of Job are ended."

But then, as the book transitions to another section, the narrator adds something confounding: "So these three men ceased to answer Job, because he was righteous in his own eyes" (Job 32:1). "Righteous in [one's] own eyes" is not a compliment. Judges 21:25 tells us that "everyone did what was right in his own eyes." In the book of Judges, the things that were right in people's eyes included rape and kidnapping. Proverbs warns us about being wise in our own eyes:

Be not wise in your own eyes;
  fear the LORD, and turn away from evil. (Prov 3:7)

The way of the fool is right in his own eyes,
  but a wise man listens to advice. (Prov 12:15)

Illuminating Counsel

Answer a fool according to his folly,
> lest he be wise in his own eyes. (Prov 26:5)

Do you see a man who is wise in his own eyes?
> There is more hope for a fool than him. (Prov 26:12)

The sluggard is wiser in his own eyes
> than seven men who can answer sensibly. (Prov 26:16)

A rich man is wise in his own eyes,
> but a poor man of understanding will find him out. (Prov 28:11)

And Isaiah says:

Woe to those who are wise in their own eyes,
> and shrewd in their own sight. (Isa 5:21)

To be "righteous [or "wise"] in [one's] own eyes" is to be *self-righteous*. A self-righteous person is a person who is overly confident in his own goodness. A self-righteous person is conceited. He thinks he's better than other people. Jesus illustrates this attitude, and condemns it, in his parable of the Pharisee and the tax collector. Jesus addresses the parable "to some who trusted themselves that they were righteous, and treated others with contempt" (Luke 18:9).

Is Job self-righteous? Maybe Job 32:1 means the *friends* viewed Job as self-righteous. We, the readers, of course know that the friends are wrong. Or are they? In Job 32, it's not the friends, but the *narrator* who tells us Job is "righteous in his own eyes." In the Bible, the narrator is always omniscient. The narrator even repeats the point:

Then Elihu the son of Barachel the Buzite, of the family of Ram, burned with anger. He burned with anger at Job *because he justified himself rather than God.* He burned with anger also at Job's three friends because they had found no answer, although they had declared Job to be in the wrong. Now Elihu had waited to speak to Job because they were older than he. And when Elihu saw that there was no answer in the mouth of these three men, he burned with anger. (Job 32:2–5)

To "justify [oneself] rather than God" hardly seems like a good thing to do. In the aforementioned parable of Jesus, the Pharisee prays about how awesome he is. He mentions all the wonderful things he does, such as fasting and tithing. He's grateful that he's a better person than the tax collector. The tax collector also prays but, unlike the Pharisee, he doesn't boast in anything he has done. He can't even bring himself to look up to heaven. He bows his head, "beats his breast," and says, "God, be merciful to me, a sinner" (Luke 18:13). Jesus says the second man "went to his house justified, rather than the other" (Luke 18:14). Anyone who justifies himself rather than God will not be

118

justified; self-righteous people are, by definition, not righteous. The narrator of the book of Job seems to be saying that, to some extent, Job has become like the Pharisee.

Who is Elihu? Why didn't the narrator mention him before? Some people think Elihu's speech was not originally part of the book. The narrator's explanation is that Elihu is young and therefore remained silent while his elders—Job and the three friends—argued with each other. Elihu listened patiently. When the friends give up trying to convince Job, Elihu can no longer hold his peace. He's *angry. Very* angry. *He burns with anger*! He agrees with the friends, but he thinks they did a miserable job prosecuting Job. Elihu, therefore, takes over the prosecution's case. He says to Job:

> You say, "I am pure, without transgression;
> > I am clean, and there is no iniquity in me.
> Behold, he finds occasions against me,
> > he counts me as his enemy,
> he puts my feet in the stocks
> > and watches all my paths."
> Behold, in this you are not right. I will answer you,
> > for God is greater than man.
> Why do you contend against him,
> > saying, "He will answer none of man's words"?
> For God speaks in one way,
> > and in two, though man does not perceive it.
> In a dream, in a vision of the night,
> > when deep sleep falls on men,
> > while they slumber on their beds,
> then he opens the ears of men
> > and terrifies them with warnings,
> that he may turn man aside from his deed
> > and conceal pride from a man;
> he keeps back his soul from the pit,
> > his life from perishing by the sword. (Job 33:9–18)

Job wanted the spotlight off of him and onto God. Elihu puts the spotlight right back onto Job. For Elihu, it's Job who should be on trial, not God. God is just. Job is not.

Many people view Elihu negatively, thinking of him as a "blowhard."[16] He does talk a *lot*. His speech is quite superfluous and verbose, taking up five whole chapters. He prepares people for what he's going to say but has a hard time getting straight to the point. However, when he does get to the point, it's difficult to argue he's wrong.

Elihu vindicates God. His theology of suffering is similar to C. S. Lewis's. Lewis said, "God whispers to us in our pleasures, speaks in our consciences, but shouts in our pain. It is his megaphone to rouse a deaf world."[17] God doesn't inflict humans

16. Alter, *The Art of Biblical Poetry*, loc. 1908.

17. Lewis, *The Problem of Pain*, 91.

with suffering because God is sadistic. God inflicts humans with suffering because he wants humans to turn from their sins. Elihu says, when a sufferer heeds God's shout and repents, God "accepts him; [God] sees his face with a shout of joy and he restores to man his righteousness" (Job 33:26). God does this over and over again "to bring back [man's] soul from the pit, that he may be lighted with the light of life" (Job 33:30).

I can hardly think of a book in the Tanakh where a man is simultaneously presented as totally righteous and yet so thoroughly rebuked with words that could have been written by the prophets themselves. Such is the case with the juxtaposition of Job's defense of himself in chs. 29–31 and Elihu's prosecution of Job in chs. 32–35. It seems like they're talking about two different people. For example, Elihu says:

> What man is like Job,
>> who drinks up scoffing like water,
> who travels in company with evildoers
>> and walks with wicked men?
> For he has said, "It profits a man nothing
>> that he should take delight in God." (Job 34:7–9)

Elihu is saying that Job is not the happy man of Ps 1. Job walks in the counsel of the wicked, stands in the way of sinners, and sits in the seat of scoffers. Elihu continues:

> Job opens his mouth with empty talk,
>> He multiplies words without knowledge. (Job 35:16)

Elihu ends his speech by saying that God "does not regard any who are wise in their own conceit [literally "heart"] (Job 37:24). This is an *inclusio*. The notion of being self-righteous brackets Elihu's speech. The point isn't subtle. According to the friends, the narrator, and Elihu, Job is arrogant.

But how could Job be arrogant if, earlier in the book, both the narrator and God say Job "was blameless and upright" and "feared God and turned away from evil" (Job 1:1, 8; 2:3)?

Recently I learned how a negative experience can arouse one's arrogance. A course I taught in my university was given to a new hire. This decision disappointed me, to say the least. It's not that the new hire isn't qualified to teach the course. It's that, from my perspective, it felt like I was being punished unjustly. I began thinking of all the reasons why I deserve to teach that course more than the other guy. I'm a very good teacher. I make sure my powerpoint is very organized. Everything is available for my students from the very beginning of the semester. I memorize my students' names before the first day. I return students' emails within an hour after they're sent. I grade essays within a week of when they're submitted. I grade exams the very same day they're taken. I bake bread for my students. I buy them pizza when I fear I'm overloading them. I also volunteer my time to work with students who are not even in

my classes. I went through extensive training to become a docent at two museums so that I can take students there.

I, I, I, I, I! As if it's all about me. Oh, how conceited I am! The dean's decision wounded my pride. In seeking to justify myself, I momentarily forgot why I teach. I don't serve my students to feed my ego. I serve my students because I love my students. Klyne Snodgrass gave me the best advice about teaching. "Leave your ego at the door of the classroom," he said. It's frightening how easy it is for a teacher to become arrogant.

So yes—Job was an extraordinary man. Through no fault of his own, he experiences two tragedies. He loses all of his children and all of his wealth. Even so, Job holds on to his integrity. He continues to bless God. But then Job himself is afflicted. He's struck with a terrible disease. He still blesses God, but this time he blesses God *only with his lips*. (Notice how we're reinterpreting the prologue!) Outwardly he blesses God, even rebuking his wife for telling him to do otherwise. Inwardly, however, for the first time, he's truly conflicted. Dare we say the prosecutor was right?! "All that a man has he will give for his life" (Job 2:4). Why? Because every human has an ego. Job could remain warmhearted toward God after losing his children and his wealth, but being struck by disease pushed him over the edge. He now wishes he were never born. He still doesn't want to say anything negative about God, though. Instead, he says as little about God as possible. But when his friends blame him for the horrendous things that God had done to him, Job's pride is wounded. He feels he has no choice but to say what's really on his mind. God is unjust! In order to prove God is unjust, Job recounts all the good deeds he had done over the course of his lifetime. His good deeds were done for the betterment of his neighbors, but he recounts them in order to justify himself and condemn God. The friends give up trying to convince Job of God's goodness. Then Elihu breaks his silence and does his best to get through to Job, to no avail. Everyone can see how Job's sufferings have caused him to become arrogant. Job remains obstinate. Then, after being silent for thirty-five chapters, God finally speaks . . .

GOD'S SPEECHES

God speaks to Job through a whirlwind, which indicates that God is not happy. The reader can almost hear thunder emanating from God's mouth when he says:

> Who is this that darkens counsel by words without knowledge?
> Dress for action like a man [Hebrew: *gever*];
>> I will question you, and you make it known to me. (Job 38:2–3)

What does "counsel" mean? "Counsel" is advice. It's a word that's used synonymously with wisdom. For example, in Prov 8:14, wisdom says:

> I have counsel and sound wisdom [literally "success"]
>> I have insight; I have strength.

Illuminating Counsel

Likewise, Prov 22:20 says: "Have I not written for you thirty sayings of counsel and knowledge . . ."

To *darken* counsel, therefore, is to cover up wisdom (cf. Rom 1:21–22). God says Job is covering up wisdom by speaking about things that he doesn't understand. In other words, Job is a fool.

Whereas Job has darkened counsel, God seeks to *illuminate* counsel. God illuminates counsel by pummeling Job with questions about creation:

> Where were you when I laid the foundation of the earth?
> Tell me, if you have understanding.
> Who determined its measurements—surely you know!
> Or who stretched the line upon it?
> On what were its bases sunk,
> or who laid its cornerstone,
> when the morning stars sang together
> and all the sons of God shouted for joy? (Job 38:4–7)

> Or who shut in the sea with doors
> when it burst out from the womb . . . ? (Job 38:8)

> Have you commanded the morning since your days began,
> and caused the dawn to know its place . . . ? (Job 38:12)

> Have you entered into the springs of the sea,
> or walked in the recesses of the deep?
> Have the gates of death been revealed to you,
> or have you seen the gates of deep darkness?
> Have you comprehended the expanse of the earth?
> Declare, if you know all this. (Job 38:16–18)

> Can you lift your voice to the clouds,
> that a flood of waters may cover you? (Job 38:34)

> Can you hunt the prey for the lion,
> or satisfy the appetite of the young lions? (Job 38:39)

> Do you know when the mountain goats give birth?
> Do you observe the calving of the does? (Job 39:1)

> Is the wild ox willing to serve you?
> Will he spend the night at your manger? (Job 39:9)

Darkening and Illuminating Counsel

> Do you give the horse his might?
>> Do you clothe his neck with a mane?
> Do you make him leap like the locust? (Job 39:19–20)

> Is it by your understanding that the hawk soars
>> and spreads his wings toward the south? (Job 39:26)

All of these questions are negative assertions. Job is just a creature. He wasn't around when the earth's foundation was laid. Job can't create anything.

God concludes his first speech by saying:

> Shall a faultfinder contend with the Almighty?
>> He who argues with God, let him answer it. (Job 40:1)

Job cannot answer it:

> Behold, I am of small account; what shall I answer you?
>> I lay my hand on my mouth.
> I have spoken once, and I will not answer;
>> twice, but I will proceed no further. (Job 40:4–5)

But God is not done with Job. God, speaking out of the whirlwind a second time, again tells Job to "dress for action"—literally "gird up your loins"—"like a man" (Job 40:7). God is telling Job to "man up"! "I will question you, and you make it known to me," God says. He continues:

> Will you even put me in the wrong?
>> Will you condemn me that you may be in the right?
> Have you an arm like God,
>> and can you thunder with a voice like his?
> "Adorn yourself with majesty and dignity;
>> clothe yourself with glory and splendor.
> Pour out the overflowings of your anger,
>> and look on everyone who is proud and abase him.
> Look on everyone who is proud and bring him low
>> and tread down the wicked where they stand.
> Hide them all in the dust together;
>> bind their faces in the world below.
> Then will I also acknowledge to you
>> that your own right hand can save you. (Job 40:7–14)

Job does not have an arm like God. Job's own right hand cannot save him.

God then goes on to describe two creatures. The first creature is a land animal called Behemoth:[18]

---

18. Behemoth is often compared to the hippopotamus. I agree with Walton that Behemoth is a mythological creature. See Walton, *Job*, 406–7.

123

Illuminating Counsel

> Behold, Behemoth,
>> which I made as I made you;
>> he eats grass like an ox.
> Behold, his strength in his loins,
>> and his power in the muscles of his belly.
> He makes his tail stiff like a cedar;
>> the sinews of his thighs are knit together.
> His bones are tubes of bronze,
>> his limbs like bars of iron. (Job 40:15–18)

Job has no advantage over Behemoth since both Job and Behemoth are creations of God.

God asks only one question regarding Behemoth:

> Can one take him by his eyes,
>> or pierce his nose with a snare? (Job 40:24)

The answer is *no*.

The second creature is called Leviathan.[19] Leviathan was mentioned in Job 3:8. Unlike Behemoth, which is mentioned only in Job, Leviathan is mentioned in other parts of the Tanakh. Isaiah 27:1 says:

> In that day the LORD with his hard and great and strong sword will punish Leviathan the fleeing serpent, Leviathan the twisting serpent, and he will slay the dragon that is in the sea.

Thus Leviathan is some kind of a sea monster. Psalm 74:13–15 says:

> You divided the sea by your might;
>> you broke the heads of the sea monsters on the waters.
> You crushed the heads of Leviathan;
>> you gave him as food for the creatures of the wilderness.
> You split open springs and brooks;
>> you dried up ever-flowing streams.

Leviathan represents chaos.[20] By slaying Leviathan, God brings order into the world.

The description of Leviathan in Job takes up all of ch. 41 and consists almost entirely of rhetorical questions:

> Can you draw out Leviathan with a fishhook
>> or press down his tongue with a cord? (Job 41:1[40:25])

The answer is *no*.

---

19. Leviathan is often compared to a crocodile, even a dinosaur. Again, I think this is incorrect.

20. Walton prefers to describe Leviathan as an "anti-cosmos" creature. See Walton, *Job*, 120–21.

Darkening and Illuminating Counsel

Can you put a rope in his nose
or pierce his jaw with a hook? (Job 41:2[40:26])

No.

Will he make many pleas to you?
Will he speak to you soft words? (Job 41:3[40:27])

No.

Will he make a covenant with you
to take him for your servant forever? (Job 41:4[40:28])

No.

Will you play with him as with a bird,
or will you put him on a leash for your girls? (Job 41:5[40:29])

Definitely not. And that verse reminds us of Ps 104:26 which says that God created Leviathan to "play" in the sea, as if Leviathan is God's pet.

The questions continue until the second half of the chapter, which consists of more descriptions of Leviathan. God concludes by saying:

On earth there is not his like,
a creature without fear.
He sees everything that is high;
he is king over all the sons of pride. (Job 41:33–34[25–26])

The point of bringing up Behemoth and Leviathan is to stress Job's mental and physical frailty compared to God's power. Suffering is *not* mentioned. God could have mentioned the "bet" he made with the prosecutor, but he doesn't bring it up. If the reader wants an explanation for why there's suffering in the world, I'm afraid the reader will have to look elsewhere. The issue here isn't suffering; it's *humility*. Job allowed his suffering to make him self-righteous and arrogant. Thus, God succeeds where the friends and Elihu failed. God humbles Job.

Job's newly acquired humility can be seen in his response to God's second speech:

I know that you can do all things,
and that no purpose of yours can be thwarted.
"Who is this that hides counsel without knowledge?"
Therefore I have uttered what I did not understand,
things too wonderful for me, which I did not know.
"Hear, and I will speak;
I will question you, and you make it known to me."
I had heard of you by the hearing of the ear,
but now my eye sees you;
therefore I despise myself,
and repent in dust and ashes (Job 42:2–6)

125

Job admits his limitations. God can do all things; Job cannot. Job admits he was a fool. He admits he spoke presumptuously. He thought he knew God, but he really didn't. God's speeches were a powerful revelation to him. He now understands God and himself more clearly than ever before.

Job 42:6 is notoriously difficult to translate. The Hebrew says "I despise." It can also be translated "I reject." The Hebrew does not say "I despise *myself*." "Myself" is added by the translator. The translator is assuming Job is despising or rejecting himself, but that may not be the case. It probably means that Job is recanting the lawsuit he sought to bring against God.[21] Job drops the charges, as it were.

Job repents "in"—literally "on"—"dust and ashes." The phrase "dust and ashes" might reminds us of the ash heap in Job 2:8. Job had also said, "God has cast me into the mire, and I have become like dust and ashes" (Job 30:19). Judy Klitsner argues Job is echoing Gen 18:27 where Abraham says, "Behold, I have undertaken to speak to the Lord, I who am but dust and ashes."[22] Like Abraham, Job's encounter with the divine has made him cognizant of his humanity.

The book's message seems to be that suffering is not an excuse to become arrogant. In fact, the book of Job raises the uncomfortable proposition that suffering might *cause* one to become arrogant. Even when one suffers, one must remember that God is the source of wisdom. This is why the center of the book contains a hymn which says:

> From where, then, does wisdom come?
>> And where is the place of understanding?
> It is hidden from the eyes of all living
>> and concealed from the birds of the air.
> Abaddon and Death say,
>> 'We have heard a rumor of it with our ears.'
> "God understands the way to it,
>> and he knows its place.
> For he looks to the ends of the earth
>> and sees everything under the heavens.
> When he gave to the wind its weight
>> and apportioned the waters by measure,
> when he made a decree for the rain
>> and a way for the lightning of the thunder,
> then he saw it and declared it;
>> he established it, and searched it out.
> And he said to man,
> 'Behold, the fear of the Lord, that is wisdom,
>> and to turn away from evil is understanding.'" (Job 28:20–28)[23]

---

21. Walton, *Job*, 391.

22. Klitsner, *Subversive Sequels of the Bible*, loc. 332–62

23. There is a debate as to whether this hymn is spoken by Job. I think it is not.

THE EPILOGUE

Job 42:7 says: "After the LORD had spoken these words to Job, the LORD said to Eliphaz the Temanite: 'My anger burns against you and against your two friends, *for you have not spoken of me what is right, as my servant Job has.*'" Wait a minute! The friends defended God. Job accused God. And God says that the friends were wrong and Job was right?! I give up! I confess I do *not* fully understand the book of Job!

Our thesis was that Job became self-righteous. Job 2:10 is the key verse. It says "Job did not sin with his lips." We argued that, though Job didn't sin with his lips, he did sin with his mind. Being struck with disease truly broke through his defenses. He still praises God, but his praises are less authentic than before. The week of mourning arouses his self-pity. This is why he curses his birthday. His friends blaming him for his suffering hurts him even more. He recounts all of his good deeds to prove that he is just and God is not. He finally gets a response from God but it's not the response he wanted. God humbles Job.

But Job 42:7 indicates that we may have to go back to the drawing board in interpreting the book. Maybe we shouldn't make too much out of the word "lips" in Job 2:10. Perhaps it does not imply Job had impious thoughts. Maybe it's not Job who's on trial, but his friends, whom he calls "worthless physicians" (Job 13:4). No one seems to understand him—not his wife, his friends, Elihu, the people of his community; no one shows him sympathy. He feels utterly alone.

What about God? Does God sympathize with Job? God's speeches seem so harsh. When readers read ch. 2 and then skip to God's speeches in ch. 38, the speeches don't make sense. Why would God pummel Job with these questions when Job praises God unconditionally? Our interpretation made sense of this. God's speeches are harsh because Job was self-righteous and God needed to humble him. But could there be another purpose to God's speeches? Are God's speeches, in some way, not just humbling, but also *comforting*?

Robert Alter points out that God's speeches seem very aware of Job's soliloquy in Job 3.[24] The first hint is the use of the particular Hebrew word for man—*gever*. (Obviously, this can only be seen when reading in the original language.) Job cursed the night on which it was said a *gever* is born (Job 3:3). God told Job to brace himself as a *gever* (Job 38:3). Also, we noted how pervasive the idea of darkness is in Job 3. In Job 38, God says that Job "darkens counsel." Job speaks of darkness whereas God speaks of light. Both Job and God use the word "womb." Job speaks of death emerging from the womb whereas God speaks of life emerging from the womb. Observe:

24. Alter, *The Art of Biblical Poetry*, loc. 1992–2065

Illuminating Counsel

Job	God
"A *gever* is conceived" (Job 3:3)	"Dress for action like a *gever*" (Job 38:3)
"Let that day be darkness" (Job 3:4)	"Who is this that darkens counsel" (Job 38:2)
"Let the stars of its dawn be dark" (Job 3:9)	"The morning stars sang together" (Job 38:7)
". . . because it did not shut the doors of my mother's womb" (Job 3:10)	"Who shut the sea with doors when it burst out from the womb?" (Job 38:8)
"Why did I not . . . come out of the womb and expire?" (Job 38:11)	"From whose womb did the ice come forth?" (Job 38:29)
"Let [my birthday not] see the eyelids of the morning" (Job 3:9)	"Have you commanded the morning since your days began . . . ?" (Job 38:12)
"Why is light given to him who . . . [longs] for death . . . ?" (Job 3:20–21)	"Have the gates of death been revealed to you?" (Job 38:17)
"Let gloom and deep darkness claim it" (Job 3:5)	". . . have you seen the gates of deep darkness?" (Job 38:17)
"Let that day be darkness! May God above not seek it, nor light shine upon it" (Job 3:4)	"Where is the way to the dwelling of light, and where is the place of darkness?" (Job 38:19)
"Why is light given to him who is in misery . . . ?" (Job 3:20)	"What is the way to the place where light is distributed . . . ?" (Job 38:24)
"Let those curse it who curse the day, who are ready to rouse up Leviathan" (Job 3:8)	"Can you draw out Leviathan with a fishhook or press down his tongue with a cord?" (Job 41:1[40:25]

I hardly think these connections are coincidental. But what do they mean?

God seems to be showing Job a different perspective. Instead of mentioning suffering, God points Job to the wonders of creation. When God laid the foundation of the earth "the morning stars sang together and all the sons of God shouted for joy" (Job 38:7). As we read in Prov 8, creation is a cause for celebration! Nature is utterly sublime. Yes, nature is also bloody. The lions "lie in wait in the thicket" for their prey (Job 38:40). The young hawks "suck up blood" as they eat their prey (Job 39:30). And what God says about the ostrich is strange:

> The wings of the ostrich wave proudly,
>> but are they the pinions and plumage of love?
> For she leaves her eggs to the earth
>> and lets them be warmed on the ground,
> forgetting that a foot may crush them
>> and that the wild beast may trample them.

Darkening and Illuminating Counsel

She deals cruelly with her young, as if they were not hers;
>   though her labor be in vain, yet she has no fear,
because God has made her forget wisdom
>   and given her no share in understanding.
When she rouses herself to flee,
>   she laughs at the horse and his rider (Job 39:13–18).[25]

Nature is bloody, but it works. Countless folk tales have hated on wolves, but wolves are essential to a functioning ecosystem. Without wolves, there would be too many herbivores. If there are too many herbivores, there will be a lack of vegetation. The herbivores would then die. But wolves reduce the number of herbivores. They leave carcasses for the scavengers. Everything becomes balanced. City-folk like me rarely think of these things. I think our ancestors were much more in tune with nature than we are.

One of my professors told the class how distraught his father became when his beloved wife died. He would ask his father, "How did you sleep last night, Dad?" "On my side," his father would spiritlessly answer. There was no life in him. He was shutting down. But the spark of life would return to his father whenever the old man would observe nature. "Look at that bird," he would say. "It's making a nest in the tree! Look at that squirrel! It has found some food!" Observing nature helped heal his grieving heart.

Nature is inherently comforting. It reminds us that, despite the magnitude of our suffering, the world is far bigger than we are. It reminds us that the world is teeming with life. Creatures are *living*, not just dying.

I think this is what Job was reminded of. He wanted to die because he forgot how wondrous life truly is. God's speeches reminded him that life is a gift. The stars of the universe are awesome! So are lions, ravens, mountain goats, donkeys, wild oxen, ostriches, hawks, and the rest of God's creatures. The movie *Secretariat* begins by mentioning Job's sufferings and quotes God's description of horses:

Do you give the horse his strength
>   or clothe his neck with a flowing mane?
Do you make him leap like a locust,
>   striking terror with his proud snorting?
He paws fiercely, rejoicing in his strength,
>   and charges into the fray.
He laughs at fear, afraid of nothing;
>   he does not shy away from the sword.
The quiver rattles against his side,
>   along with the flashing spear and lance.
In frenzied excitement he eats up the ground;
>   he cannot stand still when the trumpet sounds." (Job 39:19–24, NIV 1984)

25. Regarding the book of Job's view of ostriches, Walton says, "Yahweh is adopting the perspective common to humans at the time rather than making universally verifiable statements about the ontological nature of ostriches." Walton, *Job*, 404.

Illuminating Counsel

The screenwriter's contextualization of this quote is insightful. One's troubles may be great, but horses are amazing creatures, a wonder to behold! It may seem that God bringing up horses in response to Job's complaint is a non sequitur, but I think it answers the problem perfectly. Despite all our sufferings, and no doubt they are many, we are fortunate to be alive. Look at the horse and marvel! And then be grateful that you are a human being!

I have given two interpretations of the book—one that views God's speeches as humbling Job and the other that views God's speeches as comforting Job. I don't know which one is right. Maybe both are right. Maybe neither is completely right. Interestingly enough, the word in Job 42:6 translated "repent" can also be translated "comfort." Maybe Job was *comforted* on dust and ashes.[26] One thing is sure: the book of Job is complex. We shouldn't presume there's only one point or one "moral of the story." There can legitimately be more than one possible interpretation. There will never be a "final word" on the book. This is partly why the book is so remarkable.

It's possible Job 42:7 is the work of an editor who was retconning the negative portrayal of Job in earlier parts of the book. I find that proposition unlikely, however. The importance of Job 42:7 is that the book cannot allow the reader to think the friends were right in blaming Job for his sufferings. Job 42:7 vindicates Job. It teaches us that those who suffer have a right to vent their frustrations. They have a right to lament. And while Job said things in his pain that he later recanted, the greater offense is the friends' simplistic and rigid theology, not to mention their ineptitude at comforting Job.

Job is fully vindicated at the very end of the book. We're told that God "blessed the latter days of Job more than his beginning" (Job 42:12). Everything Job lost is restored to him. Job makes intercession for his friends. I'm assuming that, since the narrator calls them his "friends," they all reconciled. Job's family visits him. They show him "sympathy" and "comfort." They even give him money. "And the LORD gave Job twice as much as he had before" (Job 42:10). Whereas he initially had seven thousand sheep, three thousand camels, five hundred yoke of oxen, and five hundred female donkeys (Job 1:3), he now has fourteen thousand sheep, six thousand camels, one thousand yoke of oxen, and one thousand female donkeys (Job 42:12). He doesn't get twice as many children, though. However, he does have seven more sons and three more daughters. Unlike his first ten children, these children outlive him. "And after this Job lived 140 years, and saw his sons, and his sons' sons, four generations. And Job died, an old man, and full of days" (Job 42:16–17).

Bart Ehrman is particularly offended by the ending of the book of Job. He believes the book implies the second set of children are "replacement children." He calls this passage in Job the most offensive part of the Bible.[27] That's certainly a cynical reading, though not necessarily illegitimate. Michael L. Brown disagrees with Ehrman, arguing

26. For a defense of this view, see Hicks, "Job 42:1–6—Did Job 'Repent'?"

27. Ehrman, "Bart Ehrman vs. Michael Brown on Suffering."

Darkening and Illuminating Counsel

that, if Job's children were "replacements" of the ones he lost, he would have had twice as many children as before, just as he had twice as many livestock. He has twice as much of everything except the children because children cannot be replaced.[28] Let me say this: I knew a woman who was married with four children. Her husband got into a car accident while the children were in the car. All five of them died. Years later she remarried and had four more children. I don't think she viewed her second set of four children as replacements for the ones she lost. People who experience tragedies are sometimes fortunate enough to start a new family. It doesn't mean the pain of the losses goes away.

I'm somewhat sympathetic to Ehrman's perspective. The ending of Job is a bit too Polyannish for me. Tragedy is real and we need to learn how to deal with it. The Bible, though, doesn't want suffering to have the last word. The ending also vindicates God. Whatever we think about God's actions in the prologue, in the end God makes everything right.

What's vitally important to recognize is that Job doesn't recant and repent with the expectation that his fortunes will be restored. The friends told him his fortunes would be restored if he repents (Job 8:5–6). But that's not *why* Job repents. He repents because he recognizes that God is God. He repents *because it's the right thing to do.* Thus the ending of the book of Job brings us back to the beginning. The prosecutor had asked the question: "Does Job fear God for no reason?" (Job 1:7). Here at the end the reader realizes that the answer is *yes.* The trial of Job has reached its verdict.

Rabbi David Wolpe makes an interesting point about this. If the world really did operate according to the Retribution Principle, if good deeds always brought blessings and bad deeds always brought curses, no one would be good for no reason. If we knew telling lies would result in stomach cancer, we wouldn't tell lies. But that's not the way the world works. Tragedy comes to all—liars and truth-tellers alike. This means that, at the end of the day, barring any notion of an afterlife, there's no lasting reward for doing good deeds. The *only* legitimate reason to do good deeds is for goodness' sake.[29]

28. ASKDrBrown, "Amazing Insights Into the Book of Job."
29. Mercatus Center, "Why Do Bad Things Happen to Good People?"

8

A Celebration of Kindness
(Ruth)

THE BOOK OF RUTH takes place "in the days when the judges ruled" (Ruth 1:1)—the pre-monarchic period of ancient Israel's history, as told in the book of Judges. This is why the Old Testament places Ruth immediately after Judges.

The period of the Judges was a dark time in Israel's history. The Israelites were ignorant of the Torah (Judg 2:10). Even well-intentioned people committed egregious acts. "Everyone did what was right in his own eyes" (Judg 21:25).

Women play a surprisingly prominent role in Judges' narratives. We see women in positions of leadership, women who kill, and women who are victimized. In many instances, women are underestimated. As the book progresses, the treatment of women seems to get worse. The book begins with a woman named Deborah who is both a prophetess and a judge. The book ends with a concubine who is abandoned by her lover to a brutal gang who rape her to death. This horrific act of murder leads to a civil war in Israel that decimates the tribe of Benjamin.

If we apply the Retribution Principle to Judges, we can surmise the reason for Israel's suffering is, in part, due to the mistreatment of women. Women are powerful. To abuse a woman is to unleash a nuclear-like force against oneself. We all come from women; to abuse a woman is destroy oneself.

Ruth and Judges are polar opposites of each other in that regard. Whereas Judges tells stories of women being horribly abused, Ruth tells a story of women being treated with kindness. Judges ends with people fractured. Ruth ends with people made whole. Thus the Old Testament's juxtaposition of Judges and Ruth is immensely insightful.

But I argue the placement of Ruth in the Ketuvim is equally insightful. Most readers of the Bible don't notice the connections Ruth has with Psalms, Proverbs, and Job. We'll note these connections as we analyze the book. We'll also look back on Ruth and note connections with the subsequent books of the Ketuvim.

A Celebration of Kindness

BITTERNESS

There's a famine in Bethlehem. This is ironic, for Bethlehem means "house of bread." Because there was no bread in the "house of bread," "a man of Bethlehem in Judah went to sojourn in the country of Moab" (Ruth 1:1). Moab is one of Israel's arch enemies. Deuteronomy 23:3 says, "no Moabite may enter the house of the LORD."

We're led to think this book is about a man. His name is Elimelech. His wife's name is Naomi. The names of their two sons are Mahlon and Chilion.

However, our expectations are quickly subverted. By v. 3, the man dies. The family, which consisted of three men and one woman, is now reduced to two to one. The two sons marry Moabite women. Their names are Orpah and Ruth. The ratio is now two to three. Then the two sons die.[1] It happens so quickly that we have no time to weep for them. The narrator, within just five verses, wipes the slate clean of men. Only the women remain.

Naomi has been "left" without her husband and "left" without her two sons. The word "left," twice used, puts a hefty emotional weight upon Naomi. Reading Ruth in the context of the Ketuvim accentuates that emotional weight. The distance between Ruth and Job in the Old Testament prevents readers from linking Naomi's sufferings with that of Job's. But the fact that the Ketuvim has Job and Ruth near each other makes that connection unavoidable. Both Job and Naomi lose all of their children. We shall also soon see that their views of God are not dissimilar.

After ten years in Moab, Naomi learns that the famine in Bethlehem has ended. There's now no reason for her to stay in Moab. Naomi resolves to return to her home in Bethlehem. But what of her two daughters-in-law? She says to them:

> Go, return each of you to her mother's house. May the LORD deal kindly with
> you, as you have dealt with the dead and with me. The LORD grant that you
> may find rest, each of you in the house of her husband! (Ruth 1:8–9)

Does Naomi wish to return to Bethlehem alone because she's consumed with self-pity? Or is it because she's looking after the best interests of her daughters-in-law? Or is it because she feels her Moabite daughters-in-law don't belong in Judah? Whatever her reason, she invokes God's name and blesses her daughters-in-law, wishing only good things for them. Her wish that they find "rest" with new husbands is ironic since Naomi, bereft of her husband and children, has been denied such rest.[2] Naomi imparts blessings, but keeps none for herself.

Her use of the word "kindly" is significant. "Kindly" is the translation of the Hebrew word *hesed*. *Hesed* is one of the most important words in the Tanakh. The Psalms are saturated with this word, but I have waited until now to comment on it.

---

1. It is not a surprise that the sons die. The names "Mahlon" and "Chilion" mean "sickness" and "end," respectively.

2. Linafelt and Beal, *Ruth*, loc. 537.

133

Hesed is usually translated "steadfast love." James Bruckner prefers to translate it "unrelenting love." I like the NASB's translation, "lovingkindness." *Hesed* is love expressed in kindness. It's a noun; something you "do." Naomi literally says, "May the LORD *do* kindness to you . . ." Orpah and Ruth had "done" kindness to both the dead (their respective husbands, Mahlon and Chilion) and the living (Naomi). Naomi wishes divine kindness be done to Orpah and Ruth.

Naomi kisses her daughters-in-law goodbye. They weep. They don't want to be separated from her. "No," they say, "we will return with you to your people" (Ruth 1:10). Naomi responds:

> Turn back, my daughters; why will you go with me? Have I yet sons in my womb that they may become your husbands? Turn back, my daughters; go your way, for I am too old to have a husband. If I should say I have hope, even if I should have a husband this night and should bear sons, would you therefore wait till they were grown? Would you therefore refrain from marrying? No, my daughters, for it is exceedingly bitter to me for your sake that the hand of the LORD has gone out against me." (Ruth 1:11–13)

Whereas the daughters-in-law's dialogue is terse, Naomi's seems a bit all over the place. Some of what she says is tricky to translate. I believe any awkwardness in the grammar is intentional. Characterization in the book of Ruth is revealed through dialogue more than narration. From her speech, we learn that Naomi is consumed with self-pity and devoid of hope. Like Job, Naomi views God as the source of her suffering. There's no dualism here. Whether she feels she did something to deserve her suffering is less clear. All we know is that she thinks God has turned against her for his own reasons, and nothing can alter that reality.

The reason Naomi mentions having more children is because of the law of Levirate Marriage. *Levir* is a Latin word. It refers to a husband's brother. The law states that if a married man dies without having a son, the brother of the man—the *levir*—is obligated to marry the widow. Their first son will actually be the dead husband's son so that his lineage will continue. The most important instance of this custom in the Bible is in Gen 38. In that chapter, Judah's firstborn son, Er, marries Tamar, who is presumably a Canaanite. Er dies. Then Judah's middle son, Onan, marries Tamar. Onan refuses to ejaculate inside of her—an act called "Onanism," which we named after him. He dies. Judah's youngest son, Shelah, is too young to marry. Judah promises Tamar that she can marry Shelah when he comes of age. But Judah has no intention of giving Shelah to her, for he views her as a proverbial "black widow." After some time passes, Tamar becomes fed up with living as a widow. She disguises herself as a prostitute. Prostitutes in those days wore veils. Judah walks by and sees her. He's in the mood. Not realizing she's his daughter-in-law, Judah has sex with her and gets her pregnant. She gives birth to twins: Perez and Zerah. Remembering this story will prove beneficial as we continue our analysis of Ruth.

134

A Celebration of Kindness

Naomi's dissuading of her daughters-in-law may be surprising to many Christians. Shouldn't Naomi *want* her daughters-in-law to go with her so that they'll follow God and join God's people? No Christian worth her salt would dissuade pagans from attending church! No Christian would ever say to a pagan, "Go back to your gods!" Why does Naomi act so unchristian? Answer: Because Naomi is *not* a Christian! It's remarkable how Christians read the Old Testament and assume that the heroes are Christians. Perhaps we should call this Christo-centrism. Naomi is not a Christian; she's a Jew. Her actions can only be understood from a Jewish perspective. Unlike Christianity, Judaism is a non-proselytizing religion. While Judaism does accept converts, converting is not encouraged. In fact, many rabbis will actually *discourage* people from converting to Judaism. If one really wants to be a Jew, one will not succumb to dissuasion. This is precisely what happens in the book of Ruth.

"Then they lifted up their voices and wept again. And Orpah kissed her mother-in-law, but Ruth clung to her" (Ruth 1:14). Up until this point, the two young women acted and spoke in unison. They now split. Orpah succumbs to Naomi's reasoning, but Ruth is not yet ready to call it quits.

I can almost see Naomi rolling her eyes at Ruth. She tries reasoning with her again: "See, your sister-in-law has gone back to her people and to her gods; return after your sister-in-law" (Ruth 1:15). Ruth doesn't listen. It's now her turn to speak:

> Do not urge me to leave you or to return from following you. For where you go I will go, and where you lodge I will lodge. Your people shall be my people, and your God my God. Where you die I will die, and there will I be buried. May the LORD do so to me and more also if anything but death parts me from you. (Ruth 1:16–17)

It's striking how different Ruth's dialogue is from Naomi's. Naomi's is expansive and, as I described it earlier, all over the place. Ruth's is staccato (more than the English conveys), almost poetical.[3]

Ruth in effect says, "*Stop* telling me to leave you! I will *never* leave you!" Ruth is as stubborn as Naomi. She pledges to be Naomi's shadow and will not compromise on that. She renounces her Moabite citizenship. Her resolve to denounce her gods and adopt Yahweh, Israel's god, is evident in her swearing upon Yahweh's name ("the LORD"). (Compare this to Jezebel's swearing in 1 Kgs 19:2.)

The English adds the word "anything" to v. 17. When the translation has Ruth saying, "May the LORD do so to me and more also if *anything* but death parts me from you," it makes it seem like she's saying "till death do us part." But the Hebrew doesn't say "anything." The Hebrew says, "May the LORD do so to me and more also if *death* parts me from you." That does *not* mean "till death do us part." It means "death will *never* do us part!"[4] "Till death do us part" implies that once Naomi is dead, Ruth will

3. Linafelt and Beal, *Ruth*, loc. 661.
4. Linafelt and Beal, *Ruth*, loc. 678.

135

Illuminating Counsel

be free to go back to Moab. That's emphatically not what Ruth says. Ruth says she will not leave Naomi even *after* Naomi dies. Ruth pledges to be buried next to Naomi.

Ruth's speech was set to music by Charles Gounod, apparently part of an oratorio that I've never found a recording of. More recently, the composer Dan Forrest composed a setting of Ruth's speech for choir. Gounod's is lovely and Forrest's is nothing less than exquisite. Why has Ruth's speech inspired such great art? Perhaps it has something to do with the stoutheartedness of immigrants joining a new nation. Or perhaps it has to do with the victory of a religion in finding a convert. I think it has more to do with its profound expression of friendship. Ruth and Naomi break the stereotype of mothers-in-law and daughters-in-law hating each other. Naomi and Ruth love each other even though they're of different nationalities, different religions, and their legal ties have been severed. Naomi has nothing to offer Ruth—there is no *levir*—and yet Ruth will not let Naomi suffer alone. All of us long for this type of love. This is why so many people have connected with the relationship of Frodo and Samwise in Tolkien's *The Lord of the Rings*. In fact, there's a scene at the end of *The Fellowship of the Ring* which reminds me of our scene in Ruth. Frodo decides he must go to Mordor alone to destroy the ring.

> 'It would be the death of you to come with me, Sam,' said Frodo, 'and I could not have borne that.'
>
> 'Not as certain as being left behind,' said Sam.
>
> 'But I am going to Mordor.'
>
> 'I know that well enough, Mr. Frodo. Of course you are. And I'm coming with you.'
>
> 'Now, Sam,' said Frodo, 'don't hinder me! The others will be coming back at any minute. If they catch me here, I shall have to argue and explain, and I shall never have the heart or the chance to get off. But I must go at once. It's the only way.'
>
> 'Of course it is,' answered Sam. 'But not alone. I'm coming too, or neither of us isn't going. I'll knock holes in all the boats first.'[5]

The essence of friendship is *loyalty*.

I have a dear friend. His name is Jimmy. I met him at a time when I was languishing from loneliness. It's interesting how, when we're children, we don't think about why we love our friends. Now that I'm older, I can say that I love Jimmy. I love him, not just because of how he makes me feel, but because of the content of his character. He's truly one of the kindest, most hospitable people I've ever known. When my mother was dying of cancer and I had to fly every month from Chicago to New York to see her, Jimmy, who lived near the airport, let me stay at his apartment. He drove me to the airport at 3:30 in the morning each time. As the months went by, I felt uneasy at the unevenness of our relationship. He gave so much and all I seemed to do was take.

5. Tolkien, *The Lord of the Rings*, 406.

A Celebration of Kindness

When I told him that I felt guilty about this, he said to me, "There are no burdens with friends." Truer words have not been spoken. Later in the Ketuvim, we read these sagacious words:

> Two are better than one, because they have a good reward for their toil. For if they fall, one will lift up his fellow. But woe to him who is alone when he falls and has not another to lift him up! Again, if two lie together, they keep warm, but how can one keep warm alone? And though a man might prevail against one who is alone, two will withstand him—a threefold cord is not quickly broken. (Eccl 4:9–12)

And this, of course, reminds me of that tremendous moment in *The Lord of the Rings* when Frodo lacks the strength to walk:

> 'Come, Mr. Frodo!' [Sam] cried. 'I can't carry it for you, but I can carry you and it as well. So up you get! Come on, Mr. Frodo dear! Sam will give you a ride. Just tell him where to go, and he'll go.'[6]

You are wealthy indeed if you have someone like Ruth or Samwise in your life.

I'm not sure, however, that Naomi appreciates Ruth. "And when Naomi saw that she was determined to go with her, she said no more" (Ruth 1:18). This is a rather cold statement in light of the warmth of Ruth's speech. Naomi seems to view Ruth as a stray cat that just won't go away. There's no indication she's happy to have Ruth come along. She's letting Ruth accompany her to Bethlehem only because she failed to persuade Ruth to remain.

When they arrive in Bethlehem, "the whole town was stirred because of them" (Ruth 1:19). The chorus of Bethlehemite women barely recognize Naomi, collectively asking themselves, "Is this Naomi?"[7] Naomi has probably not aged well. She also returns without her family. She replies to the women:

> Do not call me Naomi; call me Mara, for the Almighty has dealt very bitterly with me. I went away full, and the LORD has brought me back empty. Why call me Naomi, when the LORD has testified against me and the Almighty has brought calamity upon me?" (Ruth 1:20–21)

"Naomi" means "sweetness." "Mara" means "bitterness." Naomi believes God is against her. She went away "full"—meaning, she had a family—despite being "empty" from a famine. She is now "empty"—meaning, she no longer has a family—despite being back home in the "house of bread."

But what's Ruth—chopped liver?! The narration, like all biblical Hebrew narrations, is very minimalistic, but we can definitely detect a lack of warmth towards Ruth

---

6. Tolkien, *The Lord of the Rings*, 940–41.

7. This line is ambiguous. The women could be happily surprised to see her.

from Naomi. It's understandable, of course. Naomi is like Fantine from *Les Misérables.* Life has killed her dream.

"So Naomi returned, *and Ruth the Moabite her daughter-in-law with her,* who returned from the country of Moab" (Ruth 1:22). The narrator won't let us forget that Naomi is not alone. Nor will the narrator let us forget Ruth's nationality. The narrator tells us Naomi and Ruth "came to Bethlehem at the beginning of barley harvest" (Ruth 1:22). The chapter began with a famine. It ends with a harvest. Perhaps that's a sign of hope for our embattled heroines.

THE REDEEMER

Ruth 2:1 is parenthetical. It tells us of a man who's related to Naomi's husband, Elimelech. His name is Boaz. We need to make two points about him.

First, that Boaz is a relative of Elimelech makes him a "redeemer." "Redeemer" is actually a legal term. The Torah tells us the redeemer has four purposes:

1. He purchases land from his poor relatives in order to keep said land in the family (Lev 25:24–25).

2. He purchases the freedom of family members who have been sold as slaves (Lev 25:47–50).

3. If a family member is dead but is paid restitution, the money goes to the redeemer (Num 5:5–8).

4. The redeemer is also the one who avenges a murdered family member (Deut 19:6–13)

Of these laws, only the first is relevant to the book of Ruth. The purpose of that first law is to prevent widespread economic inequality.

The book of Ruth seems to conflate the redeemer with the levir. The law pertaining to the levir is spelled out in Deut 25:5–10. The word "redeemer" is not used in that text. Nevertheless, in the book of Ruth, the redeemer and the levir are one and the same.

Second, Boaz is called a "worthy man." This is not an insightful translation. The Hebrew says, "*ish gibbor hayil.*" We had seen the word *hayil* in Prov 31 and noted it means "strength." *Ish gibbor hayil* should be translated, "A mighty man of strength." The phrase makes it seem like Boaz is a warrior. Perhaps so. It could also mean he's wealthy (which he seems to be). Or it could mean he's a man of noble character; his "strength" is *moral* rather than physical. Whatever it means, that phrase is immensely significant, but we will have to wait until Ruth 3 for its significance to be manifested.

Meanwhile, Ruth and Naomi need to eat. Ruth, being the more hopeful of the two, takes the initiative, asking Naomi if she can glean in the fields: "Let me go to the field and glean among the ears of grain after him in whose sight I shall find favor."

A Celebration of Kindness

"Go, my daughter," Naomi says (Ruth 2:2). Naomi's response is even terser in Hebrew: *lekhi, viti.* In ch. 1, Naomi was quite loquacious. The brevity of her dialogue at the beginning of ch. 2 perhaps indicates Naomi's deflated disposition. Her verbosity in ch. 1 was necessary to convince her daughters-in-law to not go with her. She was only partially successful. Now that she's home with no need to persuade, all that remains for her to do is to sit quietly, accept her fate, and die. Ruth, on the other hand, is determined to survive, and acts towards that end.

The request to "glean" brings us to another provision of the Torah. Leviticus 19:9–10 states that the edges of a field must be left for the poor and the sojourners. Ruth happens to fit both categories.

That's an extraordinary commandment. The Torah seeks to help the poor. However, the poor are not receiving a "hand out" in the typical sense of the phrase. The poor still have to do the gleaning themselves. Ruth and Naomi are not in an ideal situation, but the Torah has ensured that they will not starve and that they don't need to feel like they're helpless.

Of all the fields Ruth could have gleaned from, she goes to the field owned by Boaz, the relative of her father-in-law. Is that a coincidence? Or is it Providence? The text doesn't say.

Boaz is the first man in the book to speak. He greets his workers. "The LORD be with you," he says. "The LORD bless you," they respond (Ruth 2:4). Was this the typical way people in ancient Israel greeted each other? Maybe it was. Maybe their greeting is just as formulaic as when people today say "bless you" after someone sneezes. Yet the invoking of God's name in blessing by Boaz and his workers reminds us of Naomi blessing her daughters-in-law in the previous chapter.

Boaz notices Ruth. Does he notice Ruth because she's the one person there whom he has never before seen or does he notice Ruth because she's attractive? Yes! Men notice attractive women. What's striking, however, is that Ruth's physical appearance is never described by the narrator. The narrator of the book of Job told us that Job's daughters were the most beautiful in the land (Job 42:15). Later in the Ketuvim, we will read of Esther, who is described as being beautiful (Esth 2:7). Why is the narrator of Ruth silent on the question of Ruth's looks if she is, in fact, beautiful? *It's because the most attractive thing about Ruth is her character.* By downplaying Ruth's looks, the writer shines the spotlight on Ruth's deeds.

Boaz asks the foreman, "Whose young woman is this?" (Ruth 2:5). Not "who," but "*whose*." Women were thought of as belonging to a man, whether a father or a husband. The foreman's response is difficult to translate. He tells Boaz that Ruth is a Moabite who returned with Naomi. Boaz knows Naomi, of course. The foreman also mentions how hard Ruth had been working. The ESV's translation probably conveys the meaning of the difficult Hebrew: "So [Ruth] came, and she has continued from early morning until now, except for a short rest" (Ruth 2:7). Ruth has a strong work ethic.

Boaz then approaches Ruth and talks to her:

Now, listen, my daughter, do not go to glean in another field or leave this one, but keep close to my young women. Let your eyes be on the field that they are reaping, and go after them. Have I not charged the young men not to touch you? And when you are thirsty, go to the vessels and drink what the young men have drawn. (Ruth 2:8–9)

Contemporary American readers ought not be dismayed about Boaz calling Ruth "daughter." When I brought this up in class, one student (who happened to be male), thought this pet name was bizarre, even creepy. Two young women in the class, one Austrian/Croatian and the other Russian, looked at each other and smiled, thinking the same thing. "In our culture," they said, "it's common for men to call women who aren't their daughters 'daughter.'" We'll have the same issue when we look at the Song of Songs, for the man in the Song calls his lover "sister." None of this is meant to be incestuous. We must remember not to divorce the characters in the Bible from their cultural context. We must also remember that we are part of a culture as well. You can imagine how off-putting it might be for someone from another culture to hear an American call his sweetheart "baby"!

Having said that, it's noteworthy that Boaz calls Ruth "daughter" rather than "sister." Calling her "daughter" indicates that he's quite older than she is. We'll return to that issue later.

Boaz wants Ruth to stay with the young women, not the young men, and he's commanded the young men not to "touch her." He knows Ruth is vulnerable because she's a woman from another country without a husband or a father, and her home country happens to be a country that does not get along with Israel. In light of #metoo, Boaz's words come across as extraordinary. He's no Harvey Weinstein or Roger Ailes. He will not tolerate sexual harassment or sexual abuse in his field. He makes sure Ruth is protected.

But are Boaz's motives so pure? *Of course* he tells Ruth to stay near the young women; he doesn't want the competition from the young men! *Of course* he commands the young men not to touch her; he wants to be the only one who will get to do that! *Of course* he's nice to her; she's caught his fancy![8]

Did the writer mean for Boaz's words to be ambiguous? I don't think it matters. Virtually anything anyone says can have more than one interpretation. The cynical interpretation cannot be deemed wrong, though I choose to view Boaz in a charitable light. I don't see anything in the book that makes me think Boaz is anything like Samson or the Levite of Judg 19, let alone the gang of Gibeah.

Ruth is tremendously humbled by Boaz's kindness: "Why have I found favor in your eyes, that you should take notice of me, since I am a foreigner?" (Ruth 2:10).[9] Boaz's response reveals that he knew more about her than he let on to his foreman:

8. Tolkien, *The Lord of the Rings*, loc. 1040.

9. The words "take notice of me" and "foreigner" are contronyms. See Sacks, *Ceremony and Celebration*, 315.

A Celebration of Kindness

All that you have done for your mother-in-law since the death of your husband has been fully told to me, and how you left your father and mother and your native land and came to a people that you did not know before. The LORD repay you for what you have done, and a full reward be given you by the LORD, the God of Israel, under whose wings you have come to take refuge! (Ruth 2:11–12)

Notice the words "all that you have *done . . .*" He is gracious, not because of her looks, but because of her deeds. These two characters are both tremendously touched by what the other has done. Boaz's description of Ruth's actions reminds us of Abraham. Abraham's sojourn into Canaan was what brought Israel into existence. Might Ruth's sojourn to the same land be as consequential? The difference between Abraham and Ruth is that Abraham's sojourn was a stunning act of obedience to a command; Ruth's sojourn is a stunning act of kindness.[10] She sacrificed her security to be with her mother-in-law.

Then comes the third benediction in the book. Naomi had blessed her daughters-in-law, Boaz and his workers had blessed each other, and now Boaz blesses Ruth, wishing that her deeds of kindness be rewarded by God.

Boaz knows that Ruth has adopted Yahweh as her god. He gives a poetic description of Ruth's conversion. Ruth has "taken refuge" under God's "wings." This phrase is found nowhere else in the Tanakh except for the book of Psalms:

- "How precious is your steadfast love, O God! The children of mankind take refuge in the shadow of your wings" (Ps 36:7[8]).

- "Be merciful to me, O God, be merciful to me, for in you my soul takes refuge; in the shadow of your wings I will take refuge, till the storms of destruction pass by" (Ps 57:1[2]).

- "Let me dwell in your tent forever! Let me take refuge under the shelter of your wings!" (Ps 61:4[5])

- "He will cover you with his pinions, and under his wings you will find refuge; his faithfulness is a shield and buckler" (Ps 91:4).

Reading Ruth in the Ketuvim highlights this connection with Psalms.

"I have found favor in your eyes, my lord," Ruth says, "for you have comforted me and spoken kindly to your servant, though I am not one of your servants" (Ruth 2:13). This is the third time Ruth has mentioned finding favor in one's eyes (see Ruth 2:2, 10). She had hoped that she would find favor in someone's eyes, and it has happened!

The word "kindly" is not a translation of *hesed*. Ruth literally says, ". . . you have comforted me and spoken upon the heart of your servant." The sentiment, however, is synonymous with *hesed* and thus "kindly" is a good translation. These characters are throwing kindness at each another, paying it back and paying it forward. Boaz's

10. Tull, *Esther and Ruth*, loc. 1214–15

141

kindness is further exemplified in the next paragraph in which he lets Ruth eat at his table and lets her glean a generous amount of grain.

When Ruth returns to Naomi, we see life return to Naomi for the first time. "Blessed be the man who took notice of you," she says (Ruth 2:19). The reader can hear the excitement in her voice. When Ruth tells Naomi who this mystery man is, Naomi reiterates the blessing with more intensity: "May he be blessed by the LORD, whose kindness has not forsaken the living or the dead!" (Ruth 2:20). This is the fourth benediction in the book. The word "kindness" here is indeed the translation of *hesed*. This is not only the second time Naomi has used that word, it's also the second time she's referred to kindness toward "the living and the dead" (Ruth 1:8). Just as her daughters-in-law had showed kindness to their husbands and to Naomi, now someone else is showing the same breadth of kindness.

But who is Naomi referring to? Is God the one who is showing kindness, or is it Boaz? Ruth 2:20 is somewhat ambiguous. It probably refers to Boaz, but even if that's the case, Naomi doesn't view God negatively. Despite her losses, she views God as the rewarder of those who do acts of kindness. We can legitimately say that God's kindness is being manifested through the generosity of Boaz.

Naomi reveals to Ruth what the narrator had told the reader in the very beginning of the chapter: Boaz is a relative of Elimelech. "[He is] one of our redeemers," she says (Ruth 2:20). This is the first time the word "redeemer" appears in the book. Naomi is ecstatic because Boaz can lift them out of their situation. How he will do that is not yet stated.

Ruth tells Naomi that Boaz instructed her to "keep close" to the young *men* (Ruth 2:21). That, however, is precisely *not* what Boaz told her! Did Ruth get confused? Boaz told the young men not to "reproach" and "rebuke" Ruth when she gleans (Ruth 2:15–16), but he explicitly told Ruth to follow the young *women*, not the young men (Ruth 2:8–9). Naomi is alarmed that Ruth would go after the young men. "It is good, my daughter, that you go out with his young women, lest in another field you be assaulted," she says (Ruth 2:22).[11] What's interesting is how similar Naomi's response is to Boaz's. Both Boaz and Naomi call Ruth "daughter." It makes sense for Naomi to do so, but the fact that we just read Boaz calling Ruth "daughter" makes us think of Naomi and Boaz as parental figures—figures of authority and action—and Ruth as the child, the one acted upon and told what to do. Likewise, both Boaz and Naomi warn Ruth of danger. This danger is very real; we should not look upon it lightly. However, it may also be true that both Boaz and Naomi have things in mind other than Ruth's safety.

---

11. The NRSV's translation of these verses is inadequate because it neutralizes the gender of the word "servants" in v. 21.

A Celebration of Kindness

THE REAL WONDER WOMAN

Whereas Ruth took the initiative in ch. 2, Naomi takes the initiative in ch. 3:

> My daughter, should I not seek rest for you, that it may be well with you? Is not Boaz our relative, with whose young women you were? See, he is winnowing barley tonight at the threshing floor. Wash therefore and anoint yourself, and put on your cloak and go down to the threshing floor, but do not make yourself known to the man until he has finished eating and drinking. But when he lies down, observe the place where he lies. Then go and uncover his feet and lie down, and he will tell you what to do. (Ruth 3:1–4)

Seeking "rest" for Ruth means Naomi is going to play matchmaker. Her method is quite bizarre. "Wash and anoint yourself" basically means "beautify yourself." The cloak is to hide her identity. She is to sneak in at night to the threshing floor but she's not to make a move until Boaz has eaten and drunk (or *is* drunk?). At that point, Ruth is to lie down and uncover Boaz's feet.

In the Tanakh, the word "feet" is sometimes a euphemism for male genitalia.[12] In Judg 3:24, for example, Eglon is said to have "covered his feet," which means he relieved himself. The same is true of Saul in 1 Sam 24:3. In 2 Sam 11:8, David tells Uriah to go home and "wash your feet"—meaning, have sex with your wife. So here in Ruth we are left with yet another ambiguity. This time, however, we probably do need to make a choice because it affects the plot. What was Naomi actually telling Ruth to do? Laying down next to Boaz uninvited is fairly scandalous in and of itself, but is Naomi also telling Ruth to *seduce* Boaz?

Some readers might think that "uncover his feet" must be understood literally because Naomi is a godly woman and she wouldn't tell Ruth to do something promiscuous. There are two problems with that interpretation:

1. The literal meaning of "uncover his feet" doesn't make much sense. Does it mean that Ruth is to take Boaz's sandals off? Or remove a blanket from his feet? What is the point of doing that?

2. It's fallacious to assume biblical characters cannot do something which violates Christian standards of morality. The narrator does not moralize. We're not told in the narrative when characters do bad things. We also know enough about the writing style by now to know there's no attempt by the narrator to sanitize these characters.

The argument in favor of the sexualized interpretation of Naomi's words is the following:

---

12. Tull, *Esther and Ruth*, loc. 1317.

Illuminating Counsel

1. "Uncover his feet" sounds euphemistic and would be consistent with similar uses of that phrase elsewhere in the Tanakh, as we mentioned.[13]

2. The seduction of Boaz would be yet another link between the book of Ruth and Gen 38.[14] In Gen 38, Tamar had to act to change the status quo because she was destitute without a husband and without a son. That's why she dresses as a prostitute and has sex with her father-in-law. Ruth is in the same predicament. She needs a husband and a son.

Thus Naomi tells Ruth to use her feminine wiles to bring about this intended result. All Ruth need do is initiate. Boaz will then take charge, being the manly man that he is. Again, Naomi and Boaz are like the parents. Ruth, as the "daughter," is expected to act submissively. Ruth's response to Naomi's instructions is terse, just as Naomi's response had been terse in the beginning of ch. 2. "All that you say I will do," Ruth says (Ruth 3:5).

Ruth seems to follow Naomi's directions to a T. She even "uncovers Boaz's feet" (Ruth 3:7). Despite doing everything "softly," Boaz wakes up startled. He senses someone is there but can't see who it is. "Who are you?" he asks. "I am Ruth, your servant," she says (Ruth 3:9). But then she goes beyond what Naomi says. Ruth is not the submissive little girl Naomi and Boaz think she is. Indeed, she was not submissive to Naomi when Naomi told her to go back to her mother's house (Ruth 1:16–17). Instead of letting Boaz take the lead, Ruth takes matters in her own hands: "Spread your wings over your servant, for you are a redeemer" (Ruth 3:9). "Wings" can refer to the fringes of a garment. However, we cannot forget the first time that that word was used in this book. It was Boaz who told Ruth that she had taken shelter under the Almighty's "wings" (Ruth 2:12). God had spread his wings over her. Now Ruth tells Boaz that *he* must spread *his* wings over her. Ruth is telling Boaz to marry her!

Boaz has a lengthy response:

> May you be blessed by the LORD, my daughter. You have made this last kindness greater than the first in that you have not gone after young men, whether poor or rich. And now, my daughter, do not fear. I will do for you all that you ask, for all my fellow townsmen know that you are a worthy woman. And now it is true that I am a redeemer. Yet there is a redeemer nearer than I. Remain tonight, and in the morning, if he will redeem you, good; let him do it. But if he is not willing to redeem you, then, as the LORD lives, I will redeem you. Lie down until the morning. (Ruth 3:10–13)

This is the fifth benediction in this short book. It's also the third use of the word *hesed* ("kindness"). The first kindness Boaz refers to is Ruth going to Bethlehem with Naomi. The second kindness is Ruth choosing Boaz over the young men. That Boaz

13. This is despite the fact that in Judges and Samuel the phrase is to "cover his feet" and in Ruth it's to "uncover [his] feet."

14. Sacks, *Ceremony and Celebration*, 306–8.

144

A Celebration of Kindness

mentions the "young men" is a hint that there might well be merit to the cynical reading of Boaz's instructions to Ruth in the previous chapter. Our suspicions about the age gap of the two are also confirmed.

Boaz agrees to marry her. Why? Because she's gorgeous? Perhaps. But the reason he gives is both surprising and sublime. "All my fellow townsmen know that you are a *worthy woman*," he says (Ruth 3:11).

Ruth is probably surprised to learn that she has been the topic of conversation, the talk of the town. She may be even more surprised that all the men respected her immensely. More than once we'd been given hints that Ruth might be victimized by men. Nothing of the sort has happened. No one has said anything remotely racist against Ruth. No one has done anything remotely misogynistic against her either. The Jewish people come across extraordinarily well in this book.

The men of the town know that Ruth is a "worthy woman." The translation "worthy woman" is understandable but inadequate. What Boaz actually says is, "for all my fellow townsmen know that you are an *eshet hayil*." Dear reader, I trust you recall that this is the phrase used to describe the "wonder woman" of Prov 31:10–31—the "woman of strength." That phrase is used only three times in all the Tanakh—twice in Proverbs (12:4 and 31:10) and once in Ruth (here in 3:11). Whereas the woman of Prov 31 is hypothetical and abstract, the book of Ruth puts flesh and bones on her. Ruth the Moabitess is the only real woman in the Bible to be called an *eshet hayil*.

We noted many advantages of the Old Testament's placement of Ruth after Judges and before 1 Samuel. However, the Tanakh's order is no less powerful. We've already noted the connection with Job—how Naomi, too, lost her children. We've noted the connection with Psalms—the talk of finding refuge under God's wings. And now we note the connection with Proverbs. The hypothetical woman of Prov 31 seemed like Superwoman. Ruth, though, teaches us that what makes any woman *strong* is the strength to do acts of kindness.[15] In that sense, women can be just as strong, even stronger, than men.

Remember, too, that when Boaz was introduced to the reader in Ruth 2:1, the narrator referred to him as an *ish gibbor hayil* ("a mighty man of strength"). That phrase is not unique to Ruth, but what we have here is an *ish gibbor hayil* about to marry an *eshet hayil*. This is a match made in heaven! And I think it's clear, too, that the "mightiness" of Boaz's "strength," like Ruth's, is the strength of his character rather than his muscles or his assets. This is why the translations call them "worthy." It would be a fine translation except that it obscures the linguistic connections between Proverbs and Ruth which are evident when reading the text in its original language.

Boaz, perhaps due to his excitement, speaks too soon. He agrees to marry Ruth but he then realizes there's a closer relative who has first rights to her. Ruth might be perturbed to hear that, but, from a literary perspective, it sets up a new conflict in

---

15. In the alternative order of the Ketuvim where Job precedes Proverbs, the connection between Prov 31:10 and Ruth 3:11 is even more pronounced.

the book which leads us toward the climax. Boaz promises to settle the matter in the morning. Ruth sneaks out. (Notice the scandalous nature of Ruth's presence there, although the couple might have done nothing more than lie next to each other.) Before she leaves, Boaz, once again, spoils her with grain.

When Ruth returns to Naomi, Naomi says, "Wait, my daughter, until you learn how the matter turns out, for the man will not rest but will settle the matter today" (Ruth 3:18). These are Naomi's final words in the book. Neither she nor Ruth speak in ch. 4. Nevertheless, they are both central to the events which transpire in the final act.

SWEETNESS

It's now morning and the reader has been left with a bit of suspense as to whether Boaz will get to marry Ruth. Boaz must resolve the issue by confronting the mysterious relative. Our English translations fail to capture what the Hebrew says. The ESV has Boaz say to the relative, "Turn aside, friend" (Ruth 4:1). The KJV's translation does a bit better with "Ho, such a one . . ." "Friend" and "such a one" are translations of the Hebrew words *ploni almoni*. *Ploni almoni* is kind of like "John Doe" or "so and so." The author's non-name for this character is humorous (though that's lost in the translation) and, whether for better or worse, it empties the narrative of its suspense. There's no way Ruth is going to end up with Mr. So and So! Prince Charming he is not!

Here's the conversation between Boaz and "Such a One":

> Then he said to the redeemer, "Naomi, who has come back from the country of Moab, is selling the parcel of land that belonged to our relative Elimelech. So I thought I would tell you of it and say, 'Buy it in the presence of those sitting here and in the presence of the elders of my people.' If you will redeem it, redeem it. But if you will not, tell me, that I may know, for there is no one besides you to redeem it, and I come after you." And he said, "I will redeem it." (Ruth 4:3–4)

What land?! What on earth is Boaz talking about?!

Let's back up for a moment. You'll recall one of the functions of the redeemer is to purchase the land belonging to their poor family members in order to keep said land within the family. But we were never told Ruth and Naomi had land. If they did, why did Ruth have to glean from Boaz's field? Was there *really* a parcel of land that the narrator didn't tell us about until now? Or is it possible Boaz is lying to Mr. So and So?[16] I say: Who cares?! This whole time we were led to believe the issue is Ruth, not the land. We don't care about the land; we care about her!

So and So agrees to redeem the land. His response to Boaz is just two words in Hebrew. We've seen this style of dialogue before with Ruth and Naomi—long speeches

---

16. Linafelt and Beal, *Ruth*, loc. 1792.

A Celebration of Kindness

followed by terse replies. Sometimes the long speeches have grammatical abnormalities. Boaz's words in Ruth 4:5 are another example of this. The text literally says:

> And Boaz said, "In the day when you acquire the field from the hand of Naomi; and from Ruth the Moabitess the wife of the deceased, you[17] acquire to perpetuate the name of the deceased in his inheritance."

What it sounds like Boaz is saying is that So and So is to acquire the field from Naomi *and* Ruth, and he's to acquire *the perpetuation of the deceased.* That doesn't make sense. The Jewish scribes who added the punctuation (along with the vowels) seemed to understand that the words translated "and from Ruth" belong to the clause about acquiring a wife, rather than the clause about acquiring a field. That's why they placed the half-cadence of the verse after "Naomi," which I indicated with a bold semi-colon.

Most scholars think the Hebrew word translated "and from" is a scribal mistake. They think the text should say what the ESV says it says (following the Latin translation of the Bible, called the Vulgate): "When you acquire the field from Naomi, you *also* acquire Ruth the Moabitess . . ."[18]

I wonder, though, if the dialogue is intentionally grammatically awkward. Boaz is, after all, bringing up a very sensitive issue. He wants to marry Ruth more than anything, but he has to offer her to another man. He's nervous. Maybe he stammers a bit. But he also needs to use finesse. Maybe the awkward syntax of the sentence is meant to confuse the nearer kinsman. Who knows?

In any case, it works! Our John Doe quickly backs down. He doesn't like the deal. He says marrying Ruth would "impair" his inheritance, though he doesn't explain how. Maybe So and So just doesn't want to marry a Moabite and the "impairing his inheritance" thing is an excuse. Or maybe he doesn't want to raise a child who will be a dead man's son. Doing so would mean that the field he just acquired would go to someone outside his branch of the family tree.

The narrator tells us that So and So removes his sandal and gives it to Boaz in the sight of the elders. "Now this was the custom in former times in Israel concerning redeeming and exchanging: to confirm a transaction, the one drew off his sandal and gave it to the other, and this was the manner of attesting in Israel" (Ruth 4:7). This custom seems oddly similar to Deut 25:7–10, which says:

> And if the man does not wish to take his brother's wife, then his brother's wife shall go up to the gate to the elders and say, 'My husband's brother refuses to perpetuate his brother's name in Israel; he will not perform the duty of a husband's brother to me.' Then the elders of his city shall call him and speak

---

17. The Masoretic Text literally says "I acquire . . ." However, Jewish textual tradition views this as a scribal mistake. All other ancient textual witnesses have "you acquire." Some scholars view "I acquire" as the better reading. I used to hold to this view but have since changed my mind.

18. Brotzman and Tully, *Old Testament Textual Criticism*, 201.

to him, and if he persists, saying, 'I do not wish to take her,' then his brother's wife shall go up to him in the presence of the elders and pull his sandal off his foot and spit in his face. And she shall answer and say, 'So shall it be done to the man who does not build up his brother's house.' And the name of his house shall be called in Israel, 'The house of him who had his sandal pulled off.'

There's an apparent discrepancy between Ruth and Deuteronomy. Whereas the removal of the sandal in Ruth is about finalizing a deal, in Deuteronomy it's about shaming the levir who refuses to fulfill his obligation. Just because the Torah prescribes something doesn't mean ancient Israel followed it literally. The book of Ruth is presenting a kinder version of this custom. So and So isn't shamed for rejecting Ruth. The reader is happy he rejected her because she will get to marry Boaz instead.

Modern readers might be offended by the notion of "acquiring" or "buying" or even "redeeming" a woman as one acquires a field. The men talk about Ruth as if she's a piece of property. My answer to that is to throw my hands up and say, "That's how women were viewed in the ancient world." That's not entirely true, of course. "Honor your father *and your mother*," says the commandment (Exod 20:12). It's a vast overstatement to assume that women were viewed as being no more important than a field. Ancient men loved their wives and their daughters, just as today. There were also women who were regarded as prophets, such as Miriam and Deborah. We mustn't overstate the case.

Robert Hubbard argues the word "acquire" does not mean Boaz is literally buying Ruth. Rather, it's simply the terminology of the time.[19] There's no word for "marry" in biblical Hebrew. Usually the Bible says a man "took" a wife. In some contexts, to "take" means to steal, but in other contexts it just means "marry." Moreover, in Gen 4:1 Eve says that she "acquired a man." She's referring to giving birth to her son.[20]

Having said that, I don't think the book of Ruth should be viewed as a love story. There's nothing romantic about ch. 4! The book of Ruth is a celebration of kindness, not eros.

The townsmen give Boaz their blessing:

> May the LORD make the woman, who is coming into your house, like Rachel and Leah, who together built up the house of Israel. May you act worthily in Ephrathah and be renowned in Bethlehem, and may your house be like the house of Perez, whom Tamar bore to Judah, because of the offspring that the LORD will give you by this young woman. (Ruth 4:11–12)

This is the sixth benediction in the book. Mention of Rachel and Leah is exceedingly rare in the Tanakh outside of Genesis. Rachel is mentioned in Jer 31:15, in 1 Sam 10:2, and here in Ruth. Ruth is the only book to mention Leah outside of Genesis. In

---

19. See Hubbard, *Ruth*, 243–44.

20. The "man" she gives birth to is Cain. The name "Cain" comes from the word which means "acquire."

A Celebration of Kindness

addition to that, this is the only text in the Tanakh outside of Genesis and the genealogy in Chronicles to mention Judah and Tamar's son, Perez. Rachel and Leah, Jacob's wives, built the house of Israel.[21] Tamar (who was presumably a *Canaanite*) built the tribe of Judah. The townsmen's wish is that Ruth will be like them. They are wishing for a *Moabite* woman to be like the matriarchs of Israel!

Ruth and Boaz get married and have a son. What follows in the text is immensely surprising, even confounding. It's also one of the most tender moments in the Bible:

> Then the women said to Naomi, "Blessed be the LORD, who has not left you this day without a redeemer, and may his name be renowned in Israel! He shall be to you a restorer of life and a nourisher of your old age, for your daughter-in-law who loves you, who is more to you than seven sons, has given birth to him." Then Naomi took the child and laid him on her lap and became his nurse. And the women of the neighborhood gave him a name, saying, "A son has been born to Naomi." (Ruth 4:14–17)

The women of Bethlehem, reprising the role they had at the end of ch. 1,[22] invoke the seventh and final benediction in the book. Seven is a significant number in the Bible. It usually denotes *completion*. Kindness has been expressed through words and deeds.

I distinctly remember reading the book of Ruth in Hebrew with my father. When we came to this part of the book, my father began to get choked up with emotion. It's extraordinary how such a simple narrative can be so moving. The writer has written characters we care about and with whom we identify. Whether or not we've experienced the great loss of losing a child—and I wish no one ever did—we can nevertheless empathize with Naomi, just as we empathized with Job. And when the women impart hope to this broken and bitter woman, it's as if they are speaking to all of us, regardless of our religion and ethnicity.

Naomi has a redeemer! All this time we were reading about *Ruth's* redeemer. Ruth's redeemer was Boaz. That meant that Boaz had the right to buy Naomi's land and marry Ruth (aside from the forgettable So and So, of course). But the book isn't really about the redemption of Ruth. It's about the redemption of Naomi. We don't realize that until the end, until this very moment. The women are using the word "redeemer" in a spiritual sense, which is different from every other instance of that word in this book. Naomi's redeemer is not the one who marries Naomi, nor the one who buys Naomi's field. Rather, Naomi's redeemer is the one who will be for her a "restorer of life." That phrase reminds us of Ps 23:3—"He restoreth my soul," or, more literally, "he restores my life." Naomi may be a supporting character but, unlike Ruth, Naomi has the larger character arc. At the end of ch. 1, she called herself Mara—"bitter"—like

---

21. They built the house of Israel by having children. This is seen as a positive thing in the text, for only women can perform that role. This does not imply that women don't have other roles aside from wife and mother. Deborah makes that perfectly clear.

22. Notice that the last word of dialogue in the book is spoken by women.

Job being "bitter in soul" (Job 3:20). Her redeemer, her "restorer of life," the one who nourishes her in her old age, is the one who turns her bitterness into sweetness. Her redeemer is the one who makes her Naomi again. More psalms come to mind. I can easily imagine Ps 30 coming out of Naomi's mouth: "You have turned my mourning into dancing" (Ps 30:11[12]).

Who is Naomi's redeemer? *Naomi's redeemer is Ruth's baby*! Is there anything that can melt away sadness and sweeten bitterness like the birth of a child? But there's more. The women declare: "A son has been born to *Naomi*"! Technically, a son had been born to *Ruth*. The women don't say that. They say Ruth gave birth to Naomi's son. Ruth is like a surrogate in the eyes of the women. This is important to the women because Naomi is the only character in the book who has lost her children. Now, as a grandmother, she has a son again, figuratively speaking. She's not literally his mother—she's not even literally his grandmother—but she becomes his nurse, which implies she's involved in his upbringing. Perhaps the word "godmother" is apropos.

This is yet another connection between Job and Naomi. The book of Job ends with Job having more children. It's impossible for Naomi to have more children because she's too old. And yet, the narrative finds a way for her. She does have another child—through Ruth! Both the book of Job and the book of Ruth end with the restoration of the embittered hero.

Speaking of Ruth, the women tell Naomi, ". . . your daughter-in-law who loves you, who is more to you than seven sons, has given birth to him." This is the only time in the book the word "love" is used. Ruth's love for Naomi was expressed through her kind act of staying with Naomi in Naomi's bitterness. The reader has been in awe of Ruth's kindness, as was Boaz and all Bethlehem. The only one who didn't seem to appreciate Ruth was Naomi. We noted this in ch. 1 where Naomi's response to Ruth's plea was lukewarm and where Naomi said she returned "empty" even though she had her daughter-in-law with her. It's the women, here at the end, who tell Naomi what we've wanted to tell her all along. Naomi was never "empty," despite the magnitude of her tragedy, because she has the best, most loyal companion anyone could ever hope for. Naomi is not alone because she has Ruth.

Does Naomi accept what the women say? The narrator has silenced Naomi. I've known people who haven't learned to appreciate what they have because they can't get over what they've lost. Most readers probably assume she accepts their words. After all, she does take the child and puts him on her lap. The book of Ruth reminds us to appreciate those who love us—the Ruths in our lives. Proverbs 18:24 says "there is a friend who sticks closer than a brother." And there's a daughter-in-law who sticks closer than seven sons.

"More to you than *seven* sons . . ." When it comes to friendship, quality trumps quantity. Having a lot of friends doesn't mean you have good friends. People have thousands of "friends" on Facebook, but many of those friends are not true friends.

A Celebration of Kindness

Your true friends are those who stick by you in your sadness. Your sadness is their sadness. And your true friends will never envy you, but will celebrate your successes.

And now the great surprise ending: Ruth's baby is the grandfather of King David! Reading the book of Ruth in the Old Testament has quite a different effect than reading it in the Tanakh. When Ruth is read in the Old Testament, the ending leaves the novice reader with a question. The novice reader has not yet heard of David. It can be inferred that David is important, but how so? Then, sixteen chapters later, the reader learns who David is. In Old Testament hindsight, Ruth becomes a bridge connecting Judges (the pre-monarchical period) with 1 Samuel (the monarchical period).

The Tanakh, however, has pushed Ruth to the back of the Bible. By the time the novice reader reads Ruth in the Tanakh, the reader already knows who David is. But that's precisely what makes the Tanakh's order more effective than the Old Testament's. Instead of being left to wonder who this David is, the reader reads with amazement that this Ruth the Moabite is David's great-grandmother. The Old Testament's order makes 1 Samuel a sequel to Ruth. The Tanakh's order makes Ruth a *prequel* to 1 Samuel. I think the latter is far more interesting, especially since the book of Ruth waits until the very end to mention David. The reader thinks the book of Ruth is about Ruth. It *is* about Ruth, but it's about much more than her. The characters in the book don't realize that. They never learn that their actions—their little acts of kindnesses—have profound and long-lasting consequences.

David helps us understand Ruth more than Ruth helps us understand David. Recognizing that David is Ruth's great-grandson causes us to realize the importance of Ruth's actions, particularly the initial decision to leave Moab and live in Bethlehem with Naomi. If Ruth hadn't made that decision, there would be no David. If there's no David, there would have been no Jerusalem, no Solomon, no temple, and—from a Christian perspective—no Jesus. Ruth's act of leaving with Naomi is one of the most consequential acts in the entire Bible. Moreover, David's lineage makes us realize the importance of Tamar. If Tamar had not disguised herself as a prostitute and had sex with her father-in-law—if she never conceived Perez—there would likewise be no David. The actions of these women—these *foreign* women—changed the course of Israel's history.

Ruth became like Rachel and Leah! I'm certain the reader is meant to see the hand of God in this. We see God's fingerprint on the genealogy. There are ten generations from Perez to David. Boaz is the seventh from Perez. We see the same thing in Genesis. There are ten generations from Adam to Noah. Enoch, the one who "walks" with God, is the seventh from Adam. Likewise there are ten generations from Noah to Abraham. Seven and ten are important biblical numbers. Though the narrator has been coy about God's actions compared to other books of the Bible, it's clear that God answered the wish of the townsmen and made Ruth's son—well, at least her son's grandson—renowned in all Israel and the world.

MOABITES

The book of Ruth has explained for us the custom of Levirate marriage. The relative of the dead husband marries the sonless widow and gives him a son so that the dead husband's lineage will continue. This is *not* what happens in Ruth. There is a genealogical shift of sorts. The women declare Ruth's son, Obed, to be Naomi's son. When the genealogy is given, Obed is said to be the son of Boaz, not the son of Mahlon. The same thing is true with Perez. According to the custom, Perez is supposed to be the son of Er. The genealogy states, however, that Perez is the son of Judah (1 Chr 2:4). Perhaps Levirate marriage worked better in theory than in practice.

More significant, however, is Ruth's subversion of Deuteronomy's view of the Moabites. Deuteronomy 23:3–6 says:

> No Ammonite or Moabite may enter the assembly of the LORD. Even to the tenth generation, none of them may enter the assembly of the LORD forever, because they did not meet you with bread and with water on the way, when you came out of Egypt, and because they hired against you Balaam the son of Beor from Pethor of Mesopotamia, to curse you. But the LORD your God would not listen to Balaam; instead the LORD your God turned the curse into a blessing for you, because the LORD your God loved you. You shall not seek their peace or their prosperity all your days forever.

As the book of Job had subverted the Retribution Principle, which is so much part and parcel of Deuteronomy's theology, so the book of Ruth subverts Deuteronomy's view of Moabites. Deuteronomy condemns the Moabites for denying the Israelites food. In Ruth, a famished Israelite family from Bethlehem ("House of Bread") goes to Moab to receive food. Deuteronomy says no Moabite is allowed in God's assembly up to the tenth generation. Ruth says that Israel's greatest king had Moabite blood in him.[23]

I don't mean to suggest that the book of Ruth thinks Deuteronomy is wrong or inherently racist. But Ruth does counterbalance Deuteronomy, preventing a racist interpretation of it. The Moabites *had* treated Israel horribly, but reading Deuteronomy alone, apart from Ruth, might breed resentment.

KINDNESS

Job's name has become synonymous with suffering, but suffering is just as much an issue in the book of Ruth as in the book of Job. Yet the book of Ruth has a different response to suffering than the book of Job and the previous books in the Ketuvim. We've noted Psalms' response to suffering is prayer. Proverbs' is wisdom. Job's is humility. Ruth's response to suffering is *kindness*. Naomi blesses people despite her bitterness.

23. Some people think 1 Samuel gives clues that David is of Moabite descent. When David is running from Saul, he entrusts his parents to the king of Moab (1 Sam 22:3–4). However, when David subdues Moab he has Moabites lie on the ground and kills two thirds of them (2 Sam 8:2).

A Celebration of Kindness

Ruth leaves everything to be with Naomi. Boaz provides food for Ruth and Naomi. Boaz is touched that Ruth has chosen him despite his age—despite the fact that, in his mind, she could have any man she wants. The townsmen have the utmost respect for Ruth. Everyone becomes awed by everyone else's kindness.

I saw the musical *Les Misérables* on my thirty-fourth birthday. Rarely have I been so moved by a piece of art or entertainment. The forces of oppression, as portrayed in the show, were overwhelming. I couldn't bear to watch a woman who was abandoned by her lover, separated from her child, exploited by a cruel couple, fired from her job, forced to sell her jewelry, her hair, (in the book, her teeth), her body; a woman who was deathly sick, used and abused by a man, falsely accused, condemned by a police officer without pity. I was devastated to see the killing of a group of idealistic young rebels yearning for a freer world. A little boy is killed. So is a hapless young woman. So much pain. So much death.

Yet among the miserable ones there was one man who had had a hard life, who made mistakes, who had been severely mistreated, and who had let that mistreatment harden his heart until one act of grace changed him forever. This one man saves the life of nearly everyone he meets. He lifts a carriage off of a man's body. He adopts an orphan girl. He has the chance to kill his enemy but instead sets him free unconditionally. He carries a wounded soldier through the sewers to safety.

Watching this show made me realize that evil works quickly and broadly. One person has the power to ruin a multitude of lives. We've seen this time and again. A man with a gun massacres twenty children in minutes and an entire nation of 300 million people are brought to their knees in mourning for a month. It seems so unfair. Yet one of our greatest weapons against evil is the power to show kindness. A single person may not be able to save the whole world, to prevent genocide, to free an oppressed people. But a single person can show kindness to another person. If every individual would look upon another individual as a neighbor rather than a stranger, what a better world it would be.

Don't just wish to have someone like Ruth in your life. Become Ruth to someone else!

I think it's fitting to end this chapter with this quote from the blogpost of the late Roger Ebert:

> "Kindness" covers all of my political beliefs. No need to spell them out. I believe that if, at the end of it all, according to our abilities, we have done something to make others a little happier, and something to make ourselves a little happier, that is about the best we can do. To make others less happy is a crime. To make ourselves unhappy is where all crime starts. We must try to contribute joy to the world. That is true no matter what our problems, our health, our circumstances. We must try. I didn't always know this, and am happy I lived long enough to find it out.[24]

24. Ebert, "Go Gentle Into That Good Night."

153

9

The Power of Love
(The Song of Songs)

THE SONG OF SONGS is the most unique book of the Bible. While the Song is set in Jerusalem and Israel's countryside, it has no overt religiosity whatsoever. With the possible exception of one difficult-to-translate word, God's name—even the word "god"—is not used. The subject of the Song is not God, but *eros*. Here we have the Bible's one and only book of erotic love poetry.

The title of the Song comes from the superscription: "The Song of Songs which is Solomon's" (Song 1:1). "Song of songs" is a biblical superlative that means the "greatest song." Like Proverbs, the authorship of the Song is attributed to Solomon. Jewish tradition says Solomon wrote the Song of Songs in his youth, Proverbs when he was middle-aged, and Ecclesiastes when he was elderly.

But should we take the superscription at face value? It's likely the superscription was written by an editor long after the composition of the Song. Moreover, the linguistics of the Song seem to point to a date of composition centuries after Solomon.[1] Hence, few modern scholars accept the antiquity of the Song of Songs.[2]

For some people, however, if the Bible says Solomon wrote it, Solomon wrote it. Case closed. This is why there's often tension between the religious community and the academy. Unlike practicing believers, many modern scholars don't believe the Bible unconditionally.

Perhaps we can find a third way. There's a linguistic loophole in the superscription that we can lawyer our way through. The preposition before the name "Solomon" (which is one letter in Hebrew), which is usually translated "of"—"The song of songs which is *of* Solomon," and hence, ". . . which is Solomon's"—can also be translated

---

1. Segal, *The Song of Songs*, 150.

2. Exum, *Song of Songs*, 67. Duane Garrett argues for a tenth-century-BCE date of composition. See Garrett, *Song of Songs*, 19.

The Power of Love

"for" or "to." We could, therefore, translate the superscription, "The song of songs which is *for* Solomon," or "The song of songs which is [written] *to* Solomon." Those translations would alter the meaning of the superscription considerably. Instead of implying that Solomon is the author, they imply the Song was, in some way, dedicated to Solomon.[3] This is admittedly a legalistic interpretation, but I'm all for it if it enables us to have our cake and eat it too. The issue of authorship is *always* a hairy matter in biblical studies. The sooner we can get past it and on to the text, the better.

Because his name is in the superscription, readers tend to assume Solomon is the male lover in the Song. This assumption invites a cynical interpretation, for we cannot disassociate the Solomon of the Song of Songs from the Solomon of the historical record—the Solomon who had seven hundred wives and three hundred concubines (1 Kgs 11:3). Solomon is the Bible's polygamist extraordinaire. "Behold, you are beautiful, my darling, behold, you are beautiful," the male lover says. Yeah, yeah, yeah; blah, blah, blah. She's just wife number 452! Next month he'll be saying the same thing to wife number 453!

I'm not opposed to cynical interpretations when they're plausible. Sometimes it's difficult *not* to be cynical when love is the subject! Even so, I don't think the author wanted us to read the Song cynically. I believe the Song was written to be a celebration of love.

But there's absolutely no reason whatsoever to infer Solomon is the male lover. It's true that the male lover is occasionally called a king (Song 1:4, 12), but he's also called a shepherd (Song 1:7).[4] There are instances in which the Song makes no sense if he's Solomon. Solomon *is* featured in the Song, but he's not the male lover. He's mentioned six times, not including the superscription, each in a rather curious way.[5] The woman describes her skin as dark like Solomon's curtains (Song 1:5). There's a strange scene in ch. 3 where he's in a procession: "Behold it is the litter of Solomon!" (Song 3:7). The text says "King Solomon made himself a carriage from the wood of Lebanon" (Song 3:9). The speaker tells the "daughters of Zion" to "look upon King Solomon, with the crown with which his mother crowned him on the day of his wedding" (Song 3:11). And then at the end of the Song we're told "Solomon had a vineyard" which he "let out" to "keepers," each of whom were to "bring for its fruit a thousand pieces of silver" (Song 8:11). Then Solomon is addressed directly for the only time: "You, O Solomon, may have the thousand, and the keepers of the fruit two hundred" (Song 8:12). I can't help but think that that's a criticism of Solomon for his polyamorous lifestyle.[6] Even if it isn't meant to be a criticism, it demonstrates that Solomon is not the male lover.

3. Longman, *Song of Songs*, 88.

4. Longman, *Song of Songs*, 6.

5. Remember the number seven is significant in the Bible.

6. Segal, *The Song of Songs*, 154.

BETTER THAN WINE

The lovers in the Song are unnamed. They are simply two young people who crave each other and express their cravings with exquisite poetry. Here's the first line of poetry in the Song:

> Let him kiss me with the kisses of his mouth!
> For your love is better than wine;
>> your anointing oils are fragrant;
> your name is oil poured out;
>> therefore [maidens][7] love you.
> Draw me after you; let us run.
>> The king has brought me into his chambers. (Song 1:2–4)

The Song begins with the woman speaking and it ends with the woman speaking. In fact, the woman's voice makes up about two-thirds of the Song. It's very fitting that the Ketuvim places Ruth and the Song adjacent to each other, for Ruth features women speaking to each other more than any other book of the Bible. These books present us with a three-dimensional view of women. Women are not objects that are judged by what they can do for men. They are not either good wives or evil temptresses. They are full-fledged human beings who express their own thoughts and desires.

She wants him to kiss her. Okay, fine. But she wants him to kiss her *with kisses*. Pray tell, what else is he supposed to kiss her with?! But that's not all. She wants him to kiss her with the kisses *of his mouth*. What other option is there?! Does she consider the possibility that he might kiss her with the kisses of his *nose*?! The redundancy seems silly, but we must remember that this is Hebrew poetry. In the Tanakh, you love with love, you hate with hatred, you get angry with anger, you kiss with kisses. The mouth is mentioned because the mouth is an object of desire.[8] He will later describe her mouth as "lovely" (Song 4:3) and "like the best wine" (Song 7:9[10]). She will describe his mouth as "most sweet" (Song 5:16). From the mouth comes forth not only kisses, but sweet words, even sweet breath (Song 7:8[9]). The mouth speaks, kisses, and tastes.

Notice the change of grammar in the second line. In the first line, she speaks *about* him: "Let *him* kiss me . . ." In the second line, she speaks *to* him: "For *your* love . . ." The change from third person to second person is a common feature in Hebrew poetry. We've already encountered it in Ps 23. Some translations have taken the liberty to erase the change of person. The JPS, for example, says, "Oh, give me of the kisses of your mouth . . ." The NET is a bit more liberal: "Oh, how I wish you would kiss me passionately!" The Blochs simply translate it, "Kiss me . . ."[9] The CEB, though, finds a way to keep

---

7. The ESV translates the Hebrew word *alamot* as "virgins." Not only is that an erroneous translation, it sounds awkward to me. Therefore, I have replaced "virgins" with the more accurate translation, "maidens."

8. Segal, *The Song of Songs*, 9.

9. Bloch and Bloch, *The Song of Songs*, 45.

the third person while also sounding contemporary: "If only he would give me some of his kisses . . ." All of these translations capture the "sense" of the Hebrew.

But "for your love is better than wine" is not an adequate translation. The Hebrew word for "love" is *ahav*. This word does occur in the Song in some very important verses, but it doesn't occur in Song 1:2. The Hebrew word in Song 1:2 is *dodekha*. *Dodekha* means "lovemaking." It's synonymously paralleled with "kisses." The NET says, "For your lovemaking is more delightful than wine." The CEB: "Oh, your loving is sweeter than wine!" Wine is not only sweet; it also intoxicates. The Blochs' translation says, "Kiss me, make me drunk with your kisses! Your sweet loving is better than wine."[10]

The Song's woman then mentions her lover's "anointing oils." He's wearing cologne. She's drawn to his scent. The Song reminds us how sensual lovemaking is.

The woman wants her lover to "draw" her to him. This reflects virtually every male-female romantic initiation. Our culture expects the man to initiate contact with the woman. In actuality, the woman sends him nonverbal cues, giving him the green light to "come hither."[11] This is precisely what happens in the beginning of the Song. She doesn't want to kiss him per se; she wants *him* to kiss her. Such is the way of a man and a maiden—the thing which confounded Agur (Prov 30:19).

Looking at other translations will help us understand the second part of Song 1:4. The JPS says, "Let us delight and rejoice in your love, savoring it more than wine." I think the JPS is correct to translate the first Hebrew word as "let us" rather than "we will." The CEB's translation is very similar: "Let's exult and rejoice in you. Let's savor your loving more than wine." "Savor" is a much better translation than the ESV's "extol." The Hebrew word literally means "remember." Lovemaking is memorable! It's sweeter and more intoxicating than wine. It's joyous! As Ruth is a celebration of kindness, so the Song of Songs is a celebration of sex.

KEEPER OF THE VINEYARDS

The woman says:

> I am very dark, but lovely,
>> O daughters of Jerusalem,
> like the tents of Kedar,
>> like the curtains of Solomon.
> Do not gaze at me because I am dark,
>> because the sun has looked upon me.
> My mother's sons were angry with me;
>> they made me keeper of the vineyards,
>> but my own vineyard I have not kept! (Song 1:5–6)

10. Bloch and Bloch, *The Song of Songs*.

11. Legato, *Why Men Never Remember and Women Never Forget*, 30.

Illuminating Counsel

The translation of Song 1:5 is controversial. The contention is over the word "but," which is the translation of one Hebrew letter. It certainly can be translated "but," yet it can also be translated "and." Some people think "but" has racist overtones.[12] It makes it seem like she's apologizing for being black—that she's saying she's beautiful *despite* her blackness. Hence the NRSV translates it, "I am black *and* beautiful."

While it's true that beauty comes in every spectrum of skin tone, it's a mistake to read modern racial issues into the Song. The woman in the Song is Jewish. Her natural skin color would have been olive. She implies she had an unnaturally strong tan. She's embarrassed about it. This is why she tells the women not to look at her. (The poetry is clever. "Do not *gaze* at me . . . because the sun has *looked* upon me.") Her brothers are to blame for her excessive tanning. They were angry with her for some unmentioned reason, though perhaps it had something to do with a boy. A father is never mentioned in the Song. The brothers seem to take on the role of guardian of their sister (see also Song 8:8–9). Not surprisingly, she thinks they're too strict. To keep her out of trouble, they make her "keep" the vineyards (no pun intended).

With the word "vineyards" we have the first clear use of the Song's favorite poetic device: the double entendre. On the surface, she's saying she worked outside in the hot sun, tending to the vineyards of others, but she didn't get to tend her own vineyard. The deeper meaning, however, is that *she* is a vineyard. She's saying she has not kept up her appearance. She confidently declares she's "lovely," but she doesn't look her best because of her tan.

I wonder, though, if there's an even deeper meaning. Because she was sent to tend the vineyards, she has not had the chance to be with her love interest—the one she refers to as "you whom my soul loves," or, as we would put it, "the love of my life." She longs for him. She calls out to him across the distance, asking where he is:

> Tell me, you whom my soul loves,
>> where you pasture your flock,
>> where you make it lie down at noon;
> for why should I be like one who veils herself
>> beside the flocks of your companions? (Song 1:7)

The Hebrew doesn't say "flock." It literally says, "Tell me . . . where you pasture, where you make lie down at noon." The words "you make [it] lie down" are the translation of one Hebrew word, which is the same verb used in Ps 23:2—"He makes me lie down in green pastures." Might this be another double entendre? Maybe she wants him to "lie *her* down," as it were.[13]

Commentators argue over whether "like one who veils herself" is the best translation. Without going into the complex textual issues, let it suffice to say she wants to know where he is so she can go to him. She doesn't want his companions. She wants only him.

---

12. Weems, *What Matters Most*, 31–34.

13. Exum, *Song of Songs*, 106–7.

The Power of Love

He speaks for the first time, responding to her, in Song 1:8:

> If you do not know,
>> O most beautiful among women,
> follow in the tracks of the flock,
>> and pasture your young goats
>> beside the shepherds' tents.

The lovers in the Song are rarely together. The Song begins with them separated, the Song ends with them separated, and the moments in the Song when they are not separated are quite brief. When they do come together, the Song quickly thrusts them apart again. Robert Alter argues the apartness of the lovers serves as a literary device to create tension; their coming together relieves the tension, like the way musical dissonance resolves to consonance.[14] Kathryn Harding, writing from a feminist perspective, views it as expressing not only the woman's desire for love but also her anxiety concerning the relationship and her yearning to find her own identity.[15] Rabbi Shmuley Boteach uses the apartness of the lovers to make a point about eroticism. "Lust is awakened through obstacles and absence," he says.[16] Absence not only makes the heart grow fonder, it keeps the flame of passion burning.

It's not always easy to know who's speaking in the Song when reading it in English. English doesn't have gender distinctions as do many other languages, including Hebrew. The translator helps us know who's speaking by giving us a subtitle. In Hebrew, the grammar makes it clear who's speaking. *Hinakh yafah*—"Behold, you are beautiful" (Song 1:15). Those two words are in the feminine form, which indicates they are spoken *to* a woman. *Hinkha yafeh*—"Behold, you are beautiful" (Song 1:16). These are the exact same words, but in the masculine form, which indicates they are spoken *to* a man. The two lovers thus exchange the same compliments to each other.

It's interesting how they have pet names for each other. She calls him "you whom my soul loves." He calls her "most beautiful among women." He also calls her *rayati*. This word comes from the Hebrew word for "friend" (it's often translated "neighbor"). The KJV translates it "my love." I prefer to translate it "my darling" in order to distinguish it from *ahav*—the more proper word for "love."[17] His compliment—"your eyes are doves" (Song 1:15)—is repeated with variation later in the Song.

MY BELOVED IS MINE

We have a tender exchange of dialogue in the beginning of the second chapter. The woman says:

---

14. Alter, "The Song of Songs," 24–32, 52.

15. Harding, "I Sought Him," 58–59.

16. Boteach, *Kosher Lust*, 122.

17. This is how Segal translates it. Segal, *The Song of Songs*, 17.

Illuminating Counsel

> I am a rose of Sharon,
>   a lily of the valleys. (Song 2:1)

(Sharon is a plain in Israel by the coast of the Mediterranean Sea.) She's saying she's beautiful, but so are a lot of other women. She's beautiful, but not special. He thinks otherwise:

> As a lily among brambles,
>   so is my love among the young women. (Song 2:2)

No, he says. You *are* special. All women are shrubs compared to you! He meant what he said when he called her "most beautiful among women" (Song 1:8)!

She returns the sentiment:

> As an apple tree among the trees of the forest,
>   so is my beloved among the young men. (Song 2:3)

He's uniquely handsome as she is beautiful. All the other young men and young women disappear in the background. The two lovers see only each other.

She then turns her "apple tree" analogy into a metaphor. He's not *like* an apple tree; he *is* an apple tree. Thus she says:

> With great delight I sat in his shadow,
>   and his fruit was sweet to my taste.
> He brought me to the banqueting house,
>   and his banner over me was love.
> Sustain me with raisins;
>   refresh me with apples,
>   for I am sick with love.
> His left hand is under my head,
>   and his right hand embraces me!

Here we have more double entendres. Making love is described as eating fruit. The lovers are tasting each other. His lovemaking is refreshing and sustaining. It's sweet as raisins and apples. It's intoxicating as wine. She is "sick with love." That phrase doesn't mean "lovesick," which in modern vernacular refers to someone who's heartbroken. The Blochs translate the line beautifully: "for I am in a fever of love."[18] The woman is conveying how intense her passions are.

Then comes a refrain:

> I adjure you, O daughters of Jerusalem,
>   by the gazelles or the does of the field,
> that you not stir up or awaken love
>   until it pleases. (Song 2:7)

---

18. Bloch and Bloch. *The Song of Songs*, 57.

The Power of Love

What does that mean? We could interpret it as something like a "do not disturb" sign.[19] She knows the "daughters of Jerusalem" want her man (Song 1:3—"maidens love you") and she's a bit jealous. So she tells them, "Back off! He's mine! Don't interfere!" But we can also interpret the refrain as her warning the "daughters of Jerusalem" about the dangers of love. She's telling them not to fall in love too quickly. Don't fall in love when you're not ready to consummate it because the heat of your passion might consume you.[20]

The next section is like a rhapsody on the apartness of the lovers.

> The voice of my beloved!
>> Look, he comes,
> leaping upon the mountains,
>> bounding over the hills.
> My beloved is like a gazelle
>> or a young stag.
> Look, there he stands
>> behind our wall,
> gazing in at the windows,
>> looking through the lattice. (Song 2:8–9)

She hears him before she can see him. Then she sees him at a great distance because he's on the mountains. He makes his way toward her, "leaping," just as she had told him to "run" (Song 1:4). He has gotten closer, but they're not yet together. He's now on the other side of her wall. He moves closer still. He can eye her through the window. Alas, they're still separated. Therefore, as she tells us, he calls to her in an effort to overcome their separation:

> Arise, my love, my fair one,
>> and come away;
> for now the winter is past,
>> the rain is over and gone.
> The flowers appear on the earth;
>> the time of singing has come,
> and the voice of the turtledove
>> is heard in our land.
> The fig tree puts forth its figs,
>> and the vines are in blossom;
>> they give forth fragrance.
> Arise, my love, my fair one,
>> and come away.
> O my dove, in the clefts of the rock,
>> in the covert of the cliff,

19. Gault, "A 'Do Not Disturb' Sign?," 95.

20. Segal, *The Song of Songs*, 23.

let me see your face,
    let me hear your voice;
for your voice is sweet,
    and your face is lovely.
Catch us the foxes,
    the little foxes,
that ruin the vineyards—
    for our vineyards are in blossom. (Song 2:10–15)

He cannot see her face or hear her voice. Thus he calls her, drawing her to himself, drawing her away from everyone and everything. How he longs to see and hear her in all her glory! Yet she's hidden from him, hidden in the "clefts of the rock." And that's hardly their only obstacle. There are "foxes" which "ruin the vineyards," which interfere with their lovemaking. These foxes, however little they may be, must be removed, for desire is stirred and cannot bear to wait any longer.

Her response leaves no doubt about their situation:

My beloved is mine and I am his;
    he pastures his flock among the lilies.
Until the day breathes
    and the shadows flee,
turn, my beloved, be like a gazelle
    or a young stag on the cleft mountains. (Song 2:16–17)

Emotionally they are united, but physically they are apart. Thus she bids him "turn" so they can be together.

I SOUGHT HIM

She says:

On my bed by night
I sought him whom my soul loves;
    I sought him, but found him not.
I will rise now and go about the city,
    in the streets and in the squares;
I will seek him whom my soul loves.
    I sought him, but found him not. (Song 3:1–2)

The notion of her seeking him while on her bed makes the whole scene seem like a dream. Indeed, while there's some sort of a drama in the Song, it's much more like a ballet than a movie.

The Power of Love

She gets up, seemingly in the middle of the night, and searches for her beloved in the city. We must pay attention to v. 3 because it will be repeated with variation in ch. 5:

> The watchmen found me
>> as they went about in the city.
> "Have you seen him whom my soul loves?" (Song 3:3)

The watchmen (literally the "keepers of the city") don't have a chance to give her an answer. She suddenly finds him:

> I held him, and would not let him go
>> until I had brought him into my mother's house,
>> and into the chamber of her who conceived me. (Song 3:4)

It might seem strange that she would bring him into her mother's house. Wouldn't they prefer to be in a more neutral location? Perhaps the emphasis on the mother is meant to hint that that's what this young woman will eventually become.[21] Her mother's "chamber" reminds us of the king's chambers in Song 1:4. Thus sexual relations is implied. We then get a second "adjure" refrain:

> I adjure you, O daughters of Jerusalem,
>> by the gazelles or the does of the field,
> that you not stir up or awaken love
>> until it pleases. (Song 3:5)

Again, either, "Back off! He's mine!" or "Guard your heart because love, though wonderful, can also be dangerous!"

BEHOLD, YOU ARE BEAUTIFUL

In ch. 4, the male voice dominates the Song for the first time. He describes her body, starting with her head, and then moves downward. This style of poetry is referred to as a *wasf*—an Arabic word which means "description."

He begins his description of her by developing what he said in Song 1:15:

> Behold, you are beautiful, my love,
>> behold, you are beautiful!
> Your eyes are doves
>> behind your veil. (Song 4:1)

Unlike Roxanne's dimwitted handsome love interest in *Cyrano de Bergerac*, the male lover in the Song rhapsodizes on the theme of his beloved's beauty. The man uses similes to describe her beauty, likening her to aspects of nature. But it is here that the

21. Segal, *The Song of Songs*, 33.

Illuminating Counsel

modern reader encounters a problem. Likening her eyes to doves seems sweet, but in Song 1:9 he likened her to one of Pharaoh's mares, which hardly sounds romantic to twenty-first-century ears. "You look like a horse" won't work on the twenty-first-century woman! Neither will this:

> Your hair is like a flock of goats
>> leaping down the slopes of Gilead. (Song 4:1)

I'm not an expert on the ways of a man and a maiden, but methinks likening your sweetheart's hair to a flock of goats probably wouldn't go over well! And maybe one shouldn't compliment a woman's teeth like this:

> Your teeth are like a flock of shorn ewes
>> that have come up from the washing,
> all of which bear twins,
>> and not one among them has lost its young.

He's saying she's beautiful because she has all her teeth.[22] That's not a very high standard of beauty. The next line, though, is endearing:

> Your lips are like a scarlet thread,
>> and your mouth is lovely.
> Your cheeks are like halves of a pomegranate
>> behind your veil. (Song 4:3)

Likening her lips to a scarlet thread may not be something that a young man today might say, but it doesn't seem as strange as likening her hair to a flock of goats.

But when it comes to her mouth, he's at a loss for words. He has nothing with which to compare her mouth, so he simply says it's "lovely." "Lovely" is the same word that she used to describe herself in Song 1:5 ("I am dark but *lovely*").

The pomegranate simile seems to work too, for the seeds sort of look like teeth.[23] Dante Gabriel Rossetti, one of the Pre-Raphaelite painters, juxtaposes a pomegranate and lips in his masterpiece, *Proserpine*.

Next he talks about her neck:

> Your neck is like the tower of David,
>> built in rows of stone;
> on it hang a thousand shields,
>> all of them shields of warriors. (Song 4:4)

What woman wouldn't want her man to liken her neck to a skyscraper?! What's really interesting is that he embellishes the simile. Instead of describing her actual neck, he describes the tower of David. It's got rows of stone and shields—a thousand

---

22. Longman, *Song of Songs*, 144.

23. Segal, *The Song of Songs*, 41.

The Power of Love

shields—shields of warriors. He talks more about the tower than about her. He's clearly excited, but is he eloquent?

Her breasts are the final destination of this *wasf*:

> Your two breasts are like two fawns,
>> twins of a gazelle,
>> that graze among the lilies. (Song 4:5)

Some may wonder what fawns have to do with breasts. Segal thinks he's referring to the heads of the fawns as they bend down to graze.[24] He probably also has her breasts in mind when he speaks of going "away to the mountain of myrrh, to the hill of frankincense" (Song 4:6). Mountain . . . hill . . . get it?

Students always give me the same reaction when I read ch. 4 in class. The flock of goats, the shorn ewes, and the two fawns make my students laugh. But then I read these words to them and the laughter ceases immediately:

> You have captivated my heart, my sister, my bride;
>> you have captivated my heart with one glance of your eyes,
>> with one jewel of your necklace.
> How beautiful is your love, my sister, my bride!
>> How much better is your love than wine,
>> and the fragrance of your oils than any spice!
> Your lips drip nectar, my bride;
>> honey and milk are under your tongue;
>> the fragrance of your garments is like the fragrance of Lebanon. (Song 4:9–11)

You can hear a pin drop in the classroom! His descriptions of her may be antiquated, but the Song remains a powerful expression of *eros*. His passion for her takes the breath away from my eighteen-year-old students, both male and female.

I would like to say more in defense of his descriptions. Certainly there are some rather weak one-to-one correspondences between her body and the thing he compares it to. The point, however, is not that the thing, such as the flock of goats or the fawns, looks exactly like her body. The comparison is between her beauty, which is nearly indescribable, and the beauty of nature. To a man in love, there is nothing in all the world more beautiful than his beloved's body. It's more lovely than the most splendid sunset, than the most colorful flower, than the most exquisite jewel. It's more delectable than the sweetest fruit, more exquisite than any painting, more marvelous than the most majestic symphony. Its beauty surpasses that of any creation—divine and human. This is why the man cannot use just one simile or metaphor to encapsulate his darling. I don't think ancient women reading the Song would have laughed or been offended by his similes. I think they would have blushed.

---

24. Segal, *The Song of Songs*, 42.

The temperature of his passion rises in Song 4:12, which is the beginning of the climax. This is where the word "garden"—one of the most important metaphors in the Song—is first used:

> A garden locked is my sister, my bride,
>> a spring locked, a fountain sealed.
> Your shoots are an orchard of pomegranates
>> with all choicest fruits,
>> henna with nard,
> nard and saffron, calamus and cinnamon,
>> with all trees of frankincense,
> myrrh and aloes,
>> with all choice spices—
> a garden fountain, a well of living water,
>> and flowing streams from Lebanon. (Song 4:12–15)

Longman argues the "garden" refers to her vagina. If that's the case, then what do the "shoots" represent? Longman says they refer to her pubic hairs.[25] I don't agree. It's not that I think the Song couldn't refer to something so intimate. Rather, I think that that interpretation is too literal. This is poetry, not code. As we said above, the similes shouldn't be interpreted as pure one-to-one comparisons with her body. In my judgment, the "garden" is not her vagina specifically, but her whole body (which, of course, includes her vagina—something he, no doubt, has a keen interest in). The "shoots" represent the aspects of her body. He mentions fruits and spices. He wants to taste and smell. I don't think he merely wants to taste her vagina; he wants to taste *all of her*.

But she's "locked." Since he cannot "enter," he will be content to take whatever he can get. Just a whiff, perhaps:

> Awake, O north wind,
>> and come, O south wind!
> Blow upon my garden,
>> let its spices flow. (Song 4:16)

She responds:

> Let my beloved come to his garden,
>> and eat its choicest fruits. (Song 4:16)

What is she *doing* with these words? *She's giving him consent!* Theoretically he could "break in," forcing his way to the garden of her body, the way a thief breaks a lock to enter a building. But he won't do that. He will *not* force himself upon her. He will not violate her in any way. He loves her, and respects women in general. Millennia later we're still struggling with this. Yes, the Song of Songs preaches. The values of the Song shame the lewd actions of fake male feminists.

25. Longman, *Song of Songs*, 156.

The Power of Love

Lovemaking is implied in the very next line, which comes across the unfortunate chapter division. He says:

I came to my garden, my sister, my bride,
   I gathered my myrrh with my spice,
   I ate my honeycomb with my honey,
   I drank my wine with my milk. (Song 5:1)

This is not pornography. The purpose of the Song is not to make the reader sexually aroused. This is poetry. The purpose of the Song is to communicate the wonder, beauty, and joy of lovemaking.

Notice that she is *his* garden. She belongs to him, though that is a voluntary decision on her part. Later she will say that he belongs to her. Love is paradoxical. Lovers belong to each other and yet they're simultaneously free. This is precisely the point Paul makes in 1 Cor 7:4. "For the wife does not have authority over her own body, but the husband does," says Paul. That sounds misogynistic. But then he adds, "Likewise the husband does not have authority over his own body, but the wife does." What a radically egalitarian statement, especially when we consider when it was written!

The couple having nothing left to say since they are busy consummating their relationship. Thus the chorus has the final word in this section:

Eat, friends, drink,
   and be drunk with love! (Song 5:1)

While sexual intimacy is implied in various places in the Song (though not as often as people think), this is the most intense instance of it. Song 5:1 is the climax of the Song. This may seem strange to modern readers because it's more or less the middle of the Song, but this is typical of biblical literature. Always pay attention to the middle of a passage because often—not always, but often—that's where the most important idea or climax is located. Passages in the Bible, which are called *pericopes*, are often shaped like a mountain. The first half ascends to the apex, and the second half descends back to sea level. The Song of Songs is also circular; the ending connects back to the beginning.[26]

WHAT IS YOUR BELOVED MORE THAN ANOTHER BELOVED?

Chapter 5 begins with a recapitulation of ch. 3: "I slept, but my heart was awake," she says (Song 5:2). How can one sleep while one's heart is awake? Is she dreaming?

Suddenly there's a knock on the door. She knows who it is. Her beloved sweetly calls to her from the other side:

26. Exum, *Song of Songs*, 45.

Illuminating Counsel

> Open to me, my sister, my love,
>> my dove, my perfect one,
> for my head is wet with dew,
>> my locks with the drops of the night. (Song 5:2)

His pet names for her are so tender. They are his way of expressing how he feels about her. "Open to me" is probably meant to be a double entendre, especially since we just read about her being a locked garden. He wants her to open the door so he can get in because he's soaking wet, but he wants her to open her body to him as well. Perhaps his wetness is also meant to imply something sexual. We don't want to over-interpret, but the Song's ambiguity leaves us with many interpretive options.

Her response to his request is odd:

> I had put off my garment;
>> how could I put it on?
> I had bathed my feet;
>> how could I soil them? (Song 5:3)

So he's soaking wet but she won't let him in because . . . she can't put on her garment?! Walking from her bed to her door would get her feet dirty?! I'm thinking she's teasing him.[27] The poet is stretching out their separation in order to create tension and anticipation. It's like the characters are moving in slow motion:

> My beloved put his hand to the latch,
>> and my heart was thrilled within me. (Song 5:4)

We can almost hear her heart beating faster. Finally, she gets up:

> I arose to open to my beloved,
>> and my hands dripped with myrrh,
> my fingers with liquid myrrh,
>> on the handles of the bolt. (Song 5:5)

The "opening" (again, "the door" is not mentioned) and the myrrh lead the reader to think this encounter will lead to sexual intimacy (cf. Song 1:13; 4:6, 14; 5:1).[28] Then, finally, she opens [the door] but, like in ch. 3, he's gone. Just like in ch. 3, she goes to the city to look for him. But here's where things take a dark turn. Remember the watchmen? Song 5:7 begins exactly as Song 3:3—"The watchmen found me as they went about in the city . . ." What happens next is shocking:

> they beat me, they bruised me,
>> they took away my veil,
>> those watchmen of the walls. (Song 5:7)

---

27. Segal, *The Song of Songs*, 54.

28. Boersma, "Scent in Song," 93. Boersma argues the scene is a "conscious fantasy" and that the scent on the woman's fingers implies she had been masturbating.

The Power of Love

Even in the Song of Songs we don't escape violence! The book of Ruth hinted at the possibility of violence against women. Ruth evaded it, but our heroine in the Song does not. The removal of the veil may imply that the assault was sexual in nature. Why else would they abuse her?

What is the effect of this episode? It happens so fast that we don't have much time to process it. The Song seems to want to emphasize her determination to find her beloved. One can imagine her clothes torn, her face scratched, and her body bruised. But she gets up and doesn't say a word about it. She turns to the "daughters of Jerusalem" and we, once again, get the "adjure" refrain, only this time it contains a significant variation:

> I adjure you, O daughters of Jerusalem,
>> if you find my beloved,
> that you tell him
>> I am sick with love. (Song 5:8)

Previously she had said to her beloved, "Sustain me with raisins, refresh me with apples, for I am sick with love" (Song 2:5). Now we see the negative side of being in love. What if her beloved is not there to "sustain" and "refresh" her? In the first iteration of the "adjure" refrain, she perhaps told the "daughters of Jerusalem" to back off. But now, the fever of her love burns so hot with unquenched fire that she seeks their aid to help her find him.

The "daughters of Jerusalem" speak for the first time. They call her "most beautiful among women," which is her beloved's pet name for her (Song 1:8). Do they really think that's what she is? Or are they being sarcastic? Their reply seems rather snarky:

> What is your beloved more than another beloved,
>> O most beautiful among women?
> What is your beloved more than another beloved,
>> that you thus adjure us? (Song 5:9)

The "daughters of Jerusalem" basically say to our heroine, "Why should we help you?!" Their question creates the perfect opportunity for our heroine to give her *wasf* of her beloved:

> My beloved is radiant and ruddy,
>> distinguished among ten thousand.
> His head is the finest gold;
>> his locks are wavy,
>> black as a raven.
> His eyes are like doves
>> beside streams of water,
> bathed in milk,
>> sitting beside a full pool.
> His cheeks are like beds of spices,
>> mounds of sweet-smelling herbs.

> His lips are lilies,
>> dripping liquid myrrh.
> His arms are rods of gold,
>> set with jewels.
> His body is polished ivory,
>> bedecked with sapphires.
> His legs are alabaster columns,
>> set on bases of gold.
> His appearance is like Lebanon,
>> choice as the cedars.
> His mouth is most sweet,
>> and he is altogether desirable.
> This is my beloved and this is my friend,
>> O daughters of Jerusalem. (Song 5:10–16)

Like his *wasf* in ch. 4, hers makes use of similes and metaphors. However, her similes and metaphors are noticeably different. Absent is any talk of goats and fawns. She likens his body to metals, stones, ivory, and trees. Her description conveys *hardness*, no doubt fitting for a masculine muscular physique. He's statuesque. When she does liken him to animals, her descriptions seem more to the point. She mentions the color of his hair—"black as a raven." His black hair contrasts with the description of his head being "the finest gold." He has dark features and yet he's radiant. She even describes what kind of hair he has—"his locks are wavy." She also likens his eyes to doves, as he did with her, but she emphasizes the moistness and whiteness of his eyes by mentioning that the doves are "beside streams of water and bathed in milk." I don't think anyone today would laugh at her description, and I suspect any man would be flattered if a woman said his arms are "rods of gold."

Her *wasf* convinces the women to help her. They say to her:

> Where has your beloved gone,
>> O most beautiful among women?
> Where has your beloved turned,
>> that we may seek him with you? (Song 6:1)

All the sudden, though, she knows where he is:

> My beloved has gone down to his garden
>> to the beds of spices,
> to graze in the gardens
>> and to gather lilies. (Song 6:2)

Segal thinks the "gardens" stand for other women and she is not a little jealous.[29] That interpretation seems a bit too literal. We must be cautious not to make the Song

---

29. Segal, *The Song of Songs*, 66.

The Power of Love

logical. The Song is like a dream: there's no true beginning or ending. It just slides from one setting to the next. So now, the Song resets itself and the lovers are back together.

AWESOME AS AN ARMY WITH BANNERS

In Song 2:16, she said, "My beloved is mine and I am his; he grazes among the lilies." In Song 6:3 she flips it around: "I am my beloved's and my beloved is mine; he grazes among the lilies." This line will be repeated one last time with a more significant variation.

He responds to her with his second *wasf*. This *wasf* is similar to his first, but there are some notable differences. For example, he compares her to the cities, Tirzah and Jerusalem:

> You are beautiful as Tirzah, my love,
> > lovely as Jerusalem,
> > > awesome as an army with banners. (Song 6:4)

I've seen gorgeous, breathtaking cities. Saint Petersburg is marvelous, especially when viewed from the Peter and Paul Fortress. I've been to Paris, as well as Venice and Florence. Copenhagen is an under-appreciated beauty. London is my favorite city. Tower Bridge is nothing less than magnificent. I even find New York, where I was born and raised, to be beautiful—at least parts of it. I had chills down my spine when I beheld the new World Trade Center for the first time. I can say the same for when I first drove on Lakeshore Drive in Chicago, with Lake Michigan on one side and the skyline on the other. It's a ravishing sight.

I've been to Jerusalem too. In the Bible, Jerusalem is called "the perfection of beauty" (Ps 50:2)—the greatest of all cities. It's a very romantic thing, indeed, for the man to compare his beloved to Jerusalem. Tirzah is not described in the Bible, but the word itself means "she is my delight." And so the woman is to her beloved.

Instead of repeating the line about her eyes being doves, he says:

> Turn away your eyes from me,
> > for they overwhelm me— (Song 6:5)

Virtually nothing in all the world is more arresting to a man than the eyes of his beloved. To be overpowered by beauty is the most glorious defeat.

He then emphasizes her uniqueness:

> There are sixty queens and eighty concubines,
> > and [maidens] without number.
> My dove, my perfect one, is the only one,
> > the only one of her mother,
> > > pure to her who bore her.

Illuminating Counsel

The young women saw her and called her blessed;
>the queens and concubines also, and they praised her.
"Who is this who looks down like the dawn,
>beautiful as the moon, bright as the sun,
>>awesome as an army with banners?" (Song 6:8–10)

The "sixty queens" reminds us of the "sixty mighty men" (Song 3:7) from Solomon's procession in ch. 3, but I'm not sure what the connection is. The mention of the queens and concubines along with the young women sandwiches the description of the man's beloved. The point seems to be that she's unique. The king has a harem, but no one in the harem can compare to her. She's as beautiful as the moon and the sun. She's "awesome" and worthy of praise. Notice that the phrase "awesome as an army with banners" forms an *inclusio* with the beginning of the *wasf*. The ESV seems to think the women call her "awesome as an army with banners." If that's correct, then they see in her exactly what the man sees. It's as if his view of her awesomeness is objective rather than subjective. If everyone praises her, she must be awesome indeed.

RETURN, RETURN, O SHULAMMITE

The next section begins with men calling upon a "Shulammite" woman to "return" so that they can "look" upon her (Song 6:13[7:1]). "Shulammite" seems like a feminine version of Solomon's name (Solomon is *Shlomo* in Hebrew), although "Shulammite" is not a proper name, since she is called "the Shulammite." The root of "Shulammite" is the word *shalom*, which means "peace" or "well-being." This word appears at the end of the Song. I assume that our heroine is this Shulammite.[30]

She's dancing. This causes a change in the direction of the *wasf*. Instead of starting with the head, the man begins with her feet and works his way upward:

How beautiful are your feet in sandals,
>O noble daughter! (Song 7:1[2])

We get descriptions of parts of her body previously unmentioned. Her thighs are described as being "like jewels" (Song 7:1[2]). Her navel "is a rounded bowl that never lacks mixed wine" (Song 7:2[3]). Longman thinks "navel" is a euphemism for her vulva.[31] The metaphor of the bowl filled with wine lends itself to such a view. Her belly "is a heap of wheat, encircled by lilies" (Song 7:2[3]). Could this be referring to her pubic hairs? It's true that sometimes biblical words for body parts encompass a greater region than their English counterparts. A "hand" can include the wrist, for example. Longman also thinks her description of his "body" in ch. 5—that his body

---

30. I part ways with Segal here, for he views the desire of the Shulammite negatively—raw lust devoid of love. See Segal, *The Song of Songs*, 121–22.

31. Longman, *Song of Songs*, 194–95.

172

The Power of Love

is "polished ivory" (Song 5:14)—is referring to his penis, especially since ivory might cause one to think of a tusk.[32]

I do not interpret the text this way. My interpretation is a bit more conservative. I take "body" to refer to his chest down to his waist, and I take "navel" to refer to her navel. Maybe it encompasses more, but the text doesn't require us to be that specific. The metaphors and similes are not meant to be exact likenesses, as we discussed above. And for whatever reason, a woman's navel is very attractive in and of itself.[33] It's not unusual at all that he would refer to it.

The other thing is that his description emphasizes the roundness, or curves, of her body. Her "*rounded* thighs are like jewels." Her navel is a "*rounded* bowl." (What bowl isn't rounded?!) Her belly is a heap of wheat "*encircled* with lilies."

The curves of her body present a nice contrast to the aspects of her body that are straight. Her neck "is like an ivory tower" (Song 7:4[5]). Her nose "is like a tower of Lebanon." The point is not that she has a big nose, or at least a disproportionally big nose. (I certainly don't think a young man today should tell his sweetheart that her nose looks like the Eiffel Tower!). The point is her nose is straight and majestic.

When he gets to her head, he says her eyes are "pools" (Song 7:4[5]), and her hair is like Carmel, which is a mountain in northern Israel. Her "flowing locks" are like "purple," which was the color of royalty. Hence he says "a king is held captive in the tresses" (Song 7:5[6]). He concludes by saying:

> How beautiful and pleasant you are,
> > O loved one, with all your delights!
> Your stature is like a palm tree,
> > and your breasts are like its clusters.
> I say I will climb the palm tree
> > and lay hold of its fruit.
> Oh may your breasts be like clusters of the vine,
> > and the scent of your breath like apples,
> and your mouth like the best wine. (Song 7:6–9[7–10])

I don't think anything he says here is laughable. She is healthy looking—thin and curvy. She is sweet and delightful. The imagery conveys his desire for her. She responds with one of the sexiest lines in the Song:

> It goes down smoothly for my beloved,
> > gliding over lips and teeth. (Song 7:9[10])

She then repeats the "I am his, he is mine" refrain, but does so with a significant variation:

---

32. Longman, *Song of Songs*, 173.

33. Longman thinks men are attracted to the navel because of its proximity to the vulva. See Longman, *Song of Songs*, 195.

I am my beloved's,

and his desire is for me. (Song 7:10[11])

In this iteration of the sentiment, she adds the words: "his desire." This is the translation of one word in Hebrew: *teshukato*. This word—*teshukah*—appears only three times in the Tanakh: in Gen 3:16, in Gen 4:7, and here in Song 7:10[11]. Let's set aside Gen 4:7 because it doesn't deal with men and women. Genesis 3:16 is the pronouncement of God's punishment to Eve: "Your *desire* [shall be for your husband], and he shall rule over you." This statement conveys inequality. Song 7:10[11], however, says that the man desires *her*. Song 7:10 replaces "and he shall rule over you" with "his desire" and thereby creates the symmetry that is lacking in Gen 3:16. The Song of Songs is subverting the inequality of Gen 3:16. The refrain indicates a perfectly egalitarian relationship.

SET ME AS A SEAL UPON YOUR HEART

Chapter 8, the final chapter, recapitulates a lot of what came before it while also introducing new ideas. For instance, the lovers continue to deal with separation, but this time the separation is social rather than spatial:

Oh that you were like a brother to me

who nursed at my mother's breasts!

If I found you outside, I would kiss you,

and none would despise me.

I would lead you and bring you

into the house of my mother—

she who used to teach me.

I would give you spiced wine to drink,

the juice of my pomegranate.

His left hand is under my head,

and his right hand embraces me!

I adjure you, O daughters of Jerusalem,

that you not stir up or awaken love

until it pleases. (Song 8:1–4)

Apparently, she cannot kiss him in public because it would be taboo. It's interesting that the Song sees nothing wrong with an unmarried man kissing an unmarried woman. The Song seems critical of overly prudish attitudes. This is not to say the Song promotes promiscuity. It doesn't. More on that shortly.

The mention of her mother in v. 2, along with his mother in v. 5, perhaps implies their lovemaking will naturally lead to childbearing.[34] That theme, however, is not developed. The lovers do not make love primarily for the purpose of procreation. They make

34. Segal, *The Song of Songs*, 89.

The Power of Love

love simply to make love. And then we get the final statement of the "adjure" refrain. One can only wonder what the original melody of that refrain sounded like.

We now come to the key verses of the Song. The reason these verses are so important is that they provide us with some kind of a description (though not quite a definition) of the main subject of the Song, which is *love*:

> Set me as a seal upon your heart,
>> as a seal upon your arm,
> for love is strong as death,
>> jealousy is fierce as the grave.
> Its flashes are flashes of fire,
>> the very flame of the LORD.[35]
> Many waters cannot quench love,
>> neither can floods drown it.
> If a man offered for love
>> all the wealth of his house,
>> he would be utterly despised. (Song 8:6–7)

She had said she wanted him to kiss her with the kisses of his mouth. Now she tells him to "set" her as a "seal" upon his heart and arm. A "seal" is a stamp that functioned as one's signature. She wants herself to be stamped, so to speak, upon his heart. She wants to become one with him.[36]

Then comes the key statement: "love is strong as death." This is the only time "death" is mentioned in the Song. It's interesting that the Song mentions death at all. I contend that the Song, while celebrating love, never forgets the harsh reality of the world. The Song had previously mentioned a brutal act of violence (Song 5:7). This means that the Song, like all the other books we've discussed thus far, deals with suffering to some extent. And like its predecessors in the Ketuvim, the Song has its own answer to suffering and the problem of death. Whereas Psalms deals with suffering by prayer, and Proverbs urges us to pursue wisdom, and Job teaches humility, and Ruth celebrates kindness, the Song presents romantic love as the response to suffering. Since love is as strong as death, love is a suitable weapon to fight death—and not only death, but all suffering, including violence.

How might love be used as such a weapon? Trible argues the Song creates a picture of a restored garden of Eden. When the lovers are together, they are, in a sense, reentering the Edenic paradise.[37] There are many obstacles in the way of the lovers, such as the brothers, the other women, the "foxes," the watchmen, and the sheer distance between them. But when they do come together, everything seems right. The love the woman has for her man brings him "peace" (Song 8:10), and vice versa. That's why

---

35. The ESV's translation is conservative. An alternative translation will be discussed below.

36. Exum, *Song of Songs*, 250–51.

37. Trible, *God and the Rhetoric of Sexuality*, 141–61.

even in the darkest times we celebrate at a wedding. It's why, in Judaism, a wedding is not cancelled for a funeral. It's why Jews in Nazi ghettos got married despite their suffering. We *need* such celebrations in our lives.

But there's one caveat which cannot go unmentioned. The Song does *not* say that love is *stronger* than death. The Song makes plenty of "better than" arguments. His lovemaking is better than wine, she said in Song 1:2. He said the same thing about her in Song 4:10. The Song, then, could have easily said that love is stronger than death. But no—death is still the most powerful thing in the world, for nothing can cheat death or escape death's grasp. The best we can hope for is something that is *as* strong as death. For the Song of Songs, that thing is love.

I'm purposely using the word "love" as something distinct from "kindness." The Hebrew word translated "love" is *ahav*, not *hesed*. Kindness is a particular expression of love, but the love the Song speaks of is *eros*—romantic and sexual love. The reason the Song elevates eros is that two humans are never closer to each other than when they have sex. In sex they become "one flesh" (Gen 2:24).

Song 8:6 uses "love" in parallel with the word *kin'ah*, which means "jealousy." This translation seems troubling, though. Is the parallelism synonymous or antithetical? "Jealousy" is typically thought to be a negative emotion, the "green eyed monster" Iago warns Othello about. Othello illustrates the power of jealousy *over* love. The NET and the JPS, though, interpret *kin'ah* to be a synonymous parallelism. Hence they translate it "passion." The CEB translates it "passionate love."

But jealousy can have a positive connotation. Think about it: if Othello really did see Cassio kiss Desdemona and he *wasn't* jealous, we would conclude he really didn't love her. Because love involves consensual possessiveness, jealousy is an inherent part of love. It's only bad when taken to the extreme (just like so many other things, such as anger and fear). Love makes us strong, yet simultaneously makes us vulnerable. That's why finding out your spouse has committed adultery hurts so much. And so, while "passion" is a safe translation, I tend to think *kin'ah* should be translated "jealousy."

Verse 7 contains one of the central messages of the Song. To purchase love is to do something shameful. This message is reiterated in Song 8:11–12:

> Solomon had a vineyard at Baal-hamon;
>> he let out the vineyard to keepers;
>> each one was to bring for its fruit a thousand pieces of silver.
> My vineyard, my very own, is before me;
>> you, O Solomon, may have the thousand,
>> and the keepers of the fruit two hundred.

Who is speaking? I think it's the woman. I'll explain why in just a moment. She says Solomon had a "vineyard." The word "vineyard" is first mentioned in Song 1:6. It's a double entendre. It refers to a woman. This text implies that Solomon is renting a woman to other men. The thousand pieces of silver just happens to remind us of

The Power of Love

Solomon's seven hundred wives and three hundred concubines.[38] The speaker will have no part in such a transaction. "My vineyard, my very own" is the translation of two Hebrew words: *carmi sheli*. Those are the exact words the woman said in Song 1:6, translated by the ESV "but *my own vineyard* I have not kept." This is why it makes good sense to interpret the speaker in Song 8:11–12 as the woman.[39] Her statement seems like it's a criticism of Solomon for his view of women and sex. The Song holds monogamy as the standard for real love (as Gen 2:24 implies). "I am my beloved and my beloved is mine"—there's no room for anyone else. How interesting that both Proverbs and the Song are attributed to Solomon and yet they both stand contrary to the way Solomon ended up living his life!

The Song of Songs, therefore, while clearly challenging prudishness, which stereotypically has been part of the religious ethos, also challenges a libertine view of sex which is prevalent in the West. It's opposed to polygamy and polyamory. It's opposed to "hooking up" and "friends with benefits." It's opposed to swiping pictures on an app as if the faces are objects rather than people. The Song has the highest view of sex imaginable, but it insists that sex is most meaningful when it's an expression of the emotional love between two people.[40]

WHAT SHALL WE DO WITH THE SONG OF SONGS?

The Song of Songs was one of the three most controversial books of the Tanakh. The other two are Ecclesiastes and Esther. That these books were so controversial in their day is ironic because they're probably the most palatable of all the books of the Bible to the average reader today. To the ancient Jews, however, they were controversial for two reasons: First, these are the only books of the Tanakh to not use God's name, Yahweh. Second, the subject matter of these books seemed objectionable. Let's deal with these issues in turn.

The Song of Songs contains no religiosity. Yes, it mentions Jerusalem, but it doesn't mention the temple. It makes no mention of prayer. It says nothing about the Torah or the covenant. It's seemingly a secular book about love.

There's one word which might be a direct reference to God. It's the Hebrew word *shalhevetya* in Song 8:6. The key part of that word is the "ya" at the end. "Ya" can be a shortened version of God's name, Yahweh. We saw this in the most famous use of it—"hallelu-*ya*" (unfortunately spelled "ja"). But does this "ya" refer to God's name, or is it merely a superlative? Some translations, like the ESV, translate it "the very flame of the LORD," whereas the NRSV translates it "a raging flame."

It seems out of place that the Song would all the sudden mention God at the end when there's not a hint of religiosity anywhere else. There's an argument in favor of

38. It's a mystery what the "200" refers to.

39. Longman, *Song of Songs*, 218.

40. Segal, *The Song of Songs*, 156.

177

translating "ya" as God's name, however. It has been noted that the word for "death" and the word for "flame" are reminiscent of the names of two Canaanite deities—Mot (death) and Resheph (flame). It would fit, then, that the poet would also use a word reminiscent of Yahweh, especially since the poet is talking about power. Linafelt argues that the word *shalhevetya* is multivalent. The "ya" does function as a superlative, but ancient Jewish readers would have also thought of Yahweh.[41]

In any case, even if the "ya" is meant to be a reference to God, it's not the full spelling of the divine name. Moreover, the generic word for "God" (*elohim*) is not used. So why is this book in the Bible?

One of the greatest rabbis, Rabbi Akiva, defended the Song with these immortal words:

> God forbid [anyone should deny the sacredness of the Song of Songs]—no man in Israel ever disputed about the Song of Songs [that he should say] that it does not render the hands unclean, for all the ages are not worth the day on which the Song of Songs was given to Israel; for all the Writings are holy, but the Song of Songs is the Holy of Holies. And if aught was in dispute the dispute was about Ecclesiastes alone.[42]

"Rendering the hands unclean" is meant in a positive sense. If a text renders the hands unclean, it is Scripture. If it does not render the hands unclean, it is not Scripture.[43] Akiva squashes the notion that the Song should be excluded from the canon. Dispute Ecclesiastes if you wish, he says, but not the Song of Songs! He uses the superlative title to form a wordplay. The Song of Songs is the "Holy of Holies"—a phrase that usually refers to the most holy room of the sanctuary. Note also the word "writings." Perhaps he means all Scripture (that is, the whole Tanakh), but at the very least he means the Ketuvim. According to Akiva, the Song of Songs is the holiest book of the Ketuvim!

But that's not the only thing Akiva said about the Song. In another instance, he said, "Whoever sings the Song of Songs with a tremulous voice in a banquet hall and (so) treats it as a sort of ditty has no share in the world to come."[44] In other words, don't go to the club and quote the Song to pick up women! This statement implies that Akiva viewed the Song religiously rather than erotically. He never said, or implied, the Song of Songs is the holiest book of the Ketuvim because of its eroticism. It's likely he viewed it as the holiest book of the Ketuvim because he interpreted it allegorically.[45] This is how the Song of Songs has been interpreted by both Judaism and Christianity.

---

41. Linafelt, *The Hebrew Bible as Literature*, 52–53.

42. Sanhedrin 101A in Danby, trans., *The Mishnah*, 778.

43. For an explanation about what "renders the hands unclean" means, see Lim, "Defilement of the Hands," 501–15.

44. Sanhedrin 12:10. Murphy, *The Song of Songs*, 13.

45. Longman, *Song of Songs*, 20–21.

The Power of Love

Judaism interpreted the Song as an allegory of the love of God and Israel. Christianity interpreted it as an allegory of the love of Christ and the church.

By allegory, I don't mean *analogy*. An analogical reading is fairly straightforward: just as the man and the woman are immensely in love, so too God and Israel are immensely in love. But that's not how either Judaism or Christianity interpreted the Song. They interpreted every word and phrase to have a corresponding reality. In Jewish interpretations, the Song begins in the Egyptian exile and ends with the coming of the Messiah. Hippolytus, a third-century Christian theologian, interpreted the woman's breasts as the Old Testament and the New Testament![46]

During the Enlightenment, the allegorical interpretation started to be questioned. A new interpretation emerged. The Song began to be viewed as a drama, complete with plot and characters.[47] It was also once in vogue to think of the Song as part of a fertility cult.[48] Today, most scholars view the Song of Songs as nothing more than erotic love poetry,[49] not dissimilar to the love poetry of ancient Egypt.[50] Scholars are divided as to whether the Song is a unit or whether it's made up of a multitude of smaller songs.[51] Those who take the latter view cannot agree on how many songs are contained in the Song.[52] Feminist scholars disagree as to whether the Song subverts ancient patriarchy or is a patriarchal male fantasy writ large.[53] An enormous amount of ink has been spilled over this little book.

The irony is thick. The ancient commentators took the plain meaning of the text for granted and focused on the spiritual meaning. Modern scholars tend to ignore any kind of spiritual meaning and instead focus on the plain meaning of the text. And while ancient commentators wrote encyclopedically on the Song, most modern readers of the Bible ignore it. The Old Testament's arrangement doesn't do the Song any favors, for the Song is sandwiched between the much larger Wisdom Books and the book of Isaiah, which is sixty-six chapters long. The Song is easily overlooked. With the loss of the allegorical interpretation, its subject matter seems irrelevant to ecclesiastical concerns.

Yet because the Song of Songs is about love, it's relevant to everyone. But what shall we do with it? The Song celebrates physical beauty. Beauty is good because God created it. It leads to sexual attraction, which brings pleasure and leads to the perpetuation of our species. However, beauty also makes us feel uncomfortable. I think some people would like to believe love has nothing to do with beauty. Clearly that's untrue.

46. Pope, *Song of Songs*, 114.

47. This view is rejected by the vast majority of scholars but it's accepted by Iain Provan. See Provan, *Ecclesiastes/Song of Songs*, 244–46.

48. Pope, *Song of Songs*, 210–29.

49. Longman, *Song of Songs*, 43.

50. Longman, *Song of Songs*, 50–51.

51. Exum, *Song of Songs*, 33–37.

52. Exum, *Song of Songs*, 33.

53. Exum, *Song of Songs*, 80–81.

Beauty also reminds us of our inequality, which haunts us. Most people don't look like movie stars or Instagram models. People "follow" them, admire them, and envy them. They don't realize that the models themselves might also be insecure with their looks. Our culture presents us with impossible standards of beauty. People believe they have to look a certain way to have self-worth. But beauty doesn't last. Proverbs reminds us that "beauty is vain" (Prov 31:30). It's also subjective. Oxytocin causes people to ignore the imperfections in their lovers. Eventually that wears off. Jonathan Haidt describes the effect as waking up from a dream, looking at the person lying next to you, and seeing them drooling.[54]

How should singles read the Song? The Song might make them feel lonelier than they already are. Some people are sexually repressed. The Song might pour salt on that wound, making it seem like singleness is a tragedy.

How should marrieds read the Song? The Song might sadden many couples because it reminds them that they have lost the passion they once felt. "Annie's Song" is one of the greatest love songs of our time, yet John Denver and Annie, like so many couples, had a stormy marriage that ended in divorce. Even when marriages don't end in divorce, many marriage beds are ice cold. More and more people today don't think it's worth getting married. As a friend said to me, "It's better to be single than wish you were." How many people wish they were single?

A twenty-year-old student asked me if true really exists. How did one so young become so cynical? I was far more idealistic at her age. I confess time has hardened me. I do think true love exists—I *know* it does—but I also think it's rarer than we would like to believe.

I don't believe in the concept of "soulmates." A relationship requires a lot of work. A marriage either gets better or it gets worse. It never remains static. And luck is a huge factor.[55] You're very lucky if you meet someone who's willing to work on the marriage with you. If you're willing to work on the marriage but your spouse is not, no matter how hard you try, the marriage will fail. The stigma placed on divorced people is a failure to understand that truth.

I would say the most important theological idea in the Song of Songs is not God's love for humanity and humanity's love for God, but that God created sex. Like everything else, it's not perfect. Still, whether we are single or married, content or heartbroken, we can read this little gem and appreciate this most pleasant and mysterious aspect of life. Life is hard enough as it is. What would life be like without eros? Indeed, we owe our very existence to it.

54. Haidt, *The Happiness Hypothesis*, 126.
55. Prager, "The Role of Luck."

10

Eat, Drink, and Rejoice
(Ecclesiastes)

OF THE BOOK OF Ecclesiastes, celebrated author Thomas Wolfe wrote:

> Of all I have ever seen or learned, that book seems to me the noblest, the wisest, and the most powerful expression of man's life upon this earth—and also the highest flower of poetry, eloquence, and truth. I am not given to dogmatic judgments in the matter of literary creation, but if I had to make one I could say that Ecclesiastes is the greatest single piece of writing I have ever known, and the wisdom expressed in it the most lasting and profound.[1]

Wolfe's view of Ecclesiastes is not unique. Ecclesiastes has inspired many of the most brilliant thinkers in history.[2]

Yet, despite its influence, Ecclesiastes is not an easy book to understand and reading it in English makes understanding it even more difficult. We must therefore spend a considerable amount of time parsing the first two verses if we are to begin on the right foot.

KING KOHELET

The superscription: "The words of the Preacher, the son of David, king in Jerusalem" (Eccl 1:1). First things first: the Hebrew does not say "the Preacher." The Hebrew says, "The words of *kohelet*, son of David, king in Jerusalem." *Kohelet* is a cognate of the word *kahal*. *Kahal* means "he assembled." The nounal form, *kehillah*, means "assembly." This is why the Greek title of the book is Ecclesiastes. "Ecclesiastes" derives from the Greek word *ekklesia,* which is usually translated "church" in the New Testament.

---

1. Wolfe, *You Can't Go Home Again*, 570.
2. For example, Shakespeare's Sonnet 59 begins with a quote from Eccl 1:9.

181

A *kohelet* is the leader of an assembly, hence the translation "the preacher."[3] The problem, however, is that there's no definite article in front of the word. The Hebrew says *kohelet*, not *ha-kohelet*. Now, there *is* a place in Ecclesiastes where the speaker is called *ha-kohelet* (Eccl 12:8), but most of the time the word appears without the definite article. *Kohelet* is the speaker's name. "I *Kohelet* have been king over Israel in Jerusalem," he says (Eccl 1:12).

But now we have a problem. There was no such king in Jerusalem named Kohelet. This is probably why the English translations translate the name with the definite article instead of transliterating it. (This is the opposite of how they translate *ha-satan* in Job!) The "son of David" who was king in Jerusalem was Solomon. I suppose any descendant of David might have referred to himself as "son of David," but they would have been kings of *Judah*, not *Israel*, since the kingdom was divided in the days of Solomon's son, Rehoboam. Besides, Ecclesiastes sounds very Solomonic. In saying that, I don't mean that the linguistics sound like tenth-century-BCE Hebrew. Actually, the Hebrew sounds like it comes from at least the Persian period—the fifth century or later.[4] But Ecclesiastes is unique among biblical books because it contains an autobiographical section. Kohelet speaks about himself in first person. The portrait he paints looks an awful lot like Solomon. He speaks of himself as being wiser than anyone else and he speaks of his excesses. That's a dead ringer.

And yet, if it's meant to be Solomon, why does the name "Solomon" not appear in the book? Solomon appears in the superscription of Proverbs and in the superscription of the Song of Songs. In Ecclesiastes, he's called Kohelet. This is a mystery.[5]

The topic of authorship is always controversial because tradition says one thing and scholars say something else. Most religious people are convinced Solomon wrote Ecclesiastes. Just like with the Song of Songs, people say, "The Bible says it, therefore it's so." But it's not that simple with Ecclesiastes.

Let's ignore the issue of the word *kohelet* for a moment and look at a passage at the end of the book. Ecclesiastes 12:9–12 says:

> Besides being wise, the Preacher also taught the people knowledge, weighing and studying and arranging many proverbs with great care. The Preacher sought to find words of delight, and uprightly he wrote words of truth.

Who's speaking here? Whoever it is, it's not Kohelet ("the Preacher"). It's someone talking *about* Kohelet. Kohelet's teachings throughout the book are told through the mouth of someone else. This other person is teaching his son what Kohelet said: "My son, beware of anything beyond these. Of making many books there is no end, and

---

3. Some translations, such as the NET, NIV, and CEB translate *kohelet* "the teacher."

4. Alter, *The Wisdom Books*, 338.

5. Longman notes that the root KHL appears frequently in 1 Kgs 8, which is about Solomon's dedication of the temple. See Longman, *The Fear of the Lord is Wisdom*, 32–33. See also Sacks, *Ceremony and Celebration*, 113–16.

much study is a weariness of the flesh" (Eccl 12:12). To say Solomon wrote Ecclesiastes, therefore, ignores the fact that there are two speakers in Ecclesiastes.[6] This also means that the conclusion at the very end of the book is not Kohelet's conclusion; it's the father's. That there are two speakers in the book may have been the intent of the original author (a third person besides Kohelet and the father),[7] or it may be the result of redaction. In the latter case, we would posit that another author added the father's voice to the book, perhaps to make the book more palatable to second temple Judaism.

It seems altogether plausible that Kohelet's kingship is a literary device. Kohelet *must* have unlimited wisdom and unlimited resources in order for his points to be valid. If he only has $100 to spend on pleasure, we could say to him, "It's no wonder you aren't happy. In order to *really* experience life, you need to be rich." If he only obtains a little wisdom, we could say to him, "In order to benefit from wisdom, you must become *very* wise." But Kohelet is the richest, wisest person in the world. There's nothing he can't have or do. These "facts" stifle preliminary objections to his arguments. Moreover, it puts the reader in a position of intellectual vulnerability. Because we don't have the vast wisdom and wealth Kohelet has, we are in no position to dispute his conclusions.

Some will disagree with everything I just said and fall back on "the Bible says it, therefore it's true." Fine. I understand the nature of that perspective. If you want to believe Kohelet is the actual Solomon, I have no objection. My only contention is that you admit "Solomon" is not the only speaker in the book because that's an indisputable fact.

Solomon, of course, is very relevant to Ecclesiastes. The writer does not present Kohelet as just any king. He is Solomonic through and through. This causes the reader to read Ecclesiastes through a Solomonic lens. That is, we read the book in light of the fact that Solomon was the wiseman who became a fool. Solomon is a tragic figure in the sense that he had a rise and fall with no rebound. He's back now, speaking to us as an elderly man re-examining his own life, as well as life in general.

KOHELET'S THESIS

Ecclesiastes 1:2 reads:

> *Havel havalim, amar Kohelet, havel havalim! Hakol havel.*

Even if you can't pronounce the words correctly, you can see the phonetic emphases in the verse. The H, L, and K sounds are prominent.[8] We are again reminded how the Bible is best read aloud.

---

6. Longman, *The Fear of the Lord is Wisdom*, 32.

7. Segal, *Kohelet's Pursuit of Truth*, 125–26.

8. Segal, *Kohelet's Pursuit of Truth*, 12.

Illuminating Counsel

You can, perhaps, also note that *havel* and *havalim* are very similar words. In fact, *havel* is the construct form of the noun *hevel*. *Havalim* is the plural of *hevel*. So let's partially translate the line in order to isolate the important words:

> *Havel* of *havelim*, said[9] Kohelet, *havel* of *havelim*! All is *havel*!

We see that *hevel* is the key word in the verse, and hence the key word in the entire book. The superlative—*havel* of *havalim*—serves to intensify the author's point. The word is used five times in this eight-word sentence. As Segal notes, no other sentence in the Tanakh emphasizes a word as much as Eccl 1:2 emphasizes *hevel*.[10] *Hevel* is used thirty-seven times in the book.

But what does *hevel* mean? Most English translations follow the King James Version in translating it "vanity." The superlative is therefore translated, "Vanity of vanities." This is not "vanity" in the narcissistic sense. It's not describing a person who is overly concerned with his looks. Rather, this is vanity in the third commandment sense: "You shall not take the name of the Lord your God in vain."[11] The NIV translates *hevel* as "meaningless." The superlative then becomes: "Utterly meaningless!" The NET translates it "futile." The CEB translates it "pointless." "Perfectly pointless, says the Teacher . . . Everything is pointless."

The problem is *hevel* means none of those things. *Hevel* literally means "breath" or "vapor." Hence Robert Alter translates the superlative "Merest breath."[12] I prefer Segal's translation, "Vapor of vapors," not just because it sounds cool, but also because it effectively mimics the Hebrew superlative.[13] What's interesting is that we had just read a similar Hebrew superlative. It's the title of the previous book: *Shir Hashirim*—"The Song of Songs." Turn the page from the Song of Songs and we read, "Vapor of vapors," which would be a better title than "Ecclesiastes." Segal suggests there might be a connection, especially since "Vapor of vapors" is one of the only examples of this kind of superlative that is negative.[14] The typical construction of this kind of superlative is positive: "Song of songs" is the greatest song. "Holy of holies" is the most holy thing. "King of kings" is the greatest king. "Vapor of vapors" is not like any of these. Whatever it means, it clearly conveys something negative—"The most vaporous thing."

What kind of speech is "vapor of vapors"? Answer: It's a metaphor! Notice, then, what the translations have done. They have taken a metaphor ("vapor") and interpreted it ("vanity"). The reader of the translations has no clue the Hebrew author was using a metaphor. In my judgment, the translators have done the reader a tremendous

---

9. The verb is past tense. Segal is correct to translate it accordingly to reflect that Kohelet's words are being reported by the father. See Segal, *Kohelet's Pursuit of Truth*, 13.

10. Segal, *Kohelet's Pursuit of Truth*, 12.

11. Though the word "vain" in the third commandment is the translation of a different word.

12. Alter, *The Wisdom Books*, 340.

13. Segal, *Kohelet's Pursuit of Truth*, 12, 136.

14. Segal, *Kohelet's Pursuit of Truth*, 12.

disserve. The metaphor should be translated literally. I'm not suggesting that a metaphor can never be interpreted by the translator, but when you have a metaphor as the key word of a book, it becomes necessary to retain it. By translating *hevel* as "vanity," the translator has overstepped his bounds and is now doing exegesis—interpreting instead of translating. I know that all translation involves interpretation to an extent, but the translators go too far here. Sometimes *restraint* ought to be the operative principle of biblical translation.

The problem with translating *hevel* as "vanity" or "meaningless" is that those words might not necessarily convey what the metaphor means. Iain Provan illustrates this by pointing us to Eccl 11:10.[15] The NIV translates it:

> So then, banish anxiety from your heart
> > and cast off the troubles of your body,
> > for youth and vigor are meaningless.

Is youth *meaningless*? Why would anyone think such a thing? If youth is, in fact, meaningless, what reason is there to "banish anxiety"? The thought becomes a non sequitur. But the text doesn't say what the NIV says it says. The text says, ". . . for youth and the dawn [of life] are *vapor*." Ah, now the onus is on the reader to interpret the metaphor for herself. What does "vapor" mean in this context? Not "meaningless," but "*fleeting*." Not infrequently does the Tanakh use the word "vapor" as a metaphor to denote the brevity of life. In fact, *hevel* is the name of the very first person to die in the Tanakh. The hellacious English transliteration of that name is Abel. Abel is killed by his brother Cain—*Kayin*, in Hebrew.

We can also note Ps 39:5: "Surely all mankind stands as a mere breath!" The Hebrew is more poetic: *Akh kol-hevel kol-adam nitzav selah*. The word that has prominence in that verse is *kol*, which means "all." *All* humanity is *all* vapor! Or, we can say, "The whole of humanity is wholly vaporous." As the psalm says, we are a "handbreadth" and our lives are fleeting (Ps 39:4–5).

If the issue in Ecclesiastes were meaninglessness, I think the central question of the book would be different. If the book were an examination of whether life has meaning, the central question would be something like, "Why are we here?" But the central question of the book, stated in Eccl 1:3, is:

> What does man gain by all the toil
> > at which he toils under the sun?

That's not the same question. They may be similar perhaps, but "what does man gain?" ("gain" being the key word) is not about meaning but about *profit*, be it happiness or money or longevity or whatever.[16] This question is restated in Eccl 3:9. The question brackets the two poems of the book: the poem of circularity in Eccl 1:5–11

---

15. Provan, *Ecclesiastes/Song of Songs*, 52.

16. Provan, *Ecclesiastes/Song of Songs*, 54.

and the "seasons" poem in Eccl 3:2–8. We can see from these poems that death's shadow is constantly in view. The first poem begins by speaking of generations "going and coming" and the first line in the second poem says, "There is a time to be born and a time to die." As we shall see, Kohelet believes that death renders life problematic. In fact, while the question of Eccl 1:4 is rhetorical, the thesis in Eccl 1:2 sort of serves as an answer to the question. What *does* man gain from all his toil? Answer: *vapor. Vapor of vapors.* Lots and lots of *vapor.* Lots of *nothing.* Death makes losers of us all.

This is not to say that *hevel* refers only to life's brevity. Provan argues *hevel* in Ecclesiastes also refers to our inability to control life.[17] As the text states:

What is crooked cannot be made straight,
  and what is lacking cannot be counted. (Eccl 1:15)

Michael Fox prefers to translate *hevel* as "absurdity."[18] My teacher, James Bruckner, translates *hevel* as "frustration." He thinks the point Kohelet is making is that life is inherently frustrating. Substitute the word "vanity" in the English translations for "frustration" or "frustrating" and you will see it makes good sense. We might also add to that the idea of "futility." Certainly, Kohelet's catchphrase "shepherding the wind" implies all these things.

The power of maintaining *hevel* as a metaphor is that it allows the word's meaning to be flexible. Once the metaphor is translated away, the meaning becomes fixed and verses like Eccl 11:10 become (ironically) meaningless. In Ecclesiastes, there's no reason to think *hevel* means only one thing.

Therefore, the belief that Ecclesiastes is about the "meaning of life" should mostly be blamed on the English translations. Some of the blame, though, goes to the impulse to conform Hebrew biblical books with preconceived theological notions. In that vein, many Christians read Ecclesiastes as if it's a Christian book. The interpretation goes something like this: "Solomon tried living his life in a worldly way. He came to the conclusion that life is meaningless. But then he found God and realized that God is the only thing, or one, that brings meaning to life." This makes for a very compelling sermon because it's what many converts to Christianity have experienced. They tried living life without God and they ended up hitting a proverbial brick wall. Then they found Jesus, or Jesus found them, and life began to make sense to them.

But this is not what Ecclesiastes is saying at all. Aside from the fact that the book is not dealing with the "meaning of life" as that phrase is typically understood, and aside from the fact that it's fallacious to assume life can only have one meaning,[19] the thesis statement—"Vapor of vapors"—is never rescinded. In fact, it's restated in Eccl 12:8. That statement forms an *inclusio,* bracketing Kohelet's entire discourse. Kohelet

17. Provan, *Ecclesiastes/Song of Songs,* 52.

18. Fox, *A Time to Tear Down,* 35.

19. David Wolpe argues convincingly against the idea that life only has one meaning. Sinai Temple, "The Meaning of Life."

186

doesn't say, "Without God life is meaningless." He makes his famous statement within a theistic framework. The statement that Christians know and love, that the "whole duty" of human beings is to "fear God and keep his commandments," is not Kohelet's at all. It's the father's statement in Eccl 12:13–14. The common view of Ecclesiastes is fundamentally flawed through and through.

KOHELET'S AUTOBIOGRAPHY

A Christian minister told me his view of Ecclesiastes: "[Kohelet] dismantles the ways and philosophies of the world step by step." The minister is right in saying Kohelet "dismantles" preconceived notions, but the notions he dismantles are not that of "the world" (that is, anti-God philosophies). Or at least he doesn't start there. He begins his autobiography by subverting the Bible itself!

Kohelet tells us he pursued wisdom. This is precisely what Proverbs told us to do. Kohelet's pursuit of wisdom, however, is what caused him to come to the conclusion that all is "vapor." Wisdom opened his eyes to see how difficult life is. "It is an unhappy business that God has given to the children of man to be busy with" (Eccl 1:13). He would not have realized that if not for wisdom. The fool lives in ignorant bliss.

This is not to say that Kohelet thinks it's better to be a fool than to be wise. "There is more gain in wisdom than in folly," he says (Eccl 2:13). Wisdom is a valuable tool. The wise person sees whereas the fool "walks in darkness" (Eccl 2:14). But ultimately, both the wise and the fool suffer the same fate. They both die. Not only do they both die, they will both be forgotten in the course of time. Thus if we apply a comparative standard, wisdom has greater gain than folly. If we apply an absolute standard, death nullifies wisdom's benefits. In the long run, there's no gain. All is vapor and a shepherding of the wind.

As Kohelet compares the wiseman with the fool, so he compares humans with animals:

> For what happens to the children of man and what happens to the beasts is the same; as one dies, so dies the other. They all have the same breath, and man has no advantage over the beasts . . . (Eccl 3:19)

Channeling Genesis, Kohelet says, "All go to the same place. All are from the dust, and to dust all return" (Eccl 3:20). No human has advantage over another human and no human has advantage over an animal. We're all vapor. We all die.

Thus Kohelet makes two points about wisdom. First, wisdom increases sadness. Second, wisdom does not defeat death. These two points directly contradict Proverbs' claims. Proverbs says:

> Happy are those who find wisdom,
> and those who get understanding. (Prov 3:13, NRSV)

Illuminating Counsel

But Kohelet says:

> For in much wisdom is much vexation,
>> and he who increases knowledge increases sorrow. (Eccl 1:18)

Proverbs says:

> The fear of the LORD prolongs life,
>> but the years of the wicked will be short. (Prov 10:27)

But Kohelet says:

> For of the wise as of the fool there is no enduring remembrance, seeing that in the days to come all will have been long forgotten. How the wise dies just like the fool! (Eccl 2:16)

Just as Job subverts Deuteronomy, so Ecclesiastes subverts Proverbs.

Next, Kohelet decides to pursue pleasure (Eccl 2:1–11). This is the section Christians tend to focus on because Christianity opposes, as a matter of morality, the overindulgence of pleasure. Historically, Christians have sometimes gone too far in this regard, labelling things as taboo which didn't deserve such a label. Yet many non-Christians have also wrongly stereotyped Christians as being prudish. Kohelet would find the Christian teaching on pleasure to be sagacious. Pleasure is fun, but not necessarily fulfilling. Having lots of money doesn't guarantee happiness. As Kohelet says later on, "He who loves money will not be satisfied with money, nor he who loves wealth with his income" (Eccl 5:10). The same is true of sex. Having lots of sex is more likely to bring trouble than happiness if the sex is divorced from love (as we noted in our discussion of the Song of Songs). Pleasure evaporates too quickly to bring anything we humans desperately long for. All is vapor. There is no gain.

Finally, Kohelet pursues labor. He follows conventional wisdom that happiness is not found in *having* money but in *earning* money. He thus decides to keep himself busy with great projects. The problem is that he will spend so much time and effort amassing wealth only to leave it to someone (presumably his son) who lacks the wisdom to use it prudentially. Ironically, Rehoboam's foolish actions led to the division of Solomon's kingdom (1 Kgs 12). I have seen this phenomenon happen with my own eyes. I knew a man who worked hard his whole life, starting with asking to work for free to learn the business and doing tasks as menial as scrubbing toilets. He eventually become enormously successful. After his death, the business he built was run into the ground by his children. Kohelet says:

> There is an evil that I have seen under the sun, and it lies heavy on mankind: a man to whom God gives wealth, possessions, and honor, so that he lacks nothing of all that he desires, yet God does not give him power to enjoy them, but a stranger enjoys them. (Eccl 6:1–2)

188

Eat, Drink, and Rejoice

Once again, death is the problem. Not only are our lives too brief, death resets our "gains," as it were, bringing us back down to zero:

> As he came from his mother's womb he shall go again, naked as he came, and shall take nothing for his toil that he may carry away in his hand. This also is a grievous evil: just as he came, so shall he go, and what gain is there to him who toils for the wind? (Eccl 5:15–16)

Could it be that Kohelet is even daring to subvert that tremendously subversive book, the book of Job? For Job says, "Naked I came . . . naked shall I return" (Job 1:21). Job meant that in a positive sense; there's nothing left to do but praise God. But for Kohelet, it's a tragedy. It means there's no gain in life.

All of this makes one of Kohelet's statements in his autobiography stand out. "So I hated life," he says, "because what is done under the sun was grievous to me" (Eccl 2:17). As Longman notes, Kohelet doesn't say, "I hated *my* life." He says he hated *life*—meaning, life *in general*.[20]

Kohelet's autobiography is only part of the picture. He moves beyond himself and observes the world around him. What he sees confirms his experience:

> Again I saw all the oppressions that are done under the sun. And behold, the tears of the oppressed, and they had no one to comfort them! On the side of their oppressors there was power, and there was no one to comfort them. And I thought the dead who are already dead more fortunate than the living who are still alive. But better than both is he who has not yet been and has not seen the evil deeds that are done under the sun. (Eccl 4:1–3)

Kohelet agrees with Job that non-existence is better than existence except that Job speaks in the midst of his suffering whereas Kohelet's view comes from a rational interpretation of empirical evidence. The world is cold and cruel. Life is unfair. And where is God in all this? Is there any cosmic justice?

KOHELET'S POEMS

The book of Ecclesiastes opens with a poem:

> A generation goes, and a generation comes,
>> but the earth remains forever.
> The sun rises, and the sun goes down,
>> and hastens to the place where it rises.
> The wind blows to the south
>> and goes around to the north;
> around and around goes the wind,
>> and on its circuits the wind returns.

20. Longman, *Ecclesiastes*, 100.

All streams run to the sea,
  but the sea is not full;
to the place where the streams flow,
  there they flow again.
All things are full of weariness;
  a man cannot utter it;
the eye is not satisfied with seeing,
  nor the ear filled with hearing.
What has been is what will be,
  and what has been done is what will be done,
  and there is nothing new under the sun.
Is there a thing of which it is said,
  "See, this is new"?
It has been already
  in the ages before us.
There is no remembrance of former things,
  nor will there be any remembrance
of later things yet to be
  among those who come after. (Eccl 1:4–11)

Verses 4–7 are about the circularity of the world. He speaks of generations, the sun, the wind, and the waters. Everything moves in circles. Generations come and go, as the sun rises and sets and then rises again. Kohelet emphasizes the circularity of the blowing of the winds. Likewise, the waters of rivers have no real destination. They never arrive. The rivers flow into the sea but they keep flowing, in effect creating a circle.

What does all this mean? We can interpret it in a number of ways. The popular Disney movie, *The Lion King*, has a song called "The Circle of Life." Mufasa comforts Simba with the notion that life moves in cycles. Death is not meaningless, for in death we release our energy into the earth and we become food for worms which help the soil. This gives rise to vegetation which feeds the herbivores. The circularity of life reminds us that the world will not end with our generation. As Steve Jobs said, "Death is very likely the single best invention of life. It's life's change agent. It clears out the old to make way for the new."[21] One generation can do so much damage, but that generation will die and their children will have a chance to begin the world anew, at least to an extent.

Yet Kohelet views the circularity of life in a negative way. He says the circularity of life demonstrates that there's no fulfillment. As Dennis Prager has observed, "human nature is insatiable" and "that is why no single obstacle to happiness is greater than human nature."[22] The eye and ear are never satisfied. We will always want more than what we have, whether it's money, sex, knowledge, or whatever else we desire. In addition

21. Stanford, "Steve Jobs' 2005 Commencement Address."
22. Prager, *Happiness Is a Serious Problem*, 16.

Eat, Drink, and Rejoice

to this, Kohelet insists "there is nothing new under the sun." "Under the sun" is one of his many catchphrases. We're stuck "under the sun," unable to go over it, as it were. Perhaps you disagree with Kohelet that there's nothing new. Kohelet did not know of airplanes, cars, and smartphones. Yet we recall the motto: "the more things change, the more they stay the same." He would have agreed with that. The lack of newness is meant to communicate the point that human nature is fixed. One can argue that thirty centuries on, what Kohelet observed about human nature still holds true.

The poem's ending creates an *inclusio*. The first line is about death; the last line is about death. Not only do we die, we become forgotten. How many people today know the names of their great-grandparents? We view our lives to be important, but in a century hardly anyone will know who we were and what we did.

The second poem is more famous. Kohelet begins with a title of sorts: "For everything there is a season, and a time for every matter under heaven" (Eccl 3:1). Then comes the poem, which is quite different from every other poem in the Bible:

> a time to be born, and a time to die;
> a time to plant, and a time to pluck up what is planted;
> a time to kill, and a time to heal;
> a time to break down, and a time to build up;
> a time to weep, and a time to laugh;
> a time to mourn, and a time to dance;
> a time to cast away stones, and a time to gather stones together;
> a time to embrace, and a time to refrain from embracing;
> a time to seek, and a time to lose;
> a time to keep, and a time to cast away;
> a time to tear, and a time to sew;
> a time to keep silence, and a time to speak;
> a time to love, and a time to hate;
> a time for war, and a time for peace. (Eccl 3:2–8)

This poem was set to music by the '60s band The Byrds in a song titled "Turn! Turn! Turn!" There are videos of them on YouTube performing the song. In one video, there are young women in the background dancing to it. They look so cute as they work their '60s moves! In another video, there is this adorable little girl in the audience singing along as she waves her arms. Yet I can't help but think that, despite the great fun they're all having, they haven't the faintest clue what the words of the song mean! By contrast, one of my students told me that she always weeps without fail whenever she reads this poem. Her tears are joyous, for she views it as a poem of hope. Indeed, The Byrds' title is quite apt. "Turn! Turn! Turn!" observes, quite rightly, that this second poem makes the same point as the first. Like the first poem, this poem is about the circularity of life. This means we're faced with the same issue as before.

Illuminating Counsel

The poem is ambiguous.[23] We can read it positively. We're in winter now, and winter is horrid, but, as Sam said to Frodo, "it will be spring soon and the orchards will be in blossom and the birds will be nesting in the hazel thicket." We can also add theology to this. God has foreordained the seasons of life. Bad times must come, but good times will return. When a loved one dies, it's the time to mourn. Soon, we will dance again. The early 1940s were a time of war. Then came peace and the rebuilding of war-torn nations. And so on. The poem is deterministic in a positive way.

Kohelet, however, does not interpret the poem positively. Ecclesiastes 3:11 is the key verse. It's a bit tricky to interpret. Kohelet admits there's beauty in life: "[God] has made everything beautiful in its time." This is why my student sheds tears. But Kohelet continues: "Also, he has put eternity in man's heart . . ." This line is loved by Christians, for it seems like an empty bottle which Christians gladly fill with Christian theology of afterlife and resurrection. Kohelet, though, is not done: ". . . yet so that he cannot find out what God has done from the beginning to the end." Kohelet's point is—yes, God has fixed a season for everything, but we don't know what season we're in and what season is coming next. This knowledge, this program which God set up, has not been made known to us. Kohelet's views are explained more clearly in Eccl 8:16–17:

> When I applied my heart to know wisdom, and to see the business that is done on earth, how neither day nor night do one's eyes see sleep, then I saw all the work of God, that man cannot find out the work that is done under the sun. However much man may toil in seeking, he will not find it out. Even though a wise man claims to know, he cannot find it out.[24]

I had a conversation with one of my cousins at a wedding. Despite the happy occasion, we talked about how our family has suffered. Her mother had survived breast cancer. My mother had died of lung cancer. My cousin said to me, "What I'm thinking is: what the heck will come next?!" She herself ended up getting breast cancer. Thankfully, she, too, survived. Neither of us foresaw that our aunt, the youngest sibling of our parents, would die a few years later of lung cancer, four months after her diagnosis. We just cannot prepare for the seasons of life the way we can prepare for winter and spring.

KOHELET'S RESPONSE TO SUFFERING

For these reasons, many consider Ecclesiastes to be a very depressing book. And they would be forgiven for thinking so. Kohelet has brilliantly dismantled any notion of utopia on earth. He has delved into the nature of suffering. This is, in essence, no different from every other book we've looked at thus far. Each book discusses suffering in its own way. Psalms discusses suffering through prayer-poems written from

23. Segal, *Kohelet's Pursuit of Truth*, 19–20.
24. Segal, *Kohelet's Pursuit of Truth*, 31–33.

Eat, Drink, and Rejoice

the perspective of a sufferer. Proverbs, very rationally, discusses suffering as a consequence of folly. Job sets up one man's life as a test case of sorts—the ultimate sufferer. Ruth told us a story which involved women losing their husbands and one who lost her children as well. The Song of Songs is more coy about suffering than the others, but we did read about a woman who is abused, and the Song's key verse mentions death. Ecclesiastes is the most pensive of the lot. The book is not a story, despite the autobiographical section. Kohelet is not in the "thick of it" the way Job is. Rather, Kohelet is standing somewhat at a distance and looking at all of life. He's an empiricist.[25] He describes what he sees and the view is not good.

I'm not sure many would want to argue that life is not tremendously difficult. We in the West have things far better than the vast majority of human beings who have ever lived. Yet even for us, life is hard. We've all experienced pain and loss.

Kohelet, though, doesn't surrender to the fact that life is vaporous. Like all the other books of the Ketuvim thus far, Kohelet has a response to suffering. His response is different from everything we've read in the other books. His response to suffering is to *rejoice*. He makes this point no less than seven times—seven being the biblical number signifying completion. Observe:

> There is nothing better for a person than that he should eat and drink and find enjoyment in his toil. This also, I saw, is from the hand of God, for apart from him who can eat or who can have enjoyment? (Eccl 2:24–25)

> I perceived that there is nothing better for them than to be joyful and to do good as long as they live; also that everyone should eat and drink and take pleasure in all his toil—this is God's gift to man. (Eccl 3:12–13)

> So I saw that there is nothing better than that a man should rejoice in his work, for that is his lot. (Eccl 3:22)

> Behold, what I have seen to be good and fitting is to eat and drink and find enjoyment in all the toil with which one toils under the sun the few days of his life that God has given him, for this is his lot. Everyone also to whom God has given wealth and possessions and power to enjoy them, and to accept his lot and rejoice in his toil—this is the gift of God. For he will not much remember the days of his life because God keeps him occupied with joy in his heart. (Eccl 5:18–20)

> And I commend joy, for man has nothing better under the sun but to eat and drink and be joyful, for this will go with him in his toil through the days of his life that God has given him under the sun. (Eccl 8:15)

---

25. Segal, *Kohelet's Pursuit of Truth*, 3.

> Go, eat your bread with joy, and drink your wine with a merry heart, for God has already approved what you do. Let your garments be always white. Let not oil be lacking on your head. Enjoy life with the wife whom you love, all the days of your [vaporous] life that he has given you under the sun, because that is your portion in life and in your toil at which you toil under the sun. Whatever your hand finds to do, do it with your might, for there is no work or thought or knowledge or wisdom in Sheol, to which you are going. (Eccl 9:7–10)

> So if a person lives many years, let him rejoice in them all; but let him remember that the days of darkness will be many. All that comes is vanity. Rejoice, O young man, in your youth, and let your heart cheer you in the days of your youth. Walk in the ways of your heart and the sight of your eyes. But know that for all these things God will bring you into judgment. Remove vexation from your heart, and put away pain from your body, for youth and the dawn of life are vanity [literally "vapor"]. (Eccl 11:8–10)

Does it still sound like the book is a "Debbie Downer"?

There are numerous things we must unpack here. There's the key word—*simcha*—which means "joy." Many Christians seem to think that happiness is a short-term thing; it's what you feel after having a good day at work. Joy, on the other hand, according to many, is the long-term contentment which you have even when you're crying your eyes out. Such a view betrays an ignorance of Hebrew. Jonathan Sacks is correct when he notes that in Hebrew, "happiness" is long-term whereas "joy" is what you feel in the moment.[26] We saw this in the very first psalm: "*Happy* is the one who does not walk in the counsel of the wicked . . . but who meditates on the Torah of Yahweh day and night" (Ps 1:1–2). "Day and night"—as in, *every* day and *every* night. That's a long-term state of being. When the Bible talks about rejoicing, on the other hand, it refers to what you do in a short period of time, such as a holiday. Your heart may be broken into a thousand little pieces, but on the holiday you rejoice. Kohelet seems to be saying there is no happiness. The Declaration of Independence says that one of our "unalienable rights" is the "pursuit of happiness." I think Kohelet would say that pursuing happiness is no different than "shepherding the wind." Happiness is vapor. You don't find happiness and it doesn't come to you when you amass lots of stuff. You have to pursue other things in order to obtain happiness. Even then, happiness seems elusive. Joy, on the other hand, is what everyone can do here and now. Joy is a choice. None of the painful realities of life can inhibit us from making that choice.

There is a problem, however—an internal problem in Ecclesiastes which is only noticeable if reading it in Hebrew. We noted Eccl 2:1 where Kohelet said to himself, "Come now, I will test you with pleasure . . ." The word "pleasure" immediately raises yellow flags for Christians because, as we noted, there's a Christian aversion to pleasure

---

26. Sacks, *Ceremony and Celebration*, 126–29.

Eat, Drink, and Rejoice

which sometimes goes too far but other times is salubrious. In Hebrew, though, the word translated "pleasure" is *simcha*—the word for joy. Thus in ch. 2, Kohelet says that joy is vaporous, but elsewhere he commends rejoicing as being the best thing one can do. How can we resolve this tension?

In ch. 2, Kohelet pursued joy in order to obtain happiness. Likewise, he pursued wisdom to obtain what Proverbs promised. He hoped that these pursuits would bring him "gain." They didn't. Vapor, vapor, all is vapor. Therefore, we must conclude that the joy he mentions in those seven passages is a rejoicing that does *not* seek gain. The rejoicing he commends is a surrender to the fact that death robs one of any gain. To pursue joy in the hope that it will bring you lasting happiness and gain is to set yourself up for disappointment. Life is vaporous. To rejoice with the knowledge that life is vaporous, to rejoice *despite* life's vaporousness, is the best anyone can do. It's not ideal, but it's as good as it gets.

One of my students summarized Kohelet's point perfectly: don't expect too much out of life. Don't expect more out of life than it's capable of giving.[27] There's no pot of gold at the end of the rainbow. There's no magical feeling called happiness. Life is not easy and it's not romantic. If we think otherwise, just remember that your loved ones will die as will you someday, sooner than you may think. As the saying goes, "The days are long and the years are short." If we recognize these things, if we lower our expectations, we can actually do fairly well. Our ship is going to sink; we can choose to despair or we can choose to live with gusto. "Eat, drink, and be merry for tomorrow we die."

That last sentence is a quote from Isa 22:13. Paul quotes it in 1 Cor 15:32—"If the dead are not raised," he says, "'let us eat and drink, for tomorrow we die.'" In Isaiah and 1 Corinthians, the phrase is negative, and yet this is Kohelet's main point. Kohelet's view of life seems antithetical to the Christian ethos. This is perhaps why many secularists, such as the agnostic scholar Bart Ehrman and the atheist neuroscientist Sam Harris (who usually says only disparaging things about the Hebrew Bible), enjoy reading Ecclesiastes.[28] From their point of view, the dead are *not* raised indeed; therefore *carpe diem*.

Christians, then, face the same problem with Ecclesiastes as with the other books of the Ketuvim. There's no life after death in these books. Some may argue that the Torah contains hints of life after death, but the notion is denied in Ecclesiastes. Or, perhaps more accurately, Kohelet is ambivalent about it. In Eccl 3:21, he's agnostic on the matter: "Who knows whether the spirit of man goes upward and the spirit of the beast goes down into the earth?" We shall soon see that he later softens that position.

Jews and Christians who read Ecclesiastes with the lens of their theologies will run into friction here. How much afterlife theology should be imposed on this text? Ecclesiastes is Scripture, but can we say Kohelet is wrong? Or as one student said to me, what about faith? Why does Kohelet say nothing about having faith in God?

27. I'm paraphrasing the views of Matthew McLester.

28. Ehrman says Ecclesiastes is his favorite book of the Bible. See Ehrman, "Ehrman-Butt Debate."

Compare Kohelet's advice to Paul's: "Rejoice in hope, be patient in suffering, be constant in prayer" (Rom 12:12). In a way, they're both saying the same thing except that Kohelet phrases it like a deist and Paul phrases it like a Christian.[29]

Kohelet never uses the name Yahweh. He calls God *Elohim*. This is the generic word for "god." Curiously, he also calls God "Creator" (Eccl 12:1). He believes in a divine judgment, but it's doubtful that he means the kind of postmortem final judgment as in Christian theology. So Kohelet is no atheist, but he doesn't seem to have an "orthodox" view of God. God has set up the world as it is. It's a world filled with beauty and pain. The rules of life are not spelled out. Like all things, they must be ascertained through experience and reason. God will judge every act, and so the choices we make will be consequential. But God will not come to our rescue or redeem the world, and Kohelet's god doesn't seem like the type of god one would have a relationship with.

The power of Kohelet's perspective is that he seeks hope in this life rather than in the hereafter. The afterlife is fine to believe in. No doubt it's a belief that empowers people. But it seems unreasonable to seek hope in the hereafter without trying to find hope in the here-and-now. If the afterlife is our only hope, then we are admitting that life on Planet Earth is hopeless and miserable. Kohelet will not surrender to such a perspective. The life we have here and now matters. Life can be joyous despite its pains. If there is no life after death, if the atheists are right and death ends existence, then even so, according to Kohelet, life would still have its moments of joy. If the atheists are wrong and the theists are right, if we wake up after we die, how much better would that be?[30]

Kohelet's response to suffering is among the most hopeful things ever uttered. He no doubt inspired the words of the rabbis who said that the one who is rich is the one who rejoices in what he has.[31] The rabbis did *not* say, "The one who is rich is the one who is *content*." Joy is better than contentment. If all I have is an apple, then let me get as much pleasure from that apple as humanly possible. If Jeff Bezos doesn't rejoice in his billions, then I, with my apple, am richer than he is. Another rabbi said that God will judge us for all the legitimate pleasures we withheld from ourselves. Many people think religion is only about denial. Denial has its place, but so does the passion-filled life.

But it's all a choice. The power is in our hands. It's up to us to decide whether we will squeeze joy out of the short time we have here on Earth or whether we will let life's frustrations rob us of the pleasure we deserve.

---

29. For comments about Kohelet's view of God, see Sacks, *Ceremony and Celebration*, 112–13, and Alter, *The Wisdom Books*, 340–41.

30. Of course, in Christian theology it will not be good for those who are not saved by faith in Christ.

31. *Pirkei Avot* 4:1.

Eat, Drink, and Rejoice

KOHELET'S CONTRADICTIONS

At this point we can ask ourselves whether we agree with Kohelet. Is there truly nothing new under the sun? Are we really destined to be forgotten? Is everything "vapor"? Is rejoicing in the little we have the best we can do? Can we do better than that? Again—what about faith in God?

Feel free to disagree with Kohelet. Kohelet disagrees with himself! This is the astounding thing about his discourse. He contradicts himself at various points.[32] We noted Kohelet's extreme pessimism in Eccl 4:2–3:

> And I thought the dead who are already dead more fortunate than the living who are still alive. But better than both is he who has not yet been and has not seen the evil deeds that are done under the sun.

Along those lines, he later says this:

> If a man fathers a hundred children and lives many years, so that the days of his years are many, but his soul is not satisfied with life's good things, and he also has no burial, I say that a stillborn child is better off than he. (Eccl 6:3)

It appears to be his way of thinking that in many cases, perhaps even in most cases, it's better not to be born. But then he says this:

> But he who is joined with all the living has hope, for a living dog is better than a dead lion. (Eccl 9:4)

This is precisely the opposite of what he said before. He initially stated that not existing is better than existing. But in Eccl 9:4, he explicitly says that it's better to exist. "To be" is the correct answer to Hamlet's question. Note that dogs were considered filthy animals because they were not domesticated in ancient Israel, and dogs are, by nature, scavengers. Lions, which were in the Middle East at the time, were considered mighty. But a living filthy thing is better off than a dead mighty thing, according to Kohelet. This statement is incredible. Countless millions of people have been touched by the words of the late illustrious physicist Stephen Hawking:

> However difficult life may seem, there is always something you can do and succeed at. It matters that you don't just give up. Where there is life there is hope.

I find those words immensely inspiring, especially coming from someone who accomplished so much despite living with such a devastating and debilitating illness for so long. But Kohelet said it first! Thousands of years ago, Kohelet said that the one who is joined to life has hope. And hope is the thing that prevents us from putting a bullet in our head. Hope is what enables us to persevere despite adversity.

---

32. Segal, *Kohelet's Pursuit of Truth*, 110–12. Sacks says, "Kohelet uses contradiction the way Socrates used questions, to force his listeners to think beyond conventional wisdom, and understand the complexity and many-sidedness of life." Sacks, *Ceremony and Celebration*, 111.

Illuminating Counsel

Kohelet also says contradictory things about women. At first, he says this:

> And I find something more bitter than death: the woman whose heart is snares and nets, and whose hands are fetters. He who pleases God escapes her, but the sinner is taken by her. Behold, this is what I found, says the Preacher, while adding one thing to another to find the scheme of things—which my soul has sought repeatedly, but I have not found. One man among a thousand I found, but a woman among all these I have not found. (Eccl 7:26–28)

He later says:

> Enjoy life with the wife whom you love, all the days of your [vaporous] life that he has given you under the sun, because that is your portion in life and in your toil at which you toil under the sun. (Eccl 9:9)

Alter says the statement in Eccl 7 is not a description of all women but of immoral women—the adulterous kind of woman Proverbs warns about.[33] Either way, Kohelet's statement in Eccl 9:9 softens his position. There *are* good women! Ecclesiastes may not focus on femininity like the previous books in the Five Scrolls, but "misogynistic" is probably not an accurate description of Kohelet's viewpoint.

And then there's Kohelet's view of life after death, which we touched on earlier. In Eccl 3:21 he says, "Who knows whether the spirit of man goes upward and the spirit of the beast goes down into the earth?" But in Eccl 12:7 he says, "the dust returns to the earth as it was, and the spirit returns to God who gave it." In ch. 3, Kohelet is agnostic on the matter. In ch. 12, he seems certain.[34]

These contradictions are part of the charm of the book. We can explain them in various ways. First, it's very normal for people to contradict themselves. One moment I think one thing. The next moment I disagree with what I previously thought. I go back and forth on all sorts of issues. Second, his contradictions are evidence of an evolution in his thinking. This should remind us not to take everything Kohelet says as if it's "gospel truth." We ought to wrestle with his perspective. We ought not to accept his viewpoint uncritically.

KOHELET'S PROVERBS

Ecclesiastes imparts wisdom, not only through Kohelet's lectures, but also through proverbs. What's interesting is that his proverbs are so . . . *him*. One can tell that

---

33. Alter, *The Wisdom Books*, 372.

34. Kohelet seems familiar with Gen 2:7, which says God formed the man from the dust of the ground and breathed the "breath" or "spirit" into him. Therefore, it's very possible that all Kohelet is saying is that everything returns to its source. The dust returns to the ground, and the spirit, which is God's, returns to God. In other words, his statement may have nothing to do with life after death. However, the point that Kohelet contradicts himself still stands.

Eat, Drink, and Rejoice

Kohelet's proverbs are not from the book of Proverbs. His proverbs are imbued with his pessimistic yet hopeful outlook on life. For example, he states:

> It is better to go to the house of mourning
>> than to go to the house of feasting,
> for this is the end of all mankind,
>> and the living will lay it to heart.
> Sorrow is better than laughter,
>> for by sadness of face the heart is made glad.
> The heart of the wise is in the house of mourning,
>> but the heart of fools is in the house of mirth. (Eccl 7:2–4)

Kohelet had said that increasing knowledge increases sorrow (Eccl 1:18). Now he says that some sorrow may not be such a bad thing. Going to a funeral teaches you about life by reminding you of your mortality. Kohelet is not too hot on laughter either. No talk of it being the best medicine here! And notice his wonderfully paradoxical statement that sadness brings glee. Do I agree that sorrow is better than laughter? I don't know. Sometimes a little too much sorrow can put me into a depression. However, some sorrow has proven beneficial to me. As long as I have hope, and as long as I'm not emotionally deflated, a little prick of the heart here and there makes me a deeper, kinder person. What do you think? Again, don't just eat up Kohelet's words. Think about them. Discuss them. Wrestle with them.

Then there's this statement, utterly unique in the Bible:

> In my [vaporous] life I have seen everything. There is a righteous man who perishes in his righteousness, and there is a wicked man who prolongs his life in his evildoing. Be not overly righteous, and do not make yourself too wise. Why should you destroy yourself? Be not overly wicked, neither be a fool. Why should you die before your time? (Eccl 7:15–17)

If you thought the Bible wants us to be righteous to the extreme, Kohelet would say you have another think coming! Kohelet thinks being too religious isn't good. Don't be a fanatic, he's saying. Everything in moderation, even righteousness and wisdom. Being so righteous that you make yourself a martyr is, to Kohelet, a waste. I tend to agree. I've heard students complain about certain professors who mistake their opinions for facts. If the student disagrees with the professor, the student will be penalized. Should the student stand on principle? It depends. Sometimes it's not worth it. Don't be so principled that you fight a battle you cannot win which will only result in you receiving a bad grade. Choose your battles carefully.

It's remarkable how applicable Kohelet's teachings are. Consider a proverb like this:

> Through sloth the roof sinks in,
>> and through indolence the house leaks. (Eccl 10:18)

Cutting corners comes at a price. Then there's this one:

Illuminating Counsel

> Bread is made for laughter,
>> and wine gladdens life,
>> and money answers everything. (Eccl 10:19)

There's a soberness to this line. We have here another expression of Kohelet's penchant for living life with gusto. He also (finally) says something positive about laughter! But then he reminds us that he doesn't have a romantic view of life. We need money. We work for money. Money makes the world go round, as they say. Maybe we don't like that thought, but Kohelet is dead set against us having an unrealistic view of life.

Kohelet extols wisdom. We must never forget that though Ecclesiastes subverts Proverbs, it does so within the family of wisdom books. Hence Kohelet says:

> A man's wisdom makes his face shine,
>> and the hardness of his face is changed. (Eccl 8:1)

He never meant to imply that wisdom isn't good. Through his realist view of life, he says:

> I have also seen this example of wisdom under the sun, and it seemed great to me. There was a little city with few men in it, and a great king came against it and besieged it, building great siege works against it. But there was found in it a poor, wise man, and he by his wisdom delivered the city. Yet no one remembered that poor man. But I say that wisdom is better than might, though the poor man's wisdom is despised and his words are not heard. The words of the wise heard in quiet are better than the shouting of a ruler among fools. Wisdom is better than weapons of war, but one sinner destroys much good. (Eccl 9:13–18)

Kohelet knows that a wise person does not always get the recognition he or she deserves. He also knows that luck is real and that some get good breaks and others don't (see Eccl 9:11–12). But if the choice is between being wise or being a fool, the correct decision is self-evident. Wisdom reigns, even if wisdom should bring us sorrow and even if wisdom is not as strong as death.

One of my favorite pieces of advice from Kohelet is Eccl 11:1:

> Cast your bread upon the waters,
>> for you will find it after many days.

If that seems cryptic, he states the same sentiment more clearly in Eccl 11:6:

> In the morning sow your seed, and at evening withhold not your hand, for you do not know which will prosper, this or that, or whether both alike will be good.

Eat, Drink, and Rejoice

I think Kohelet is advising us to take chances. Don't be so reserved, he's saying. Don't listen to the naysayers. As people say, "Everything is impossible until someone does it." It's possible that the seed you sow can grow to be a mighty tree. Indeed, I wrote this book not knowing if it was going to be published. It could have been rejected by the publisher and all my work would have been for naught. But I cast my bread upon the waters and it paid off. I love that such practical advice is found in the Bible![35]

KOHELET'S FINAL MESSAGE

It seems Kohelet's view of life becomes softer as the book progresses. He had to expound on the harsh realities of life in order to find a philosophy of joy that will last. He has learned much from his experiences and his investigations of life, and he wants others to learn from his conclusions and especially from his mistakes. He therefore cautions the young to "remember" God before it's too late:

> Remember also your Creator in the days of your youth, before the evil days come and the years draw near of which you will say, "I have no pleasure in them"; before the sun and the light and the moon and the stars are darkened and the clouds return after the rain, in the day when the keepers of the house tremble, and the strong men are bent, and the grinders cease because they are few, and those who look through the windows are dimmed, and the doors on the street are shut—when the sound of the grinding is low, and one rises up at the sound of a bird, and all the daughters of song are brought low—they are afraid also of what is high, and terrors are in the way; the almond tree blossoms, the grasshopper drags itself along, and desire fails, because man is going to his eternal home, and the mourners go about the streets—before the silver cord is snapped, or the golden bowl is broken, or the pitcher is shattered at the fountain, or the wheel broken at the cistern, and the dust returns to the earth as it was, and the spirit returns to God who gave it. (Eccl 12:1–7)

What we have here is a single point which Kohelet stretches into the size of a paragraph of exquisite prose so eloquent that it stands on the edge of poetry.[36] Some of the phrases here may be obscure to the average reader (what does it mean for the silver cord to be snapped?), but we get the gist of it. This is the most magnificent expression of old age, of declining towards death, in the Bible.

All of Kohelet's advice is summarized in the maxim "remember your Creator." This is a reminder that while Kohelet has at least one foot outside of orthodoxy, he certainly was no atheist. Would he have been an atheist if he were living in the post-Darwinian age? Who knows? What is clear from what Kohelet says is that forgetting God would, ironically, cause us to forget that everything is vapor. Forgetting God

35. Ecclesiastes 11:1 is a key part of the plot of the movie *Just Cause*.

36. Some commentators say it is poetry.

means forgetting that we're mortal. Forgetting God means forgetting right from wrong. (Kohelet is never ambivalent about the objective nature of morality.) Proverbs states that the beginning of wisdom is the fear of God. Kohelet cautions us to fear God while we're young, before it's too late.

The phrase, "Youth is wasted on the young," comes to mind. It would be wonderful if old people could inhabit young bodies like in *Benjamin Button*. Alas. The young must walk a tight rope. They must enjoy their youth, but they can only really enjoy it if they obtain the wisdom that life is vaporous. They must not be afraid to cast their bread upon the waters, but they must also know that acting recklessly will land them in a heap of trouble and bring them misery. This is the power of biblical religion. Faith in God imparts wisdom to the young so that they don't have to learn "the hard way" through the pain of experience.

THE FATHER'S CONCLUSION

Kohelet's words end in Eccl 12:8 with his thesis that everything is vapor. Ecclesiastes 12:9–14 are the words of the father teaching his son. The setting of the book is not a cathedral with a pulpit. It's a father sitting with his son, perhaps in the son's bedroom, or perhaps the two of them walking alone along a path.

The father thinks highly of Kohelet and his teachings. The collecting of proverbs (Eccl 12:9), no doubt, reminds us of Solomon. I find it interesting that the father says Kohelet sought "words of delight" (Eccl 12:10). The father recognizes that Kohelet's primary message is ultimately positive rather than negative.

Ecclesiastes 12:11–12 are also curious:

> The words of the wise are like goads, and like nails firmly fixed are the collected sayings; they are given by one Shepherd. My son, beware of anything beyond these. Of making many books there is no end, and much study is a weariness of the flesh.

Whereas the father just told his son that Kohelet's words are delightful, he also acknowledges that the truth hurts. Our teachers of wisdom are like shepherds, and we are their sheep; they prod us with their goads to get us on the paths of righteousness. It's painful, but necessary.

The father seems to want his son to have a mind that is cautiously open. A mind too open to all ideas—a metaphorical "sponge"—will lead to disaster, for the student will read indiscriminately and accept some very bad ideas. The father, then, tries to scare his son by telling him there's no end to writing books (which a visit to a college library will prove) and studying is wearisome. Of course, no student needs to be told such a thing! I wonder, though, if this is the first hint that the father is himself subverting Kohelet. It was Kohelet who said knowledge brings sorrow. The father basically agrees but for different reasons.

Eat, Drink, and Rejoice

Finally we come to "the end of the matter":

> Fear God and keep his commandments, for this is the whole duty of man. For God will bring every deed into judgment, with every secret thing, whether good or evil. (Eccl 12:13–14)

In my experience, Christians quote these verses more than any other from Ecclesiastes. I rarely hear the verses about rejoicing quoted. That ought to tell us something. The father's conclusion seems far more pious, certainly more orthodox, than anything Kohelet said.

Longman argues that the father is taking elements from the three sections of the Tanakh. "Fearing God" is the motto of the Writings. "Keeping" the "commandments" is the primary message of the Law (especially Deuteronomy). The "judgment" message is prominent in the Prophets.[37]

Segal notes that the father is not making these statements up out of whole cloth. Rather, they're based on things Kohelet has said.[38] In Eccl 5:7, Kohelet says, "when dreams increase and words grow many, there is vanity; but God is the one you must fear." In Eccl 8:5, Kohelet says, "Whoever keeps a command will know no evil thing, and the wise heart will know the proper time and the just way." And we already quoted Eccl 3:17: "God will judge the righteous and the wicked, for there is a time for every matter and for every work."

Yet Segal is correct in stating that Kohelet's statements don't mean the same thing as the father's.[39] For example, Kohelet's exhortation to "keep a command" is about keeping the command of the king. His advice is pragmatic rather than spiritual. The same is true of Kohelet's advice about fearing God. He's warning people about making rash vows. They will get you into trouble (as Jephthah could testify).

It seems, then, that the father takes what Kohelet says but makes it sound orthodox. Actually, it's probably the other way around. Kohelet took orthodox phrases and stated them unorthodoxly. The father seems to be restoring the nature of those sentiments.

That begs the question as to whether the father agrees with Kohelet. Longman argues he doesn't.[40] One can certainly argue that the father's statement nullifies everything Kohelet has said. Such a reading would cause us to render Eccl 12:9–10 as platitudinous. "Yeah, yeah, yeah . . . Kohelet is very wise and that's a good thing. But here's the conclusion: Obey the Torah and fear God because God is watching and will judge." Basically, we don't need Kohelet because we have Deuteronomy, Proverbs, and Isaiah!

What's amazing is that Kohelet's words survived—that this book was not only preserved, but was also included in the canon. And while the father has the final word, it's the words of Kohelet which make Ecclesiastes so powerful, memorable, and life-changing.

---

37. Longman, *The Fear of the Lord is Wisdom*, 40.

38. Segal, *Kohelet's Pursuit of Truth*, 96.

39. Segal, *Kohelet's Pursuit of Truth*, 95.

40. Longman, *The Fear of the Lord is Wisdom*, 41.

11

No Sorrow Like Her Sorrow
(Lamentations)

HISTORY

IT WAS A GORGEOUS Tuesday morning but the weather didn't reflect the anxiety I felt about what lay in store for me that day. I was a senior in college suffering from a severe case of senioritis. I had a class at 2 p.m. which I was thoroughly unprepared for. My plan: cram, cram, and cram some more to fool my professor into thinking that I had been diligently and steadily working all week. But one can't cram on an empty stomach. So first, breakfast; then cramming.

I made my way down the stairs to the dining hall. The room was empty except for the workers and one student. When the student saw me, he began speaking to me so fast that he nearly choked on this food. I had seen this kid around campus but had never spoken to him. I didn't even know his name. But never will I forget him and the look he had on his face—a look of utter shock and dismay. The undying need to tell someone—*anyone*—the news was aching in his bones. "A plane crashed into one of the Twin Towers!" I looked on the TV screen in disbelief. I don't remember eating breakfast. I don't remember leaving the dining hall. My next memory is in my dorm with as many people that could fit in my neighbor's tiny room while we all soaked up the news. We saw the second plane hit the second tower in real time. Also in real time, we saw both towers collapse. I left the room, walked out into the empty hallway, and let out a loud F-bomb. I didn't know a girl was behind me. I was embarrassed that she heard me. I had a reputation for speaking with squeaky clean language. I apologized to her but she was understanding. We all felt the same way.

We were glued to the TV, watching the news re-play the images over and over and over again. Classes were cancelled. In fact, classes were cancelled for the rest of the week. This was my first lesson in the difference between good stress and bad stress.

204

No Sorrow Like Her Sorrow

Good stress is being stressed out about a class. (Of course, in my case the stress was entirely self-inflicted.) Bad stress is when thousands of people are murdered.

My alma mater is in Westchester County, New York, about thirty miles north of New York City. I grew up in Queens. The Twin Towers were an icon to New Yorkers. Although the neighborhood I grew up in is farther away from the Towers than any other neighborhood in New York, from certain hilly places one could see the Manhattan skyline. As a child I always knew my father was driving west on the highway when the magnificent Towers were in view. As a senior in high school I took music lessons a few blocks from the Towers. After they collapsed, the first person I called was my former music teacher. I wanted to make sure he wasn't hurt. He wasn't, thank God, and he didn't feel like staying on the phone with me long. He probably had calls of his own to make.

Manhattan was shut down. The professors who lived in Manhattan had to spend the night in the university gymnasium. I spent the night off campus at a friend's place. We watched President Bush's address in which he quoted Ps 23. The next day I drove home to Queens to stay with my father. As I was driving on the Whitestone Bridge, I looked to my right and saw the giant dust cloud over where the World Trade Center used to stand.

My students are too young to remember the events of that day. For those of us who are more seasoned, we not only remember the day, we remember exactly where we were when we first heard what had happened. It's permanently baked into our memory.

I recently heard a Christian man say that ancient Judah's 9/11 was the destruction of the temple in 587 BCE. I understand the point of that analogy. 9/11 is the closest thing we have to relate to what the Jews of the sixth century BCE experienced. Even so, the analogy fails. As traumatic as that Tuesday was, there's no comparison between September 11, 2001, and the ninth of Av, 587 BCE. The latter was exponentially more horrific and traumatic.

It isn't just that more people died when the Babylonians, under King Nebuchadnezzar, sacked Jerusalem. The difference is that for the United States, there was a September 12. For ancient Judah, there was no tenth of Av. The destruction of the temple was effectively the end of the nation. Some survivors escaped to Egypt (Jeremiah was forcibly brought there), some remained in Judah (essentially to rot), and the rest were brought to Babylon (there were already Jews exiled in Babylon from Nebuchadnezzar's invasion in 597; Ezekiel was one of them). David's kingdom was broken. The Davidic king, Zedekiah, saw his sons executed right before his eyes. Then the Babylonians gouged out his eyes. Thousands upon thousands of people were slaughtered. Pregnant women had their wombs ripped open, their babies dashed against rocks. Men were castrated. What had happened to the tribes in the northern kingdom (called "Israel") by the Assyrian empire had now happened to the last remaining tribe. The people of Judah dodged a bullet in 701 BCE when Sennacherib had hemmed Hezekiah in Jerusalem "like a bird in a cage."[1] They survived that awful siege. It seemed like divine

1. ANET, 288.

providence. But King Zedekiah's ill-advised rebellion against Nebuchadnezzar had sealed Judah's fate.

The book of Lamentations is about that event. It's certainly the most lugubrious book of the Bible, dwarfing even the melancholic intensity of the lament psalms and Job. The Psalter, while containing laments, also contains lyrics of jubilation. Job, while exploring the depths of human suffering (particularly in ch. 3), breaks out into a theological debate. Lamentations, however, is doleful from the first sentence to the last sentence.

THEOLOGY

Why was the temple destroyed? Here are the facts: In 612 BCE, the Babylonians and the Medes destroyed the city of Nineveh, the capital of the Assyrian empire. The Assyrian empire was thus ended and Babylon, first under Nabopolassar, and then under his son, Nebuchadnezzar, became the dominant power in the western part of the Middle East. Pharaoh Neco II was keen on curbing the power of Babylon. His army marched eastward toward Haran to join forces with whomever was left of the Assyrian army to fight Babylon. King Josiah of Judah—Judah's most righteous king—tried to stop Neco but was killed in the battle of Megiddo in 609 BCE. Josiah's son, Jehoahaz succeeded him. Neco, now controlling Judah, quickly removed Jehoahaz and installed as king another son of Josiah, Jehoiakim. Then Egypt fought Babylon at Carchemish in 605 BCE, but Babylon won. Babylon now controlled Judah. In 598 BCE, Jehoiakim rebelled against Nebuchadnezzar. Nebuchadnezzar responded with a siege against Jerusalem that lasted three months. Jehoiakim died during the siege and his son, Jehoiachin—also known as Jeconiah (or Coniah)—succeeded him as king. But Nebuchadnezzar dethroned Jeconiah, exiling him to Babylon (along with thousands of priests, one of whom was Ezekiel), and set up Jehoiakim's younger brother, Mattaniah, whom Nebuchadnezzar renamed Zedekiah, as his vassal. Ten years later, Zedekiah rebelled against Nebuchadnezzar. Nebuchadnezzar again laid siege against Jerusalem, only this time he decided to go full throttle. He destroyed the city, the temple, and the kingdom entirely.

Those are the facts. Then there's the theology. Theology is, in this case at least, an interpretation of facts. Facts leave God out of the picture. Theology adds the "God dimension" into the mix. The theology of the Hebrew Bible informs us that Jerusalem—the City of God—did not fall by natural causes. It could *not* have fallen by natural causes because God made a covenant with David; Jerusalem was under God's protection. So why, then, was the temple destroyed? The temple was destroyed because Judah broke the covenant God had made with Israel at Sinai.

Thus the theology of the book of Lamentations is rooted in Deuteronomy's Retribution Principle. This theology, as we mentioned, is the dominant theology in the Hebrew Bible. In Ps 1 we saw it applied generally to all humanity: God rewards the

No Sorrow Like Her Sorrow

righteous and punishes the wicked. But throughout the Prophets we see it applied to the covenant. Keep the covenant and you will live; break the covenant and you will die. "Death," in this sense, means exile. The land will vomit you out of its mouth as it had vomited out the nations who were living in it before you (Lev 18:24–28).

The Retribution Principle overrides the Zion Theology. As you will recall, the Zion Theology is prominent in Psalms. This theology, expressed so clearly in Pss 46–48, stated that Jerusalem was indestructible because it's God's city. Tied together with the Zion Theology is the Davidic covenant. In Ps 2, the nations try to kill the Davidic king. God laughs at their attempts. We also see this theology expressed in the book of Isaiah, particularly in Isa 7, which is an historical account of the Syro-Ephraimite Conflict that began in 736 BCE. Israel and Aram sought to depose King Ahaz of Judah and install a puppet king in order to force Judah to help them fight Assyria. "It shall not stand, and it shall not come to pass," God says in Isa 7:6. The magnificent prophecies of Isa 9 and Isa 11, so dear to Christians, are a response to that conflict. David's kingdom will last forever.

But it didn't. The execrable Zedekiah was Judah's last king. And the nations—Babylon, specifically—did, in fact, destroy Jerusalem. Psalms struggles with this fact, most profoundly in Ps 89, as we already noted. Was the Zion Theology a fraud? Was the Davidic covenant a sham? Only the Retribution Principle can provide the answer. The Zion Theology was correct, but the Retribution Principle took precedence over it.

Therefore, we can say that Lamentations helps the exiles come to terms with their cognitive dissonance regarding the Zion Theology and the destruction of the royal and holy city. But championing the Retribution Principle also means that Lamentations "blames the victim." According to Lamentations, it's Judah's fault Jerusalem was destroyed. It's Judah's fault the Babylonians slaughtered them. Had Judah been faithful to the covenant, none of the atrocities that befell them would have transpired.

But we've already looked at Job. Whereas Lamentations provides an answer to Psalms' Zion Theology, Job provides an answer to Lamentations' Retribution Principle. Job's theology is not just non-Deuteronomistic; it is anti-Deuteronomistic. Job makes it clear that the Retribution Principle cannot explain all suffering.

The ninth of Av is the saddest day in the Jewish calendar. It commemorates the destruction of, not only the first temple, but also the second temple. (Spoiler Alert: the first temple was rebuilt in 516 BCE but was destroyed by the Romans in 70 CE.) It's also a day to remember the wandering in the wilderness and the most tragic events of Jewish history, even the Holocaust. It's a day of fasting and sadness. Lamentations is chanted in the synagogue while the reader is sitting on the floor—the mourner's posture. Studying the Torah—the holiest part of the Tanakh—is forbidden on the ninth of Av. The only other book that is allowed to be read on the ninth of Av along with Lamentations and the laments of Jeremiah is the book of Job.[2]

---

2. Fried, "The Book of Job," 157.

Illuminating Counsel

This creates a remarkable insight: Whereas Lamentations makes the sufferers believe they are the cause of their suffering, Job says the opposite. The book of Job indirectly reminds the Jewish community that antisemitism is not the fault of Jews.[3] That the whole world hates Jews and wants to annihilate Jews doesn't mean that there's anything wrong with Jews. Indeed, suffering in general is not always the fault of the sufferer. Job enables the Jewish community to vent their pain to God without guilt.[4]

Because Lamentations comes after Job in the order of the Ketuvim, it may feel like we are regressing theologically. But perhaps viewing the Retribution Principle with the book of Job in hindsight has its advantages. We already know by this point that Job subverts the Retribution Principle—that the Retribution Principle is not the Bible's sole explanation for suffering. Therefore, we can look for the positive aspects of the Retribution Principle because we're under no pressure to defend the Retribution Principle as the be-all-end-all explanation for suffering. And there's one very important aspect of the Retribution Principle that cannot go unmentioned. It's true that the downside to it (setting aside the matter of its truthfulness) is that it blames the victim. The upside, though, is that the Jews (in this case) are inclined to look inward to explain their own sufferings rather than give in to the human propensity to blame all problems on external sources, which is called "scapegoating."[5] What's absolutely striking about Lamentations is that Babylon is never mentioned.[6] There's an unnamed "enemy" but it's clear that the real destroyer of Judah is God, not humans. Now, we mustn't overstate the case. Lamentations does call upon God to exact vengeance on Judah's enemies. And interestingly enough, Edom, rather than Babylon, is mentioned. Even so, the resentment in Lamentations is rather tame compared to what it could be. The book is about sorrow, not vengeance.

POETRY

Lamentations is almost entirely written in acrostic form. Each chapter is an acrostic except for the final chapter. Yet interestingly, the final chapter has twenty-two verses—one verse for each letter of the Hebrew alphabet. In chs. 2 and 4, the Hebrew equivalent of O and P are switched. Chapter 3 is somewhat of an anomaly too. Like chs. 1, 2, and 4, it's an acrostic, but ch. 3's verses are much shorter than the verses in the other chapters, which are actually quite long, even for biblical poetry. In ch. 3, the first three verses begin with the Hebrew equivalent of A, the next three with B, the next three with C, and so on. Hence ch. 3 has sixty-six verses.

Lamentations is hardly the only set of biblical poems which are in acrostic form. We've already encountered acrostics in various psalms (such as Pss 9 and 10 and Ps

3. I am intentionally using the word "antisemitism" despite it being anachronistic.

4. Fried, "The Book of Job," 163–64.

5. Sacks, *Not in God's Name*, 247.

6. Berlin, *Lamentations*, 1.

208

119) as well as the "Woman of Strength" poem of Prov 31. The power of an acrostic is not only that it gives the poet a structure (something hardly unimportant), but also that the poet is utilizing all his resources. Every letter becomes a key part of the poetry. This is the equivalent of a composer writing in every key or using every instrument in the orchestra. Obviously the acrostic nature of Lamentations is not easy to maintain in translation; it's usually lost in the process. Yet it's another reminder that this poetry is meant to be read aloud so that we can hear every consonant at work.

Douglas Stuart argues the structure of Lamentations—with the apex of the acrostic being in ch. 3 and the acrostic nonexistent in ch. 5—gives the book a depressive feel. The book diminishes to a "whimper," he says.[7] Likewise, many scholars think that the poetry of Lamentations has a particular meter which is referred to as Kinah Meter. (*Kinah* is the Hebrew word for "lamentation.") In Lamentations, the last two versets of each verse appear to be shorter than the previous three. In other words, the meter is 3:2. The shorter line creates a depressive feel, as if each sentence ends with a sigh.[8]

I made a recording of myself reading Lamentations in English. I read it with Barber's Adagio for Strings—one of the saddest pieces of music ever written—playing in the background. The mood of that music fits Lamentations perfectly. Lamentations is "one, long, awful, magnificent sob."[9]

Let us now delve into the text itself. Our goals are to note the main points, to note the feminine aspects, to ask from whence hope for battered Zion is found, and to note Lamentations' contribution to the question of how we respond to suffering.

LONELINESS

> How lonely sits the city
> > that was full of people!
> How like a widow has she become,
> > she who was great among the nations!
> She who was a princess among the provinces
> > has become a slave. (Lam 1:1)

"How" is the translation of the the Hebrew word *eikha*, which is what the book is called in Hebrew. This is not only the first word of ch. 1, but also of ch. 2 and ch. 4. It's probably better translated as "Alas," not just because "alas" happens to begin with the first letter of the English alphabet, but also because *eikha* seems to function as a sigh.[10]

---

7. Stuart, *Old Testament Exegesis*, 54.

8. Wright, *The Message of Lamentations*, 31. Stuart, though, thinks Kinah Meter is a misunderstanding of the meter in Lamentations. See Stuart, *Old Testament Exegesis*, 179.

9. A quote from the novel *The Phantom of the Opera* by Gaston Leroux.

10. Wright, *The Message of Lamentations*, 59.

The very first verse marks out the tragedy of the situation. The city (Zion-Jerusalem) was once "full of people." Now she's "lonely." She was once "great." Now she's "like a widow." She was once a "princess." Now she's a "slave."

Notice the city is personified as a woman. We've seen this in the psalms, such as Ps 46. It also reminds us of the way Proverbs personifies wisdom. The effect of the personification of Zion allows the reader to identify with the city because the city is a *she*, not an *it*. The personification also enables the poet to magnify the sadness of the city. "She weeps bitterly in the night, with tears on her cheeks" (Lam 1:2). She is so sad, so crushed, so devastated that she weeps instead of sleeping. This is repeated throughout. She herself says, "For these things I weep; my eyes flow with tears" (Lam 1:16). "My stomach churns; my heart is wrung within me" (Lam 1:20).

Because the people sinned, "she became filthy." Her "nakedness" has been uncovered. She "groans" and "turns her face away." "Her uncleanness is in her skirts" (Lam 1:8–9). Does this imply that she was sexually assaulted?[11] See what you think:

> The enemy has stretched out his hands
>> over all her precious things;
> for she has seen the nations
>> enter her sanctuary,
> those whom you forbade
>> to enter your congregation. (Lam 1:10)

If we're meant to understand that personified Zion was raped, to "stretch out his hands over all her precious things" would mean that the rapist stretched out his hands and touched her body. To "enter her sanctuary" would mean he penetrated her. If this is correct, it's a very clever use of double entendre—one worthy of the Song of Songs. It might even remind us of Song 5:7, where the woman in the Song is violated by the watchmen of the city. But the woman in the Song of Songs had a lover. Zion has no one. Zion was once like the woman in the Song of Songs. Now look what has become of her.

The word "groan" has prominence. "Her priests groan" and "her virgins have been afflicted" (Lam 1:4). "All her people groan as they search for bread" (Lam 1:11). This is the first mention of starvation. She speaks for herself and says she is "groaning" (Lam 1:21). Her "groans are many" because her children have been slaughtered (Lam 1:22). "In the street the sword bereaves; in the house it is like death" (Lam 1:20).

It's emphasized repeatedly that "she has none to comfort her" (Lam 1:2). "She has no comforter" (Lam 1:9), ". . . for a comforter is far from me," she says (Lam 1:16). Zion has no one to "revive [her] spirit" (Lam 1:16), literally "return my life to me." Her experience is the opposite of the psalmist's experience in Ps 23:3, where he says that God "restores my soul." Notice how Lamentations subverts the book of Ruth. Naomi had a redeemer—the little baby who was to her a "restorer of life" and "nourisher of

---

11. Niveen Sarras interprets those verses as referring to rape. See Sarras, "Daughter Zion," 86–87.

No Sorrow Like Her Sorrow

[her] old age" (Ruth 4:15). Zion has no one. She stretches out her hands hoping for someone to hold them or pick her up, "but there is none to comfort her" (Lam 1:17). It's not because there's no one there; it's because no one cares: "They have heard my groaning, yet there is no one to comfort me. All my enemies have heard of my trouble; they are glad that you have done it" (Lam 1:21).

The poetry of ch. 1 oscillates between the speaker's words and Zion's words. The first thing Zion says is, "O LORD, behold my affliction, for the enemy has triumphed" (Lam 1:9). Her hope is that someone will notice her suffering. "Look, O LORD, and see for I am despised" (Lam 1:11). But no one seems to care. "Is it nothing to you, all you who pass by? Look and see if there is any sorrow like my sorrow" (Lam 1:12). She will not give up calling out to God. "Look, O LORD, for I am in distress" (Lam 1:20). Zion knows that she deserves her suffering. "I have been very rebellious," she says (Lam 1:20). "The LORD is in the right; I have rebelled against his word" (Lam 1:18). She speaks of her transgressions being "bound to a yoke" and placed on her neck (Lam 1:14). But maybe God will notice how severe the punishment is and show mercy.[12]

ANGER

Chapter 1 had spoken of unnamed enemies but also made it clear that God is the source of Zion's pain. Chapter 2 picks up on that last point and develops it:

> How the LORD in his anger
>> has set the daughter of Zion under a cloud!
> He has cast down from heaven to earth
>> the splendor of Israel;
> he has not remembered his footstool
>> in the day of his anger.
>
> The LORD has swallowed up without mercy
>> all the habitations of Jacob;
> in his wrath he has broken down
>> the strongholds of the daughter of Judah;
> he has brought down to the ground in dishonor
>> the kingdom and its rulers.
>
> He has cut down in fierce anger
>> all the might of Israel;
> he has withdrawn from them his right hand
>> in the face of the enemy;
> he has burned like a flaming fire in Jacob,
>> consuming all around. (Lam 2:1–3)

12. Berlin, *Lamentations*, 9.

Illuminating Counsel

What's emphasized here is God's *anger*. Three times ch. 2 says God has become "like an enemy" (Lam 2:3–5). It is God who "laid waste his booth like a vineyard" (Lam 2:6). God has "scorned his alter" and "disowned his sanctuary" (Lam 2:7). God "determined to lay in ruins the wall of the daughter of Zion" (Lam 2:8). As a result, "the elders of the daughter of Zion sit on the ground in silence" and "the young women have bowed their heads to the ground" (Lam 2:10).

Lamentations 2:10 is a turning point. In Lam 2:10, the poetry switches to first person. However, it is the narrator (the poet?) who's speaking, not Zion, though they both say similar things:

> My eyes are spent with weeping;
>> my stomach churns;
> my bile is poured out to the ground
>> because of the destruction of the daughter of my people,
> because infants and babies faint
>> in the streets of the city. (Lam 2:10)

Have you ever wept so hard that you felt sick? The poet is describing uncontrollable weeping—weeping that is so intense that the person is vomiting bile. The reason the speaker weeps so bitterly is because of the sight of babies starving. "Where is bread and wine?" they cry (Lam 2:11).[13] They "faint like a wounded man" and "their life is poured out on their mother's bosom" (Lam 2:11). The speaker wants to comfort his city, but the speaker is concerned that Zion has suffered too much to be comforted. "For your ruin is vast as the sea; who can heal you?" (Lam 2:13).

Zion cannot count on any human to help her. She was failed by her prophets, in whom she trusted (Lam 2:14). The onlookers "clap their hands" and "hiss" as they see her in agony; they mock her in her distress (Lam 2:15–16). What, then, is Zion's hope?

Once again, the point is the same: Zion's only hope is that the God who afflicted her will realize that though Zion deserved to be punished, the punishment was unduly harsh. For this reason the speaker encourages Zion to cry out, to weep, to pray (Lam 2:19).

> Look, O LORD, and see!
>> With whom have you dealt thus?
> Should women eat the fruit of their womb,
>> the children of their tender care?
> Should priest and prophet be killed
>> in the sanctuary of the Lord? (Lam 2:20)

How can God not have compassion when he sees starvation so severe that mothers are eating their own children?

---

13. "Bread" is a mistranslation. The word *dagan* means "grain." Berlin says the point about "grain and wine" is that they don't spoil. See Berlin, *Lamentations*, 72.

No Sorrow Like Her Sorrow

STEADFAST LOVE

How many ways do you think you could describe affliction and torture? The poetry in Lam 3 is as intense as anything in the Bible:

> I am the man who has seen affliction
>> under the rod of his wrath;
> he has driven and brought me
>> into darkness without any light;
> surely against me he turns his hand
>> again and again the whole day long.
> He has made my flesh and my skin waste away;
>> he has broken my bones;
> he has besieged and enveloped me
>> with bitterness and tribulation;
> he has made me dwell in darkness
>> like the dead of long ago.
> He has walled me about so that I cannot escape;
>> he has made my chains heavy;
> though I call and cry for help,
>> he shuts out my prayer;
> he has blocked my ways with blocks of stones;
>> he has made my paths crooked.
> He is a bear lying in wait for me,
>> a lion in hiding;
> he turned aside my steps and tore me to pieces;
>> he has made me desolate;
> he bent his bow and set me
>> as a target for his arrow.
> He drove into my kidneys
>> the arrows of his quiver;
> I have become the laughingstock of all peoples,
>> the object of their taunts all day long.
> He has filled me with bitterness;
>> he has sated me with wormwood.
> He has made my teeth grind on gravel,
>> and made me cower in ashes;
> my soul is bereft of peace;
>> I have forgotten what happiness is;
> so I say, "My endurance has perished;
>> so has my hope from the LORD." (Lam 3:1–18)

The speaker is a *gever*—a strong man. This immediately reminds us of Job. In fact, everything said here could have been said by Job. But Job reminds us of Jeremiah. Both

Illuminating Counsel

Job and Jeremiah curse their birthdays (Job 3:1–26; Jer 20:14–18). And since Lamentations is associated with Jeremiah, it seems natural that we would identify the speaker in Lam 3 as Jeremiah. Jeremiah, though, bears connections with the "suffering servant" in Isa 50:6 and Isa 53 (more precisely Isa 52:13—53:12). Isaiah 53 seems reminiscent of Ps 44. Both the righteous community of Ps 44 and the righteous servant of Isa 53 are described as "sheep led to the slaughter" (Ps 44:11, 22[12, 23]; Isa 53:7). And, of course, the New Testament likens Isaiah's righteous servant to Jesus (1 Pet 2:22–24).

So who is this guy in Lam 3? I don't think it matters. Ultimately he's a literary device. To make the suffering more acute, the poet describes the suffering of an individual. In ch. 1, it was personified Zion. In ch. 2, it was the unnamed speaker. In ch. 3, it's the strong man.

God is portrayed very harshly, but after reading Psalms and Job we should be used to this. God is the source of this man's suffering. But Lam 3:21 is a turning point. The man says he recalls something to mind and it brings him hope:[14]

> The steadfast love of the LORD never ceases;
>   his mercies never come to an end;
> they are new every morning;
>   great is your faithfulness.
> "The LORD is my portion," says my soul,
>   "therefore I will hope in him." (Lam 3:22–24)

The words "steadfast love" are a translation of *hesed*. Yes, God punished. Yes, God is wrathful. But God is also merciful and kind. All the biblical writers hold these two truths together.

I love the notion of God's mercies (or "compassions") being new every morning. There's something gracious about the morning. However bad we messed up yesterday, today we can make things right. Today may have been hellacious, but tomorrow we get to start over.

It's no coincidence that this—the *only* hopeful passage in Lamentations—is in the middle of the book. It's not only in the middle of the book; it's in the middle of the middle of the book. As we mentioned, this is typical of biblical literature. The great hopeful sentiment of Lam 3 is the apex of the book. However, that means that it's all downhill from here. Observe:

> The LORD is good to those who wait for him,
>   to the soul who seeks him.
> It is good that one should wait quietly
>   for the salvation of the LORD.
> It is good for a man that he bear
>   the yoke in his youth. (Lam 3:25–27)

---

14. This turning point is reminiscent of the turning point in Ps 73:17 when the psalmist went into the sanctuary.

No Sorrow Like Her Sorrow

Do you see the descent? God is good and will bring salvation. However, we will have to wait and be patient for that salvation to come. In the meantime, we ought to take our lashes:

> Let him sit alone in silence
> > when it is laid on him;
> let him put his mouth in the dust—
> > there may yet be hope;
> let him give his cheek to the one who strikes,
> > and let him be filled with insults. (Lam 3:28–30)

The "strong man" is telling us to "man up," if you'll pardon the expression, to endure. Don't complain when you're getting punished for your own sins. Take it. Accept your punishment. And the thought that enables us to persevere through the pain is that God's salvation will come eventually. "For the Lord will not cast off forever," we're told (Lam 3:31).

Lamentations 3 calls upon the people of Judah to repent. The man tells the people to confess their sins to God (Lam 3:40–42). "We have transgressed and rebelled, and you have not forgiven" (Lam 3:42).

The problem is once the people start talking about their sins, they end up describing their sufferings. The lofty idea of God's steadfast love is minimized. Instead, we hear more about how God has made the people "scum and garbage" (Lam 3:45). We're told of weeping: "My eyes flow with rivers of tears, because of the destruction of the daughter of my people" (Lam 3:48). The people have not given up on God but justice (or vengeance) is more important to them in the short run than forgiveness. Of those who destroyed Zion, the people pray, "You will pursue them in anger and destroy them from under your heavens, O LORD" (Lam 3:66).

DESTRUCTION

Lamentations 4 brings back the word *eikha*—"Alas!" Jerusalem has been destroyed. The "gold has grown dim" and the "holy stones lie scattered" (Lam 4:1).

The theme of starvation seen in previous chapters is now amplified:

> The tongue of the nursing infant sticks
> > to the roof of its mouth for thirst;
> the children beg for food,
> > but no one gives to them. (Lam 4:4)

The speaker (the man of ch. 3?) states explicitly that the fortunate ones in Jerusalem were those who were killed by the sword. The starvation in the city was so harrowing that mothers were eating their own children:

Illuminating Counsel

> The hands of compassionate women
>> have boiled their own children;
> they became their food
>> during the destruction of the daughter of my people. (Lam 4:10)

Maybe this is hyperbole, but 2 Kgs 6:24–31, which is an historical narrative, describes a siege against the city of Samaria which caused a severe famine that led to cannibalism. Likewise, the description of people wandering through the streets drenched in blood (Lam 4:14) also seems realistic.

I'm friends with a police sergeant. I asked him how he sleeps at night after spending all day dealing with murders and murderers. He has seen a lot but the one thing he said he cannot get used to—the thing that keeps him up at night—is when a child has been sodomized or killed. The police officers go into the scene of the crime and begin weeping. He has to be proactive in rotating the officers in and out of the room. The sight of a child suffering to that extent is appalling even for people used to viewing corpses. Thus Lamentations' descriptions of the suffering of children makes it the most grim of all biblical books.

Lamentations 4 reprises the points already stated in the previous chapters. There are human enemies—and here Edom (though not Babylon) is named (Lam 4:21–22). Ultimately, however, God is the one who caused it: "The LORD gave full vent to his wrath" (Lam 4:11). The reason God did this is because Judah broke the covenant: "This was for the sins of her prophets, the iniquities of her priests, who shed . . . the blood of the righteous" (Lam 4:13). There is no hope: "Our eyes failed, ever watching vainly for help" (Lam 4:17). There's also a reference to Zedekiah, the last king of Judah: ". . . the LORD's anointed was captured in their pits" (Lam 4:20). And the people plead for justice: ". . . your iniquity, O daughter of Edom, he will punish; he will uncover your sins" (Lam 4:22).

PRAYER

Lamentations 5 is a prayer: "Remember, O LORD, what has befallen us; look, and see our disgrace" (Lam 5:1). The speaker is now the entire nation; the grammar is the first person plural ("we" and "our"). The sentiment is the same as what we've seen in the previous chapters. The people of Judah want God to see how much they've suffered in the hope that God will show mercy. So the first eighteen verses are a summation of all the sufferings we've read throughout the book. Jerusalem has been destroyed. Parents have been killed. Children have been killed. The population is destitute. The women are raped. The men are slaves.

Lamentations 5:15 is a particularly potent verse:

> The joy of our hearts has ceased;
>> our dancing has been turned to mourning.

216

No Sorrow Like Her Sorrow

This is a subversion of Ps 30:11[12]:

You have turned for me my mourning into dancing;
   you have loosed my sackcloth
   and clothed me with gladness . . .

The exuberance of the thanksgiving Psalms is gone. Psalm 137 had said that the captives "hung up" their lyres (Ps 137:2). Lamentations 5:14 says that the "young men have [stopped playing] their music."

But is there hope?

But you, O LORD, reign forever,
   your throne endures to all generations." (Lam 5:19)

God's sovereignty is a fact in the minds of the people. Their beliefs have not changed. That doesn't mean, though, that they have hope:

Why do you forget us forever,
   why do you forsake us for so many days? (Lam 5:20)

That question is more emotional than rational. Rationally, the answer is that they broke the covenant, but it still doesn't make sense entirely. How can God cease loving his people? How can God not show mercy?

Then comes the famous plea:

Restore us to yourself, O LORD, that we may be restored!
   Renew our days as of old—(Lam 5:21)

Finally they pray what's most on their hearts. They want to be *restored*. They believe they don't deserve it, but they ask for it anyway. These words have been set to music in what has become quite a popular song in Judaism. It has always been the plea of the Jewish people. The Jews endured the longest exile of any people in history. For two thousand years, whether in Ukraine, Spain, France, Libya, Syria, Yemen, Argentina, or America, at the end of every Passover, they have said, "Next year in Jerusalem."

Unfortunately, the last line of Lamentations does not end on a positive note:

unless you have utterly rejected us,
   and you remain exceedingly angry with us. (Lam 5:22)

Jewish tradition does whatever it can to squeeze every drop of hope out of a text, even one as hopeless as this. Therefore, in Jewish tradition, Lam 5:21 is repeated after Lam 5:22 so that the book ends on a hopeful note:

Restore us to yourself, O LORD, that we may be restored!
   Renew our days as of old—
unless you have utterly rejected us,
   and you remain exceedingly angry with us.

Illuminating Counsel

Restore us to yourself, O LORD, that we may be restored!
Renew our days as of old.

The only hope is the prayer for restoration. The reality remains, however, that people praying this prayer were not entirely confident it would be answered. It's a prayer prayed in desperation, not in certainty.

COMFORT

Is hope found in Lamentations? Or do we have to go outside of Lamentations to find hope? As we saw, there's a sweet spot in the center of the book. However, the hope found there is a flickering flame amidst thick darkness all around. Lamentations, then, is not like the dynamic psalms that modulate to a major key. It's not like Job and Ruth which end with the restoration of the sufferer. Personified Zion, like Job and Naomi, is bereaved of her children, but unlike Job and Naomi, all she has at the end is a plea.

If we cannot find much hope within Lamentations, we can certainly find hope outside of Lamentations. It's long been observed that the part of Isaiah which scholars refer to as Deutero-Isaiah, or Second Isaiah, is a companion piece to Lamentations. Throughout Lamentations, we heard over and over again that there's no one to comfort poor Zion. Second Isaiah comes to the rescue:

Comfort, comfort my people, says your God.
Speak tenderly to Jerusalem,
    and cry to her
that her warfare is ended,
    that her iniquity is pardoned,
that she has received from the LORD's hand
    double for all her sins. (Isa 40:1–2)

But Zion cries out:

The LORD has forsaken me;
    my Lord has forgotten me. (Isa 49:14)

This is almost identical to Lam 5:20—

Why do you *forget* us forever,
    why do you *forsake* us for so many days?

But God responds:

Can a woman forget her nursing child,
    that she should have no compassion on the son of her womb?
Even these may forget,
    yet I will not forget you. (Isa 49:15)

218

No Sorrow Like Her Sorrow

God *did* forsake Zion, but God will not *forget* Zion. The lamenters in Lam 5:1 asked God to remember them. This God has done:

> For the LORD comforts Zion;
>> he comforts all her waste places
> and makes her wilderness like Eden,
>> her desert like the garden of the LORD;
> joy and gladness will be found in her,
>> thanksgiving and the voice of song. (Isa 51:3)

> Break forth together into singing,
>> you waste places of Jerusalem,
> for the LORD has comforted his people;
>> he has redeemed Jerusalem. (Isa 52:9)

> O afflicted one, storm-tossed and not comforted,
>> behold, I will set your stones in antimony,
> and lay your foundations with sapphires. (Isa 54:11)

LAMENTING

There *is* hope for Zion. But that Lamentations does not end that way tells us something profound about suffering. I know of a man who lost his wife when he was in his twenties. He was weeping so hysterically at her funeral that he had to be carried out. He later remarried and had a son. His son was born with a terrible illness. The boy died while still a youth. Then the man's second wife divorced him. When I spoke to him and told him of my own sorrows, he told me that when people are grieving, they don't need to "cheer up," contrary to the hymn, "Farther Along," which says, "Cheer up, my brother . . . we'll understand it all by and by." No. When people are grieving, they need to lament. Sometimes lamenting is the only appropriate, natural, and healthy response to suffering. Sometimes people need to sit in their pain and weep. Those who perpetuated suffering need to grieve over their misdeeds. Those who have been oppressed need to shed their tears. We've touched on these issues already in Psalms and Job, but Lamentations brings the point home. Lamentations isn't variegated like Psalms. There's no joy here. It's not the time for joy. Lamentations isn't a philosophical discourse on wisdom like Job. Lamentations does just one thing: it expresses sorrow.

And oh how it expresses it! What magnificent poetry—as sublime as anything else in the Bible! The poet of Lamentations turned grief into art. Leonard Cohen said, "Never lament casually. And if one is to express the great inevitable defeat that awaits us all, it must be done within the strict confines of dignity and beauty."[15]

15. Cohen was paraphrasing the poet Federico Garcia Lorca. See Alan Showalter, "Leonard Cohen's Prince of Asturias Speech."

Illuminating Counsel

Lamentations is a very Jewish book. It represents all the sufferings of the Jewish people, not just the suffering that occurred on the ninth of Av, 587 BCE. The people that gave the world the Bible have been hated—and hated intensely—by so many, even by people who loved the Bible. Pogrom after pogrom, expulsion after expulsion, from holocaust to holocaust to *the* Holocaust, Jewish history is wet with tears and blood. I wish for Lamentations to draw people's attention to that.

But I also wish for Lamentations to draw our attention to all the sufferers in the world—to the parents who've lost their children, to the children who've lost their parents, to the victims of crime and terrorism, to the miserable ones living in abject poverty, to those who suffer from disease and their caretakers who carry their burdens—I hope Lamentations will arouse our compassion and make us kinder people. I hope Lamentations will cause us to pray and act on behalf of the lonely and afflicted.

12

The Brave Hidden Jew
(Esther)

THE THREE MAJOR THEMES in the book of Esther are: misogyny, antisemitism, and the hiddenness of God.

Esther is the only book of the Bible to unambiguously *not* mention God. It is likely that the original form of the book did, in fact, mention God. That older, and shorter original version is preserved in the Greek manuscript of Esther known as the "Alpha Text." But the only Hebrew version we have of Esther has all references to God removed. It is perhaps for this reason that Esther is the only book of the Hebrew Bible that is not in the Dead Sea Scrolls.

THE KING

The book of Esther, which is written entirely in prose, begins rather strangely. We're not introduced to our heroes until a bit later. Instead we're told of the Persian king, Ahasuerus. In modern Hebrew, his name is pronounced *Achashverosh*. This is a Hebrew version of the name *Khshayarsha*, which the Greeks pronounced *Xerxes*. Xerxes, the son of Darius I, is the king who fought the Spartans, as seen in the movie *300*. The Septuagint, for some reason, posits he's Artaxerxes (presumably Artaxerxes I, the son of Xerxes). Both Xerxes and Artaxerxes I reigned in the fifth century BCE. There's another Achashverosh in Dan 9:1 who is the father of another Darius who was of Median descent. This is probably not the Achashverosh in Esther and, interestingly enough, the Septuagint translates Achashverosh in Daniel as Xerxes. Then there's an Achashverosh in Ezra 4:6, which the Septuagint transliterates *Asoueros*.[1] All of this is confusing, so I shall simply refer to the Achashverosh in Esther as "the king."

---

1. This is how the name is spelled in the New English Translation of the Septuagint (NETS).

Illuminating Counsel

The book of Esther begins by telling us how powerful the king is. He rules over 127 provinces from India to Ethiopia (Esth 1:1).[2] He likes showing off his wealth and having people celebrate it. He parades his wealth around for 180 days. Then, in the city of Susa, he throws a party for seven days. There is only one rule: "There is no compulsion" (Esth 1:8). This means there are no rules; you can drink as much as you want. This king could out-party any college student. By day three, even the biggest party animals would be telling him they have to go and study!

The king has a wife. Her name is Vashti. The king's party is a male-only affair. Vashti is having her own party for women. On the seventh day of the king's feast, the king summons Vashti to appear at his party "with her royal crown, in order to show the peoples and the princes her beauty, for she was lovely to look at" (Esth 1:11). Jewish tradition interprets this to mean that she was to appear at the party wearing *nothing* but her crown.[3] Vashti refuses to come.

Vashti's insubordination enrages the king. He turns to his officials for advice, as was his custom. The officials tell him that this situation is very bad, indeed. If everyone hears that Vashti disobeyed the king without penalty, all the women of the empire will start disobeying their husbands. And so the advisors tell the king to banish Vashti, to replace her with someone more worthy (that is, someone who's obedient), and to pass an irrevocable law ordering all women to honor their husbands. The king likes this idea. He banishes Vashti and passes a law that every man is to be "master in his own household" (Esth 1:22). We need to make three points about this:

1. Vashti is a strong woman who is righteously disobedient. We, the reader, ought to support her and sympathize with her.

2. The king may be powerful but he's also indecisive and impressionable. He reacts to situations but he only does what his advisors tell him to do. He lacks the wisdom to discern whether the advice he receives is sagacious or not. This can cut both ways. It means, as we just saw, that he will take bad advice. It also means that it's possible he will take good advice.

3. The opening chapter presses hard the theme of misogyny. It's not a spoiler to say that the book is about a woman. The book, then, is undoubtedly anti-misogyny. This is quite extraordinary for a book that's well over two thousand years old. But the book is not preachy on the matter. If nothing else, telling a story with a female heroine within a misogynistic society makes for a compelling read. It creates dramatic tension. The woman is an underdog.

In order to find a replacement for Vashti, virgins throughout Susa are kidnapped, placed in a harem ("house of women" in Hebrew), and given extensive

---

2. The Hebrew says "Cush." This is best understood as Nubia, which is modern-day Sudan, not Ethiopia.

3. Tull, *Esther and Ruth*, loc. 250.

222

The Brave Hidden Jew

beauty treatments. Naturally, only the most attractive women are taken. The king gets to have sex with each of them. Eventually he will choose one of them to be his queen. The rest, I suppose, stay in his harem. There's to be only one queen, but the king is not monogamous.

THE HEROES

Finally we're introduced to our heroes: "Now there was a Jew in Susa the citadel whose name was Mordecai" (Esth 2:5). He had adopted his little cousin, Hadassah, because her parents had died. Hadassah's alias is Esther. We're told "the young woman had a beautiful figure and was lovely to look at" (Esth 2:7). She ends up being one of the virgins who's taken into the king's harem.

At this point in history, Jerusalem and Judah have been reestablished. The Jews began returning to Jerusalem in 538 BCE. Many Jews didn't return, however. Mordecai's family were among those Jews who stayed in the diaspora. They built a life there. Picking up and moving isn't easy.

There's something strange about Mordecai and Esther. Mordecai is not a Hebrew name. It actually comes from the name Marduk. Marduk is the chief god of the Babylonian pantheon. Hadassah *is* a Hebrew name. It means "myrtle tree." But the name Esther is Persian. It means "star." It also sounds like the name of the goddess Ishtar. Ishtar was the Mesopotamian goddess of war and fertility. So our Jewish heroes are named after pagan deities![4]

However, the name Esther has a dual meaning. Esther is simultaneously Persian *and* Hebrew. Esther means, "I will hide." "Esther had not made known her people or kindred, for Mordecai had commanded her not to make it known" (Esth 2:10). Esther *hides* her Jewish identity from the world.

Esther makes an impression in the harem. "Now Esther was winning favor in the eyes of all who saw her" (Esth 2:15). She becomes the king's favorite and he makes her his queen in place of Vashti. This is no surprise, dramatically speaking. The reader sees this coming a mile away. The question, though, is why Esther makes such an impact. I'm sure many people would say that the light of God shined from Esther's face. She was just so godly that everyone who saw her knew that God was with her! But that doesn't seem right to me. After all, Esther hides her Jewish identity. She doesn't "let her line shine," as the saying goes. It's possible to hide one's Jewishness and still keep Jewish customs—it's been done before—but it's not easy. How Jewish can one really be while married to a pagan tyrant?

Ruth and Esther are opposites. Whereas Ruth the Moabitess becomes a Jew and marries a Jew, Esther the Jew hides her Jewish identity and marries a non-Jew.

4. Levenson, *Esther*, 58.

223

Illuminating Counsel

The reason the king fancies Esther is hinted at twice in the text. Mordecai had "commanded" Esther to hide her Jewish identity (Esth 2:10). The text later says, "Esther had not made known her kindred or her people, as Mordecai had commanded her, *for Esther obeyed Mordecai just as when she was brought up by him*" (Esth 2:20). What was the king looking for in a woman? Someone beautiful—of course—but also someone who's *obedient*. Someone who will come when summoned, or not show up unsummoned.[5] Esther is that obedient girl. Mordecai commands her to do something, and she obeys, just as she *always* obeyed. Vashti and Esther are opposites.[6]

There's a plot to assassinate the king. Mordecai discovers it and tells Esther. Esther tells the king. The king has the conspirators hanged (Esth 2:19–23). Thus Mordecai saves the king's life. It's recorded in the king's chronicles but Mordecai is not given any special honor. We don't hear about it again until much later in the book.

But why would he save this king's life? Why would he save the life of a misogynistic tyrant who had his adopted daughter kidnapped? Does that make sense to you? The story will only get stranger as it progresses.

THE VILLAIN

The king is a chauvinist pig, but he's not the villain of the story. The real villain is introduced in ch. 3. When his name is read in the synagogue on Purim (more on that later), the congregation uses "graggers," or noisemakers, to make as much noise as possible to blot it out. That name is Haman. Haman is called "the Agagite." This reminds us of the rivalry between King Saul and King Agag of the Amalekites (see 1 Sam 15), especially since Esth 2:5 had told us that Mordecai is from the tribe of Benjamin—the same tribe as King Saul.

Mordecai is overlooked for saving the king's life. Instead Haman is promoted to be the king's second-in-command. Perhaps this is a response to the assassination plot.[7] The king commands everyone who sees Haman to bow down to him. This is the king's way of solidifying his power.

But Mordecai refuses to bow. This happens repeatedly. People try reasoning with him but he's adamant that he's not going to bow to Haman. Why not? Some readers will think it's idolatry to bow to a human, but that's not true. Plenty of people who are faithful to God also pay homage to human rulers (see 1 Sam 24:8 and 1 Kgs 1:16). God, of course, is not mentioned in the book, and so God is not the stated reason Mordecai doesn't bow. Mordecai actually does give the reason he won't bow: "And

---

5. Regarding Esther adorning herself only with what Hegai, the king's eunuch advised (Esth 2:15), Levenson says, "This too may foreshadow her deference to another older man, Mordecai, in her moment of decision (4:16)." See Levenson, *Esther*, 62. I will argue, though, that Esther has to break the rules, which is out of her character, in order to save her people.

6. Hazony's view is far more nuanced. See Hazony, *God and Politics in Esther*, 25.

7. Hazony, *God and Politics in Esther*, 32.

The Brave Hidden Jew

when they spoke to him day after day and he would not listen to them, they told Haman, in order to see whether Mordecai's words would stand, *for he had told them that he was a Jew*" (Esth 3:4). Mordecai doesn't bow because he's a Jew![8]

I'm not sure if Mordecai had previously told anyone that he's a Jew. His name is not Jewish. He is, after all, the man who told Esther to hide her Jewish identity. It's possible that Mordecai was a Jew who had assimilated into Persian society.[9] If that's the case, it means that this confrontation with Haman is his "coming out." He finally reveals who he truly is. He's a Jew. It may not make sense to some readers, but *that* is the reason he doesn't bow to Haman.

Haman is an egomaniac. He's furious that Mordecai won't bow to him. Haman wants to kill Mordecai but he "disdained to lay hands on Mordecai alone. So, as they had made known to him the people of Mordecai, Haman sought to destroy all the Jews" (Esth 3:6). This is the "final solution." Before Hitler, there was Haman.

Haman goes to the king to make his dream of annihilating the Jews a reality. He says to the king:

> There is a certain people scattered abroad and dispersed among the peoples in all the provinces of your kingdom. Their laws are different from those of every other people, and they do not keep the king's laws, so that it is not to the king's profit to tolerate them. If it please the king, let it be decreed that they be destroyed, and I will pay 10,000 talents of silver into the hands of those who have charge of the king's business, that they may put it into the king's treasuries. (Esth 3:8–9)

It's true that the Jews were "scattered abroad" and "dispersed" throughout the empire. It's true that the laws of the Jews—the Torah—are unique. It's not quite true that the Jews do not obey the king's laws. Yes, Mordecai didn't obey the king's law to bow to Haman, but that doesn't mean *all* Jews disobey the king's laws. Jews would disobey the king's laws only when the king's laws conflict with the Torah. Otherwise, Jews live as subjects of the king. It's completely *untrue* that it's not in the king's "profit" to "tolerate" the Jews.

What's so eerie about Haman's words is how his half-truths have been repeated throughout history. In some form they've been echoed by the Romans, by the church, by the Nazis, by the Communists, and others.

Antisemitism is the view that Jews are inherently problematic. In 1880, a quarter of a million Germans signed a petition that was presented to Reich Chancellor Otto von Bismarck. The petition began:

> In all regions of Germany the conviction has prevailed that the rank growth of the Jewish element bears within it the most serious dangers to our nationhood.[10]

---

8. Hazony, *God and Politics in Esther*, 30.

9. Hazony, *God and Politics in Esther*, 31.

10. Dawidowicz, *A Holocaust Reader*, loc. 344–45.

The petition later states:

> In view of these conditions and of the massive penetration of Semitic elements into all positions which impart power and influence . . . it certainly does not appear unjustified from either the ethical or the national point of view to ask: What future awaits our fatherland if the Semitic element remains in a position for another generation to make such conquests on our native soil as have been made in the last two decades? If the concept of a fatherland is not to be stripped of its ideal meaning; if the conception that it was our fathers who wrested this soil from the wilderness, who fertilized it in a thousand battles with their blood, is not to be lost to our Volk; if the intimate relationship of German custom and German morality with the Christian world view and Christian tradition is to be preserved-then a foreign stock, that has been accorded visitors' and resident rights by our humane legislation, but whose feeling and thinking is further from us than is that of any people of the whole Aryan world, must never be permitted to rise to dominance on German soil.[11]

Is there any substantive difference between this petition and Haman's? Haman's antisemitism is more primitive in that it lacks the Germanic nationalism and pseudo-scientific racial hierarchy that we see in Nazi ideology, but it's otherwise essentially the same. Both argue that Jews are aliens. Both argue that Jewish presence ruins the land. Both argue the land is better off without Jews.

The expulsions, pogroms, forced conversions, etc., are the antisemite's solutions to the "Jewish problem." Eventually, the antisemite realizes that those solutions don't work. The only way to deal with the Jews, the antisemite concludes, is to annihilate them. About two thousand years ago, the rabbis said: "For, not only one arose to try to destroy us. Rather, in every generation they try to destroy us. But God saves us from their hands."[12] The rabbis were speaking of Pharaoh. Pharaoh enslaved the Jews to curb their power. Then he killed their babies. Eventually he tried to wipe them out while their backs were against the sea. Pharaoh was not the only one. The Amalekites tried to annihilate the Jews (Exod 17:8–16). In Ps 82, seven nations try to annihilate the Jews. Haman tried to annihilate the Jews. Hitler tried to annihilate the Jews. Sadly, even today, people are determined to annihilate the Jews.

The truth is it *was* in the king's "profit" to tolerate the Jews. This is emphasized repeatedly in the Bible and I will come back to it later. Suffice it to say for now, Jews are a blessing to the nations. I don't think it's out of bounds to use real modern statistics to illustrate this point. Jews are only .02 percent of the world's population, but they've received 22.5 percent of the Nobel Prizes. One would think no one would notice the disappearance of such a small people, but the whole world would be a lot worse off if the Hamans and the Hitlers of the world had had their way.

11. Dawidowicz, *A Holocaust Reader*, loc. 350–56

12. This quote is from the section in the Haggadah called *Vehi She'amda*.

The Brave Hidden Jew

So Haman offers to pay ten thousand talents of silver to have the Jews annihilated.[13] The king green-lights the plan. The king is impressionable, remember?

Haman casts *purim*, that is, lots, to determine when the Jews will be annihilated. "Letters were sent by couriers to all the king's provinces with instruction to destroy, to kill, and to annihilate all Jews, young and old, women and children, in one day, the thirteenth day of the twelfth month, which is the month of Adar, and to plunder their goods" (Esth 3:13). That's awful, of course, but the silver lining is that the Jews have some time until it happens. Annihilation Day could have been the very next week. Chapter 3 ends ominously: "The king and Haman sat down to drink, but the city of Susa was thrown into confusion" (Esth 3:15).[14]

And it's all Mordecai's fault! Well, we can't *really* blame him, but we *can* note the awful irony. If Mordecai had *not* saved the king's life, Haman would not have been promoted. And if Mordecai had not refused to bow to Haman, and had not told everyone the reason he didn't bow is because he's a Jew, the Jews would not have been targeted for annihilation. This is very compelling storytelling because not only do we have a true villain (perhaps the Bible's most villainous villain), we also have very flawed heroes who seem to make dubious decisions. And where is God when you need him?

THE DECISION

> When Mordecai learned all that had been done, Mordecai tore his clothes and put on sackcloth and ashes, and went out into the midst of the city, and he cried out with a loud and bitter cry. He went up to the entrance of the king's gate, for no one was allowed to enter the king's gate clothed in sackcloth. And in every province, wherever the king's command and his decree reached, there was great mourning among the Jews, with fasting and weeping and lamenting, and many of them lay in sackcloth and ashes. (Esth 4:1–3)

All the Jews are mourning because they have been targeted for annihilation, but Esther has no idea what's going on! She's the one who's closest to the king—the man who green-lit this heinous plan—and yet Esther is totally clueless.

Esther is informed that the Jews are mourning and she offers to give Mordecai clothes to wear instead of sackcloth so that he can enter the palace and talk face to face; no one is allowed to wear mourner's clothing in the jolly king's palace. Mordecai refuses. They will have to communicate through a messenger.

---

13. Tull notes that this is the opposite of what Oskar Schindler did. Schindler spent his fortune to save Jews from genocide. See Tull, *Esther and Ruth*, loc. 397.

14. The king and Haman drinking amidst the chaos of the city reminds us of Joseph's brothers eating while Joseph was thrown into the waterless pit. See Gen 37:24–25.

Illuminating Counsel

Mordecai gives Esther a copy of the written decree ordering the annihilation of the Jews. Mordecai is not without hope, however. Esther is the Jews' "ace in the hole." Esther can talk to the king on behalf of the Jews. Esther can save the Jewish people!

I'm assuming this means she will have to stop pretending she's not Jewish. The man who commanded her to hide her Jewish identity now tells her to "come out," just as he "came out." One could retort that she doesn't have to tell the king she's a Jew in order to intercede on behalf of the Jews. However, I think the idea is that the king would be more likely to stop the annihilation of the Jews if he realized his dear wife is also a Jew. Esther must come out of hiding!

But there's a problem. She can't go to the king, she says. There's a protocol. No one—man or woman—is allowed to approach the king unsummoned. That includes the queen. The penalty for approaching the king unsummoned is death. The only loophole in the protocol is if the king grants clemency, indicated by the lowering of his golden scepter. But, she says, she hasn't been summoned to the king in a month. Methinks that means he's having sex with other women in his harem. Clearly Esther thinks she has lost favor in the king's eyes—that there's no chance he'd lower his scepter—and therefore approaching the king would be suicide.

We're approaching the middle of the book. You know what that means! We're now engaging with the most important ideas. Mordecai's response to Esther is perhaps the key piece of dialogue in the book:

> Do not think to yourself that in the king's palace you will escape any more than all the other Jews. For if you keep silent at this time, relief and deliverance will rise for the Jews from another place, but you and your father's house will perish. And who knows whether you have not come to the kingdom for such a time as this? (Esth 4:13–14)

Let's deconstruct what Mordecai says. Esther said if she *does* intercede for the Jews, she will die. Mordecai says if she does *not* intercede for the Jews, she will die.

Mordecai's proposition is complicated by his statement that Esther is *not* the only hope for the Jews. If Esther will not intercede, someone else will. Who? Mordecai doesn't say. Deliverance will come "from another place." How does Mordecai know that? And if Mordecai is correct—if it's a foregone conclusion that deliverance will come to the Jews—why is Mordecai so insistent that his little cousin risk her life to intercede? It's more than that, though. If "relief and deliverance" will indeed come to the Jews despite Esther's silence, why will Esther and her "father's house" die?

We cannot escape the thought that Mordecai is manipulating Esther. I say "manipulating" rather than "persuading" because he's saying things that don't appear to be logical. He says:

1. Esther must approach the king to rescue the Jews.

2. If she doesn't, the Jews will still be delivered.

3. Even though the Jews will be delivered, Esther will die.

The Brave Hidden Jew

Ironically, Esther will live only if she commits the capital offense of approaching the king unsummoned.

Is Mordecai right? Or is Mordecai saying what he's saying because he knows Esther approaching the king is the *only* hope the Jewish people have for deliverance?

Why would Esther die if she does *not* intercede? My answer is that Esther would die because she's a Jew. If that interpretation is correct, it means that Mordecai is saying that Esther cannot hide her real identity. That's interesting because Jews don't look different from anyone else. Blacks in majority white countries cannot hide their skin color. But Jews usually look like the majority. Yes, Jews dress differently and pray differently and have a different diet, but all those things can be changed. Jews can *fully* assimilate into the dominant culture. But Mordecai is saying otherwise. Mordecai is saying that Esther is, and always will be, Jewish. She can change her name, she can eat pork, she can marry the king, but none of that will save her because underneath it all she's a Jew. Mordecai won't bow because he's a Jew. Esther won't survive because she's a Jew.

The Jews of Germany in the first half of the twentieth century were the most assimilated Jews in Europe. They fought for Germany in World War I. They said they were German first and Jews second. But it didn't matter to the Nazis. It didn't matter if Jews converted to Christianity. It didn't matter if Jews were atheists. It didn't matter if Jews were only a quarter Jewish. A Jew is a Jew is a Jew. Jews cannot hide from their Jewishness. And if they cannot hide from their Jewishness, they might as well embrace it.

JOSEPH AND MOSES

At this point we need to pause in order to connect some dots. The first point to make is that Esther bears similarities to Joseph. Esther and Joseph are young (Esth 2:7; Gen 37:2). Esther and Joseph are attractive (Esth 2:7; Gen 39:6). Esther and Joseph both have two names; Joseph's Egyptian name is Zaphenath-paneah (Esth 2:7; Gen 41:45). Esther and Joseph are kidnapped (Esth 2:8; Gen 37:28). Esther and Joseph impress the people who are over them (Esth 2:9, 15; Gen 39:3–4, 21–23). Esther and Joseph rise to prominence in the palace (Esth 2:17; Gen 41:37–41). Esther and Joseph end up saving the Jewish people (Esth 8:7–8; Gen 45:4–13; 50:20).

The stories of Esther and Joseph are exilic stories. Technically, the "Exile" (with a capital E) refers to the Babylonian exile which began in 597 BCE. This means that—again, technically—Joseph's story is pre-exilic and Esther's is post-exilic. However, Joseph's story is about exile in general. Joseph and his family end up living outside of the land of Israel. Esther and Mordecai remained in the diaspora (the land outside the land of Israel) despite the fact that the temple in Jerusalem had been rebuilt. So both Joseph's family and Esther's Jews are minorities in the lands in which they lived.

As we've just pointed out, the contours of the two stories are the same. A Jew in exile, who hits rock bottom, rises to prominence in the Gentile king's court and ends up saving the Jewish people from extinction. The book of Esther is a variation on the

229

Joseph story in numerous ways. For one thing, Esther is, of course, a woman. Moreover, in the book of Esther the "Joseph" figure is bifurcated. It's not just Esther who rises to prominence in the Gentile king's court to save the Jewish people; Mordecai does as well (Esth 10:1–3).

There are two important sub-themes within these stories. The first theme has to do with the wisdom of the Jewish people. This is particularly emphasized in the Joseph story. Pharaoh says of Joseph, "Can we find a man like this, in whom is the Spirit of God?" (Gen 41:38). And then Pharaoh says to Joseph, "Since God has shown you all this, there is none so discerning and wise as you are" (Gen 41:39). We already pointed out how ironic this is in Esther. The whole world has profited from the tiny Jews. The message is that the dispersion of the Jewish people is a way of God fulfilling his promise to bless all the nations of the world through them (Gen 12:3).

The second theme, though, is the danger of assimilation. Jews living in non-Jewish nations might be tempted to assimilate (or forced to assimilate) and thereby lose their Jewish identity. This doesn't mean the Bible views assimilation in general as something bad. Ruth assimilated; she became a Jew. If people want to assimilate, they should have the right to do so. If people move to another country voluntarily, perhaps they have an obligation to do so. And to some extent, assimilation is inevitable. But the Tanakh isn't concerned with immigration per se; it's concerned with Jews. If Jews assimilate, there will be none left.

Because many people don't read the Bible from a Jewish perspective (which is understandable), the theme of assimilation in the Joseph story often goes unnoticed. But consider: Joseph not only becomes the second-in-command of Egypt, he also marries an Egyptian woman, the daughter of a priest. Joseph dressed as an Egyptian and spoke Egyptian so well his brothers didn't suspect he was anything other than Egyptian (Gen 42:8). Yes, he gives his sons Hebrew names, but look at the meaning of those names. "Manasseh" comes from the word that means "forget"—"God has made me forget all my hardship and all my father's house," Joseph says (Gen 41:51). "Ephraim" comes from the word that means "fruitful"—"God has made me fruitful in the land of my affliction," Joseph says (Gen 41:52). Joseph had moved on. That's why, after he becomes Prime Minister, he never goes back to his father to tell his father he's alive.[15]

Joseph, therefore, becomes an Egyptian. However, Judah's speech changes him. Judah's speech emphasizes their father (Gen 44:18–34). Joseph realizes he can't forget his father's house. He can't move on entirely. Judah's speech reminds Joseph who he is: he's a child of Israel—or, as his descendants would later be called, a Jew.[16]

Then there's Moses. Moses is also a Jew who rises to prominence in the Gentile king's court. But Moses is the mirror image of Joseph. Joseph begins as a Jew and becomes an Egyptian. Moses begins as an Egyptian and becomes a Jew. The qualifiers are

---

15. Sacks, *Genesis*, loc. 5345. Sacks says, "Joseph did not communicate with his father because he believed his father no longer wanted to see him or hear from him."

16. Koptak, "Rhetorical Identification in Preaching," 11–18.

The Brave Hidden Jew

that Joseph recovers his Jewish identity toward the end of his story just as Moses was born and raised in a Jewish home in the very beginning of his story. Moses presumably had to discover he was a Jew. Even when he runs away from Egypt, the Midianite women think he's Egyptian (Exod 2:19). He names his son Gershom, which comes from the word that means "sojourner"—"I have been a sojourner in a foreign land," he says (Exod 2:22). Moses doesn't know what he is or where he belongs!

Look at Esther's connections with Moses. Both Esther and Moses have names which have meanings in two different languages. Moses is both an Egyptian name as well as a Hebrew name. In Egyptian, it means "child of." In Hebrew, Moses is Moshe. Moshe comes from the word *mashah*, which means "drew out." Pharaoh's daughter names him Moshe because she "drew him out of the water" (Exod 2:10). Esther and Moses have hidden identities in the palace. Esther and Moses are assisted by a relative—Esther by her cousin, Mordecai, and Moses by his brother, Aaron. Esther and Moses rescue the Jewish people from annihilation—not from a famine as does Joseph, but from a genocidal maniac (Esth 3:6; cf. Exod 15:9). Their rescuing of the Jews is commemorated by holidays: Purim and Passover, respectively. Purim is in the twelfth month. Passover is in the first month. The two holidays are thus a month apart from each other.

We should also add that Esther's story and Moses's story both feature misogyny. In the case of Esther, the misogyny is overt. In the Moses story, the misogyny is "soft." Pharaoh is threatened by the males, and so he has the male babies killed and the females left alive. He underestimates the power of women. He ends up defied and defeated by women: the Hebrew midwives, Moses's mother, Moses's sister, and his own daughter. Esther and Mordecai are composites of Joseph, but Esther herself is a combination of Moses and Exodus's heroic women.

So let's put all of this together. Joseph is a Jew who becomes an Egyptian but eventually becomes a Jew again. Likewise, Moses is a Jew who becomes an Egyptian but eventually becomes a Jew again. Esther is a Jew who becomes a Persian but eventually becomes a Jew again. Mordecai told her to hide her Jewish identity. His logic was not that he was embarrassed about being a Jew, but that being a Jew could get one into trouble. He was right. Even so, we can question the nobility and wisdom of hiding ones identity. Is this what Jews in the diaspora should do?

These Jews are among the greatest heroes of the Bible. But in order to be heroes, they had to accept their true identity. They needed to accept their Jewishness.

GOD

Let's return to Esth 4. Mordecai adds another point in his attempt to get Esther to risk her life. He raises the possibility that she became queen for the purpose of saving the Jewish people. He suggests that all that had happened had happened for a reason. It was her destiny to save the Jewish people from the wicked Haman.

Illuminating Counsel

But Mordecai only suggests this. "Who knows?" he says. He's not dogmatic about it. Maybe it's all fate. Maybe it isn't. He's not claiming to have received revelation. He's simply planting a thought in Esther's head to get her to intercede for the Jews.

This brings us back to Joseph. A third feature of this "court Jew" biblical trope is the providence of God. The book of Esther presents a very interesting variation on this theme. Compare what Joseph says about God's providence with what Mordecai says:

> As for you, you meant evil against me, but God meant it for good, to bring it about that many people should be kept alive, as they are today. (Gen 50:20)

> And who knows whether you have not come to the kingdom for such a time as this? (Esth 4:14)

Joseph is totally certain. Joseph knows that everything that happened was part of God's plan. Mordecai does not have that certainty. If ever there was a place where the book of Esther should have mentioned God, surely it's here. All Mordecai had to say was, "God has raised you up in the kingdom for such a time as this." He doesn't say that. Can you imagine Joseph saying, "You meant evil against me, but *who knows* whether God meant it for good to bring it about that many people should be kept alive, as they are today?" Of course, it's true that Mordecai is speaking before the fact (the saving of the Jews) whereas Joseph is speaking with the clarity of hindsight. Even so, Mordecai never revises what he says. God is not mentioned in the book!

What about the many coincidences in the book of Esther? Out of all the women that could have been chosen queen, it was a Jewish girl who was chosen at the very time when an antisemite would plot the annihilation of the Jews. Mordecai saves the king's life and refuses to bow to Haman, seemingly causing the downfall of the Jews, but it actually causes the downfall of Haman. Haman's wife tells him to build gallows for Mordecai to be hanged on (Esth 5:14). On that very night, the king happened to have a case of insomnia (Esth 6:1). He wants to be lulled to sleep by a reading of his chronicles. Out of all the things that could have been read from his chronicles that evening, what is read is the account of how Mordecai saved the king (Esth 6:2). At that very moment Haman walks in.[17] Haman is told to parade Mordecai around the city so that Mordecai can receive the honor due him (Esth 6:6–11). Haman ends up being hanged on the very gallows he built for Mordecai (Esth 7:9–10). The day on which the Jews were to be annihilated ends up being the day they are victorious over their enemies. Talk about poetic justice!

Coincidences make for compelling storytelling, but do these coincidences indicate that God is active in the book? Is God absent? Or is God merely playing hide and seek, taking a cue from Isa 45:15 which says, "Truly, you are a God who hides himself"?

Some won't like to hear this, but the truth is coincidences are ambiguous. They might be indicators of the providential hand of God. Then again, they might

---

17. The text makes it seem like there's no gap of time between the events.

be meaningless. How we interpret the coincidences in the book of Esther says more about us than about the text.

We have the same issues in the Joseph story. If Joseph had never been sold as a slave, if he had never been thrown into prison for being (falsely) accused of attempted rape, he would never have been made second-in-command of Egypt. In other words, if the brothers had listened to Reuben and *did the right thing* by bringing Joseph back to his father instead of selling him, the whole family would have died and there would have been no Jewish people! No wonder Joseph saw the hand of God at work!

But in Esther, we're never given that definitive statement that this was all God's doing. Therefore, if God is indeed in the book of Esther, the reader of the book must have faith *within the book*. What do I mean by that? Think of the book of Exodus. The reader doesn't need to have faith within Exodus because God is everywhere in Exodus. The reader reads about God speaking to Moses and performing miracles. The reader needs to have faith that God is working *today*, but not that God worked within the book. The book of Esther, though, is wholly different. The reader has to have faith that God is working within the book because God is invisible in the book. The reader has to have faith that God is *hiding* rather than absent. Interpreting the book of Esther is like interpreting the events of one's life. Amazing things happen. George Washington's hat had bullet holes in it and yet he was never once injured in battle. Had one of those bullets been one inch in another direction, all of American history, indeed world history, would have been different. To some, including Washington himself, it was Providence at work. To others, it was just coincidence. Mordecai would say, *Who knows*?! Faith, then, is a choice.

COURAGE

Esther tells Mordecai:

> Go, gather all the Jews to be found in Susa, and hold a fast on my behalf, and do not eat or drink for three days, night or day. I and my young women will also fast as you do. Then I will go to the king, though it is against the law, and if I perish, I perish. (Esth 4:16)

Esther had to change. She had to become more like Vashti. In the beginning, Esther was very obedient. She was a rule-keeper. We surmised that that's why the king fancied her. But now she realizes that she must break the rules in order to rescue her people. She also realizes that she must take charge. Earlier, the text had said that Esther obeyed Mordecai's commands. Now, the text tells us, "Mordecai . . . did everything as Esther had ordered him" (Esth 4:17).[18]

Esther approaches the king unsummoned (Esth 5:1). This is her "David and Goliath" moment. What she does takes as much courage as any act in the Bible.

18. The word translated "ordered" comes from the same root as the word translated "commanded."

Illuminating Counsel

The king lowers his golden scepter (Esth 5:2). He liked her a lot more than she thought. She asks for a private banquet—just her, the king, and Haman. She doesn't want to make her request known in the court. But when the banquet occurs, Esther loses her nerve. She doesn't say anything. So she asks for a second private banquet. It's in that second banquet that she reveals everything:

> If I have found favor in your sight, O king, and if it please the king, let my life be granted me for my wish, and my people for my request. For we have been sold, I and my people, to be destroyed, to be killed, and to be annihilated. If we had been sold merely as slaves, men and women, I would have been silent, for our affliction is not to be compared with the loss to the king. (Esth 7:3–4)

Notice she says, "I and my people." That's the first time she reveals who she really is. She then exposes "wicked" Haman, whom she calls "a foe and an enemy" (Esth 7:6). There's something refreshing about calling an evil person what he is.

The king silently walks out. It's an ambiguous gesture. This creates dramatic tension. Will he punish Haman? Or will he punish Esther for being a Jew and a rebellious woman?

Haman begs Esther for mercy. The king comes back in, sees Haman too close to his wife, and gets the wrong idea. He thinks Haman is assaulting his wife. The reader doesn't mind that the king misreads the situation. He then orders Haman to be executed.

So the king isn't a villain. He's an anti-hero. He just needed to start listening to better advice than that of his chauvinistic advisors and his antisemitic hatchet man. How ironic that the book begins with him punishing a woman and it ends with him listening to a woman!

Esther is a hero. She risks her life to save the Jewish people from annihilation. Here we note more connections with Ruth. Yes, Ruth and Esther are opposites. Ruth becomes a Jew whereas Esther hides her Jewish identity. For both of them, being a Jew is a risk. Ruth takes a risk in becoming a Jew because she might not be accepted as a Jew by the Jewish community. Esther takes a risk by coming out as a Jew because she might not be accepted by Persian society. Esther reveals herself to the two misogynistic men who ordered the annihilation of the Jews. It's almost like revealing one's Jewishness to Hitler and Goering! The decision to become Jewish works out for both Ruth and Esther. Ruth and Esther make decisions which have profound consequences for the Jewish people. If Ruth had not gone with Naomi to Bethlehem, there would be no David. If Esther had not approached the king, the Jews would have been annihilated.[19] From the Christian perspective, we can summarily say: No Ruth, no Jesus. No Esther, no Jesus.

The book of Esther, then, is as much about suffering as any of the other books of the Ketuvim. It foreshadows the Nazi Holocaust! Some ancient rabbis were afraid that

19. Mordecai's comment to the contrary notwithstanding!

The Brave Hidden Jew

people might read Esther and get ideas about annihilating the Jews.[20] They weren't wrong. But Esther teaches us that the way to respond to catastrophe is by being courageous. Ronald Reagan said, "Evil is powerless if the good are unafraid."

In the Psalms, courage is linked to faith. Psalm 23:4 says, "Even though I walk through the valley of the shadow of death I will fear no evil, for you are with me." Psalm 27:1 says, "The LORD is my light and my salvation; whom shall I fear?" But is this truly courage? Courage is usually defined as, not the absence of fear, but doing the right thing despite feeling fear. In that vein, I'm not sure David is courageous for standing up to Goliath. From our point of view he's courageous because we'd be terrified to fight Goliath. David is also the *only* one who is willing to fight Goliath. But David is totally unafraid of Goliath because of his faith (1 Sam 17:37).

Because the book of Esther doesn't mention God, we can't definitively say that Esther acts in faith. Unlike David, Esther is not certain that she will survive. Unlike Moses, God doesn't give her assurance that she'll be successful. Esther teaches us that we must do the right thing even if we're not sure where God is.[21] Esther is therefore courageous in a way virtually no one else in the Bible is. For this reason, I find Esther to be one of the most relatable and inspiring of all the Bible's heroes.

When faced with suffering, sometimes we turn to prayer. Prayer expresses our emotions and fosters a faith which informs us that though we lack control, God is at the helm and will answer us according to his righteousness.

We must also seek wisdom. For one thing, wisdom teaches us how to respond to suffering. Moreover, acting wisely will minimize future suffering.

But in order to be truly wise we must be humble. Suffering reminds us how small we are in the universe and how limited our understanding is. Humility causes us to look at the wonders of the world around us rather than think we are the center of everything.

We must also act in kindness. Suffering is not an excuse to be selfish.

Likewise, love is so important to life. "He who finds a [spouse] finds a good thing" (Prov 18:22). Love brings people into a temporary paradise amidst the pains and fragilities of life.

We must also rejoice. Life is short and filled with suffering. We must therefore be intentional about rejoicing. Don't wait for joy to find you. Go to it and grab hold of it.

When times get very hard, though, lamenting is the only appropriate response. Only in expressing our sorrow can we be liberated from it.

But sometimes we don't have time to lament. Sometimes we have to step up and act despite fear. Sometimes we have to find it within ourselves to be courageous even if we lack the faith which supplies that courage.

---

20. See Sacks, "God's Hidden Call."

21. This idea comes from Yoram Hazony. See Sean Giordano, "Prager Discusses the Book of Esther."

ARROGANCE AND HUMILITY

I can't help but think of the books of the Bible in terms of music. The book of Esther seems like a variation on themes from the book of Exodus. One of the major sub-themes of Exodus is arrogance and humility. Pharaoh is the arrogant man extraordinaire whereas Moses is totally humble. In Esther, those roles are played out by Haman and Mordecai. Haman expects people to bow to him. He gets very excited when he's invited to a private dinner by the royal family: "And Haman went out that day joyful and glad of heart" (Esth 5:9). But he can't be happy if Mordecai doesn't bow to him: "But when Haman saw Mordecai in the king's gate, that he neither rose nor trembled before him, he was filled with wrath against Mordecai" (Esth 5:9). Haman says, "Even Queen Esther let no one but me come with the king to the feast she prepared. And tomorrow also I am invited by her together with the king. Yet all this is worth nothing to me, so long as I see Mordecai the Jew sitting at the king's gate" (Esth 5:12–13). When the king asks Haman what he thinks should be done to the man the king wishes to honor, Haman assumes the king is speaking of him. So he goes to town with ideas:

> For the man whom the king delights to honor, let royal robes be brought, which the king has worn, and the horse that the king has ridden, and on whose head a royal crown is set. And let the robes and the horse be handed over to one of the king's most noble officials. Let them dress the man whom the king delights to honor, and let them lead him on the horse through the square of the city, proclaiming before him: 'Thus shall it be done to the man whom the king delights to honor.'" (Esth 6:7–9)

Imagine the look on Haman's face when he learns that he has to do all those things for Mordecai!

Mordecai, by contrast, doesn't seek his own fame. He saves the king's life without getting credit for it and it doesn't seem to bother him. He saves the king because it's the right thing to do. True, he doesn't bow to Haman, but why should he? Haman is arrogant and deserves to be humbled. Mordecai is humble and deserves to be exalted to a position of honor:

> On that day King Ahasuerus gave to Queen Esther the house of Haman, the enemy of the Jews. And Mordecai came before the king, for Esther had told what he was to her. And the king took off his signet ring, which he had taken from Haman, and gave it to Mordecai. And Esther set Mordecai over the house of Haman. (Esth 8:1–2)

Reading Esther in light of Proverbs is interesting. Proverbs has a lot to say about pride and humility, as we mentioned:

- "When pride comes, then comes disgrace, but with the humble is wisdom" (Prov 11:2).

The Brave Hidden Jew

- "Pride goes before destruction, and a haughty spirit before a fall" (Prov 16:18).

- "Before destruction a man's heart is haughty, but humility comes before honor" (Prov 18:12).

- "The reward for humility and fear of the LORD is riches and honor and life" (Prov 22:4).

- "One's pride will bring him low, but he who is lowly in spirit will obtain honor" (Prov 29:23).

Haman and Mordecai are like test cases of these proverbs. Everything, in the end, seems to come back to the issue of wisdom.

THE RETURN OF JOY

The decree to annihilate the Jews was irrevocable. Therefore, in order to stop it, another decree has to be issued which allows the Jews to defend themselves. Unlike the mourning and chaos that resulted from the first decree, the second decree is received with jubilation:

> Then Mordecai went out from the presence of the king in royal robes of blue and white, with a great golden crown and a robe of fine linen and purple, and the city of Susa shouted and rejoiced. The Jews had light and gladness and joy and honor. And in every province and in every city, wherever the king's command and his edict reached, there was gladness and joy among the Jews, a feast and a holiday. And many from the peoples of the country declared themselves Jews, for fear of the Jews had fallen on them. (Esth 8:15–17)

Esther 9 tells of how the Jews defended themselves against their would-be annihilators. Thus the book takes a violent turn. This has actually caused the book of Esther to be fodder for antisemites. Martin Luther wrote this of the Jews:

> They are real liars and bloodhounds who have not only continually perverted and falsified all of Scripture with their mendacious glosses from the beginning until the present day. Their heart's most ardent sighing and yearning and hoping is set on the day on which they can deal with us Gentiles as they did with the Gentiles in Persia at the time of Esther. Oh, how fond they are of the book of Esther, which is so beautifully attuned to their bloodthirsty, vengeful, murderous yearning and hope. The sun has never shone on a more bloodthirsty and vengeful people than they are who imagine that they are God's people who have been commissioned and commanded to murder and to slay the Gentiles.[22]

---

22. Luther, *On the Jews and Their Lies*, loc. 340.

Illuminating Counsel

So the Jews defend themselves against people trying to commit genocide against them, and Luther says this shows us how the Jews want to commit genocide against the Gentiles. Behold, antisemitism's logic!

It's true, of course, that the violence in the Bible, even in Esther, *can* inspire fanaticism. Baruch Goldstein, a Jewish physician, brutally murdered twenty-nine Palestinian Muslims and injured 125 more in the Cave of the Patriarchs in Hebron on February 25, 1994. Purim and the Muslim holiday Ramadan were overlapping that year.[23]

However, the fighting in Esth 9 is meant to be understood as defensive, even if preemptive. Three times we're told the Jews did not lay hold of the plunder (Esth 9:10, 15–16). This is in contrast to Haman's plan. Haman not only wanted to annihilate the Jews, but to plunder their goods as well (Esth 3:13; 8:11). Furthermore, the holiday which they instituted—Purim—commemorates the day *after* their victory (Esth 9:16–19).[24] In other words, Purim commemorates survival, not killing.

Purim is a joyous holiday because the Jews survived an attempted genocide. And here we see a beautiful chain of subversions which are crystal clear when reading the Ketuvim:

> You have turned for me my mourning into dancing;
>> you have loosed my sackcloth
>> and clothed me with gladness . . . (Ps 30:11[12])

> The joy of our hearts has ceased;
>> our dancing has been turned to mourning. (Lam 5:15)

> [The days of Purim are] the days on which the Jews got relief from their enemies, and as the month that had been turned for them from sorrow into gladness and from mourning into a holiday; that they should make them days of feasting and gladness, days for sending gifts of food to one another and gifts to the poor. (Esth 9:22)

Lamentations had subverted the joyful redemption of Ps 30. Esther subverts Lamentations right back. Lamentations is about the seeming destruction of the Jews. Esther is about the redemption and survival of the Jews. Joy has returned!

The giving of gifts on Purim is such a contrast to the wickedness of Haman. Haman fights for death; the Jews fight for life. Haman wants to take; the Jews celebrate their freedom by giving. Proverbs 11:23 summarizes the book of Esther quite well:

> The desire of the righteous ends only in good,
>> the expectation of the wicked in wrath.

---

23. Jobes, *Esther*, 19. I must say, I find it a bit off-putting that this incident is the very first thing Jobes mentions in her commentary on Esther. Esther is about an attempted genocide of the Jews. One would think there are other historical examples that would better set the tone of Esther.

24. Bush, *Ruth-Esther*, 328.

The Brave Hidden Jew

Giving is a cure for sorrow. Giving makes people joyous, and joyous people love to give. It's a wonderful cycle. Proverbs 11:24–25 states:

> One gives freely, yet grows all the richer;
>> another withholds what he should give, and only suffers want.
> Whoever brings blessing will be enriched,
>> and one who waters will himself be watered.

On Purim, Jews eat a triangular cookie called *Hamantaschen* in Yiddish. The cookie is meant to be Haman's hat. In Hebrew, it's called *Oznei Haman*—"Haman's ears." I admit I like the Yiddish name better than the Hebrew. The thought of eating Haman's ears makes me lose my appetite! In any case, Hamantaschen has some kind of a sweet filling inside. The most traditional filling is made of poppy but they come in all sorts of flavors, such as apricot, lemon, raspberry, and chocolate. The sweet stuff is *hidden* inside, just as Esther was hidden; just as, according to Judaism and Christianity, God is present but hidden.

Rabbi Dov Greenberg points out how life-changing a cookie can be.[25] Instead of feeling resentment toward the pre-incarnate Hitler, Jews have turned their mortal enemy into a dessert! Resentment truly is a thief of joy. We struggled through the imprecatory Psalms. We also noted the resentment in Lamentations. The resentment in Lamentations could have been a whole lot worse, but it's still there. In Esther, the fighting notwithstanding, resentment has entirely disappeared. It's been morphed into the shape of a delicious cookie!

Antisemitism has not, and must not, define the Jewish people. Likewise, others' opinion of you should not define you. Life is too short to spend our days hating on others. Turn your enemy into a dessert and rejoice!

MRS. HAMAN'S ENIGMATIC STATEMENT

Haman's wife might remind us of Job's wife. Job's wife saw Job suffering and told him to "curse God and die" (Job 2:9). She wanted to put him out of his misery. Unlike Job's wife, Haman's wife has a name—Zeresh. She sees Haman suffering because of Mordecai. She, likewise, gives him advice to cure him of his dispiritedness: "Let a gallows fifty cubits high be made, and in the morning tell the king to have Mordecai hanged upon it. Then go joyfully with the king to the feast" (Esth 5:14). Haman has the gallows built and goes to the king for permission to hang Mordecai. Instead, as we noted, he has to parade Mordecai around the city, honoring Mordecai for saving the king.

Now Haman is really upset! He hurries back to his house "mourning and with his head covered" (Esth 6:12). He was humiliated and the reader loves every second of it. Haman tells his wife and friends what happened. They respond thusly: "If Mordecai,

---

25. Greenberg, "Matzah, Jelly Donuts, and Hamtashen."

before whom you have begun to fall, is of the Jewish people, you will not overcome him but will surely fall before him" (Esth 6:13).

Of course, arrogant Haman is a fool and won't listen, but what are we to make of Zeresh's words? Did she not know Mordecai was a Jew when she told Haman to build the gallows? If she did, why did she tell him to build the gallows in the first place? More importantly, why does she (and the "wise men") tell Haman the Jews are indestructible? The answer to that question is found in the next book of the Ketuvim.

13

The Wise Jew Who Refused to Hide
(Daniel)

JUDAISM AND CHRISTIANITY DISAGREE about Daniel. Christianity considers Daniel a prophet because Daniel receives visions of the future. Jesus himself calls Daniel a prophet (Matt 24:15). That's why the book of Daniel is placed in the Prophets section of the Old Testament, after Ezekiel. But Judaism doesn't consider Daniel a prophet. The reasons for this aren't clear. There's evidence that Jewish communities before the destruction of the second temple in 70 CE did, in fact, consider Daniel a prophet.[1] The Talmud (written long after the destruction of the second temple) lists the names of everyone it considers a prophet and Daniel made the cut.[2] But the Talmud—Baba Batra—also places Daniel in the Ketuvim rather than the Prophets. It's possible the book of Daniel was once in the Prophets but was later moved to the Ketuvim when the Ketuvim was formed.[3] Goswell thinks the reason for Daniel's placement in the Ketuvim is because Daniel's narrative content bears similarities to the other books of the Ketuvim.[4] Maimonides, the greatest Jewish philosopher, said Daniel is not a prophet because he received visions which are considered a lesser form of revelation than the revelation the prophets received.[5] In any case, I hope to demonstrate that while the placement of Daniel in the Prophets makes sense, Daniel's placement in the Ketuvim is a stroke of editorial brilliance.

Before I get to that, I have a confession: I don't love the book of Daniel. I *like* the book of Daniel, but I don't love it as I do the other books of the Ketuvim. For a long

1. Finley, "The Book of Daniel," 197.

2. Megillah 14a. It lists seven female prophets and forty-six male prophets.

3. Goswell, "Canonical Position(s)," 138–40.

4. Goswell, "Canonical Position(s)," 133–34, 140.

5. Maimonides, *The Guide for the Perplexed*, 241–45. Goswell says Maimonides' view "is nothing more than a theory . . . to account for the accepted arrangement of the biblical books . . ." See Goswell, "Canonical Position(s)," 136–37.

241

time I wasn't sure why Daniel doesn't move me the way all the other books we've discussed thus far do. Then I read Robert Alter's translation and commentary on Daniel and I realized what it is. Daniel has no character development.[6] The book begins when Daniel is young, perhaps a teenager, and it ends when he's old. His life spans two empires—the Babylonian and the Persian. One normally changes dramatically from youth to twilight years. Yet Daniel's characterization is the same at the end of the book as it is in the beginning. The world changes. Daniel, at least as he's portrayed, does not.

Instead of a progressing story, such as we have in Ruth and Esther, Daniel is episodic. The first half of the book (Dan 1–6) is a series of "court tales." The second half of the book is a series of visions. The first half is written in straightforward prose. The second half is written in a highly figurative language referred to as *apocalyptic*. The apocalyptic style is not poetry. It's a stylized prose that contains verbal and numerical symbolism. So the first half of Daniel is easy to understand. The second half of Daniel is a bear.

The episodes break down as follows:

- Dan 1—Daniel refuses to eat the king's food.

- Dan 2—The king has a dream about a statue that represents four kingdoms.

- Dan 3—Three Jews are thrown into a fiery furnace for not worshiping idols.

- Dan 4—The king has a dream about a special tree that is cut down.

- Dan 5—The king arrogantly uses the holy vessels from the temple.

- Dan 6—Daniel is thrown into a den of lions for praying to God.

The visions break down as follows:

- Dan 7—Daniel sees a vision of four beasts which represent four kingdoms.

- Dan 8—A ram and a goat represent future kingdoms.

- Dan 9—Daniel prays a prayer of repentance on behalf of the Jews. He is told how Jerusalem will be devastated.

- Dan 10–12—More details of the battles which will occur as well as the final vindication of God's people.

Half of Daniel is written in Aramaic. Aramaic is a Semitic language, very similar to Hebrew. Hebrew and Aramaic can be compared to Spanish and Portuguese. The Aramaic section begins within Dan 2:4. The verse begins in Hebrew, saying, "And the Chaldeans spoke to the king in Aramaic . . ." Then the language switches to Aramaic, as if it's recording the precise words the Chaldeans spoke. But the narrative remains in Aramaic even after the Chaldeans are done speaking. It doesn't switch back to Hebrew until Dan 8:1. It then remains in Hebrew until the end.

---

6. Alter, *Strong as Death is Love*, loc. 3010.

The Wise Jew Who Refused to Hide

Why is half of Daniel written in Aramaic? We know that after the exile Hebrew fell into disuse as a spoken language. Eventually Aramaic became the tongue of the Jewish people. But that doesn't explain why half of Daniel is written in *Hebrew*. If the writer thought he needed to write in Aramaic so the average Jew could understand the book, why not write the entire book in Aramaic?

The writer's choice to switch to Aramaic, and then back to Hebrew, is not arbitrary. The languages help form the structure of the book. As we said, the basic structure is two symmetrical halves:

- Court Tales (Dan 1–6)

- Visions (Dan 7–12)

But the last five chapters of the first half are in Aramaic and the last five chapters of the second half are in Hebrew. The first chapter of the court tales is in Hebrew. The first chapter of the visions is in Aramaic. So we can diagram it like this:

	Court Tales	Visions
Hebrew	Dan 1	
Aramaic	Dan 2	
	Dan 3	
	Dan 4	
	Dan 5	
	Dan 6	
		Dan 7
Hebrew		Dan 8
		Dan 9
		Dan 10
		Dan 11
		Dan 12

Notice the languages form a chiastic structure:

A (Hebrew)
   B (Aramaic)
   B (Aramaic)
A (Hebrew)

Illuminating Counsel

In addition to that, the Aramaic section has a chiastic structure within itself which is formed by the thematic material:[7]

A—Dream of Four Kingdoms (Dan 2)
   B—Attempted Persecution (Dan 3)
      C—King Humbled (Dan 4)
      C—King Humbled (Dan 5)
   B—Attempted Persecution (Dan 6)
A—Vision of Four Kingdoms (Dan 7)

Thus, like every other book of the Bible, Daniel is artistically written, employing a very carefully planned out and intricate literary structure. But *unlike* every other book of the Bible, Daniel uses a second language as a literary device.[8] I think Daniel's use of Aramaic is stylistic. The use of Aramaic creates a book within the book. It also binds the two halves of the book together.[9] It's quite clever!

THE FOOD PROBLEM

"In the third year of the reign of Jehoiakim king of Judah, Nebuchadnezzar king of Babylon came to Jerusalem and besieged it" (Dan 1:1). This verse is problematic. Jehoiakim began reigning in 609–8 BCE. The third year of his reign would have been about 605 BCE. That's also the year Nebuchadnezzar inherited the kingdom of Babylon from his father. But we know of no such siege in 605 BCE. We know about the siege in 597 BCE, which is when Jehoiakim died and his son, Jehoiachin (a.k.a. Jeconiah), took over but was then quickly deposed and sent to Babylon along with many priests. Ezekiel became a prophet in the fifth year of that exile, in 592 BCE (Ezek 1:2). It seems we just need to accept Dan 1:1 even though we don't have any historical evidence corroborating it.[10]

Nebuchadnezzar orders certain Jews to be taken from Jerusalem to the palace in Babylon. "Among these [are] Daniel, Hananiah, Mishael, and Azariah" (Dan 1:6). They're young, handsome, intelligent, and of the upper crust of society (Dan 1:3–4). They're put into some sort of three-year-long reeducation program. It seems the king wanted to take the best specimens of the Jewish people and turn them into Babylonians so that they would serve the king loyally in his palace. Daniel and his associates are given Babylonian names. Daniel's name is changed to Belteshazzar, and Hananiah, Mishael, and Azariah are given the names Shadrach, Meshach, and Abednego (Dan 1:7).

7. Baldwin, "Daniel: Theology of," in VanGemeren, *New International Dictionary of Old Testament Theology and Exegesis*, 499–500.

8. Ezra-Nehemiah is an exception, for that book does contain Aramaic, though not as extensively as does Daniel.

9. Baldwin, *Daniel*, 20.

10. Baldwin, *Daniel*, 86.

The Wise Jew Who Refused to Hide

The text says, "The king assigned them a daily portion of the food that the king ate, and of the wine that he drank" (Dan 1:5). That sounds delicious. No doubt the king had Michelin-Star-worthy food. But Daniel views the food as unholy, so he "resolved that he would not defile himself with the king's food, or with the wine that he drank" (Dan 1:8). He asks the eunuch to supply him with only vegetables. The eunuch worries that without the protein, Daniel and his friends will look gaunt and that this might have negative consequences—*for the eunuch*. But Daniel urges the eunuch to let him try the vegetables for ten days to see what happens. A miracle is implied—Daniel and his friends look healthier than everyone else. This, along with their intellect and knowledge, causes them to receive high positions in the palace.

We're never told what's wrong with the food. It's difficult to resist thinking the meat was not kosher—that it didn't conform to the dietary laws (called *kashrut*) as stipulated in Lev 11 and Deut 14. Kashrut, in a sense, only applies to meats. All vegetables are permitted. Scholars, however, tell us that it's a mistake to assume the food was not kosher.[11] Maybe the meat was sacrificed to idols. What's clear is that Daniel thought eating the king's food would compromise his religious convictions. He, therefore, chose to abstain—a choice that carried some risk. God blesses his decision.

NEBUCHADNEZZAR'S FIRST DREAM

Nebuchadnezzar dreams a dream. He wakes up troubled by it. He wants to know the interpretation. He calls all of his advisors to give him the interpretation. They're eager to do so. However, he wants to be sure their interpretation is the correct interpretation. After all, how is he to know they're not spouting nonsense to curry favor? So in order to prove their interpretation is correct, he doesn't tell them what his dream was about. They have to not only tell him the interpretation of the dream, they have to tell him the dream itself! The advisors tell the king that his request is unreasonable. The king then orders all his advisors to be executed. This includes Daniel, Hananiah, Mishael, and Azariah.

Daniel hears about this. He goes to Hananiah, Mishael, and Azariah and tells them to pray. Daniel then receives a revelation from God. He tells Arioch, the king's hatchet man, that he can tell the king both the dream and the interpretation. Daniel does so. We'll discuss the dream in more detail below. For now, we note that Nebuchadnezzar is so impressed with Daniel that he

> gave Daniel high honors and many great gifts, and made him ruler over the whole province of Babylon and chief prefect over all the wise men of Babylon. Daniel made a request of the king, and he appointed Shadrach, Meshach, and Abednego over the affairs of the province of Babylon. But Daniel remained at the king's court. (Dan 2:48–49)

11. Baldwin, *Daniel*, 91–92.

The promotion of Daniel and his friends is a reoccurring theme throughout the episodes (Dan 3:30; 5:29; 6:28).

THE IDOLATRY PROBLEM

This is the only episode that doesn't feature Daniel. Shadrach, Meshach, and Abednego get to be the stars of the show. Nebuchadnezzar decides to erect a massive golden idol. He commands everyone to worship the idol when they hear the court musicians playing music. Perhaps he wants to inculcate some sort of Pavlovian response in his subjects. He also implements negative reenforcement. If anyone doesn't worship the idol, into a fiery furnace they go!

But Shadrach, Meshach, and Abednego (Hananiah, Mishael, and Azariah) refuse to obey the king's edict. Chaldeans (at this time, Chaldeans are almost synonymous with Babylonians; Nebuchadnezzar was Chaldean) rat out the three young Jews. They're brought to Nebuchadnezzar who demands an answer as to why they refuse to worship. They respond:

> O Nebuchadnezzar, we have no need to answer you in this matter. If this be so, our God whom we serve is able to deliver us from the burning fiery furnace, and he will deliver us out of your hand, O king. But if not, be it known to you, O king, that we will not serve your gods or worship the golden image that you have set up. (Dan 3:16–18)

This is one of the most powerful statements of faith in the entire Bible. The key words are "*But if not . . .*" The three young Jews believe that God is able to perform a miracle to rescue them. But their obedience to God doesn't depend on God performing such a miracle. Their obedience is truly unconditional. They will neither test God nor attempt to manipulate God. Even if God doesn't perform a miracle—even if God lets them die—they will still be faithful to him. Miracle or no miracle, they will walk into a fiery furnace—which Nebuchadnezzar, in his fury, made seven times hotter than before—rather than worship an idol.

Of course, they do get their miracle. The fire consumes the guards who throw Shadrach, Meshach, and Abednego into the furnace, but "the fire had not had any power over the bodies of [Shadrach, Meshach, and Abednego]. The hair of their heads was not singed, their cloaks were not harmed, and no smell of fire had come upon them" (Dan 3:27). Even so, their statement to Nebuchadnezzar alters the way Jews and Christians have viewed faith. Cancer, tragedy, oppression—these things are not excuses to be unfaithful to God. Whether God heals or not, obedience must be unconditional, else it is not obedience. Notice how this is precisely the point Job makes, at least in the prologue: "God gives, God takes away . . . Naked I come, naked I go . . . Shall we accept good from God and not bad also?"

246

NEBUCHADNEZZAR'S SECOND DREAM

Daniel 4 is narrated by Nebuchadnezzar, as if it's taken from his personal diary. The use of first person narrative is exceedingly rare in the Tanakh, though it seems to become more common in the post-exilic literature (which Daniel is a part of). It provides a nice contrast to the preceding chapters by giving us a different point of view.

Nebuchadnezzar dreamed a dream. It was a disturbing dream but the king responds to it a bit less severely than the way he did with his previous dream. This time he calls his wise men to interpret but doesn't make them tell him the dream. It doesn't matter. They're unable to provide the interpretation. Daniel is brought in. The reader learns of Nebuchadnezzar's dream when he explains it to Daniel.

He dreamed of a big tree that reached to the heavens. It was a wonderful tree with leaves and fruit that fed man and beast. Birds nested in it and animals found shade under it. But then a heavenly "watcher" orders the tree to be cut down and stripped. Only the stump is to remain.

The curious thing is that the watcher speaks of the stump as if it's a person: "Let him be wet with the dew of heaven. Let his portion be with the beasts in the grass of the earth. Let his mind be changed from a man's, and let a beast's mind be given to him; and let seven periods of time pass over him" (Dan 4:15–16). It doesn't take a prophet to figure out that Nebuchadnezzar is the stump. When Nebuchadnezzar begins boasting of his greatness, he ends up losing his mind and acting like an animal. He eventually comes to his senses and acknowledges that God is the king of the world. This is one of the most fantastical and bizarre stories in the Bible, though keep in mind that lycanthropy is a real, albeit rare, condition.[12] The first person narrative gives the scene an air of authenticity.

THE WRITING ON THE WALL

There's a new king in Babylon. Well, sort of. His name is Belshazzar. He's actually the son of King Nabu-na'id, or Nabonidus as he's called in Greek. Nabonidus was the final king of the neo-Babylonian empire. Belshazzar was a co-regent. The odd thing, however, is that he's called the son of Nebuchadnezzar (Dan 5:1, 13, 18, 22). There are three possible explanations for the discrepancy:

1. The writer got his history wrong.

2. Belshazzar is using the word "father" figuratively (father = ancestor).

3. The writer has some other purpose—literary or theological—for linking Belshazzar with Nebuchadnezzar.

   I'm going with option 3.

12. Baldwin, *Daniel*, 131.

Belshazzar arrogantly decides to feast from the holy vessels which were from the temple in Jerusalem—the temple Nebuchadnezzar destroyed. Belshazzar does this while praising his gods.

The strangest thing happens next. A mysterious hand writes something on a wall. Is the hand connected to a person? The text says, "Immediately the fingers of a human hand appeared and wrote on the plaster of the wall of the king's palace, opposite the lampstand. And the king saw the hand as it wrote" (Dan 5:5). It certainly doesn't seem like there's a body connected to that hand. Is this the origin of Thing from *The Addams Family*?

"Writing on the wall" is an idiom in American English. It refers to something which is a foregone conclusion. Sam Smith wrote and sang a song called "Writing on the Wall" for the 2015 James Bond movie *Spectre*. It won the Golden Globe and the Oscar for Best Original Song. This reveals the Bible's influence on Western culture, even if most people today have no clue the phrase is from the Bible. I wonder if Sam Smith knows his source material.

In any case, Belshazzar cannot read or understand what the hand wrote. This is clearly similar to Nebuchadnezzar not knowing the meaning of his dreams. Like Nebuchadnezzar, Belshazzar calls his wise men to interpret. Just as in the previous episodes, they cannot. And just as in the previous episodes, Daniel is called in and provides the correct interpretation.

The writing says MENE, MENE, TEKEL, and PARSIN. The key to the interpretation is to recognize that it's a riddle whose answers are contained within. Each word is a wordplay. The king's reign has been "numbered" (*mena*); his rule is at an end. The king has been "weighed" (*tekiltah*), measured, and found wanting. The king's kingdom has been "divided" (*perisat*) and given to the Medes and Persians (Dan 5:24–28).[13]

That very night Belshazzar is killed, but not before he promotes Daniel. Someone named Darius the Mede takes over. This Darius is not to be confused with Darius the Great of the Achaemenid Empire. There is no historical source corroborating Darius the Mede.

DANIEL IN THE LION'S DEN

Daniel has been climbing the ladder of power despite the fact that he's a Jew. "Then this Daniel became distinguished above all the other high officials and satraps, because an excellent spirit was in him. And the king planned to set him over the whole kingdom" (Dan 6:3). Daniel's success rouses the jealousy of the "high officials and the satraps." They seek to destroy him but they know they cannot touch his pristine character. They therefore decide to attack his religion. "We shall not find any ground for complaint against this Daniel," they say, "unless we find it in connection with the law of his God"

---

13. "Persians" in Aramaic and Hebrew is *paras*, which might make it a double wordplay with PARSIN.

(Dan 6:5). So they influence King Darius the Mede to issue an irrevocable decree that no one shall pray ("make petition") to any god except the king for thirty days.

The decree is issued and Daniel knows about it. He purposely violates it, as the high officials and satraps knew he would. Daniel prays to God facing Jerusalem—a practice still done by Jews to this day. The high officials and satraps rat out Daniel to the king like schoolyard bullies. "Daniel, who is one of the exiles from Judah, pays no attention to you, O king, or the injunction you have signed, but makes his petition three times a day," they say (Dan 6:13). They might as well call him a "dirty Jew"!

The king is deeply conflicted because he has the highest respect for Daniel. He's so manipulated by his underlings, however, that he acts against his values and orders Daniel to be thrown into the den of lions. All he offers Daniel are his "thoughts and prayers"—"May your god, whom you serve continually, deliver you" (Dan 6:16). He is genuinely concerned, though. He can neither sleep nor eat knowing that Daniel is being mauled to death.

But when the king rushes to the den, he sees Daniel alive and well. Daniel, like his three counterparts in ch. 3, received a visit from a heavenly messenger. No harm came upon Daniel and the king could not be more happy. He then orders those who "maliciously accused" Daniel to be thrown to the lions—not only them, but their families as well. They receive no comparable miracle. The six episodes end with this note: "So this Daniel prospered during the reign of Darius and the reign of Cyrus the Persian" (Dan 6:28). We will discuss "Cyrus the Persian" in the next chapter.

This is the climax of the episodes. The image of Daniel not being harmed by the lions was very important to the early Christians, many of whom were thrown to lions by the Romans. Daniel in the lion's den became a symbol of resurrection.

THE VISIONS

Whether Daniel is a prophet or not is a "small potatoes" controversy. The larger controversy is about when the book of Daniel was written. Judaism and Christianity posit that Daniel was written during Daniel's lifetime, which was in the sixth century BCE. Secular scholarship, however, argues that Daniel was written in the second century BCE. As you may have realized by now, I hate these controversies. I'd much rather get on with talking about the book itself. But this controversy is particularly significant because it's connected to the interpretation of a key part of the book.

Daniel 2 and Dan 7 are connected. Indeed, they form an *inclusio*, bracketing the Aramaic section. In Dan 2, King Nebuchadnezzar has a dream of a statue of a human-shaped figure. The statue has a gold head, silver chest and arms, bronze belly and thighs, iron legs, and a mix of iron and clay feet (Dan 2:32–33). In Dan 7, Daniel has a vision of four beasts. The first beast is like a lion with eagles' wings. The wings are eventually plucked off. It's made to stand on its two legs and given the mind of a human. The second beast is like a bear. It's raised on one side and has three ribs in its

Illuminating Counsel

mouth. The third beast is like a leopard with four heads and wings. The fourth beast is indescribable except that it has iron teeth and ten horns. Among the ten horns emerges a little horn that has eyes and a mouth (Dan 7:3–8).

In both the dream and the vision, the statue and the beasts are destroyed. Compare:

> As you looked, a stone was cut out by no human hand, and it struck the image on its feet of iron and clay, and broke them in pieces. Then the iron, the clay, the bronze, the silver, and the gold, all together were broken in pieces, and became like the chaff of the summer threshing floors; and the wind carried them away, so that not a trace of them could be found. But the stone that struck the image became a great mountain and filled the whole earth. (Dan 2:34–35)

> I looked then because of the sound of the great words that the horn was speaking. And as I looked, the beast was killed, and its body destroyed and given over to be burned with fire. As for the rest of the beasts, their dominion was taken away, but their lives were prolonged for a season and a time. (Dan 7:11–12)

What does all this mean? In Dan 2, Daniel interprets the dream for the king. In Dan 7, a heavenly messenger interprets the vision for Daniel. It's interesting how in the episodes Daniel is the giver of information but after chapter 7 he's the receiver of information. The interpretation of the dream is basically the same as the interpretation of the vision. Compare:

> You, O king, the king of kings, to whom the God of heaven has given the kingdom, the power, and the might, and the glory, and into whose hand he has given, wherever they dwell, the children of man, the beasts of the field, and the birds of the heavens, making you rule over them all—you are the head of gold. Another kingdom inferior to you shall arise after you, and yet a third kingdom of bronze, which shall rule over all the earth. And there shall be a fourth kingdom, strong as iron, because iron breaks to pieces and shatters all things. And like iron that crushes, it shall break and crush all these. And as you saw the feet and toes, partly of potter's clay and partly of iron, it shall be a divided kingdom, but some of the firmness of iron shall be in it, just as you saw iron mixed with the soft clay. And as the toes of the feet were partly iron and partly clay, so the kingdom shall be partly strong and partly brittle. As you saw the iron mixed with soft clay, so they will mix with one another in marriage, but they will not hold together, just as iron does not mix with clay. And in the days of those kings the God of heaven will set up a kingdom that shall never be destroyed, nor shall the kingdom be left to another people. It shall break in pieces all these kingdoms and bring them to an end, and it shall stand forever . . . (Dan 2:37–44)

> These four great beasts are four kings who shall arise out of the earth. But the saints of the Most High shall receive the kingdom and possess the kingdom forever, forever and ever. (Dan 7:17–18)

The Wise Jew Who Refused to Hide

Now, what's the problem we, the readers, are faced with? We have the interpretation of the dream and vision, but we need an interpretation of the interpretation! What are the four kingdoms? The text starts us off: the first kingdom is Babylon. But we're not given much help figuring out the rest. Of course, we know enough about history to know what empires arose after Babylon. The problem, though, is whether to consider the empire of the Medes as something separate from the empire of the Persians.

The Median Empire took down the Assyrian Empire with the help of the Babylonians. Babylon then ruled the western part of the Middle East. Media ruled the eastern part of the Middle East. According to Herodotus (a Greek historian referred to by Cicero as the "father of history"), the aforementioned Cyrus the Persian was actually half Mede. His father, Cambyses I, the king of Persia, married Mandana, the daughter of Astyages, king of Media.[14] Cyrus rebelled against Astyages and defeated him. Thus was born the Achaemenid empire, named after Cyrus's (legendary?) ancestor, Achaemenes. Eventually, this new Persian Achaemenid Empire conquered the entire Middle East.

To my mind, then, the Median Empire and the Persian (Achaemenid) Empire are two different entities. However, the book of Daniel seems to put them together. Daniel 5:28 says that Belshazzar's kingdom will be given to "the Medes and Persians." Daniel 6:8, 6:12, and 6:18 refer to "the law of the Medes and Persians." (See also Esth 1:19.) If the Median kingdom and the Persian kingdom are considered one and the same, it would seem the fourth kingdom would have to be Rome. This is the common Christian interpretation:

First Kingdom	Babylon
Second Kingdom	Media-Persia
Third Kingdom	Greece
Fourth Kingdom	Rome

This interpretation fits exceedingly well with the New Testament. Jesus's self-descriptor, "Son of Man," undoubtedly comes from Dan 7:13–14—

> and behold, with the clouds of heaven
> > there came one like a son of man,
> and he came to the Ancient of Days
> > and was presented before him.
> And to him was given dominion
> > and glory and a kingdom,
> that all peoples, nations, and languages
> > should serve him;

14. Some scholars doubt the historicity of Cyrus's Median heritage.

his dominion is an everlasting dominion,
 which shall not pass away,
and his kingdom one
 that shall not be destroyed.

By calling himself the "Son of Man," Jesus was indicating that he is the person Dan 7:13 is referring to. Moreover, in Jesus's eschatological discourse recorded in Mark 13 and Matt 24, he refers to the "abomination of desolation" (Matt 24:15; Mark 13:14), which is a direct reference to Dan 9:27, 11:31, and 12:11. Revelation 17 also has allusions to Daniel, specifically Dan 8. Revelation concerns Rome and the Roman persecution of Christians. Like every other part of the OT, the NT views the book of Daniel as a large prophecy of Jesus and the birth of the church.

Positing the fourth kingdom to be Rome is very convenient for Christianity and Christian apologetics because it implies the Messiah *had* to come during the days of the Roman Empire. If the Messiah didn't come during the days of the Roman Empire, he's not coming at all.[15] During the lifetimes of Jesus and his apostles, God established the eternal kingdom, namely the church.

But what if Media and Persia are not meant to be linked together? The interpretation would then look like this:

First Kingdom	Babylon
Second Kingdom	Media
Third Kingdom	Persia
Fourth Kingdom	Greece

Does positing the fourth kingdom to be Greece instead of Rome hold water?

In Dan 8, Daniel has a vision of a ram and a goat. The ram has two horns, one higher than the other. It's very powerful. But then the goat comes from the west. The goat has one horn between his eyes. The goat overpowers the ram. Then the goat's horn is broken and, in its stead, four horns arise. From those four horns arises yet another horn—a little one. However, the little horn becomes great and wreaks havoc. As a result, the sanctuary of "the Prince of the host" is overthrown.

Daniel 8 gives us the interpretation of this vision. The ram with the two horns represents the kingdom of the Medes and Persians. Again, they are linked together. We must contend with this. But there's more to the story. The goat is Greece and the initial horn is the first king. When that king of Greece dies, his kingdom is divided into four, none of which has the strength his kingdom had. And that last little horn is yet another king that will arise.

15. This is the argument of Michael L. Brown. See Real Messiah, "Objection 4.20."

The Wise Jew Who Refused to Hide

This is fairly easy to interpret. The first king is Alexander the Great. When Alexander died, his kingdom was divided amongst four of his generals. Antigonus took northern Syria and western Babylon. Ptolemy took Egypt and southern Syria. Lysimachus took Thrace and western Asia Minor (modern-day Turkey). And Cassander took Greece and Macedonia. However, a fifth military leader named Seleucus took over Antigonus and Lysimachus's portions. Thus was born the Seleucid dynasty which ruled the the Middle East except for Egypt. Originally the Jews in Judea were under Ptolemaic rule. Eventually the Jews came under Seleucid rule. Both the Ptolemys and the Seleucids were benevolent, allowing the Jews to worship their god.

But then, in 175 BCE, there arose among the Seleucids a tyrant. His name was Antiochus IV but he called himself Epiphanes, which means "God manifest." Antiochus ended the policy of toleration toward the Jews. He wanted to Hellenize them (that is, make them Greek). A Jewish opportunist named Jason saw this as an opportunity to rise to power. Jason's brother, Onias III, was the high priest. Jason bribed Antiochus to give him his brother's position. In exchange, Jason promised to implement Antiochus's program of Hellenization. So Onias was forced out and Jason became the high priest. He installed a gymnasium (where athletes trained naked) in Jerusalem, which was abhorrent to Judaism. But then Jason was double-crossed by his underling, Menelaus. Menelaus curried favor with Antiochus and took over Jason's position. Then Antiochus was called to battle and rumor had it he was killed. Jason saw this as an opportunity to get his position back. But Antiochus was very much alive. He invaded Jerusalem with a vengeance. He entered the temple, put a statue of Zeus in the holy of holies, and sacrificed a pig to it. The book of 1 Maccabees, one of the books in which this history is recorded, implies this offense is the "abomination of desolation" (see 1 Macc 6:7). Antiochus then initiated a program of forced Hellenization of the Jews. Any Jew who practiced Judaism was executed.

But one old priest had had enough. His name was Mattathias (Mattatiyahu in Hebrew). Mattatthias inspired his five sons to revolt against Antiochus. The leader of the group was the middle son: Judah who was called "Maccabee" (which means "hammer" in Hebrew). Their revolt, from 167 to 160 BCE, became known as the Maccabean Revolt. Against all odds, the Maccabees defeated the Seleucids and rededicated the temple. This is what Hanukkah commemorates. "Hanukkah" means "dedication."

With this history in mind, it seems probable—I would say almost certain—that the final section of the book of Daniel (Dan 7–12) is about this crisis. The tyranny imposed by Antiochus IV is the only thing that can make sense of this seemingly confusing passage in Dan 9—

> Know therefore and understand that from the going out of the word to restore and build Jerusalem to the coming of an anointed one, a prince, there shall be seven weeks. Then for sixty-two weeks it shall be built again with squares and moat, but in a troubled time. And after the sixty-two weeks, an anointed one

253

Illuminating Counsel

shall be cut off and shall have nothing. And the people of the prince who is to come shall destroy the city and the sanctuary. (Dan 9:25–26)

This passage confuses many people (especially Christians) because of the words "anointed one." "Anointed one" is a translation of the Hebrew word *mashiach*, which is where the word Messiah comes from. (*Christos* is the Greek translation of *mashiach*.) But this is not about *the* Messiah (with a capital M). An "anointed one" can refer to any king or priest. The "anointed one" who is "coming," who is also called a "prince," is the execrable Antiochus IV. The "anointed one" who is "cut off" is the high priest Onias. The "people of the prince who is to come" who destroys "the city and the sanctuary" are the Seleucids. Without knowledge of Jewish history we cannot interpret Daniel correctly.[16]

So what does this say about the four kingdoms in Dan 7? Actually, Dan 7 doesn't say they are *kingdoms*; it says the beasts are *kings*. "These four great beasts are four kings who shall arise out of the earth" (Dan 7:17). The first beast must be the king of Babylon. The second beast must be the king of Persia. We have to accept that the book of Daniel links the Medes together with the Persians. We cannot separate them. The third beast, therefore, must be the king of Greece. But the fourth beast is *not* the king of Rome. Notice the third beast has four wings. These represent the four generals who take over Alexander's kingdom. The fourth beast is Seleucus. The little horn of that beast is Antiochus IV. The "one like a son of man" (in contrast to the creatures that are *like* beasts) is not an individual. This figure represents the Jews and their victory over Antiochus. "These four great beasts are four kings who shall arise out of the earth. But the saints of the Most High shall receive the kingdom and possess the kingdom forever, forever and ever" (Dan 7:17–18). Later the text says, "As I looked, this horn made war with the saints and prevailed over them, until the Ancient of Days came, and judgment was given for the saints of the Most High, and the time came when the saints possessed the kingdom" (Dan 7:21–22).

The interpretation I'm presenting is controversial for several reasons. First, many Christians view the visions in Daniel as some of the most powerful prophecies of Jesus in the Bible. I don't want to take that away from Christians. Daniel can be about Antiochus *and* about Jesus. How can that be? Jim Bruckner would say that the prophecies are multivalent; they have more than one meaning. To that I would add that the New Testament writers, like the ancient Jewish sages, didn't interpret the Hebrew Bible scientifically. For example, John 19:37 states that Zech 12:10 ("They will look on him whom they have pierced") was fulfilled when Jesus died on the cross. However, Rev 1:7 seems to say that Zech 12:10 will be fulfilled when Jesus comes on the clouds and "every eye will see him." So the interpretation of biblical prophecy can be a bit fluid and paradoxical. Prophecies that are "fulfilled" are not fully fulfilled.

Second, this interpretation seems to suggest a late date for the composition of the book. This is why secular scholarship argues Daniel was written in the second

16. McLaughlin, *The Ancient Near East*, 83.

century BCE. The book *cannot* be about Rome, the theory goes, because the author of Daniel couldn't have known the future. He knew about the Maccabean Revolt because he lived through it. In fact, some scholars would argue the book was written in the midst of the crisis, as evidenced by Dan 11 getting facts correct up to a certain point.[17] The historical discrepancies in the book, such as the invasion in 605, Belshazzar being Nebuchadnezzar's son, the kingship of Darius the Mede, and so on, testify to the late date of Daniel. Daniel was written hundreds of years after those events and the writer got his facts mixed up. Many religious people, however, feel that Daniel must have been written in the sixth century when Daniel was alive because the visions are narrated by Daniel. It is argued that the book of Daniel can most certainly be about Rome because God knows the future. Both sides of this argument accuse the other of having preconceived biases.

I'm not concerned when the book was written. I don't know when it was written. What I'm concerned with are the themes of the book. Even if the book were written in the sixth century BCE, there can be no doubt that at least some of the visions (I'd say all of them) are concerned with the Antiochus crisis. The reason accepting that interpretation is crucial is because we must notice that the episodes and the visions, while very different stylistically, are thematically connected. They are both about two things: the perseverance of the Jews and the sovereignty of God.

JOSEPH AND ESTHER

Daniel reminds us of Joseph. Both Daniel and Joseph are young and attractive (Dan 1:4; Gen 39:2, 6). Both Daniel and Joseph are forcibly taken to a foreign land (Dan 1:3; Gen 37:28). Both Daniel and Joseph are given new names (Dan 1:7; Gen 41:45). Both Daniel and Joseph are wise (Dan 1:4; Gen 41:39). Both Daniel and Joseph interpret dreams (Dan 2; 4–5; Gen 40–41). Both Daniel and Joseph are slandered and are the recipients of discrimination (Dan 3:8; 6:5; Gen 39:14–17; 43:32) Both Daniel and Joseph rise to power in the king's court (Dan 5:29; Gen 41:37–44).

The interpretation of dreams is perhaps the most striking similarity between Daniel and Joseph. Both Daniel and Joseph are introduced to the king by someone else; in Joseph's case, the cupbearer (Gen 41:9–13), and in Daniel's case, Arioch (Dan 2:25). Both Daniel and Joseph credit God with giving them the ability to interpret. To Pharaoh's cupbearer and baker, Joseph says, "Do not interpretations belong to God?" (Gen 40:8). And to Pharaoh, Joseph replies, "It is not in me; God will give Pharaoh a favorable answer" (Gen 41:16). Likewise Daniel tells Nebuchadnezzar, "No wise men, enchanters, magicians, or astrologers can show to the king the mystery that the king has asked, but there is a God in heaven who reveals mysteries, and he has made known to King Nebuchadnezzar what will be in the latter days" (Dan 2:27–28). On that point,

17. Fleetwd1, "The Book of Daniel."

Illuminating Counsel

both Pharaoh's dreams and Nebuchadnezzar's dreams are about the future of the nation (Egypt and Babylon, respectively). And interpreting the dreams causes both Daniel and Joseph to be loved by their respective monarch (Dan 2:46; Gen 41:38–39; cf. Dan 4:9, 18).

We have already noted that Esther bears striking similarities to Joseph as well. Reading the Ketuvim enables us to see the similarities between Esther and Daniel. The Ketuvim juxtaposes them. I would say this is one of the most instructive juxtapositions of any two figures in the entire Bible. The similarities between Daniel and Joseph are rather obvious. The Daniel story is almost a retelling of the Joseph story. But while Esther and Daniel have powerful similarities, it is their differences which highlight their themes.

Both Daniel and Esther are young and attractive (Dan 1:4; Esth 2:7). Both Daniel and Esther are in a foreign land and have their names changed (Dan 1:7; Esth 2:7). Both Daniel and Esther (and Mordecai) rise to power (Dan 2:48; Esth 2:17; 10:3).

The book of Daniel and the book of Esther both deal with antisemitism. Compare Haman's words with those of the Babylonians who wish to harm Daniel and his Jewish friends:

> There is a certain people scattered abroad and dispersed among the peoples in all the provinces of your kingdom. Their laws are different from those of every other people, and they do not keep the king's laws, so that it is not to the king's profit to tolerate them. (Esth 3:8)

> There are certain Jews whom you have appointed over the affairs of the province of Babylon: Shadrach, Meshach, and Abednego. These men, O king, pay no attention to you; they do not serve your gods or worship the golden image that you have set up. (Dan 3:12)

> Daniel, who is one of the exiles from Judah, pays no attention to you, O king, or the injunction you have signed, but makes his petition three times a day. (Dan 6:13)

Remember that in Dan 6:5, the antisemites say that the only way they can destroy Daniel is if they attack Daniel's religious law. This is Haman's strategy as well.

In both the book of Daniel and the book of Esther, the Jews survive their enemies' attacks. The absolute brilliance of having Daniel in the Ketuvim along with Esther is that Daniel is the only thing that makes sense of Zeresh and the wise men's words in Esth 6:13. That Haman has "wise men" is interesting, because that word (it's one word in Hebrew) is used throughout Daniel. The "wise men" are the ones who cannot interpret the king's dreams (Dan 2:12–14, 18, 24, 48; 4:6, 18; 5:7–8, 15). It's as if Zeresh and the "wise men" read the book of Daniel, whereas Haman didn't. Slandering Jews doesn't work. Throwing Jews into a furnace and to the lions doesn't work. Hence they conclude,

256

The Wise Jew Who Refused to Hide

"If Mordecai, before whom you have begun to fall, is of the Jewish people, you will not overcome him but will surely fall before him" (Esth 6:13).[18]

Both Daniel and Esther face pressure to assimilate. Esther almost completely loses her Jewish identity. She sacrifices it for security. Only when her people are threatened with annihilation does she reveal who she truly is. Daniel, too, deals with assimilation. Daniel and his friends are given Babylonian names and are set up to become Babylonians. We must also remember to read the visions along with the episodes. The point the visions stress is that the crisis they describe is an existential crisis for the Jewish people. Like Haman, Antiochus was trying to destroy the Jews. Instead of annihilation, he was going to assimilate Jews out of existence. Hanukkah is thus connected to Purim. Both holidays are about the survival of Jewish people from wicked antisemites.

But there are two major differences between Esther and Daniel. The first difference is that Daniel does not succumb to assimilation as does Esther. The Babylonians change Daniel's name but he still calls himself "Daniel," as does the narrator (Dan 7:1).[19] We must presume Esther ate the king's food. Daniel refused to do so. Each episode in Daniel is about how Daniel and his three friends refused to conform and assimilate even when threatened with death. While Daniel and his friends do not save the Jewish people from annihilation as does Esther, they do provide a better example for how Jews in exile are to live.

This is why I used the word "faithfulness" to describe Daniel's response to suffering. The key verse is Dan 6:4. Daniel's enemies realize "they could find no ground for complaint or any fault, because he was *faithful*, and no error or fault was found in him." The book urges faithfulness to God no matter the consequences. Unlike Job, there is no arguing with God in Daniel. There are no impassioned laments in Daniel such as we find in Psalms and Lamentations. All we have in Daniel is unyielding trust.

That brings us to the second difference between Esther and Daniel. We noted how the book of Esther is ambiguous regarding God's sovereignty. God isn't even mentioned in the book. What a contrast to Daniel! God is mentioned incessantly in Daniel. God is mentioned as early as the second verse of the book. The temple is referred to as the "house of God" (Dan 1:2). God gave Daniel and his friends their abilities (Dan 1:9, 17). When Daniel receives revelation, he blesses "the God of heaven" (Dan 2:19). Whereas Mordecai's reason for not bowing to Haman was left ambiguous, Shadrach, Meshach, and Abednego make it clear that they serve God (Dan 3:16–18). They are "servants of the Most High God" (Dan 3:26). The phrase "Most High God" occurs three more times in the book (Dan 4:2; 5:18, 21). And God is not mentioned any less in the second half of the book. Daniel has a long prayer in ch. 9 in which he mentions God well over a dozen times.

Like the Joseph story, Daniel also focuses on the sovereignty of God. Here, again, we see another major contrast with the book of Esther. For Mordecai, God's sovereignty

18. This brilliant point comes from Goswell, "The Canonical Position(s)," 135.

19. The name "Daniel" means "My Judge is God."

257

Illuminating Counsel

was a question ("Who knows?"). Daniel, however, like Joseph, is absolutely certain of God's sovereignty. This is what Nebuchadnezzar's dreams and Daniel's visions are about. The superpowers of the world come and go, but God remains on the throne. Nebuchadnezzar—who perhaps did more damage to the Jewish people than anyone in the Hebrew Bible—comes to acknowledge that the Jews' god is God (Dan 3:28–29). Nebuchadnezzar's praise of God's sovereignty forms an *inclusio* in Dan 4. Nebuchadnezzar acts like an animal until he acknowledges why God is worthy of praise,

> for his dominion is an everlasting dominion,
>> and his kingdom endures from generation to generation;
> all the inhabitants of the earth are accounted as nothing,
>> and he does according to his will among the host of heaven
>> and among the inhabitants of the earth;
> and none can stay his hand
>> or say to him, "What have you done?" (Dan 4:34–35)

Likewise, Darius the Mede praises the God of Daniel, saying,

> for he is the living God,
>> enduring forever;
> his kingdom shall never be destroyed,
>> and his dominion shall be to the end.
> He delivers and rescues;
>> he works signs and wonders
>> in heaven and on earth,
> he who has saved Daniel
>> from the power of the lions. (Dan 6:26–27)

The visions make the same point. Daniel is told:

> At that time shall arise Michael, the great prince who has charge of your people. And there shall be a time of trouble, such as never has been since there was a nation till that time. But at that time your people shall be delivered, everyone whose name shall be found written in the book. (Dan 12:1)

There will be great tribulation, but God will vindicate his people. God wins in the end.

Daniel's focus on God couldn't present a greater contrast with the book of Esther. It's perhaps also significant that most orders of the Ketuvim have Esther preceding Daniel. Daniel shows us that the absence of God from Esther does not mean that God is no longer relevant. God is back![20]

---

20. The other reason the book of Esther precedes the book of Daniel is that Esther is one of the five books read on a Jewish holiday.

WISDOM

Aside from the three wisdom books, and aside from 1 Kings and 2 Chronicles which tell the story of Solomon, the book of Daniel uses the word "wisdom" more than any other book of the Tanakh. The word occurs nine times in the book. Daniel and his friends are "skillful in all wisdom" (Dan 1:4, 9, 20). This means they are extremely intelligent. But Daniel praises God for being the source of wisdom:

Blessed be the name of God forever and ever,
    to whom belong wisdom and might.
He changes times and seasons;
    he removes kings and sets up kings;
he gives wisdom to the wise
    and knowledge to those who have understanding;
he reveals deep and hidden things;
    he knows what is in the darkness,
    and the light dwells with him.
To you, O God of my fathers,
    I give thanks and praise,
for you have given me wisdom and might,
    and have now made known to me what we asked of you,
    for you have made known to us the king's matter. (Dan 2:20–23)

Daniel emphasizes the point when he explains to Nebuchadnezzar that God has enabled him to interpret dreams; the "wisdom" to interpret comes from God, not from Daniel (Dan 2:30). Daniel's ability to interpret is described as "wisdom" by the wise men in the court (Dan 5:11, 14).

This is not enough to conclude that Daniel is a wisdom book.[21] However, Daniel's place in the Ketuvim enhances the Ketuvim's emphasis of wisdom. There are three points to make about this. First, Jews are special—not because of their genetics, but because of their god. We made this point when we discussed Esther. The exilic stories—Joseph, Esther, Daniel—show us that Jews in exile bless the lands they live in. Antisemitism, then, is self-destructive. Second, the book of Daniel, like Esther, emphasizes the theme of arrogance and humility. Daniel 4 and 5 are about how arrogance brings people down. Nebuchadnezzar learns the lesson:

Now I, Nebuchadnezzar, praise and extol and honor the King of heaven, for all his works are right and his ways are just; and those who walk in pride he is able to humble. (Dan 4:37)

It's as if Nebuchadnezzar read Proverbs.

Again, this doesn't make Daniel a wisdom book. It does mean, though, that Daniel, perhaps surprisingly, fits exceedingly well in the Ketuvim. Daniel works in

21. Longman, *The Fear of the Lord is Wisdom*, 78–79, 92.

the Prophets too. But Daniel and Esther are companion pieces. Esther and Daniel compliment each other. Together they form a bridge from the Five Scrolls to the Other Books. Daniel takes us from the Babylonian period to the Persian period, setting us up for the great post-exilic book, Ezra-Nehemiah. As we move toward the finale of the Ketuvim, we will do well to not forget Daniel. Daniel's prayer in Dan 9 needs to be kept in view.

14

Returning Home
(Ezra-Nehemiah)

THE DECREE

NEVER HAVE I MET a person who said Ezra is their favorite book in the Bible. Genesis, yes. Exodus, yes. Psalms, definitely. I knew a young woman who told me Proverbs is her favorite book. But Ezra, no. The same goes for Nehemiah. Does anyone even read them?

Ezra-Nehemiah (they're one book in Hebrew) may not be popular like the previous books of the Ketuvim. And yet, there are aspects of Ezra-Nehemiah which are of the utmost importance, not only to biblical studies, but to human history. That statement is not intended as an exaggeration. And not only important, but inspiring as well.

Ezra-Nehemiah begins with events that happened before Ezra and Nehemiah were born:

> In the first year of Cyrus king of Persia, that the word of the LORD by the mouth of Jeremiah might be fulfilled, the LORD stirred up the spirit of Cyrus king of Persia, so that he made a proclamation throughout all his kingdom and also put it in writing . . . (Ezra 1:1)

The year is 539 BCE. Cyrus II, a.k.a. Cyrus the Great (*Koresh* in Hebrew), king of Persia, enters Babylon and wins over the city without a fight. The Babylonians view him as a liberator because he restores the worship of Marduk which Nabonidus, the final king of Babylon, had neglected in favor of the moon god, Sin.

In 538 BCE, Cyrus issues a decree written on what is now called the Cyrus Cylinder, housed in the British Museum. The cylinder says this:

> . . . I returned to (these) sacred cities on the other side of the Tigris, the sanctuaries of which have been ruins for a long time, the images which (used) to live therein and established for them permanent sanctuaries. I (also) gathered all their (former) inhabitants and returned (to them) their habitations.

Illuminating Counsel

> Furthermore, I resettled upon the command of Marduk, the great lord, all the gods of Sumer and Akkad whom Nabonidus has brought into Babylon to the anger of the lord the gods, unharmed, in their (former) chapels, the places which make them happy. May all the gods whom I have resettled in their sacred cities ask daily Bel and Nebo for a long life for me and may they recommend me (to him); to Marduk, my lord, they may say this: "Cyrus, the king who worships you, and Cambyses [II], his son, . . . all of them I settled in a peaceful place . . . I endeavoured to fortify/repair their dwelling places . . . [1]

Compare that to Cyrus's decree in Ezra-Nehemiah:

> Thus says Cyrus king of Persia: The LORD, the God of heaven, has given me all the kingdoms of the earth, and he has charged me to build him a house at Jerusalem, which is in Judah. Whoever is among you of all his people, may his God be with him, and let him go up to Jerusalem, which is in Judah, and rebuild the house of the LORD, the God of Israel—he is the God who is in Jerusalem. And let each survivor, in whatever place he sojourns, be assisted by the men of his place with silver and gold, with goods and with beasts, besides freewill offerings for the house of God that is in Jerusalem." (Ezra 1:2–4)

What do you notice about the two decrees? They don't match! Cyrus's decree on the cylinder is about Cyrus serving Marduk, the chief god of Babylon. The temples Cyrus pledges to rebuild are the houses of Mesopotamian gods. The peoples he resettles are Mesopotamian peoples. The Cyrus Cylinder doesn't mention Jews or Yahweh. This leads some scholars to doubt the authenticity of Cyrus's decree in Ezra.[2] After all, how plausible is it for the Persian king to call Yahweh "the God of Heaven" and to credit Yahweh with giving him "all the kingdoms of the earth"?

However, there's another decree mentioned in Ezra that's far more reserved:

> In the first year of Cyrus the king, Cyrus the king issued a decree: Concerning the house of God at Jerusalem, let the house be rebuilt, the place where sacrifices were offered, and let its foundations be retained. Its height shall be sixty cubits and its breadth sixty cubits, with three layers of great stones and one layer of timber. Let the cost be paid from the royal treasury. And also let the gold and silver vessels of the house of God, which Nebuchadnezzar took out of the temple that is in Jerusalem and brought to Babylon, be restored and brought back to the temple that is in Jerusalem, each to its place. You shall put them in the house of God. (Ezra 6:3–5)

Now, we have no corroborating sources for this decree either, but there's little reason to doubt its authenticity.[3] For one thing, while Ezra 1:2–4 is written in Hebrew, this decree is written in Aramaic, which was the lingua franca of the time. Cyrus

1. ANET, 316.
2. McLaughlin, *The Ancient Near East*, 64–65.
3. McLaughlin, *The Ancient Near East*, 64.

262

Returning Home

would have communicated his message to the Jews in Aramaic. The Cyrus Cylinder, for example, is written in Babylonian because it was meant to be read by the Babylonians. Second, this decree doesn't have Cyrus credit Yahweh with commissioning him. Third, we know for a fact that Jews returned to Jerusalem and rebuilt the temple during the Persian Achaemenid Empire. The only explanation is what we read in Ezra: Cyrus issued a decree allowing that to happen.

The two decrees of Cyrus in Ezra, even if embellished, are perfectly consistent with what we know of Cyrus's character. He ruled in a way decidedly different from the Assyrians and the Babylonians. He introduced a policy of toleration. He defeated Astyages, but let him live. He defeated Nabonidus, but let him live. Instead of dislocating peoples, he sent them home. Instead of forcing peoples to follow his religion, he let them worship their own gods. Instead of destroying temples, he rebuilt them.

Cyrus is the reason the Jews returned to their homeland. Who ever heard of a people whose nation had been destroyed, who had been exiled, returning to their land after just seventy years (which is what Jeremiah prophesied)?[4] It's perhaps as close to a miracle as anything in history. Cyrus was the right man at the right time.

Now, consider the consequences of Cyrus's decree. Had Cyrus *not* allowed the Jews to rebuild the temple, we can surmise they would never have returned to their homeland. There would not have been a restored nation of Israel. Would Judaism have survived? Would there be Jews today?

There was a Jewish community on an island on the Nile in southern Egypt called Elephantine. We have the manuscripts of their writings. They're referred to as the Elphantine Papyri. They're older than all of the manuscripts we possess of the Bible. We know from the Elephantine Papyri that this Jewish community had a temple, but their religion was thoroughly polytheistic, which is altogether different from Judaism as we know it today. Their religion didn't survive.

The Jewish community in Babylon did survive. Centuries after Cyrus, Babylon became a center of Jewish life. Some of the most important Jewish writings came from Babylon (called the Babylonian Talmud). But would the Jewish community in Babylon have done as well if the nation of Israel had not been reestablished? Would their identity as Jews have survived? I have my doubts. Certainly, had the Jews not returned to Jerusalem, Jesus of Nazareth would not have been Jesus of Nazareth! There would be no Christianity as we know it. I imagine there would not have been Islam either. Everything would be different. Cyrus's decree changed the world!

This is why the Tanakh praises Cyrus like no other non-Jewish ruler. The first time Cyrus is mentioned in the Tanakh is in Second Isaiah. He's probably the one referred to in these verses:

---

4. The reference to Jeremiah in Ezra 1:1 is about the prophecy that the exile will last seventy years. See Jer 25:11–12; Jer 29:10; Dan 9:2; and Zech 1:12.

Illuminating Counsel

Who stirred up one from the east
    whom victory meets at every step?
He gives up nations before him,
    so that he tramples kings underfoot;
he makes them like dust with his sword,
    like driven stubble with his bow.
He pursues them and passes on safely,
    by paths his feet have not trod.
Who has performed and done this,
    calling the generations from the beginning?
I, the LORD, the first,
    and with the last; I am he. (Isa 41:2–4)

I stirred up one from the north, and he has come,
    from the rising of the sun, and he shall call upon my name;
he shall trample on rulers as on mortar,
    as the potter treads clay. (Isa 41:25)

Cyrus is explicitly mentioned in Isa 44 and Isa 45:

Thus says the LORD, your Redeemer,
    who formed you from the womb:
"I am the LORD, who made all things,
    who alone stretched out the heavens,
    who spread out the earth by myself . . .
who says of Cyrus, 'He is my shepherd,
    and he shall fulfill all my purpose';
saying of Jerusalem, 'She shall be built,'
    and of the temple, 'Your foundation shall be laid.'" (Isa 44:24, 28)

Thus says the LORD to his anointed, to Cyrus,
    whose right hand I have grasped,
to subdue nations before him
    and to loose the belts of kings,
to open doors before him
    that gates may not be closed:
"I will go before you
    and level the exalted places,
I will break in pieces the doors of bronze
    and cut through the bars of iron,
I will give you the treasures of darkness
    and the hoards in secret places,
that you may know that it is I, the LORD,
    the God of Israel, who call you by your name.

Returning Home

> For the sake of my servant Jacob,
>> and Israel my chosen,
> I call you by your name,
>> I name you, though you do not know me. (Isa 45:1–4)

So Cyrus, the king of Persia, is Yahweh's shepherd and anointed! "His anointed" is the translation of the Hebrew word *meshicho*, which is transliterated "messiah." According to Second Isaiah, David's heir is not the one who will rescue Israel. The Jews might have wanted David's heir to come to their rescue. The prophet proclaims their hero is none other than Cyrus the Persian!

Of course, we must be careful not to overstate the case. Cyrus shouldn't be thought of as a champion for human rights.[5] Cyrus was a conquerer. His policy of toleration was a means of securing his power. He realized that giving people a measure of freedom would make them more likely to be content to live as subjects of his empire. The empire he founded became the largest the world had ever seen. The restored nation of Israel was not really a nation. It was a Persian province called Yehud.[6] The Jews, like all other subjects of the empire, had to pay their taxes. Eventually, taxes became such a burden that peoples began to become discontent with their Persian overlords.[7] When Alexander the Great conquered the Persian Empire, the Egyptians greeted him as a liberator and made him a Pharaoh.

That said, if I had a choice whether to live under the Assyrians, the Babylonians, or the Persians, I'd choose the Persians in a heartbeat. And the consequences of Cyrus's policy of toleration were more far-reaching than Cyrus could have ever known. Thomas Jefferson possessed two copies of Xenophon's biography of Cyrus, *Cyropaedia*. Jefferson was inspired by Cyrus. So was Ben Gurion—the first Prime Minister of the modern state of Israel. Cyrus is one of the most important figures in Jewish history.

Cyrus ended the exile. According to Ezra-Nehemiah, after Cyrus issued his decree, a few Jews returned with the "vessels" of the temple which the Babylonians had carried away (Ezra 1:7). These Jews were led by one Sheshbazzar, who is referred to as "prince of Judah" (Ezra 1:8). We don't know anything about this man. He quickly disappears from the text.[8] Soon after, a second wave of Jews return, this time numbering in the thousands. One of these Jews is named Zerubbabel. Zerubbabel is Jeconiah's grandson, and hence the rightful heir to the throne of David. But the Persians are in power, and so Zerubbabel becomes the governor rather than the king. The kingdom of David is never reestablished.

---

5. This is what the Shah of Iran—Mohammad Reza Pahlavi—claimed in the 1970s.

6. "Judah" in Hebrew is *Yehuda*.

7. Fensham, *The Books of Ezra and Nehemiah*, 14.

8. He's mentioned in Ezra 1:8, 11; 5:14, 16.

Ezra 2 is a chapter of numbers. We don't need to get bogged down in the details of how many Jews returned. You should know two things: some scholars question the numbers in Ezra, and many Jews remained in Babylon. Jews actually faired quite well in Babylon, as it turns out. Wealthy Jews in Babylon gave support to the returnees, but returning still proved to be difficult.[9]

We're introduced to another man. His name is Jeshua, which is a shortened version of Joshua. Jeshua is the high priest.[10] He and Zerubbabel lead the people in the construction of the temple. The first thing to be rebuilt is the altar. This allows for the sacrifices to commence. The sacrifices begin on the first day of the seventh month, which is the month of Tishrei. The Bible doesn't say this, but the first day of Tishrei is Rosh Hashanah—the Jewish New Year. How can the New Year be in the *seventh* month? The Jewish New Year is meant to be the birthday of the world—the anniversary of the creation. In other words, the Jewish New Year is really about the world, not about Jews! This tradition arose much later. The first day of Tishrei in the Bible is referred to as the [Festival of] Trumpets (see Lev 23:23–25 and Num 29:1–6).[11] The tenth day of Tishrei is Yom Kippur, the Day of Atonement, the holiest day in the Jewish calendar. The fifteenth day of Tishrei is yet another holiday called Sukkot, or the Festival of Booths (or Tabernacles) in English. We're told the returnees celebrated this holiday (Ezra 3:4). We're also told they followed the instructions for the sacrifices "as it was written in the Law of Moses the man of God" (Ezra 3:2).

The returnees are motivated to rebuild the alter by their fear of the "people of the land" (Ezra 3:3). This sets the pattern for what is to come. Ezra-Nehemiah is all about restoration. Ezra 1–6 is about the restoration of the temple. Ezra 7–10 is about the restoration of the Torah (the law). Nehemiah 1–7 is about the restoration of Jerusalem.[12] Nehemiah 8–10 is the culmination of the restoration of the Torah. Nehemiah 11–12 is the culmination of the restoration of the nation of Israel. Nehemiah 13 is about Nehemiah's second term and his reforms. We will discuss these things in more detail below.

THE RESTORATION OF THE TEMPLE

It is now the year 520 BCE. Persia is ruled by Darius I, also known as Darius the Great. Cyrus had died in battle in 530. He was succeeded by his son, Cambyses II, who died unexpectedly in 522. Darius I was Cambyses's general. He put down a revolt and became emperor. He had expanded the empire and founded its capital, Persepolis.

---

9. Fensham, *The Books of Ezra and Nehemiah*, 11.

10. In Hebrew, his name is pronounced *Yeshua*. This is the name of Jesus before it was filtered through Greek and Latin.

11. It's simply called "Trumpets." The word for "trumpet" is *shofar*. This is a ram's horn. The blowing of the shofar is a significant part of Rosh Hashanah and Yom Kippur.

12. Throntveit, *Ezra-Nehemiah*, 3.

Returning Home

It is in the year 520 that the foundation of the temple is completed under the leadership of Jeshua and Zerubbabel. We're told:

> And when the builders laid the foundation of the temple of the LORD, the priests in their vestments came forward with trumpets, and the Levites, the sons of Asaph, with cymbals, to praise the LORD, according to the directions of David king of Israel. (Ezra 3:10)

The sons of Asaph were singers (Ezra 2:41). Do you know where we read the name Asaph? In the book of Psalms! Twelve psalms have a superscription which says "A Psalm of Asaph." Psalm 73, which we looked at in detail, is one of those psalms. And these singers and musicians are praising Yahweh "according to the directions of David king of Israel." Whose name is all over Psalms? David's! I hope that things are now clicking for you.

There's more. We're told "they sang responsively, praising and giving thanks to the LORD," saying:

> For he is good,
> for his steadfast love endures forever toward Israel. (Ezra 3:11)

That refrain, sans "toward Israel," appears only in the book of Psalms and one other book which is also in the Ketuvim and which I'll mention shortly. Psalm 106:1, Ps 107:1, Ps 118:1, and Ps 118:29 say, "Give thanks to the LORD, for he is good; for his steadfast love endures forever!" It's interesting that Ezra 3:11 says the singers sang "responsively." Psalm 136 is set up to be a "call and response" song. The leader says a line that mentions something God has done, and the congregation responds by saying, "For his steadfast love endures forever." That refrain occurs in all twenty-six verses of the psalm!

So "all the people shouted with a great shout when they praised the LORD, because the foundation of the house of the LORD was laid" (Ezra 3:11). But all is not well. We're told:

> many of the priests and Levites and heads of fathers' houses, old men who had seen the first house, wept with a loud voice when they saw the foundation of this house being laid, though many shouted aloud for joy, so that the people could not distinguish the sound of the joyful shout from the sound of the people's weeping, for the people shouted with a great shout, and the sound was heard far away. (Ezra 3:12–13)

Ezra may not be anyone's favorite book, but there's genuine emotion here. The word *cacophony* comes to mind. One can almost hear the cacophony of praising and weeping when one reads this passage. Those who praise, praise loudly. Those who grieve, grieve loudly. The Tanakh is so passionate! No matter what people feel, they feel things to the nth degree.

Illuminating Counsel

Here we have a generation gap. The youngsters are excited that they will soon have a temple. The more seasoned among them, however, are old enough to remember Solomon's temple. This new temple, or at least the foundation of it, doesn't seem impressive. The older folks recognize that things will never be as they once were.[13]

But Jeshua and Zerubbabel are not the only leaders of the people. There are also two prophets. Their names are Haggai and Zechariah. These prophets are mentioned in Ezra-Nehemiah and they also have their own books. Haggai deals with this very problem:

> Who is left among you who saw this house in its former glory? How do you see it now? Is it not as nothing in your eyes? Yet now be strong, O Zerubbabel, declares the LORD. Be strong, O Joshua, son of Jehozadak, the high priest. Be strong, all you people of the land, declares the LORD. Work, for I am with you, declares the LORD of hosts, according to the covenant that I made with you when you came out of Egypt. My Spirit remains in your midst. Fear not. For thus says the LORD of hosts: Yet once more, in a little while, I will shake the heavens and the earth and the sea and the dry land. And I will shake all nations, so that the treasures of all nations shall come in, and I will fill this house with glory, says the LORD of hosts. The silver is mine, and the gold is mine, declares the LORD of hosts. The latter glory of this house shall be greater than the former, says the LORD of hosts. And in this place I will give peace, declares the LORD of hosts." (Hag 2:3–9)[14]

There was a question as to whether the second temple was greater than the first. The first temple had the ark of the covenant. The ark disappeared. (This is the premise for *Indiana Jones and the Raiders of the Lost Ark*.) The first temple was also filled with the "glory" of Yahweh (1 Kgs 8:10–11). This apparently didn't happen to the second temple. Yet Haggai's promise is that Yahweh will make the second temple greater than the first.

I resonate with the message "Be strong!" Everything in life requires strength, even building the temple. Or perhaps we should say *especially* building the temple. This is because the Jews faced opposition from the "peoples of the land," whom they feared.

These peoples are described as "adversaries" of the Jews. They were brought to the land by the Assyrians, specifically Sennacherib's son, Esarhaddon. They are the ancestors of the Samaritans whom we read about in the New Testament. They worship Yahweh, but their religion is more syncretistic than Judaism. In any case, they offer to help rebuild the temple, but the Jews don't trust them and reject their offer, saying, "You have nothing to do with us in building a house to our God; but we alone will build to the LORD, the God of Israel, as King Cyrus the king of Persia has commanded

---

13. I'm using Haggai to interpret the reaction of the older folks. It's possible they were wailing because they remembered the destruction of the temple rather than comparing the new temple with the old one.

14. Haggai calles Jeshua "Joshua."

268

us" (Ezra 4:3). This causes the "people of the land" to intimidate the Jews and bribe "counselors against them to frustrate their purpose" (Ezra 4:5).

Then arose another problem for the Jews. A man named Tattenai, a governor of a nearby province, along with another man named Shethar-bozenai and his associates, question the Jews on their right to rebuild the temple. The Jews tell them that Cyrus had issued a decree allowing them to rebuild. Tattenai is skeptical, so he writes a letter to Darius to uncover the truth.

This is where we read that second decree of Cyrus. Darius affirms Cyrus's policy. He commands Tattenai to leave the Jews alone. In fact, the royal revenue from Tattenai's province is to fund the building of the temple. Tattenai is to provide everything the Jews need. Darius concludes by saying:

> Also I make a decree that if anyone alters this edict, a beam shall be pulled out of his house, and he shall be impaled on it, and his house shall be made a dunghill. May the God who has caused his name to dwell there overthrow any king or people who shall put out a hand to alter this, or to destroy this house of God that is in Jerusalem. I Darius make a decree; let it be done with all diligence. (Ezra 6:11–12)

Harsh? Yes. But finally someone is on the side of the Jews! They were being bullied and the king stands up for them. The result? The temple is completed in 516 BCE! The following month, which is the first month of the year, the month called Nisan, the Jews celebrate Passover, a.k.a. the Festival of Unleavened Bread:

> And they kept the Feast of Unleavened Bread seven days with joy, for the LORD had made them joyful and had turned the heart of the king of Assyria to them, so that he aided them in the work of the house of God, the God of Israel. (Ezra 6:22)

Centuries later, a tradition was established to read the Song of Songs on Passover.

THE RESTORATION OF THE TORAH

Ezra is introduced to us in Ezra 7. According to the text, Ezra is a Jew from Babylon who lives during the reign of Artaxerxes. We assume this is Artaxerxes I, the son of Xerxes. Ezra leaves Babylon and goes to Jerusalem. He arrives in Jerusalem during the seventh year of Artaxerxes's reign. This is around the year 458 BCE.

You should know that many scholars question that date. They think it's impossible for Ezra to have arrived in Jerusalem that early. According to the traditional view, Ezra arrives in Jerusalem before his counterpart, Nehemiah, but some scholars see evidence that Nehemiah was there first. And maybe "Artaxerxes" is not Artaxerxes I

269

Illuminating Counsel

but Artaxerxes II.[15] In any case, I have no opinion on the matter. My main interest is focusing on the themes of the literature.

Ezra is a priest, a descendant of Aaron. He is also a scribe. The text tells us he "was a scribe skilled in the Law of Moses that the LORD, the God of Israel, had given" (Ezra 7:6). The text also tells us Ezra "set his heart to study the Law of the LORD, and to do it and to teach his statutes and rules in Israel" (Ezra 7:10). You can see what's being emphasized. The entire chapter is saturated with the word "law," which is the translation of *torah*. Artaxerxes gives Ezra a letter with permission to go to Yehud. The introduction to the letter reminds the reader who Ezra is: "Ezra the priest, the scribe, a man learned in matters of the commandments of the LORD and his statutes for Israel" (Ezra 7:11). The letter itself begins thusly: "Artaxerxes, king of kings, to Ezra the priest, the scribe of the Law of the God of heaven" (Ezra 7:12). The king says Ezra is "sent by the king and his seven counselors to make inquiries about Judah and Jerusalem according to the Law of your God, which is in your hand" (Ezra 7:14). Artaxerxes then makes a decree: "Whatever Ezra the priest, the scribe of the Law of the God of heaven, requires of you, let it be done with all diligence" (Ezra 7:21). And Artaxerxes concludes by saying:

> And you, Ezra, according to the wisdom of your God that is in your hand, appoint magistrates and judges who may judge all the people in the province Beyond the River, all such as know the laws of your God. And those who do not know them, you shall teach. Whoever will not obey the law of your God and the law of the king, let judgment be strictly executed on him, whether for death or for banishment or for confiscation of his goods or for imprisonment." (Ezra 7:25–26)

The word translated in those verses as "law" is *dat*, not *torah*, but it amounts to the same thing. Notice the king doesn't use the name "Yahweh." His letter is also in Aramaic, not Hebrew. Because of these things, the letter feels very authentic.

Notice the pattern of events: Just as Cyrus issued a decree allowing the Jews to rebuild their temple, so Artaxerxes issues a decree allowing Ezra to teach the Jews the Torah. The Jews returned to their homeland carrying the "vessels" of Yahweh. Ezra returns to his homeland carrying the Torah of Yahweh.

Now, ask yourself a question: How did Ezra have the Torah? Answer: He had it because the Jews brought their texts with them to Babylon when they were exiled. If they didn't bring their texts, the texts would probably have been destroyed and Jewish identity would have been lost. Their texts, which became what we call the Bible, formed, shaped, and preserved Jewish identity. Ezra is now bringing those texts from Babylon back to Jerusalem.

---

15. For a concise discussion of the issue, see Throntveit, *Ezra-Nehemiah*, 1. For a longer discussion, see Williamson, *Ezra-Nehemiah*, xxxix–xliv.

Returning Home

But what did these texts consist of? Tradition (and the Bible) says that Moses is the author of the Torah. Many scholars, however, believe that the Torah is made up of four different sources which were woven together by an editor or a group of editors. (This theory is called the Documentary Hypothesis.) May I split the difference for you? Even if the Torah was indeed written by Moses, the text still required editing. After all, there are five different books in the Torah. Who arranged them? Who copied them? The Jews actually changed their script. Someone had to rewrite the text in the new script. Who wrote the end of Deuteronomy which says "there has not arisen a prophet since in Israel like Moses" (Deut 34:10)? Texts were not only written, but also copied, edited, preserved, and taught.

And on the other side, even those scholars who argue that the Torah consists of four different sources find sufficient evidence that all four of those sources are mentioned in Ezra-Nehemiah. That means that Ezra's Torah was not merely the book of Deuteronomy, or the commandments, but the *entire* Torah as we have it today: Genesis, Exodus, Leviticus, Numbers, and Deuteronomy.[16] And that means that, in all likelihood, Ezra was, what we might call, the Editor-in-Chief of the Torah![17]

Most people, religious or not, have heard of Moses. Not many have heard of Ezra. And yet the Bible portrays Ezra as a second Moses. All of Ezra-Nehemiah is reminiscent of Exodus. There is a second exodus: the Jews leaving Babylon to go to Jerusalem. There is also a second giving of the Torah: Ezra coming to Jerusalem to teach the Jews the Law of God.

I would like to propose that without Ezra we would not have the Bible. I'm not sure if I can prove that, but I think it's implied in the text. This is the man who is most responsible for preserving the biblical text, both as a literary form and as a living tradition. No Ezra, no Bible.

The chapter where we see the full restoration of the Torah is Neh 8, which is my friend Nathan Clayton's favorite chapter in the Bible. It's the month of Tishrei, the seventh month. Again! Remember, seven is the biblical number signifying completion. The people gather "as one man," just as they did when they built the altar (Neh 8:1; cf. Ezra 3:1). They're in a public place—a "square before the Water Gate" (Neh 8:1). The text says:

> And they told Ezra the scribe to bring the Book of the Law of Moses that the LORD had commanded Israel. So Ezra the priest brought the Law before the assembly, both men and women and all who could understand what they heard, on the first day of the seventh month. And he read from it facing the square before the Water Gate from early morning until midday, in the presence of the men and the women and those who could understand. And the ears of all the people were attentive to the Book of the Law. (Neh 8:1–3)

16. Friedman, *Who Wrote the Bible?*, 159.

17. Friedman, *Who Wrote the Bible?*, 223–25.

Illuminating Counsel

It's not only the seventh month; it's also Rosh Hashanah, just like in Ezra 3. What's remarkable, though, is that the assembly that has assembled to hear the Torah is made up, not only of men, but of women and children as well. The Bible is for everyone!

The text goes on:

> And Ezra the scribe stood on a wooden platform that they had made for the purpose. And beside him stood Mattithiah, Shema, Anaiah, Uriah, Hilkiah, and Maaseiah on his right hand, and Pedaiah, Mishael, Malchijah, Hashum, Hashbaddanah, Zechariah, and Meshullam on his left hand. And Ezra opened the book in the sight of all the people, for he was above all the people, and as he opened it all the people stood. And Ezra blessed the Lord, the great God, and all the people answered, "Amen, Amen," lifting up their hands. And they bowed their heads and worshiped the Lord with their faces to the ground. Also Jeshua, Bani, Sherebiah, Jamin, Akkub, Shabbethai, Hodiah, Maaseiah, Kelita, Azariah, Jozabad, Hanan, Pelaiah, the Levites, helped the people to understand the Law, while the people remained in their places. They read from the book, from the Law of God, clearly, and they gave the sense, so that the people understood the reading. (Neh 8:4–8)

So much of this has become part of Jewish tradition. In the synagogue (a Jewish house of worship), the Torah is "housed" in an ark, which in Hebrew is called the *Aron Hakodesh* ("The Holy Ark"). On the Sabbath (*Shabbat* in Hebrew), which is Saturday, the Torah is taken from the ark to be read. When the ark is opened, everyone in the congregation stands up. The Torah is undressed (it's ornamented with a cover and something like a necklace) and placed on a table which is on a "platform." In Hebrew, this platform is called a *bimah*, but *bimah* is actually a Greek word.[18] In fact, the word "platform" in Neh 8:4 is translated *bimah* in the Septuagint! The Torah is divided into *parashot*, plural of the Hebrew word *parashah*, which basically means "portion." There are fifty-four *parashot*. One portion is read—or, more literally, chanted—each Sabbath, so that the entire Torah is read in a year. The completion of the Torah is celebrated on a holiday called *Simchat Torah* ("Rejoicing of the Torah"), which is on the twenty-second day of Tishrei. (There's that seventh month again!) Each weekly portion is itself divided into seven parts, so that there can be up to seven readers total. In some traditions, the seventh reader is a child. The person reading is "called" to "go up" to the *bimah*. This is referred to as an *aliyah*, which means "ascent." The person reading, or chanting, is surrounded by others who are following along, perhaps correcting mistakes. Before the reading, the reader says a blessing:

> Blessed are you, Lord our God, King of the universe, who has chosen us from among all the nations and given us his Torah. Blessed are You Lord, who gives the Torah.[19]

18. "Synagogue" is also a Greek word.

19. See Chabad, "Blessings and Procedures."

Returning Home

After the reading, another blessing is said:

> Blessed are you, Lord our God, King of the universe, who has given us the Torah of truth and planted eternal life within us. Blessed are you Lord, who gives the Torah.[20]

After each blessing, the congregation responds resoundingly with "Amen!"

Then there's the tradition called *Hagbah*, which means "lifting." In some Jewish communities, after the reading, someone lifts up the scroll, spreads out his arms, and turns around so that everyone can see the words. Then the scroll is dressed, paraded around the congregation, and returned to the ark. In some communities, as it's being returned, the congregation sings a hymn called *Etz Hayim*, which means "Tree of Life":

> She is a tree of life to those who lay hold of her;
>> those who hold her fast are called blessed.
> Her ways are ways of pleasantness,
>> and all her paths are peace.
> Restore us to yourself, O LORD, that we may be restored!
>> Renew our days as of old.

This hymn is made up of three verses from the Bible: Prov 3:18, Prov 3:17, and Lam 5:21. All three of those verses are from the Ketuvim!

Then there's a sermon, or *drash*, which comes from the Hebrew word which means "seek."[21] The sermon is based on the reading of the Torah and the reading of the Prophets (called the *Haftarah*), which is read after the Torah. The sermon seems to correspond to Neh 8:7–8. Those verses are a bit confusing, which is ironic, but also interesting. There were several Levites who went among the people to "help them understand the Law." The ESV says, "They read from the book, from the Law of God, *clearly*, and they gave the sense, so that the people understood the reading." The KJV says, "They read from the book ... *distinctly* ..." The NET says, "They read from the book ... *explaining it and imparting insight* ..." The JPS says, "They read from the book ... *translating it*." Why such different translations? What were these Levites doing?

The Hebrew word in question is *mephorash*. This word comes from the same root as the word *parashah*, which, as we just said, refers to a "portion."[22] That's why the KJV translates it "distinctly," though that translation doesn't help us understand the verse. The JPS assumes the Levites are translating the Torah from Hebrew into Aramaic. At this time in history, Hebrew began to fall into disuse. Jews were now speaking Aramaic. Nehemiah himself complains that half of the Jews "could not speak the language

---

20. Chabad, "Blessings and Procedures."
21. The cognate of this word is translated "study" in Ezra 7:10.
22. This word is related to the Aramaic word *parsin* in Dan 5:25–28. The king's kingdom is *divided*.

273

of Judah" (Neh 13:24).[23] However, *mephorash* doesn't mean "translating." We actually see the Hebrew word for "translating" in Ezra 4:7:

> In the days of Artaxerxes, Bishlam and Mithredath and Tabeel and the rest of their associates wrote to Artaxerxes king of Persia. The letter was written in Aramaic and *translated.*

The Hebrew word rendered "translated" is *meturgam.* Centuries after Ezra, the Bible was translated into Aramaic. These translations (there are several of them) are often more like paraphrases than translations. Even so, they're referred to as the Targum, or Targumim in plural.[24]

So what's going on in Neh 8:8? Maybe the Levites are translating, but if so, they're doing more than that. They're *interpreting.* They're explaining what the text means. The rabbis said the biblical text is crying out to us, saying, "Interpret me!" Think about how awesome that is. What we are doing right now is participating in a project of interpretation that has been going on for 2,400 years!

The reading of the Torah made the Jews weep. Why would they weep? Presumably, they felt guilty for not obeying God's commandments. This reminds us of Josiah's reaction when the Book of the Law was found and read to him (see 2 Kgs 22:11). But Nehemiah, Ezra, and the Levites don't want the Jews to weep:

> And Nehemiah, who was the governor, and Ezra the priest and scribe, and the Levites who taught the people said to all the people, "This day is holy to the LORD your God; do not mourn or weep." For all the people wept as they heard the words of the Law. Then he said to them, "Go your way. Eat the fat and drink sweet wine and send portions to anyone who has nothing ready, for this day is holy to our Lord. And do not be grieved, for the joy of the LORD is your strength." So the Levites calmed all the people, saying, "Be quiet, for this day is holy; do not be grieved." And all the people went their way to eat and drink and to send portions and to make great rejoicing, because they had understood the words that were declared to them. (Neh 8:9–12)

Kohelet had said there's a time to weep and a time to laugh (Eccl 3:4). The people had suffered because of their sins and the sins of others, but now they were restored. The time to weep has passed.

These verses are personal to me in an odd way. I used to be obese. After my mother died of lung cancer in 2013, I felt like death was knocking on my door, coming for me next. So I resolved to fight death. I reasoned that the best way to fight death is with life. I saw a dietitian and I stuck to my diet and exercise regimen with fierce determination. It took me about a year and a half to get to my goal weight. I lost one hundred pounds. I'm more proud of this accomplishment than any other.

---

23. In the Tanakh, the Hebrew language is never referred to as "Hebrew."

24. I trust, dear reader, that you can see the linguistic connection between *meturgam* and *targum.*

Returning Home

But I was strict with my diet almost to a fault. I didn't starve myself by any means—I wanted to eat to build muscle—but I wouldn't dare put anything unhealthy in my mouth, even for a taste. (I no longer have that problem, by the way.) I had a fitness mentor named Tierney. Tierney is a devout Christian. She said to me, "Isn't there some verse somewhere that says, 'Eat the fat'?" I had to look it up. It's Neh 8:10! She was giving me permission to be a bit more lenient with my diet. Life is too short to never enjoy eating something less than perfectly healthy. There's no dieting on special occasions. Eat the fat! Drink the sweet wine! Rejoice!

And that's what the Jews did. They learned about Sukkot—the Festival of Booths—from the Torah, so they celebrated it, just as we read in Ezra 3:4:

> And there was very great rejoicing. And day by day, from the first day to the last day, he read from the Book of the Law of God. They kept the feast seven days, and on the eighth day there was a solemn assembly, according to the rule. (Neh 8:17–18)

Eventually, a tradition developed to read Ecclesiastes on Sukkot.

The synagogue tradition is not entirely taken from Neh 8, but it's similar enough to make the point that the Jewish tradition is a living tradition whose roots are in the Hebrew Bible. The Jewish tradition goes back to the Hebrew Bible in a way the Christian tradition does not. The holidays in the Hebrew Bible are Jewish holidays, not Christian holidays. Jews venerate the Torah in a way Christians do not. I'm not saying Judaism is greater than Christianity. What I'm saying is that Christians must remember that they adopted the *Jewish* Bible. Even Paul says that Christians share the spiritual blessings of the Jews (Rom 15:27).

The other thing to point out here is that Ezra and Nehemiah are not the highest authority in the land. The highest authority is the book. I know that some might say that that's terrible because no book is infallible—and clearly the Jews believed the Torah *is* infallible. On the other hand, the only way to have a just society is to be a society of laws, not men, as the founders of the United States put it. No human can be above the law, just as no one human can be the source of wisdom. Ezra-Nehemiah takes what Proverbs says about wisdom and applies it to the book. Thus Jewish life ever since has been characterized by *studying* and *learning*.

THE RESTORATION OF JERUSALEM

In some ways, Ezra-Nehemiah is the most extraordinary book of the Bible. Why do I say that? Ezra-Nehemiah is made up of first-person narratives. Scholars refer to these first-person narratives as the Ezra Memoir and the Nehemiah Memoir. These first-person narratives make the book feel very authentic. Nehemiah's memoir has an endearing characteristic. As he's telling his story, he offers up miniature prayers to God. Sometimes he tells us he prayed. Other times he writes the prayers out. These prayers

275

Illuminating Counsel

are sprinkled throughout the book. The very last verse in Nehemiah says, "Remember me, O my God, for good" (Neh 13:31).

Nehemiah is a Jew who lives in the diaspora—in Susa, which is where Esther lived. He's King Artaxerxes's cupbearer. We assume this is Artaxerxes I. Being the king's cupbearer is an important job. It means the king trusts Nehemiah not to poison him.

Nehemiah receives some bad news about the state of affairs of Jerusalem. "The remnant there in the province who had survived the exile is in great trouble and shame. The wall of Jerusalem is broken down, and its gates are destroyed by fire" (Neh 1:3). He's very sad about this, as you can imagine. The king sees that he's sad and questions him about it. Nehemiah tells the king the situation. The king gives Nehemiah permission to go to Jerusalem to rebuild its wall.

Let's review: Cyrus allows the Jews to go to Jerusalem to rebuild the temple. Artaxerxes allows Ezra to go to Jerusalem to teach the Jews the Torah. Artaxerxes allows Nehemiah to go to Jerusalem to rebuild the wall. These texts show the Persian kings in the most positive light.

There are interesting differences between Ezra and Nehemiah. Ezra explicitly mentions that he came to Jerusalem without an armed guard. He says:

> For I was ashamed to ask the king for a band of soldiers and horsemen to protect us against the enemy on our way, since we had told the king, "The hand of our God is for good on all who seek him, and the power of his wrath is against all who forsake him." (Ezra 8:22)

Again, the text feels so authentic. He wishes he had an armed guard but he was afraid to ask, lest the king would think Yahweh was weak. Nehemiah doesn't have that problem. "Now the king had sent with me officers of the army and horsemen," he says (Neh 2:9).

Nehemiah goes to Jerusalem in the twentieth year of Artaxerxes I's reign. This would have been around 445 BCE. He becomes the governor of of the Jews, as we read in Neh 8:9. (That verse, by the way, is the only verse that has Ezra and Nehemiah together in the narrative.) Nehemiah returns to Susa twelve years later, in the year 433 BCE. He then returns to Jerusalem for a second term as governor for an unknown period of time.

The account of the rebuilding of the wall is one of the most tedious passages in the Ketuvim, and yet it's strangely inspiring. Nehemiah tells us *everyone* who worked. He's very specific about what they did. "The sons of Hassenaah built the Fish Gate. They laid its beams and set its doors, its bolts, and its bars" (Neh 3:3). "Joiada the son of Paseah and Meshullam the son of Besodeiah repaired the Gate of Yeshanah" (Neh 3:6). "Hanun and the inhabitants of Zanoah repaired the Valley Gate" (Neh 3:13). And so on. There's even a gate called the Dung Gate! It was repaired by Malchijah the son of Rechab, ruler of the district of Beth-haccerem (Neh 3:14). What's amazing, though, is that everyone is doing something. Who'd have thought *teamwork* was a biblical value?! I'm a tennis

Returning Home

guy, but the thing I love about team sports is that everyone is necessary; everyone plays his or her part for the benefit of the whole. I also play chess. In chess, every piece is important. Even a little pawn can be promoted to a powerful queen. Everyone is valuable, and every work is valuable, no matter how small it might seem.

The completion of the wall is met with a great celebration:

> So both choirs of those who gave thanks stood in the house of God, and I and half of the officials with me; and the priests Eliakim, Maaseiah, Miniamin, Micaiah, Elioenai, Zechariah, and Hananiah, with trumpets; and Maaseiah, Shemaiah, Eleazar, Uzzi, Jehohanan, Malchijah, Elam, and Ezer. And the singers sang with Jezrahiah as their leader. And they offered great sacrifices that day and rejoiced, for God had made them rejoice with great joy; the women and children also rejoiced. And the joy of Jerusalem was heard far away. (Neh 12:40–43)

We started the book (Ezra-Nehemiah) with a mixture of joy and sadness. Sadness has now dissolved. There's only joy now. The restoration of Jerusalem is complete!

And notice what they're doing: they're singing! What do you think they're singing? The text implies they're singing from the book of Psalms:

> And they performed the service of their God and the service of purification, as did the singers and the gatekeepers, according to the command of David and his son Solomon. For long ago in the days of David and Asaph there were directors of the singers, and there were songs of praise and thanksgiving to God. (Neh 12:45–46)

We can almost hear the exact psalms that they're singing:

> When the LORD restored the fortunes of Zion,
> > we were like those who dream.
> Then our mouth was filled with laughter,
> > and our tongue with shouts of joy;
> then they said among the nations,
> > "The LORD has done great things for them."
> The LORD has done great things for us;
> > we are glad. (Ps 126:1–3)

> For the LORD has chosen Zion;
> > he has desired it for his dwelling place:
> "This is my resting place forever;
> > here I will dwell, for I have desired it.
> I will abundantly bless her provisions;
> > I will satisfy her poor with bread.
> Her priests I will clothe with salvation,
> > and her saints will shout for joy. (Ps 132:13–16)

Behold, how good and pleasant it is
>when brothers dwell in unity!
It is like the precious oil on the head,
>running down on the beard,
on the beard of Aaron,
>running down on the collar of his robes!
It is like the dew of Hermon,
>which falls on the mountains of Zion!
For there the LORD has commanded the blessing,
>life forevermore. (Ps 133:1–3)

Come, bless the LORD, all you servants of the Lord,
>who stand by night in the house of the LORD!
Lift up your hands to the holy place
>and bless the LORD!
May the LORD bless you from Zion,
>he who made heaven and earth! (Ps 134:1–3)

It would seem Psalms' Zion Theology has been vindicated after all! And we can imagine other psalms they sang. Psalm 100, for sure. Psalm 136. Psalm 150. All praise and thanksgiving. No laments!

THE COURT JEWS

It's now time to connect the remaining dots. We're almost finished. Soon you will see how brilliant the arrangement of the books of the Ketuvim truly is.

Ezra and Nehemiah are both "court Jews." They are Jews who live in the diaspora and who rise to prominence in the Gentile king's court. Ezra is not quite the same as Nehemiah. Ezra is from Babylon but the king lived in Susa, apparently. But since Ezra has received a letter from the king, we assume that Ezra was of importance to him. Maybe he worked for the king as a scribe.

Ezra and Nehemiah have powerful connections with Joseph, Moses, Esther, Mordecai, and Daniel. Here is a chart indicating what these figures and their stories have in common:

	Dual Meaning Name	Two Names	Assimilation	Slander	Wisdom/ Interpretation of dreams	God's Sovereignty
Joseph		√	√	√	√	√
Moses	√		√	√		√

Returning Home

	Dual Meaning Name	Two Names	Assimilation	Slander	Wisdom/ Interpretation of dreams	God's Sovereignty
Esther/ Mordecai	√	√	√	√		√
Daniel		√	√	√	√	√
Ezra/ Nehemiah			√	√		√

Here's an explanation of what we see in these stories:

- *Joseph* is betrayed by his brothers and slandered by his master's wife. He interprets dreams and rises to prominence in the king's court. He's deemed to be wise. He assimilates and becomes Egyptian, even having an Egyptian name, though he eventually comes to remember who he is. He increases the power of the king. He saves the Jewish people from the famine. He is certain of God's sovereignty. He remains in exile. It's only after his death that his bones are brought to the land of Israel.

- *Moses* grows up in the king's court but becomes a Jew again. The name "Moses" is both Egyptian and Hebrew. Moses rescues the Jewish people from Pharaoh.

- *Esther* and *Mordecai* both assimilate and become Persian, especially Esther, though both of them "come out" as Jews. Esther's real name is Hadassah. The name "Esther" is both Persian and Hebrew. Esther "comes out" at the end of her story. Haman slanders the Jews. Esther's most important action is approaching the king. In doing so, she saves the Jewish people from annihilation. God's sovereignty is subtly brought up as a possibility, but not a certainty. Esther and Mordecai remain in exile.

- *Daniel* is forcibly brought to Babylon. He's given a Babylonian name. He resists assimilation even when it's forced upon him. He interprets dreams and rises to prominence in the king's court. He endures slander by those who are envious of him. He's certain of God's sovereignty. He remains in exile.

- Ezra and *Nehemiah* are in exile but return to Jerusalem. They approach the Gentile king. Nehemiah is slandered. Nehemiah increases the power of the poor. Nehemiah saves his people from their enemies. Nehemiah is certain of God's sovereignty. Ezra and Nehemiah fight against the assimilation of the Jews.

Let's first deal with what I anachronistically call antisemitism. Joseph the "Hebrew" is slandered by Potiphar's wife; she accuses him of trying to rape her. Pharaoh slanders the Israelites by calling them a "fifth column." Haman slanders the Jews to the

Illuminating Counsel

king, telling him that the Jews are no good and it's "not to the king's profit to tolerate them" (Esth 3:8). Daniel's enemies slander him to the king, telling the king that Daniel is disloyal.

As you can see, these are all variations on the same theme. We must pay special attention to Esther, though. When Haman slanders the Jews, the king issues a decree calling for the annihilation of the Jews. Esther approaches the king to intercede on behalf of the Jews. The king sides with the Jews and the Jews are thereby victorious.

Ezra 4:6 mentions Ahasuerus, who I suppose is Xerxes. The text says: "And in the reign of Ahasuerus, in the beginning of his reign, they wrote an accusation against the inhabitants of Judah and Jerusalem." If this Ahasuerus is the same king as the guy in Esther, that's a very interesting connection indeed. Then Ezra 4:7 mentions Artaxerxes, who, as we said, is the son and successor of Ahasuerus. This is confusing because Ezra 1–6 takes place during the reigns of Cyrus II, Cambyses, and Darius I—a century or so before Artaxerxes. The text is arranged thematically, not chronologically.

Brace yourself, for we're going to make a delicious connection. In Ezra 4, a bunch of officials who opposed the Jews write a letter to Artaxerxes:

> To Artaxerxes the king: Your servants, the men of the province Beyond the River, send greeting. And now be it known to the king that the Jews who came up from you to us have gone to Jerusalem. They are rebuilding that rebellious and wicked city. They are finishing the walls and repairing the foundations. Now be it known to the king that if this city is rebuilt and the walls finished, they will not pay tribute, custom, or toll, and the royal revenue will be impaired. Now because we eat the salt of the palace and it is not fitting for us to witness the king's dishonor, therefore we send and inform the king, in order that search may be made in the book of the records of your fathers. You will find in the book of the records and learn that this city is a rebellious city, hurtful to kings and provinces, and that sedition was stirred up in it from of old. That was why this city was laid waste. We make known to the king that if this city is rebuilt and its walls finished, you will then have no possession in the province Beyond the River." (Ezra 4:10–16)

As a result of this letter, Artaxerxes is convinced the Jews are wicked! He writes a letter back and says:

> Therefore make a decree that these men be made to cease, and that this city be not rebuilt, until a decree is made by me. And take care not to be slack in this matter. Why should damage grow to the hurt of the king? (Ezra 4:21–22)

All of this is the context for . . . wait for it . . . Neh 1! (Now you see why Ezra and Nehemiah ought to be viewed as one book!) The work on the reconstruction of Jerusalem has ceased by order of the king himself. Nehemiah hears about the awful condition Jerusalem is in, how the Jews are vulnerable to their enemies, and he's very sad. He approaches the king. The king sees how sad he is. He tells the king what's going

280

Returning Home

on. Just like in Esther, the king reverses his decision and decides in favor of Nehemiah and the Jews![25]

Yoram Hazony points out a way in which Nehemiah subverts Joseph.[26] Joseph, for all the good he did, actually increases the power of the Pharaoh. Joseph does this to help the Egyptians. The Egyptians were broke and starving. So Joseph gave Pharaoh ownership of their land:

> So Joseph bought all the land of Egypt for Pharaoh, for all the Egyptians sold their fields, because the famine was severe on them. The land became Pharaoh's. As for the people, he made servants of them from one end of Egypt to the other. (Gen 47:20–21)

The result is that the Egyptians have to pay Pharaoh a fifth of everything they have. Nehemiah does the opposite. Instead of increasing the power of the rich, he does whatever he can to increase the power of the poor:

> I took counsel with myself, and I brought charges against the nobles and the officials. I said to them, "You are exacting interest, each from his brother." And I held a great assembly against them and said to them, "We, as far as we are able, have bought back our Jewish brothers who have been sold to the nations, but you even sell your brothers that they may be sold to us!" They were silent and could not find a word to say. So I said, "The thing that you are doing is not good. Ought you not to walk in the fear of our God to prevent the taunts of the nations our enemies? Moreover, I and my brothers and my servants are lending them money and grain. Let us abandon this exacting of interest. Return to them this very day their fields, their vineyards, their olive orchards, and their houses, and the percentage of money, grain, wine, and oil that you have been exacting from them." (Neh 5:7–11)

Nehemiah, despite being governor, refuses to make use of his position for financial gain. "The former governors who were before me laid heavy burdens on the people and took from them for their daily ration forty shekels of silver. Even their servants lorded it over the people. But I did not do so, because of the fear of God," he says (Neh 5:15).

How do Ezra and Nehemiah fight against assimilation? They both discover that many Jews have married non-Jews. (Though their circumstances were very different, this is what Joseph and Esther had done.) Ezra is so distressed over the matter that he prays to God and calls the Jews to repent. "While Ezra prayed and made confession, weeping and casting himself down before the house of God, a very great assembly of men, women, and children, gathered to him out of Israel, for the people wept bitterly" (Ezra 10:1). Ezra tells them, "You have broken faith and married foreign women, and so increased the guilt of Israel. Now then make confession to the LORD, the God of

---

25. Hazony, *God and Politics in Esther*, 92.

26. Hazony, *God and Politics in Esther*, 59–60.

281

Illuminating Counsel

your fathers and do his will. Separate yourselves from the peoples of the land and from the foreign wives" (Ezra 10:10–11).

Nehemiah is equally irate when he discovers the Jews have intermarried. Nehemiah takes a slightly different approach than Ezra, however. Both of them call the Jews to repent and separate themselves from non-Jews. However, when Ezra finds out about the intermarriages, he pulls out his hair: "As soon as I heard this, I tore my garment and my cloak and pulled hair from my head and beard and sat appalled," he says (Ezra 9:3). When Nehemiah finds out, he pulls out *other people's* hair: "And I confronted them and cursed them and beat some of them and pulled out their hair" (Neh 13:25). I wouldn't fool with Nehemiah!

The whole matter is not easy to digest. We had spent a considerable amount of time talking about Ruth. Ruth seemed to subvert Deuteronomy's prohibition against the Moabites. It seemed that as the Tanakh progresses from the Torah to the Ketuvim, the Tanakh becomes softer and more tolerant. But Ezra-Nehemiah is about the restoration of the Torah. And so it's perhaps not surprising that Ezra-Nehemiah subverts Ruth by affirming Deuteronomy:

> On that day they read from the Book of Moses in the hearing of the people. And in it was found written that no Ammonite or Moabite should ever enter the assembly of God, for they did not meet the people of Israel with bread and water, but hired Balaam against them to curse them—yet our God turned the curse into a blessing. As soon as the people heard the law, they separated from Israel all those of foreign descent. (Neh 13:1–3)

Of course, we must bear in mind that Ruth converted and became a Jew. The Jews in Ezra-Nehemiah are not marrying foreign women who converted. They're marrying polytheists. By marrying these women, they were becoming like Solomon; they were compromising their religion. In fact, Nehemiah mentions Solomon and his foreign wives (Neh 13:26). The Jews had suffered so much because they worshiped idols. They had come so far. Nehemiah did not want them to repeat the sins of the past.

We can say, then, that the Bible's prohibition against intermarriage is religious, not ethnic or racial. There's no thought here that Jews are ethnically superior to anyone else.

Throughout our survey, I've been making the point that the books of the Ketuvim deal with life's most profound issues. Indeed, they even deal with inter-religious marriage! Inter-religious marriage is not uncommon in American culture. Catholics marry Protestants, Christians marry Jews, atheists marry believers. It may seem intolerant to question the wisdom of such "mixed" marriages, as if the questioner would also be opposed to blacks marrying whites. And we also live in a culture where men can marry men and women can marry women. So what's wrong with inter-religious marriages?

Judaism discourages inter-religious marriages but recognizes the reality that they sometimes occur. If there's an inter-religious marriage with children, the child is

282

considered a Jew if the mother's a Jew. For example, the Canadian rapper Drake is half black and half Jewish, but his mother is a Jew, and therefore Drake is a Jew. He even became a Bar Mitzvah.

Christianity opposes inter-religious marriages too. Paul says, "Do not be unequally yoked with unbelievers" (2 Cor 6:14). But Paul also dealt with situations where two polytheists married each other but one of them became a Christian. He tells Christians who are married to pagans to not divorce, but also to not fret if the unbeliever leaves (2 Cor 7:12–16). This is far less strict than Ezra, who tells the Jews to divorce, though perhaps we should think of it as *annulment* rather than divorce.

I know couples who are of different religions who love each other dearly. Most of them, though, are not religious. For them, religion is merely a matter of culture. The children celebrate both Hanukkah and Christmas. If one spouse is religious, the nonreligious spouse might yield and allow the child to be raised in the religion of the other. But if both spouses are religious, it might be much harder to make it work.

Many Christians assume that the prohibition against Jews marrying non-Jews has to do with the purity of the bloodline to prepare the way for the Messiah. I think that view is totally wrong. The reason Ezra and Nehemiah get upset is because of Jewish identity. It has nothing whatever to do with the Messiah. If Jews assimilate, there will be no Jews left in the world. Marrying non-Jews and adopting their religion—doing what Solomon did—is a surefire way for Jews to assimilate themselves out of existence. The failure of Christians to understand this—the failure of Christians to read the Jewish Bible as a *Jewish* book—has caused so much pain for Jews throughout the centuries. Christians have not realized that if Jews become Christians (as Christians practice Christianity; that is, with the abolition of the Torah and Jewish holidays, customs, and traditions), Jews will cease to be Jews. The problem, of course, is that Christians, throughout the ages have assumed that there's no purpose for Jews to be Jews since the Messiah, Jesus, has already come. As I said in the beginning, the only way to truly appreciate the Hebrew Bible is to appreciate the Jews as a *living* people.

PERSISTENCE

Like every other book we've discussed, Ezra-Nehemiah deals with suffering, though in the case of Ezra-Nehemiah, it might be more accurate to use the word "adversity." We've already noted that in the days of Jeshua and Zerubbabel, the "peoples of the land" opposed the Jews. This theme reoccurs during the tenure of Nehemiah. The whole problem with the wall being broken down is that the Jews are vulnerable to their enemies. When Nehemiah arrives in Jerusalem, we're introduced to two of the leaders of the peoples of the land: "But when Sanballat the Horonite and Tobiah the Ammonite servant heard this, it displeased them greatly that someone had come to seek the welfare of the people of Israel" (Neh 2:10). Then we're introduced to a third guy: Geshem the Arab. The three of them hear that the Jews are rebuilding the wall.

Illuminating Counsel

Nehemiah says, "But when Sanballat the Horonite and Tobiah the Ammonite servant and Geshem the Arab heard of it, they jeered at us and despised us and said, 'What is this thing that you are doing? Are you rebelling against the king?'" (Neh 2:19).

These three men are basically bullies. They taunt Nehemiah and the Jews in order to intimidate them and get them to stop building:

> Now when Sanballat heard that we were building the wall, he was angry and greatly enraged, and he jeered at the Jews. And he said in the presence of his brothers and of the army of Samaria, "What are these feeble Jews doing? Will they restore it for themselves? Will they sacrifice? Will they finish up in a day? Will they revive the stones out of the heaps of rubbish, and burned ones at that?" Tobiah the Ammonite was beside him, and he said, "Yes, what they are building—if a fox goes up on it he will break down their stone wall!" (Neh 4:1–3[3:33–35])

You can almost hear them laugh when Tobiah says that.

What's important to note is how Nehemiah responds to them. He tells them, "The God of heaven will make us prosper, and we his servants will arise and build, but you have no portion or right or claim in Jerusalem" (Neh 2:20). That's a strong and direct response, though it doesn't put an end to the bullying. When the enemies mock the Jews, Nehemiah offers up a prayer and then says in his memoir, "So we built the wall" (Neh 2:6). I love that! The bullies can mock all they want; we're going to keep working! The enemies respond by plotting to "come and fight against Jerusalem and to cause confusion in it" (Neh 2:8). But Nehemiah says that the Jews "prayed to our God and set a guard as a protection against them day and night" (Neh 2:9).

Of course, being bullied tends to lower morale. Thus we read:

> In Judah it was said, "The strength of those who bear the burdens is failing. There is too much rubble. By ourselves we will not be able to rebuild the wall." And our enemies said, "They will not know or see till we come among them and kill them and stop the work." At that time the Jews who lived near them came from all directions and said to us ten times, "You must return to us." So in the lowest parts of the space behind the wall, in open places, I stationed the people by their clans, with their swords, their spears, and their bows. (Neh 4:10–13[4–7]).

Nehemiah then tells the Jewish officials: "Do not be afraid of them. Remember the Lord, who is great and awesome, and fight for your brothers, your sons, your daughters, your wives, and your homes" (Neh 4:14[8]). Nehemiah counters the bullying by inspiring his people. He then tells us that they all resumed their work on the wall.

The bullies then decide to attack Nehemiah personally. Sanballat, who's clearly the ringleader, sends word to Nehemiah to set up a meeting. Nehemiah knows what's going on, though. "But they intended to do me harm," he says (Neh 6:2). Nehemiah tells them that he's too busy working on the wall to meet with them. They keep

284

Returning Home

pestering him, but he ignores them. (This reminds me of scammers who keep calling me telling me I need to buy a car warranty from them!)

Sanballat then changes his approach:

> In the same way Sanballat for the fifth time sent his servant to me with an open letter in his hand. In it was written, "It is reported among the nations, and Geshem also says it, that you and the Jews intend to rebel; that is why you are building the wall. And according to these reports you wish to become their king. And you have also set up prophets to proclaim concerning you in Jerusalem, 'There is a king in Judah.' And now the king will hear of these reports. So now come and let us take counsel together." (Neh 6:5–7)

In essence, this is no different than what we saw in Esther and Daniel. Today we would call all of them antisemites. They are extorting Nehemiah and the Jews by threatening to slander them to the king. How would you respond to that? Nehemiah tells them, "No such things as you say have been done, for you are inventing them out of your own mind" (Neh 6:8). Nehemiah knows they want to scare the Jews so that they will stop working, but there's really nothing to be afraid of. He calmly calls their bluff.

Then Sanballat and company hire a man to deceive Nehemiah. This man tells Nehemiah that Sanballat *et al.* are trying to kill him and that he should find sanctuary by living in the temple. Nehemiah, as we've seen, is not naive:

> I understood and saw that God had not sent him, but he had pronounced the prophecy against me because Tobiah and Sanballat had hired him. For this purpose he was hired, that I should be afraid and act in this way and sin, and so they could give me a bad name in order to taunt me. (Neh 6:12–13)

Nehemiah offers up another prayer and the Jews finish the wall. Then we read a most satisfying verse: "And when all our enemies heard of it, all the nations around us were afraid and fell greatly in their own esteem, for they perceived that this work had been accomplished with the help of our God" (Neh 6:16). This is reminiscent of Esther 8:17—"And many from the peoples of the country declared themselves Jews, for fear of the Jews had fallen on them."

So what's Ezra-Nehemiah's response to suffering and adversity? Interestingly, Nehemiah is a pray-er, and so, while he's not a poet, his response reminds us of Psalms, especially the imprecatory Psalms. I'd add something else, though. The word that comes to my mind is *persistence*. No matter what the bullies did, no matter how much they bullied, no matter how much they tried to intimidate, Nehemiah did not back down. He had a job to do and he made sure it got done no matter the obstacles.

It's a sad fact that not everyone you meet is on your side. We've discussed the sin of envy, but what happens when others envy you? What happens when you're bullied because people are envious of who you are and what you've accomplished? Nehemiah would tell you to pray and get on with your life and work. Their envy is their problem, not yours. You have a task to do. Be persistent and do it!

285

15

Ending with a New Beginning
(Chronicles)

UNIQUE FEATURES

CHRONICLES IS A CONDENSED version of Samuel and Kings. It's a rewrite of the history of the monarchy from a post-exilic perspective.

Rabbi David Wolpe says Chronicles is "Samuel made boring."[1] He certainly has a point. For one thing, Chronicles doesn't begin with David's story. Chronicles doesn't even begin with Samuel's story. Chronicles begins with a genealogy. The genealogy starts with Adam and goes all the way to those who returned from the exile. The first *nine* chapters of Chronicles are nothing but names!

One of the features that makes David's story as told in Samuel so interesting is Saul's obsessive pursuit of David. We have an envious, unstable king trying to kill his heroic son-in-law whom he once "greatly loved" (1 Sam 16:21). The hero of Israel becomes a fugitive in his own nation. He hides in a cave. He has the chance to kill his crazy father-in-law but he can't bring himself to do it because he respects the office of "Yahweh's anointed one." When his father-in-law is killed in battle, he mourns for him as if he were his own father.

In Chronicles, all of that is *gone*. Saul is barely mentioned. He has one chapter and that's it. How about the story of David and Bathsheba? What an amazing scandal of sex, betrayal, and murder! *Gone*. Amnon, David's heir, raping his half-sister Tamar, and Tamar's brother, Absalom, killing Amnon? *Gone*. Absalom rebelling against David, having sex with David's concubines on a roof in broad daylight, getting killed by Joab while being caught in a tree by his long hair, and David breaking down when he hears of Absalom's death? *Gone*. All of the best parts of the David story are not found in Chronicles.

---

1. Wolpe, *David*, loc. 139.

Ending with a New Beginning

What about Solomon? Chronicles sanitizes him. The harem of seven hundred wives and three hundred concubines? *Gone.* The idolatry? *Gone.* Earlier we discussed Solomon's legacy. Is Solomon's legacy positive or negative? If all we read was Kings, we'd have to conclude his legacy is negative. He never rebounds. He never repents. But the Ketuvim vindicates him. His name is on three books: Proverbs, the Song of Songs, and Ecclesiastes.[2] Ecclesiastes might be thought of as Solomon's way of renouncing his past mistakes. True, Solomon is mentioned in a negative way in Ezra-Nehemiah, but Chronicles has the final word. Chronicles makes Solomon's legacy positive.

And what of the great stories in Kings involving Elijah and Ahab? They're gone too. Chronicles barely mentions the kingdom of Israel. Chronicles instead focuses almost entirely on the kingdom of Judah.

So if we have Samuel and Kings, and they are better books, why do we need Chronicles? What does Chronicles bring to the table?

The key to understanding Chronicles is to focus not so much on what Chronicles cuts from Samuel and Kings, but what Chronicles adds to Samuel and Kings.

One of the most obvious differences between Chronicles and Samuel-Kings is that Chronicles focuses on the building of the temple. Now, Kings focuses on the building of the temple too. But Chronicles focuses on David's role in the building of the temple. In 2 Sam 7, David comes up with the idea to build the temple. It's rejected. He's told his son will build the temple. That's that. In Chronicles, however, David makes preparations for Solomon to build the temple. These preparations begin in 1 Chr 22 and they go all the way to 1 Chr 29. So all of the juicy parts of David's story are removed in order to make space for the building of the temple. *Eight* chapters of David's preparations!

It makes sense for the writer/redactor of Chronicles (referred to by scholars as the Chronicler) to focus on the temple since that is what the post-exilic community was focused on, as we read in Ezra-Nehemiah. Chronicles also focuses on the Levites. Go to biblegateway.com and type in "Levites" in the search engine. Samuel and Kings use the word "Levites" a total of four times. Chronicles uses the word "Levites" over eighty times! Ezra-Nehemiah use the word "Levites" well over fifty times. These post-exilic books use the word "Levites" more than all the other books of the Bible combined! Chronicles emphasizes the Levites' role in temple worship (2 Chr 5, 7, 30). It mentions the priests and Levites from Israel defecting to Judah (2 Chr 11). It mentions the priests and Levites being appointed as judges (2 Chr 17, 19). It mentions the Levites collecting the tax when Joash repairs the temple (2 Chr 24).

Chronicles tells a story of king Uzziah going into the temple and performing the priestly duty of burning incense. The priests criticize him for this:

---

2. His name is not mentioned in Ecclesiastes but Kohelet is equated with Solomon, as we discussed earlier.

287

Illuminating Counsel

> It is not for you, Uzziah, to burn incense to the LORD, but for the priests, the sons of Aaron, who are consecrated to burn incense. Go out of the sanctuary, for you have done wrong, and it will bring you no honor from the LORD God. (2 Chr 26:18)

Uzziah is then punished by God. He becomes a leper to the day of his death and lives in solitary confinement, "for he was excluded from the house of the LORD" (2 Chr 26:21).

Chronicles shows us the primacy of the priest over the king. The implication is clear. Pre-exilic Israel was led by the kings. Post-exilic Israel was led by the priests and Levites.

Chronicles also focuses on prayer. We learn of Jabez, whose mother bore him in "pain." Jabez prays to God and says, "Oh that you would bless me and enlarge my border, and that your hand might be with me, and that you keep me from harm so that it might not bring me pain" (1 Chr 4:10). God grants Jabez's request.[3]

David has an extraordinary prayer which we only read in Chronicles:

> Blessed are you, O LORD, the God of Israel our father, forever and ever. Yours, O LORD, is the greatness and the power and the glory and the victory and the majesty, for all that is in the heavens and in the earth is yours. Yours is the kingdom, O LORD, and you are exalted as head above all. Both riches and honor come from you, and you rule over all. In your hand are power and might, and in your hand it is to make great and to give strength to all. And now we thank you, our God, and praise your glorious name. (1 Chr 29:10–13)

This is the *only* time in the Bible that the phrase, "Blessed are you, O LORD," is used (Hebrew: *Barukh atah Adonai*). The Psalms say, "Blessed be the LORD," but not "Blessed are *you*." These words form the beginning of every Jewish blessing. Interestingly, David's prayer also provides the added ending to the "Lord's Prayer" in the New Testament: "For thine is the kingdom, the power, and the glory forever. Amen." Thus David's prayer in Chronicles is the root of two traditions—one in Judaism and one in Christianity!

We also have Solomon's prayer of dedication for the temple in 2 Chr 6. That's not unique since the same prayer is found in 1 Kings 8. What *is* unique, however, is God saying, "if my people who are called by my name humble themselves, and pray and seek my face and turn from their wicked ways, then I will hear from heaven and will forgive their sin and heal their land" (2 Chr 7:14).

The word "seek" is incredibly significant in Chronicles. In Hebrew, there are two words for "seek." One word is *bakash*. The other word is *darash*. Most of the Hebrew Bible uses the word *bakash*. Chronicles uses both words with *darash* being more prominent. *Darash* is the same root as the word used in Ezra-Nehemiah for "study," and the Hebrew word for "sermon." Furthermore, while the word "seek" appears frequently in Samuel and Kings, it always refers to seeking *things*, whether donkeys, a

---

3. See my discussion of Jabez in Teram, *You Are Israel*, 58–59.

Ending with a New Beginning

country, or someone's life (i.e., to kill them). In Chronicles, though, the word is applied to God. The most important thing one can do, according to Chronicles, is to seek God. The one chapter in Chronicles about Saul tells us that

> Saul died for his breach of faith. He broke faith with the LORD in that he did not keep the command of the LORD, and also consulted a medium, seeking guidance. He did not seek guidance from the LORD. (1 Chr 10:13–14)

David is the opposite of Saul. He says to his people, "Then let us bring again the ark of our God to us, for we did not *seek* it in the days of Saul" (1 Chr 13:3). He tells them God punished them because they did not seek God (1 Chr 15:13). He tells Solomon to "seek the LORD" (1 Chr 22:19) and to "seek out the commandments of the LORD" (1 Chr 28:8). "If you seek him, he will be found by you," David says (1 Chr 28:9).

The priests who defected to Judah did so not only because Jeroboam kicked them out but also because they had "set their hearts to seek the LORD" (2 Chr 11:16). But ironically, King Rehoboam of Judah "did not set his heart to seek the LORD" (2 Chr 12:14).

Chronicles tells us about King Asa. He instructs Judah "to seek the LORD" and "to keep the law and the commandment" (2 Chr 14:4; cf. 15:12–13). However, we're also told that he develops some kind of a foot disease. Just as Saul didn't seek God but instead sought a medium, we're told that "even in his disease [Asa] did not seek the LORD, but sought help from physicians" (2 Chr 16:12). He's never healed of his malady.

On the other hand, Asa's son, Jehoshaphat, "did not seek the Baals, but sought the God of his father" (2 Chr 17:3–4). Later on in his reign, Judah is attacked. The text tells us

> Jehoshaphat was afraid and set his face to seek the LORD, and proclaimed a fast throughout all Judah. And Judah assembled to seek help from the LORD; from all the cities of Judah they came to seek the LORD. (2 Chr 20:3–4)

He prays to God, asking for help to defeat his enemies (2 Chr 20:5–12).

And, of course, the two greatest kings of Judah, Hezekiah and Josiah, seek God. Of Hezekiah, we're told "every work that he undertook in the service of the house of God and in accordance with the law and the commandments, seeking his God, he did with all his heart, and prospered" (2 Chr 31:21). And of Josiah, who became king when he was just eight years old, we're told "in the eighth year of his reign, while he was yet a boy, he began to seek the God of David his father" (2 Chr 34:3).

Between Hezekiah and Josiah is Hezekiah's son, Manasseh. Manasseh was the most wicked king Judah had. He worships the Baals and burns his children to death as a sacrifice (2 Chr 33:1–9). Yet, in Chronicles—*only* in Chronicles, not in Kings—Manasseh repents. We're told:

> And when he was in distress, he entreated the favor of the LORD his God and humbled himself greatly before the God of his fathers. He prayed to him, and

289

Illuminating Counsel

> God was moved by his entreaty and heard his plea and brought him again to
> Jerusalem into his kingdom. Then Manasseh knew that the LORD was God.
> (2 Chr 33:12–13)

How inspiring is it that the most wicked king repented?! If *he* could repent, *anyone* can repent.

What is the implication of Chronicles' emphasis on prayer and "seeking" God? As my friend, Nathan Clayton, puts it, the question Samuel and Kings ask is, "Why the exile?" The question Chronicles asks is, "The exile happened—now what?" Chronicles is not merely a historiography. It's a book that contains a message to a people who have suffered and are rebounding. It's a message to those seeking *reorientation*.

After the temple was destroyed, sacrifices had ceased. The only way the Jews could repent was by offering up prayer. This is precisely what Solomon says in his prayer in 2 Chr 6:

> If they sin against you—for there is no one who does not sin—and you are
> angry with them and give them to an enemy, so that they are carried away
> captive to a land far or near, yet if they turn their heart in the land to which
> they have been carried captive, and repent and plead with you in the land of
> their captivity, saying, "We have sinned and have acted perversely and wick-
> edly," if they repent with all their heart and with all their soul in the land of
> their captivity to which they were carried captive, and pray toward their land,
> which you gave to their fathers, the city that you have chosen and the house
> that I have built for your name, then hear from heaven your dwelling place
> their prayer and their pleas, and maintain their cause and forgive your people
> who have sinned against you. (2 Chr 6:36–39)

Prayer had replaced sacrifice as a means of atonement. It is for this reason Daniel and Ezra-Nehemiah both feature prayers of confession of sin. Daniel prays in Dan 9. Ezra prays in Ezra 9. And Nehemiah prays in Neh 1. Daniel says, "We have sinned and done wrong and acted wickedly and rebelled, turning aside from your commandments and rules" (Dan 9:5). Ezra says, "O my God, I am ashamed and blush to lift my face to you, my God, for our iniquities have risen higher than our heads, and our guilt has mounted up to the heavens" (Ezra 9:6). Nehemiah says, "Even I and my father's house have sinned" (Neh 1:6). And then either Ezra or the Jews pray this very long prayer in Neh 9. They renew the covenant in writing and seal it with their names.

Chronicles also emphasizes music. Even in the midst of the massive genealogy, Chronicles pauses to tell those who "ministered with song before the tabernacle of the tent of meeting until Solomon built the house of the LORD in Jerusalem, and they performed their service according to their order" (1 Chr 6:32). We're told "David also commanded the chiefs of the Levites to appoint their brothers as the singers who should play loudly on musical instruments, on harps and lyres and cymbals, to raise sounds of joy" (1 Chr 15:16). Also:

290

Ending with a New Beginning

> [David] appointed some of the Levites as ministers before the ark of the LORD, to invoke, to thank, and to praise the LORD, the God of Israel. Asaph was the chief, and second to him were Zechariah, Jeiel, Shemiramoth, Jehiel, Mattithiah, Eliab, Benaiah, Obed-edom, and Jeiel, who were to play harps and lyres; Asaph was to sound the cymbals, and Benaiah and Jahaziel the priests were to blow trumpets regularly before the ark of the covenant of God. Then on that day David first appointed that thanksgiving be sung to the LORD by Asaph and his brothers. (1 Chr 16:4–7)

First Chronicles 23 and 25 tell about David setting up the choir. "David and the chiefs of the service also set apart for the service the sons of Asaph, and of Heman, and of Jeduthun, who prophesied with lyres, with harps, and with cymbals" (1 Chr 25:1). David's choir and orchestra were no innovation. Chronicles tells us that it was God who commanded David to set them up:

> And [Hezekiah] stationed the Levites in the house of the LORD with cymbals, harps, and lyres, according to the commandment of David and of Gad the king's seer and of Nathan the prophet, for the commandment was from the LORD through his prophets. (2 Chr 29:25)

Chronicles also contains psalms. First Chronicles 16 contains parts of Ps 96, Ps 105, and Ps 106.[4] Earlier, I had mentioned the refrain, "for his steadfast love endures forever." That refrain occurs in only three books of the Bible: Psalms, Ezra-Nehemiah, and Chronicles. It's all over the place in Chronicles: 1 Chr 16:34, 1 Chr 16:41, 2 Chr 5:13, 2 Chr 7:3, 2 Chr 7:6, and 2 Chr 20:21. That refrain is connected to the glory of God filling the (first) temple:

> and it was the duty of the trumpeters and singers to make themselves heard in unison in praise and thanksgiving to the LORD, and when the song was raised, with trumpets and cymbals and other musical instruments, in praise to the LORD,
>
> > "For he is good,
> >   for his steadfast love endures forever,"
>
> the house, the house of the LORD, was filled with a cloud, so that the priests could not stand to minister because of the cloud, for the glory of the LORD filled the house of God. (2 Chr 5:13–14)

John W. Kleinig says this is the key verse to Chronicles' "theology of praise."[5] The idea is that music—voices and instruments—reveals the glory of God. This message was particularly meaningful to the post-exilic community because, as we said, the

---

4. Klein, "Psalms in Chronicles," 264.

5. Kleinig, "Bach, Chronicles, and Church Music," 54.

Illuminating Counsel

second temple was never filled with the cloud. But though it may not have had the cloud, it had music! The psalms were sung and the singing was accompanied by instruments. Thus, even without the cloud, God's glory was revealed. God's presence is manifested through music!

WORSHIP

Chronicles doesn't whitewash David completely. It tells the story of David counting the people (1 Chr 21; cf. 2 Sam 24).[6] For some reason, this was a sin against God. It resulted in a terrible plague which God sent that killed seventy thousand people.

In Samuel and Kings, David basically dies after the sinful census. In Chronicles, the census is followed by David's preparations for building the temple (1 Chr 22–29). I hardly think that's insignificant, but what does it mean?

On one hand, we can simply say that the connection between the two passages is the location of the temple. First Chronicles 21 ends with David praying on the threshing floor belonging to a Jebusite named Ornan. In 1 Chr 22:1, David says, "Here shall be the house of the LORD God and here the altar of burnt offering for Israel."[7] It's a perfect segue.

On the other hand, I think there's a deeper meaning. David and Israel are redeemed by and through David's preparations for building the temple. The message seems to be that the worship of God brings atonement and healing. This point is reinforced by the fact that 1 Chr 22–29 is a chiasmus with the center being the Aaronic priests:[8]

A—David's Speech: to Solomon and the Assembly (1 Chr 22:2–19)
   B—Civil Rulers: David appoints Solomon as King (1 Chr 23:1)
      C—Levities: Assistants to Priests (1 Chr 23:2–32)
         D—Priests (1 Chr 24:1–19)
      C—Levites: Musicians and Gatekeepers (1 Chr 24:20—26:32)
   B—Civil Rulers: David Appoints Government Officials (1 Chr 27:1–34)
A—David's Speech: to Solomon and the Assembly (1 Chr 28:1—29:30)

As you can see, the text is artistically arranged. The Levites sandwich the priests. The civil rulers sandwich the Levites. And David's speeches are the *inclusio*. The priests at the center remind us of atonement, since the high priest was the one who made atonement for the people on Yom Kippur—the Day of Atonement.

---

6. One of the Chronicler's most prominent redactions is changing "God incited" David to count the people to "Satan incited David . . ." This time, "Satan" does not have the definite article. For an explanation, see Stokes, "The Devil Made David Do It," 91–106.

7. I owe this point to Nathan Clayton.

8. Ahn, *The Persuasive Portrayal*, 72, n. 40. Ahn's source is Dorsey, *The Literary Structure of the Old Testament*, 147.

Ending with a New Beginning

Chronicles is speaking to a people who had suffered tremendously. Earlier we noted how Isaiah provides the comfort to Zion which Lamentations lacks. But Isaiah is not in the Ketuvim. Chronicles is. Think of suffering Zion—the suffering of the Jews—when you read the words a prophet named Azariah spoke to King Asa:

> The LORD is with you while you are with him. If you seek him, he will be found by you, but if you forsake him, he will forsake you. For a long time Israel was without the true God, and without a teaching priest and without law, but when in their distress they turned to the LORD, the God of Israel, and sought him, he was found by them. In those times there was no peace to him who went out or to him who came in, for great disturbances afflicted all the inhabitants of the lands. They were broken in pieces. Nation was crushed by nation and city by city, for God troubled them with every sort of distress. But you, take courage! Do not let your hands be weak, for your work shall be rewarded." (2 Chr 15:2–7)

These words perfectly match the situation of the exiles!

King Hezekiah is far more important in Chronicles than in Kings. In Kings, his story begins in ch. 18. He makes important reforms but then has to deal with the Assyrian siege on Jerusalem, which was an existential crisis. Jerusalem survives. Hezekiah becomes deathly ill and prays for more time. His request is granted to him. Then he's visited by envoys from Babylon who want to get a tour of Hezekiah's house. Isaiah says this is a foreshadow of the Babylonian destruction of Jerusalem. And that's it. That's all Kings says about Hezekiah. Just three chapters—1 Kgs 18–20.

By contrast, Hezekiah's story in Chronicles is four chapters long. It begins in 2 Chr 29 and goes all the way to 2 Chr 32. In Chronicles, Hezekiah's reforms are far more extensive than they are in Kings and they center around—you guessed it—the priests and the Levites. Hezekiah says to them:

> Hear me, Levites! Now consecrate yourselves, and consecrate the house of the LORD the God of your fathers, and carry out the filth from the Holy Place. For our fathers have been unfaithful and have done what was evil in the sight of the LORD our God. They have forsaken him and have turned away their faces from the habitation of the LORD and turned their backs. They also shut the doors of the vestibule and put out the lamps and have not burned incense or offered burnt offerings in the Holy Place to the God of Israel. Therefore the wrath of the LORD came on Judah and Jerusalem, and he has made them an object of horror, of astonishment, and of hissing, as you see with your own eyes. For behold, our fathers have fallen by the sword, and our sons and our daughters and our wives are in captivity for this. Now it is in my heart to make a covenant with the LORD, the God of Israel, in order that his fierce anger may turn away from us. My sons, do not now be negligent, for the LORD has chosen you to stand in his presence, to minister to him and to be his ministers and make offerings to him. (2 Chr 29:5–11)

Illuminating Counsel

If you didn't know any better, you'd think these words were spoken by Ezra!

The text goes on to emphasize all of the works of the priests and Levites, how they made sacrifices to God. Hezekiah then invites the Israelites in the northern kingdom to come down to Jerusalem to observe the Passover, for the Passover had not been celebrated. Josiah restores the Passover too (2 Kgs 23; 2 Chr 35). Only in Chronicles, though, does Hezekiah restore the Passover. Everything was so chaotic because of the prior unfaithfulness of the people that Hezekiah had to have the Passover celebration a month after Passover. (Imagine celebrating Christmas on January 25.) Then Hezekiah prays (emphasis on prayer):

> May the good LORD pardon everyone who sets his heart to seek God, the LORD, the God of his fathers, even though not according to the sanctuary's rules of cleanness. (2 Chr 30:18–19)

Again, imagine those words prayed over the Jews who returned to Jerusalem from Babylon. They couldn't offer sacrifices because the temple was destroyed. But they did offer up their prayers. They sought God. Chronicles says, "And the LORD heard Hezekiah and healed the people" (2 Chr 30:20). They celebrate the Passover with joy and gladness, and the chapter ends on this note: "Then the priests and the Levites arose and blessed the people, and their voice was heard, and their prayer came to [the LORD's] holy habitation in heaven" (2 Chr 30:27).

When you read Chronicles you quickly realize that Chronicles emphasizes *worship*. In Kings, the word "worship" is used to refer to worshiping other gods. In Chronicles, the word "worship" is used to refer to the Israelites worshiping Yahweh. When the "glory" of God filled the temple, the people "bowed down with their faces to the ground on the pavement and worshiped" (2 Chr 7:3). After Jehoshaphat prays, we're told he "bowed his head with his face to the ground, and all Judah and the inhabitants of Jerusalem fell down before the Lord, worshiping the LORD" (2 Chr 20:18). And of course with Hezekiah we're told:

> The whole assembly worshiped, and the singers sang, and the trumpeters sounded. All this continued until the burnt offering was finished. When the offering was finished, the king and all who were present with him bowed themselves and worshiped. And Hezekiah the king and the officials commanded the Levites to sing praises to the LORD with the words of David and of Asaph the seer. And they sang praises with gladness, and they bowed down and worshiped. (2 Chr 29:28–30)

Chronicles, like all the other books of the Ketuvim, deals with the problem of suffering. It's a book written to a community that had sung the cries of Lamentations! And, like all the other books of the Ketuvim, Chronicles provides a response. Its response to suffering is *worship*. This means seeking God, praying to God for forgiveness,

Ending with a New Beginning

and celebrating the healing which God brings. Chronicles is misunderstood. It's really about *redemption*.

PLACEMENT IN THE KETUVIM

We've now come to the end. We're ready to answer the remaining questions. First, why is Ezra-Nehemiah in the Ketuvim? Second, why is Chronicles in the Ketuvim? Third, why is Chronicles at the *end* of the Ketuvim? My answers to these questions are not "official." They are based on my observations and reasoning.[9]

Ezra-Nehemiah completes the "court Jew" theme. It's true that in the Old Testament, Esther and Ezra-Nehemiah are placed in the same section—the History Books. However, Daniel is separated from them, for Daniel is in the Prophets. The brilliance of the Ketuvim is that it recognizes that Daniel is actually more closely related to Esther and Ezra-Nehemiah than to Jeremiah and Ezekiel. Moreover, the Old Testament order places Esther *after* Ezra-Nehemiah. This is understandable. While both Ezra and Nehemiah live after Esther (Esther is married to the father of Artaxerxes), the book of Ezra-Nehemiah begins with events that happen before Esther. Thematically, however, Ezra-Nehemiah work better when they come *after* Esther. This is because Ezra and Nehemiah are the only "court Jews" who return to the land of Israel. All of that is lost in the Old Testament, but prominent in the Tanakh.

Having Ezra-Nehemiah after Daniel gives much more meaning to Daniel than having Daniel precede Hosea, as in the Old Testament. Not only are prayers of repentance featured in Daniel and Ezra-Nehemiah, the events of Ezra-Nehemiah are, in a large sense, an *answer* to Daniel's prayer in Dan 9.[10]

Ezra-Nehemiah also completes the narrative arc of the Tanakh. The books of Genesis through Joshua tell the story of how Israel entered the land. The books of Judges through Kings tell the story of how Israel was expelled from the land. The book of Ezra-Nehemiah tells the story of how Israel returned to the land. The Old Testament tells the same story, but the Old Testament doesn't end that way. The Tanakh ends with the restoration of Israel.

Ezra-Nehemiah forms an *inclusio* with the beginning of the Bible. The books of Genesis through Deuteronomy are about God giving the Torah to Israel. The book of Ezra-Nehemiah is about the Torah being restored to Israel. Perhaps there's also a connection with the book of Joshua. Moses delivers the Israelites from Egypt, gives them the Torah, and Joshua brings them into the promised land where the walls of Jericho fall. In Ezra-Nehemiah, the Jews return to their land, they receive the Torah, and they rebuild the wall of Jerusalem.

---

9. For a very good and detailed explanation for the placement of Chronicles, see Goswell, "Putting the Book of Chronicles in its Place," 283–99.

10. Goswell, "The Canonical Position(s)," 135–36.

Illuminating Counsel

Ezra-Nehemiah also forms an *inclusio* with the beginning of the Ketuvim. Psalm 1 says the happy person is the one who meditates on the Torah day and night. Ezra-Nehemiah is all about the study of the Torah (Ezra 7:10; Neh 8:13).

Chronicles has a connection with Psalms that Samuel and Kings don't have. Chronicles gives us the background to the superscriptions of the psalms. Chronicles tells us how David set up the choir and the orchestra. Chronicles explains the function of the psalms in the temple. And Chronicles is the culmination of what the psalms are: the intersection of prayer and worship. Thus Chronicles forms an *inclusio* in the Ketuvim. The Ketuvim begins with psalms. The Ketuvim ends with psalms. The book of Psalms begins with the Torah and ends with worship. Ezra-Nehemiah is about the restoration of the Torah. Chronicles is about the formation of temple worship!

Chronicles also forms an *inclusio* with Genesis! (I'm getting goosebumps as I write this!) The Tanakh begins with Genesis. The Tanakh ends with Genesis, for Chronicles begins with Genesis. "Adam" is the very first thing we read in Chronicles! Chronicles, therefore, gives us a review of all of the workings of God from the very beginning to the very end—or at least the end of the Tanakh's narrative. Chronicles contextualizes the Ketuvim within the larger framework of the Tanakh.

How does Chronicles end? It tells us how Jerusalem was sacked by Babylon, which is the way Kings ends, but then it adds the decree of Cyrus:

> Now in the first year of Cyrus king of Persia, that the word of the LORD by the mouth of Jeremiah might be fulfilled, the LORD stirred up the spirit of Cyrus king of Persia, so that he made a proclamation throughout all his kingdom and also put it in writing: "Thus says Cyrus king of Persia, 'The LORD, the God of heaven, has given me all the kingdoms of the earth, and he has charged me to build him a house at Jerusalem, which is in Judah. Whoever is among you of all his people, may the LORD his God be with him. Let him go up.'" (2 Chr 36:22–23)

This is a bit strange, though. In the Old Testament, Chronicles is *before* Ezra and Nehemiah. That arrangement makes perfect sense. Since Chronicles ends chronologically with the decree of Cyrus, and Ezra begins chronologically with the decree of Cyrus, the decree of Cyrus functions as a bridge connecting the two books—connecting the exile to the post-exilic period. The only problem with the Old Testament's order is that it's so difficult to read Chronicles after having just read through Samuel and Kings. But leaving that aside, we must ask why the Tanakh puts Chronicles *after* Ezra-Nehemiah.

When Chronicles comes after Ezra-Nehemiah, Cyrus's decree becomes an *inclusio*! Ezra-Nehemiah begins with Cyrus's decree. Chronicles ends with Cyrus's decree. Now think more broadly. The Tanakh begins with *creation*. The Tanakh ends with Cyrus's decree. Do you see how important Cyrus's decree is?!

Ending with a New Beginning

Cyrus's decree calls for Jews everywhere to return to the land of Israel. Chronicles' version is slightly different than Ezra-Nehemiah's. Chronicles' last word—the very last word in the Tanakh—is *veya'al*, which means "Let him go up." So think about how this relates to Genesis. In Genesis, God creates the world and creates Israel. In Chronicles, with Cyrus's decree, God is re-creating Israel. In Genesis, God calls Abraham to leave Mesopotamia and go to Canaan, which is the land of Israel, the "promised land." In Chronicles, with Cyrus's decree, all Jews are called to be like Abraham and go to that land. Genesis ends with the Israelites in Egypt. In Exodus, Moses delivers them and brings them home, or at least he brings them to the edge of the land. Cyrus is like Moses. He brings the Jews home.

Cyrus's decree still speaks 2,500 years later. Today, when a Jew emigrates to Israel, it's called "making *Aliyah*"—"going up." The Tanakh, then, doesn't really have an ending. It will not end in tragedy. Neither will it have a definitive "happily ever after" ending, lest one think Jewish history ends with the Tanakh. No, the Tanah ends with a new beginning. The story goes on.[11]

Look what has happened: In Ezra-Nehemiah and Chronicles, Abraham, Moses, and David—the three most important figures in the Tanakh—have been brought together. Psalms combines prayer with poetry, singing, and instrumental music. Proverbs, Job, and Ecclesiastes have explored the topic of wisdom. Ezra-Nehemiah combines prayer and wisdom with Torah—the written word. And Chronicles has connected all of those things with the temple—the visible presence of the invisible God dwelling amongst his people. What a glorious finale!

11. Sacks, *Genesis*, loc. 5925–6017.

Epilogue

I HAD TWO OBJECTIVES in writing this book. First, to show you, dear reader, that the books of the Ketuvim explore many of life's most important issues. Second, to show you how reading these books together, as they're found in the Hebrew order, yields fascinating, moving, and powerful insights.

We've noted the importance of women in these books. Unfortunately, women cease to be prominent in the Ketuvim after Esther. Even so, women play an indispensable role in the story of the Bible and the history of the Jewish people.

We've noted the importance of Jewish identity. I hope that, even if you're not Jewish, you can still find a way of relating to it. After all, everyone has an identity. Everyone *needs* an identity.

We've noted how subversive these books are. I truly believe that that is part of the charm and uniqueness of the Hebrew Bible. The Hebrew Bible is a literary symphony.

One of my most emphasized points was that each of the books of the Ketuvim gives us a response to suffering. Let us recap:

- Psalms' response to suffering is *prayer*.
- Proverbs' response to suffering is *wisdom*.
- Job's response to suffering is *humility*.
- Ruth's response to suffering is *kindness*.
- The Song of Songs' response to suffering is *love*.
- Ecclesiastes' response to suffering is *joy*.
- Lamentations' response to suffering is *lamentation*.
- Esther's response to suffering is *courage*.
- Daniel's response to suffering is *faithfulness*.
- Ezra-Nehemiah's response to suffering is *persistence*.
- Chronicles' response to suffering is *worship*.

Chronicles seems to be the culmination of all of these ideas. It weaves psalms, wisdom, and Torah into a story.

Epilogue

And here is part of *my* story. On January 25, 2020, my beloved Aunt Jaynee died of lung cancer—the same disease that took my mother on November 23, 2013. Mom was the oldest of my grandparents' six children. She was the first to go. Aunt Jaynee was the youngest. She was the second to go. Mom and Aunt Jaynee form an *inclusio*.

I wanted my aunt to read the manuscript of this book. When she was well, I didn't send it to her because I thought she was too busy. When she was sick, I didn't send it to her because I knew she'd be too tired. Now she's gone. She will never read it. She will never hold it in her hands. That's why I'm dedicating it to her.

As I've grieved for my aunt, I thought about all that I've written in these pages. Not one word I wrote had any power to stop the cancer in her fifty-seven-year-old body. All I was able to do was say goodbye and weep with my family. Yet those things are gifts, as we've already discussed.

Life is so tremendously difficult. Often it doesn't make sense. Yet these Hebrew books remind us that there's hope. I've been employing what I've learned from these books as I grieve and move forward in my life. I hope they will help you too as you journey on. "May the LORD give strength to his people. May the LORD bless his people with peace" (Ps 29:11).

Acknowledgments

I AM INDEBTED TO so many people that it's impossible to list them all. If I mentioned you in one of the chapters in this book, it's because you have touched my life in a profound way. If you have helped me in some way but were not mentioned, please know that I'm grateful to you.

Without Joel Willitts offering me the course on the Ketuvim, this book would not exist.

I am the most fortunate teacher, for I have had wonderful, kind, and brilliant students. To all the students who took Old Testament Poetry and Wisdom Literature, and to all my students in Intro to Bible: you are my inspiration.

I am very grateful to Wipf & Stock for publishing this book and for being so patient with me.

I've had great teachers and mentors. I will always need to thank Jim Bruckner, Klyne Snodgrass, Hauna Ondrey, Max Lee, and Nathan Clayton. I'm especially grateful to Paul Koptak for his wisdom, encouragement, and friendship.

To my mother of blessed memory: "Many women have done excellently, but you surpass them all" (Prov 31:29).

Finally, the person I owe the most to is my father. My father loves the Bible more than anyone I know. He instilled the love of the Bible in me from the time I was a small child. "Grandchildren are the crown of the aged, and the glory of children is their fathers" (Prov 17:6).

Bibliography

Ahn, Suk-il. *The Persuasive Portrayal of David and Solomon in Chronicles: A Rhetorical Analysis of the Speeches and Prayers in the David-Solomon Narrative*. McMaster Biblical Studies 3. Eugene, OR: Pickwick, 2018.

Alter, Robert. *The Art of Biblical Narrative*. Rev. ed. New York: Basic, 2011.

———. *The Art of Biblical Poetry*. Rev. ed. New York: Basic, 2011.

———. "The Song of Songs: An Ode to Intimacy." *BRev* 18, no. 4 (August 2002) 24–52.

———. *Strong as Death is Love: The Song of Songs, Ruth, Esther, Jonah, Daniel: A Translation with Commentary*. New York: Norton, 2015. Kindle.

———. *The Wisdom Books: Job, Proverbs, and Ecclesiastes: A Translation with Commentary*. New York: Norton, 2010.

ASKDrBrown. "Amazing Insights Into the Book of Job." YouTube, November 7, 2019. https://youtu.be/CZSGNVFjWVk.

Baldwin, Joyce G. *Daniel*. Tyndale Old Testament Commentaries. Downers Grove, IL: InterVarsity, 2016.

Ballard Jr., H. Wayne, and W. Dennis Tucker Jr., eds. *An Introduction to Wisdom Literature and the Psalms: Festschrift Marvin E. Tate*. Macon, GA: Mercer University Press, 2000.

Bazak, Jacob. "Numerical Devices in Biblical Poetry." *Vetus Testamentum* 38, no. 3 (July 1988) 333–37.

Berlin, Adele. *Lamentations: A Commentary*. The Old Testament Library. Louisville: Westminster John Knox, 2002.

Bloch, Chana, and Ariel Bloch. *The Song of Songs: The World's First Great Love Poem*. New York: Modern Library, 2006.

Bloom, Harold. *The Book of J*. Translated by David Rosenberg. New York: Vintage, 1990.

Boersma, Matthew. "Scent in Song: Exploring Scented Symbols in the Song of Songs." *Conversations with the Biblical World* 31 (2011) 80–94.

Boteach, Shmuley. *Kosher Lust: Love Is Not the Answer*. Jerusalem: Gefen, 2014.

Brenner, Athalya, and Carole Fontaine, eds. *Wisdom and Psalms*. A Feminist Companion to the Bible (Second Series) 2. Sheffield: Sheffield Academic, 1998.

Brotzman, Ellis R., and Eric J. Tully. *Old Testament Textual Criticism: A Practical Introduction*. 2nd ed. Grand Rapids: Baker Academic, 2016.

Brueggemann, Walter. *Praying the Psalms: Engaging Scripture and the Life of the Spirit*. 2nd ed. Eugene, OR: Cascade, 2007.

———. *Spirituality of the Psalms*. Minneapolis: Fortress, 2002.

———. *Theology of the Old Testament: Testimony, Dispute, Advocacy*. Minneapolis: Fortress, 2005.

Bibliography

Brueggemann, Walter, and William H. Bellinger Jr. *Psalms.* New Cambridge Bible Commentary. New York: Cambridge University Press, 2014.

Bush, Frederic. *Ruth-Esther.* World Biblical Commentary 9. Grand Rapids: Zondervan, 1996.

Camp, Claudia V. "Woman Wisdom: Bible." In *The Encyclopedia of Jewish Women*, February 2009. Jewish Women's Archive, accessed on March 14, 2020. https://jwa.org/encyclopedia/article/woman-wisdom-bible.

Chabad. "Blessings and Instructions for Getting and an Aliya: Procedure for Getting Called Up to the Torah." Chabad.org. https://www.chabad.org/library/article_cdo/aid/382001/jewish/Blessings-and-Instructions-for-Getting-an-Aliyah.htm.

Danby, Herbert, trans. *The Mishnah: Translated from the Hebrew with Introduction and Brief Explanatory Notes.* Peabody, MA: Hendrickson, 2011.

Dawidowicz, Lucy S., ed. *A Holocaust Reader.* Library of Jewish Studies. West Orange, NJ: Behrman House, 1976.

Dorsey, David A. *The Literary Structure of the Old Testament: A Commentary on Genesis–Malachi.* Grand Rapids: Baker Academic, 1999.

Ebert, Roger. "Go Gentle Into That Good Night." RogerEbert.com, May 2, 2009. https://www.rogerebert.com/rogers-journal/go-gentle-into-that-good-night.

Ehrman, Bart D. "Bart Ehrman vs. Michael Brown on Suffering." YouTube, June 29, 2016. https://youtu.be/vQOUa2-D224.

———. "Ehrman-Butt Debate Suffering and God's Existence." YouTube, September 18, 2015. https://youtu.be/AeDQfGbcYpE.

Engineering an Empire. Season 1, episode 8, "The Persians." Directed by Hassan Ildari and Mark Cannon. Aired December 4, 2006. KPI Productions.

Exum, J. Cheryl. *Song of Songs.* The Old Testament Library. Louisville: Westminster John Knox, 2005.

Feiler, Bruce. *America's Prophet: Moses and the American Story.* New York: Morrow, 2009.

Fensham, F. Charles. *The Books of Ezra and Nehemiah.* The New International Commentary on the Old Testament. Grand Rapids: Eerdmans, 1982.

Finley, Thomas J. "The Book of Daniel in the Canon of Scripture." *Bibliotheca Sacra* 165 (April–June 2008) 195–208.

Fleetwd1. "Lecture—Rabbi Benjamin Scolnic—The Book of Daniel and the Nature of Biblical Truth." YouTube, February 10, 2015. https://youtu.be/US1HJj6a2RU.

Fox, Michael V. *A Time to Tear Down and a Time to Build Up: A Rereading of Ecclesiastes.* Grand Rapids: Eerdmans, 1999.

Frankl, Viktor E. *Man's Search for Meaning.* Boston: Beacon, 2006.

Fried, David. "The Book of Job as a Way of Relating to Jewish National Suffering." *Jewish Bible Quarterly* 44, no. 3 (September 2016) 157–65.

Friedman, Richard Elliot. *The Exodus: Why It Happened and Why It Matters.* San Francisco: HarperOne, 2017.

———. *Who Wrote the Bible?.* New York: Summit, 1987.

Fromm, Erich. *You Shall Be As Gods: A Radical Interpretation of the Old Testament and Its Tradition.* New York: Holt, Rinehart, and Winston, 1966.

Gager, John G. *The Origin of Anti-Semitism: Attitudes Toward Judaism in Pagan and Christian Antiquity.* New York: Oxford University Press, 1985. Kindle.

Garrett, Duane A. *Proverbs, Ecclesiastes, Song of Songs.* The New American Commentary: An Exegetical and Theological Exposition of Scripture 14. Nashville: Holman, 1993.

Bibliography

Gault, Brian P. "A 'Do Not Disturb' Sign? Reexamining the Adjuration Refrain in Song of Songs." *Journal for the Study of the Old Testament* 36, no. 1 (September 2011) 93–104.

Giordano, Sean. "Prager Discusses the Book of Esther with Yoram Hazony." YouTube, March 14, 2016. https://youtu.be/dRMJR2k4tzo.

Glazer, Miriyam. *Psalms of the Jewish Liturgy: A Guide to Their Beauty, Power, and Meaning.* New York: Aviv, 2009. Kindle.

Greenberg, Dov. "Easy or Hard?" Chabad.org. https://www.chabad.org/multimedia/video_cdo/aid/1373309/jewish/Easy-or-Hard.htm.

———. "Matzah, Jelly Donuts, and Hamantashen." Chabad.org. https://www.chabad.org/multimedia/video_cdo/aid/1373314/jewish/Matzah-Jelly-Donuts-and-Hamantashen.htm.

Goldingay, John. *Do We Need the New Testament?: Letting the Old Testament Speak for Itself.* Downers Grove, IL: InterVarsity, 2015. Kindle.

———. *The First Testament: A New Translation.* Downers Grove, IL: InterVarsity, 2018.

Gordon College. "Faith Seeking Understanding The Anguish and Joy of Jerusalem." YouTube, November 6, 2009. https://youtu.be/1ORPEZUclvI.

Goswell, Greg. "The Canonical Position(s) of the Book of Daniel." *Restoration Quarterly* 59, no. 3 (2017) 129–40.

———. "Putting the Book of Chronicles in its Place." *Journal of the Evangelical Theological Society* 60, no. 2 (June 2017) 283–99.

Greene-McCreight, Kathryn. *Darkness Is My Only Companion: A Christian Response to Mental Illness.* Grand Rapids: Brazos, 2006.

Gunkel, Hermann. *The Psalms: A Form-Critical Introduction.* Translated by Thomas M. Horner. Philadelphia: Fortress, 1967.

Haidt, Jonathan. *The Happiness Hypothesis: Finding Modern Truth in Ancient Wisdom.* New York: Basic, 2006.

Harding, Kathryn. "I Sought Him But I Did Not Find Him: The Elusive Lover in the Song of Songs." *Biblical Interpretation* 16, no. 1 (2008) 43–59.

Hazony, Yoram. *God and Politics in Esther.* New York: Cambridge University Press, 2016.

———. "Jonathan Sacks and Yoram Hazony: Is the Bible a Work of Philosophy?" YouTube, October 23, 2012. https://youtu.be/8bKJF3UjkLU.

Hicks, John Mark. "Job 42:1–6—Did Job 'Repent'?" Johnmarkhicks.com, October 14, 2011. http://johnmarkhicks.com/2011/10/14/job-421-26-did-job-repent/.

Hidabrut—Torah and Judaism. "The Book of Job—Rabbi Yitzchak Breitowitz." YouTube, January 13, 2016. https://youtu.be/e9LB4704Q9M.

Hubbard Jr., Robert L. *The Book of Ruth.* The New International Commentary on the Old Testament. Grand Rapids: Eerdmans, 1988.

Jobes, Karen H. *Esther.* The NIV Application Commentary. Grand Rapids: Zondervan, 1999.

Just Cause. Directed by Arne Glimcher. Warner Bros., 1995.

Klein, Ralph W. "Psalms in Chronicles." *Currents in Theology and Mission* 32, no. 4 (August 2005) 264–75.

Kleinig, John W. "Bach, Chronicles, and Church Music." *Logia* 21, no. 3 (2012) 51–54.

Klitsner, Judy. *Subversive Sequels in the Bible: How Biblical Stories Mine and Undermine Each Other.* Jerusalem: Maggid, 2011.

Koptak, Paul E. *Proverbs.* The NIV Application Commentary. Grand Rapids: Zondervan, 2003.

Bibliography

———. "Rhetorical Identification in Preaching." *Preaching* (November–December 1998) 11–18.

Kushner, Aviya. *The Grammar of God: A Journey Into the Words and Worlds of the Bible.* New York: Spiegel & Grau, 2015.

Legato, Marianne J. *Why Men Never Remember and Women Never Forget.* Emmaus, PA: Rodale, 2005.

Leroux, Gaston. *The Phantom of the Opera.* Tales of Mystery & the Supernatural. London: Wordsworth, 2008.

The Letter of Aristeas. Edited by R. H. Charles. Oxford: Clarendon, 1913. https://www.ccel.org/c/charles/otpseudepig/aristeas.htm.

Levenson, John D. *Esther.* The Old Testament Library. Louisville: Westminster John Knox, 1997.

Lewis, C. S. *Mere Christianity.* New York: Touchstone, 1996.

———. *The Problem of Pain.* New York: HarperCollins, 1996.

———. *Reflections on the Psalms.* San Francisco: HarperOne, 2017.

Light, Alan. *The Holy or the Broken: Leonard Cohen, Jeff Buckley, and the Unlikely Ascent of "Hallelujah."* New York: Atria, 2013.

Lim, Timothy H. "Defilement of the Hands as a Principle Determining the Holiness of Scriptures." *The Journal of Theological Studies* 61, no. 2 (October 2010) 501–15.

———. *The Formation of the Jewish Canon.* The Anchor Yale Bible Reference Library. New Haven, CT: Yale University Press, 2013.

Limburg, James. *Psalms for Sojourners.* 2nd ed. Minneapolis: Augsburg, 2002.

Linafelt, Tod. *The Hebrew Bible as Literature: A Very Short Introduction.* Very Short Introductions 478. New York: Oxford University Press, 2016.

Linafelt, Tod, and Timothy K. Beal. *Ruth and Esther.* Berit Olam: Studies in Hebrew Narrative and Poetry. Collegeville, MN: Michael Glazier, 1999.

Longman III, Tremper. *The Book of Ecclesiastes.* The New International Commentary on the Old Testament. Grand Rapids: Eerdmans, 1998.

———. *The Fear of the Lord is Wisdom: A Theological Introduction to Wisdom in Israel.* Grand Rapids: Baker Academic, 2017.

———. *Song of Songs.* The New International Commentary on the Old Testament. Grand Rapids: Eerdmans, 2001.

Luther, Martin. *On the Jews and Their Lies.* Edited by Coleman Rydie. Translated by Martin H. Bertram. 1542. Reprint, York, SC: Liberty Bell, 2004.

Maimonides, Moses. *The Guide for the Perplexed.* Translated by M. Friedländer. Reprint, Digireads, 2008.

Martyr, Justin. *Dialogue with Trypho.* https://www.newadvent.org/fathers/0128.htm.

McGuiggan, Jim. *Celebrating the Wrath of God: Reflections on the Agony and Ecstasy of His Relentless Love.* Colorado Springs: Waterbrook, 2001.

McLaughlin, John L. *The Ancient Near East: An Essential Guide.* Nashville: Abingdon, 2012. Kindle.

Mercatus Center. "Why Do Bad Things Happen to Good People? | A Conversation with Rabbi David Wolpe." YouTube, February 15, 2017. https://youtu.be/3K-kPvGYDcA.

Moore, Robert L. *Facing the Dragon: Confronting Personal and Spiritual Grandiosity.* Edited by Max J. Havlick Jr. Wilmette, IL: Chiron, 2003.

Murphy, Roland E. *The Song of Songs.* Hermenia. Minneapolis: Fortress, 1990.

Bibliography

Orlinsky, Harry Meyer. "Some Terms in the Prologue to Ben Sira and the Hebrew Canon." *Journal of Biblical Literature* 110, no. 3 (Fall 1991) 483–90.

Perdue, Leo G., and W. Clark Gilpin, eds. *The Voice from the Whirlwind: Interpreting the Book of Job.* Nashville: Abingdon, 1992.

Pope, Marvin H. *Song of Songs: A New Translation with Introduction and Commentary.* The Anchor Bible. Garden City, NY: Doubleday, 1977.

Prager, Dennis. *Happiness Is a Serious Problem: A Human Nature Repair Manual.* New York: HarperCollins, 1998.

———. "How I Found God at Columbia." Dennisprager.com, December 2, 2003. https://www.dennisprager.com/how-i-found-god-at-columbia/.

———. "The Role of Luck—Thoughts on a Birthday." Dennisprager.com, August 3, 2010. https://www.dennisprager.com/the-role-of-luck-thoughts-on-a-birthday/.

Pritchard, James B., ed. *Ancient Near Eastern Texts Relating to the Old Testament.* 3rd ed. Princeton Studies on the Near East. Princeton, NJ: Princeton University Press, 1992.

Provan, Iain. *Ecclesiastes/Song of Songs.* The NIV Application Commentary. Grand Rapids: Zondervan, 2001.

Rabbi Sacks. "A Tale of Two Women—A Shavuot Shiur by Jonathan Sacks." YouTube, June 8, 2016. https://youtu.be/nNg1Z5lijJ8.

Real Messiah. "Objection 4.20: Christians Divide the 70 Weeks in Daniel Incorrectly." YouTube, November 7, 2014. https://youtu.be/vU4nyVjzPLk.

Ryken, Leland. *Sweeter Than Honey, Richer Than Gold: A Guided Study of Biblical Poetry.* Reading the Bible As Literature. Bellingham, WA: Lexham, 2015.

Sacks, Jonathan. *Ceremony and Celebration: Introduction to the Holidays.* New Milford, CT: Maggid, 2017.

———. *Genesis: The Book of Beginnings.* Covenant and Conversation. Jerusalem: Koren, 2009.

———. "God's Hidden Call." *The Office of Rabbi Sacks,* March 22, 2016. http://rabbisacks.org/gods-hidden-call/.

———. *Not in God's Name: Confronting Religious Violence.* New York: Schocken, 2015.

Sarna, Nahum M. *On the Book of Psalms: Exploring the Prayers of Ancient Israel.* New York: Schocken, 1995.

Sarras, Niveen. "Daughter Zion Identifies with Syrian and Iraqi Women: A Reading in the Book of Lamentations." *Word & World* 37, no. 1 (Winter 2017) 84–92.

Segal, Benjamin. *Kohelet's Pursuit of Truth: A New Reading of Ecclesiastes.* Jerusalem: Gefen, 2016.

———. *A New Psalm: The Psalms as Literature.* Jerusalem: Gefen, 2013.

———. *The Song of Songs: A Woman in Love.* Jerusalem: Gefen, 2009.

Shakespeare, William. *Othello.* 2nd Norton Critical Edition. Edited by Edward Pechter. New York: Norton, 2016.

Showalter, Allan. "Leonard Cohen's Prince of Asturias Speech—No Overdubbing." YouTube, October 25, 2011. https://youtu.be/VIR5ps8usuo.

Sinai Temple. "Topic: The Meaning of Life: A Jewish Perspective with Rabbi David Wolpe." YouTube, October 13, 2014. https://youtu.be/rokizv_fs-s.

Smith, F. LaGard. *The Daily Bible.* Eugene, OR: Harvest House, 1984.

Smith, Mark S. *The Early History of God: Yahweh and the Other Deities in Ancient Israel.* San Francisco: Harper & Row, 1990.

Bibliography

Snodgrass, Klyne. *Between Two Truths: Living with Biblical Tensions*. Eugene, OR: Wipf & Stock, 1990.

Stanford. "Steve Jobs' 2005 Commencement Address (with intro by President John Hennessy)." YouTube, May 14, 2008. https://youtu.be/Hd_ptbiPoXM.

Stokes, Ryan E. "The Devil Made David Do It . . . Or Did He?: The Nature, Identity, and Literary Origins of of the Satan in 1 Chronicles 21:1." *Journal of Biblical Literature* 128, no. 1 (Spring 2009) 91–106.

Strawn, Brent A. *The Old Testament Is Dying: A Diagnosis and Recommended Treatment*. Theological Explorations for the Church Catholic. Grand Rapids: Baker Academic, 2017.

Stuart, Douglas. *Old Testament Exegesis: A Handbook for Students and Pastors*. 4th ed. Louisville: Westminster John Knox, 2009.

Telushkin, Joseph. *Words That Hurt, Words That Heal: How to Choose Words Wisely and Well*. New York: Morrow and Co., 1996.

Teram, Jonathan. *You Are Israel: How Isaiah Uses Genesis As a Means of Identity Formation*. Eugene, OR: Wipf & Stock, 2018.

Throntveit, Mark A. *Ezra-Nehemiah*. Interpretation: A Bible Commentary for Teaching and Preaching. Louisville: Westminster John Knox, 1992.

Tolkien, J. R. R. *The Lord of the Rings*. 50th anniversary ed. Boston, MA: Houghton Mifflin Hardcourt, 2012.

Trible, Phyllis. *God and the Rhetoric of Sexuality*. Philadelphia: Fortress, 1978.

Tull, Patricia K. *Esther and Ruth*. Interpretation: Bible Studies. Louisville: Westminster John Knox, 2003. Kindle.

VanGemeren, Willem A., ed. *New International Dictionary of Old Testament Theology and Exegesis*. 5 vols. Grand Rapids: Zondervan, 1997.

Walton, John H. *Job*. The NIV Application Commentary. Grand Rapids: Zondervan, 2012.

Weems, Renita J. *What Matters Most: Ten Lessons in Living Passionately from the Song of Solomon*. New York: Warner, 2004.

Williamson, H. G. M. *Ezra-Nehemiah*. World Biblical Commentary 16. Waco, TX: Word, 1985.

Wolfe, Thomas. *You Can't Go Home Again*. New York: Scribner, 2011.

Wolpe, David. *David: The Divided Heart*. Jewish Lives. New Haven, CT: Yale University Press, 2014.

Wright, Christopher J. H. *The Message of Lamentations: Honest to God*. The Bible Speaks Today. Downers Grove, IL: InterVarsity, 2015.

Subject Index

Aaron 231, 270, 278, 288
Aaronic priests 292
Abaddon 51, 116 126
Abednego 244–46, 256–57
Abel 185
Abigail 80
Abraham 49, 126, 141, 128, 167, 173, 248, 272,
    275, 288
Abraham's sojourn 141
Absalom 286
Achaemenes 251
Achaemenid Empire 248, 251, 263
Achashverosh (see Ahasuerus)
Adagio for Strings 209
Adar 227
Adonai 1, 288
adultery 39, 45, 84, 116, 176, 198
Agag 224
Agur 69, 93, 157
Ahab 287
Ahasuerus 221, 256, 280
Ahaz 207
Akiva 178
Aleppo Codex 11
Alexander the Great 253–54, 265
allegory 14, 178–79
Alter, Robert 28n1, 29n2, 31n5, 31n6, 32n7,
    34, 108,n9, 113n14, 119n16, 127, 159,
    159n14, 182n4, 184, 196n29, 198, 242,
Amalekites 224, 226
Ammonites 80
Amnon 286
Amos 6–7, 9, 111
Amoz 10
angels 24, 56, 101
anger 48–49, 56, 58, 61, 64, 89–91, 109, 118–19,
    123, 127, 156, 176, 211–12, 215, 217, 272,
    284, 290, 293
antisemitism 208, 221, 225, 226, 234, 238–39,
    256, 259, 279
    anti-Jewish 2
    Anti-semite 22, 226, 232, 256–57, 279

Antigonus 253
anxiety 53, 55–56, 90, 106, 159, 185, 204
apocalyptic 20, 242
Apocrypha 4
apologetics 252
apostles 108, 252
Aram 207
Aramaic 3, 10, 50, 242–44, 248–49, 262–63,
    273–74
Arioch 245, 255
Ark of the Covenant 268, 291
arrogance 23, 45, 79, 81–82, 84, 92, 120–21,
    235–36, 240, 242, 248, 259
Artaxerxes 221, 269–70, 274, 276, 280, 295
Aryan 226
Asa 289, 293
Asaph 39, 267, 277, 291, 2094
Ashrei 41–42
assimilation 229–30, 257, 278–79, 281, 283
assonance 34, 42, 64
Assyria 207, 269
Assyrian Empire 5, 205–6, 251, 263, 265, 268,
    293
astrologers 255
Astyages 251, 263
Athalya
atonement 290, 292
    Day of 266, 292
Augustine 10
Auschwitz 24, 115
Azariah 244–46, 272, 293

Babylon 5, 16, 33, 62–64, 205–6, 208, 216,
    244–45, 247, 251–54, 256, 261–63, 266,
    269–71 278–79, 293–94, 296
Babylonian Empire 5, 10, 64, 229, 242, 244, 257,
    260, 263, 279, 293
Babylonians 62–64, 205–7, 244, 246, 256, 261,
    263, 265
Bach, J.S. 291
Balaam 152, 282

Subject Index

Baldwin, Joyce G 244n7, 244n9, 244n10, 245n11, 247n12
Bathsheba 28, 35, 286
Batra Baba 10–13, 15
Bazak, Jacob 55n15
Beatles, the 75
beauty 39, 56, 98, 158, 163–65, 167, 171, 179–80, 192, 196, 219, 222–23
behemoth 122, 124–25
Bellinger, William H 68n26
Belshazzar 247–48, 255
Beltshazzar 244
Benaiah 292
Benjamin 34, 132, 202
Berlin, Adele 29n2
Bethlehem 133, 137–38, 144, 148, 149–52, 234
Bezos, Jeff 196
Bildad 102, 108, 110–12
bimah 272
Blochs 156–57, 160
Bloom, Harold 29n2
Boaz 18, 138–63
Boersma, Matthew 168
Boteach, Shmuley 159
Brahms, Johannes 34–35, 48
Braveheart 24
Breitowitz, Rabbi Yitzchak 100n2, 101n5
Brown, Michael L. 131
Bruckner, James 60, 70, 134, 254
Brueggemann, Walter 26, 37, 64, 68
bullying 233, 284–85
Byrds, the 191

Cain 148, 185
Cambyses 251, 262, 266, 280
Canaan 5, 141, 297
Caananite 134, 149, 178
Cancer 52, 114, 151, 156, 192, 246, 274, 299
canon 10, 19, 36, 69, 241, 257, 295
Carchemish, battle of 206
Carmel 177
Cassander 253
Cassiodorus 37
Chabad 272–73
Chaldean 246
Chesterfield, lord 84
chiasmus 57, 243–44
Christ 2, 179, 196
Christian ix, 2–4, 8, 10, 15, 37, 39–40, 50–51, 55, 107, 135, 143, 151, 179, 186–88, 192, 194–96, 205, 226, 234, 239, 251–52, 275, 283, 304–5
Christianity 1–4, 15, 37, 79, 84, 100, 135, 178–79, 186, 188, 229, 241, 249, 252, 263, 275, 283, 288, 306

Christo-centrism 135
Clayton, Nathan 271, 290, 292, 301
Cohen, Leonard 67, 219, 306
comfort 51, 54–55, 103, 130, 141, 189, 210–12, 218, 293
commandments 2, 8, 26, 74, 110, 187, 203, 270–71, 274, 289, 291
confession 241, 281, 290
consent 85, 166
courage 23–24, 71, 83, 233, 235, 293, 298
covenant 2–3, 5, 21, 38, 52, 60–61, 115–16, 125, 177, 206–7, 216–17, 268, 290–91, 293, 307
creation 5, 43–44, 47, 66, 74, 87–88, 104, 122, 128, 181, 266, 296
Cush 222
Cyrano de Bergerac 163
Cyrus 16, 249, 251, 261–66, 268–70, 276, 289, 296–97

Dante 164
Darius 221, 248–49, 255, 258, 266, 280
Darwinian 201
David 6, 27–28, 34, 36, 39–40, 53–54, 57, 61, 69, 71, 80, 84, 131, 143, 151–52, 164, 181–82, 186, 206, 233–35, 265, 267, 277, 286–92, 294, 296, 303, 304, 306–8
death 22–23, 47–48, 50–51, 43–54, 57–58, 72, 75, 79, 88, 103–4, 106–9, 117, 122, 122, 127–28, 132, 135–36, 141, 153, 175–76, 178, 186, 190, 216, 228, 235, 238, 242, 249, 257, 270, 274, 279, 286, 299–89
Deuteron-Isaiah 218
deuterocanonical 4
Deuteronomistic 21, 72, 110, 207
Deuteronomy 5, 7, 9, 19, 21, 27, 76, 110, 133, 148, 152, 188, 203, 271, 282, 295
Devil, the 292, 308
diaspora 223, 229, 231, 278
drunkenness 70, 91
dualism 114–15, 134

Eden 175, 219
Edomites 62
education 74–75
Eglon 143
Egypt 5, 14, 72, 80, 152, 179, 205–6, 230–31, 233, 253, 256, 263, 268, 281, 295, 297
Egyptian 179, 229–31, 265, 279, 281
Ehrman, Bart 130, 194
Elam 277
Eliab 291
Eliakim 277
Elihu 99, 118–21, 125, 127
Elijah 21, 108, 287

Subject Index

Elimelech 133, 138, 142, 146
Eliphaz 102, 108–10
Elephantine 263
emotions 23, 47, 53, 67–68, 71, 235
encouragement 53, 90, 107, 109, 301
English alphabet 217–18
Enoch 151
envy 46–47, 70, 83, 151, 189, 285
Ephraim 230
eros 148, 154, 165, 176, 180
eroticism 159, 178
Esarhaddon 268
Eshet Hayil 95, 145
exile 5, 16, 18, 20–21, 36, 65, 179, 207, 217, 229,
        243–44, 257, 259263, 276, 279, 286, 290,
        296
exiles 63–64, 207, 249, 256, 293
Exodus 4–5, 7, 9, 19, 100, 233, 236, 261, 271,
        297, 304
Exum, Cheryl 154, 158, 167, 175, 179, 304
Ezekiel 6–7, 9–10, 16, 18–19, 205–6, 241, 244, 295

faith 27, 47, 51–55, 56, 63, 76, 99, 195–96, 202,
        233, 235–36, 246, 281, 289, 305
faithful 25, 32–33, 95, 207, 224, 245, 257
faithfulness 23–24, 51, 57–58, 60, 66, 71, 116,
        141, 214, 257, 298
fame 236
family 27, 52, 60, 82, 96, 103, 118, 130–31, 138,
        146–47, 152, 192, 200, 223, 229, 233, 236,
        248, 299
famine 27, 109, 133, 137–38, 216, 231, 279, 281
Fear of the Lord 43, 73, 76–77, 81, 86, 92, 98,
        126, 188, 237
femininity 25–26, 31, 85, 95–96, 144, 159, 172,
        198, 209
feminist 166, 179
Fishbane, Michael 112
Form Criticism 36, 49
Fox, Michael 186
freewill 272
Friedman, Richard Elliot 100n3, 271n16, 217n17
friendship 91, 136, 150
Frodo 24, 136–37, 192
Fromm, Erich 38, 53

Gandalf 24
genealogy 151–52, 286, 290
genocide 84, 153, 27, 238
Gibeah 140
Gilead 164
gladness 57–58, 217, 219, 237–38, 294
gluttony 70
God ix, 1, 2–3, 5–6, 8,
God-breathed 8

Goldingay, John 3
Goldstein, Baruch 238
Goliath 235
gospels 2, 21
gossip 70, 91
Goswell, Greg 19n39, 241n3, 241n4, 241n5,
        257n18, 295n9, 295n10
Gounod, Charles 138
grammar 30, 55, 134, 156, 159, 216
grandiosity 79
Greece 251–54
greed 84–85
Greek 1–5, 8, 13, 28–29, 38, 67, 181, 221, 247,
        251, 253–54, 267, 272
Greeks 221
Greenberg, Dov 79n15, 239
Greene-McCreight, Kathryn 51–52
Gregorian calendar 14
grief 61, 103, 219
grieving 129, 219
guilt 60, 115, 137, 274
Gunkel, Hermann 36
gymnasium 205, 253

Habakkuk 7–9
Hadassah 223, 279
Haftarah 273
Hagbah 273
Haggadah 226
Haggai 7–9, 21, 268
Hagiographa 8
Haidt, Jonathan 180
hallelujah 67
Haman 224–27, 231–40, 256–67, 279–80
hamantaschen 239
Hamlet 29, 106–7
Hanukkah 253, 257, 283
happiness 6, 42–43, 67, 189, 190, 194–95, 213
Harding, Kathryn 159
harem 80, 84, 172, 222–23, 228, 287
Harris, Sam 205
    Rosh Hashanah 267, 272
Hawking, Stephen 197
    Eshet Hayil 85, 95, 145
Hazony, Yoram 18, 77, 224–25, 234–35, 281
Hebrew iii, iv, vii, ix, 1–4, 8–9, 11, 23, 21, 23,
        28–35, 38, 40–42, 46, 49–52, 42, 46,
        49–51, 54, 57, 60, 64, 67, 76, 85, 94–95,
        98, 100, 103–4, 121, 126–27, 133, 134,
        137, 138–39, 146–49, 154, 156–59, 172,
        174, 177–78, 181–82, 184–86, 194–95,
        206, 208–9, 242–43, 248, 253–54, 256,
        258, 261–62, 265–66, 270, 272–75, 279,
        283, 288, 298–99
Hebrews, book of 2–3

311

Subject Index

Hegai 224
Hellenization 253
hesed 23, 133–34, 141–42, 176, 214
hevel 98, 184–86
Hezekiah 61, 89, 205, 289, 291, 293–94
Hicks, John Mark 130n26
Hippolytus 179
Hitler, Adolf 225–26, 233, 239
Holocaust 22, 114, 207, 220, 225–26, 234
Hosea 6–7, 9, 295
Hubbard, Robert 148
hubris 66, 77, 84
Hymn 37, 41, 47–48, 107, 126, 219, 273

Iago 176
illness 49, 51–52, 197, 214, 219
inclusio 33, 47, 55, 65, 67–68, 96, 98, 120, 172,
   186, 191, 249, 258, 292, 295–96, 299
industriousness 71
intermarriage 282
Intertestamental literature 4, 82
Israel ix, 1–3, 5, 8–9, 14, 16, 21, 26–28, 38–40,
   45, 69, 72, 80, 95, 100, 132, 139–41,
   147–49, 151–52, 160, 173, 177–79, 182,
   197, 205–7, 211, 229, 263–73, 286–88,
   291–93, 295, 297
Israelites 27, 132, 152, 279, 294–95, 297

Jabez 288
Jacob 26, 81, 149, 211, 265
Jason (high priest) 253
Javert 101
Jeconiah 206, 244, 265
Jeduthun 291
Jefferson, Thomas 265
Jehoahaz 206
Jehoiachin 244
Jehoiakim 206, 244
Jehoshaphat 289, 294
Jehozadak 268
Jephthah 203
Jericho 295
Jeroboam 80, 289
Jerusalem 10, 16, 22, 37, 61–64, 72, 151, 154,
   157, 160–61, 163, 169–71, 174, 177,
   181–82, 205–7, 215–19, 223, 229, 242,
   244, 253, 262–64, 264, 266, 269–71,
   276–77, 279–80, 283–84, 290, 293–96,
   293, 295, 297
Jeshua 266–68, 272, 283
Jesus 2, 21, 33, 50, 60–51, 90, 92, 117–78, 151,
   186, 214, 234, 241, 251–52, 256, 263, 266,
   283
Jew (Jews, Jewish) ix,
   anti 2

Jezebel 135
Joab 80, 286
Jobes, Karen 238n23
Joseph 18, 227, 229–33, 255–57, 258, 278–79,
   281
Josiah 16, 206, 289, 294
joy 14, 23, 43, 55, 58–59, 62–63, 65, 67, 83, 88,
   108, 115–16, 120, 122, 128, 153, 167,
   193–96, 201, 216, 219, 235, 237–38, 267,
   275, 277, 290, 294, 298
Judah
   man 133–34, 148–49
   tribe/kingdom 21, 52, 69, 80, 149,
Judah 21, 52, 69, 80, 152, 205–8, 211, 215–16,
   223, 244, 249, 254, 256, 262, 265, 270,
   274, 280, 284–85, 287, 289, 293–94, 296
Judah
Judaism 2, 4, 8–10, 12, 14–16, 27, 42, 45, 91,
   100–101, 135, 178, 178, 183, 217, 239,
   241,, 249, 253, 263, 268, 275, 282, 288
judgment 66, 72, 91, 113, 181, 184, 194, 196,
   2013, 254, 270
Klitsner, Judy 26, 126
   justice 6, 70, 72, 74, 87, 94, 110, 189, 215–16,
   232
Kashrut 245
kindness 6, 23, 55, 94, 97, 132–34, 137, 140–42,
   144–45, 148, 150, 152–53, 175–76, 235,
   292
knowledge 73–75, 77, 86, 120–22, 125, 182, 188,
   190, 192, 194, 199, 245, 259
Kohelet
   association with Solomon 181–83
   autobiography 187–92
   book 11
   contradictions 197–98
   proverbs 198–202
   response to suffering 192–96
   thesis 83–87
Koptak, Paul 74, 84, 89, 95, 230
kosher (see Kashrut)
Kushner, Aviya 30

lament 23, 25, 37, 41, 49–50, 52, 56, 108, 130,
   206, 219, 235
Lamentations (book) vi, 6–7, 11–19, 22–23,
   24–26, 248–49, 257, 293–94, 298
   background history 204–6
   poetry 208–9
   theology 206–8
laughter 65, 111, 165, 199–200, 277
law
   Jewish ix, 225, 245, 256
   of Christ 2
   of gleaning 92

312

Subject Index

of levirate marriage 134, 138
of the redeemer 138
Persian 222, 225, 233, 251
Torah 4, 5, 8, 10, 16, 19–20, 30, 43–45, 203, 248, 266, 270–75, 282, 289, 293
laziness 93
Leah 148–49, 151
Lemuel 69, 85, 94–95, 98
Leningrad Codex 11–13, 27
Letter of Aristeas 4
Levenson, Jon 63, 223–24
leviathan 104–5, 124–25, 128
Levites 39, 140, 267, 272–74, 287–88, 290–94
Leviticus 4–5, 7, 9, 19, 139, 271
Lewis, C.S. 44–45, 79, 84, 119
Light, Alan 67
Linafelt, Tod 30, 133, 135, 146, 178
literature (the Bible as) 28–30, 34, 99, 108, 167, 214, 270
loneliness 21, 52, 136, 209–10, 220
longevity 72, 75, 185
Longman, Tremper III 74, 76–77, 113, 155, 164, 166, 172–73, 177–79, 182–83, 189, 203, 259
love
as kindness 134
for enemies 37, 90
for God 39, 76
for Jerusalem 61, 63
for money 188
for people 84, 114, 121, 136, 148–50
for wisdom 6, 74, 85, 88
of God 13–14, 66, 71, 214–15, 291
response to suffering 23–25, 235, 175–76, 298
romantic 26, see the chapter, "The Power of Love," 188, see also "eros"
without wisdom 75
lust 172n13
Martin Luther 237–338
LXX (see also "Septuagint") 4, 9
Lycanthropy 247
Lysimachus 263

Maccabean Revolt 57, 255
Maimonides 241
Man's Search for Meaning 24
Marduk 223, 261–62
marriage 152, 180, 282–83
Masoretic Text 147
Mattathias 253
matzah 239
McGuiggan, Jim 114
meaninglessness 185

Medes 248–49, 251, 255, 258
Media-Persia 251
Menelaus 253
Mesopotamia 223, 262
Messiah (oratorio by Handel) 67, 113
Messiah, the 2, 179, 252, 254, 265, 283
messianic 37–38, 60
misogyny 95, 145, 167, 198, 221–22, 231
Moabites 27, 133, 135, 138–39, 147, 149, 151–52, 282
money 42, 75, 92–93, 96–97, 130, 138, 185, 188, 190, 200, 281
monogamy 177, 223
Moore, Robert 84, 89
morality 45, 77, 143, 188, 202, 226
Mordecai (see the chapter "The Brave Hidden Jew")
Moses 4, 8, 11, 18, 28, 77, 108, 230–31, 233, 235–36, 266, 270–71, 278, 279, 282, 295, 297
music vii, 41, 43, 45, 47, 49, 51, 53, 55, 57, 59, 61, 63, 65, 67–68, 113, 136, 191, 205, 209, 217, 236, 246, 290–92, 297
Muslims 78, 238

Nabonidus 247, 261–63
Nabopolassar 206
Nabu-na'id 206
Nahum 7–9
Zeresh 239
Naomi (see the chapter "A Celebration of Kindness")
Narcissism 82, 184
Nebuchadnezzar 206, 244–49, 255, 257–59, 262
Neco 206
Nehemiah (see the chapter "Returning Home")
Nineveh 206

oppression 64, 102, 106, 153, 189, 219
Orpah 133–35
Othello 75, 176
Oznei Haman (see also Hamantaschen) 239

Parable of the Pharisee and Tax Collector 118
Parallelism 31–32, 34, 43, 45, 70, 73, 176
parashah 272–73
Passover 13–14, 217, 231, 269, 294
patriarchs 238
patriarchy 179
Paul (apostle) 2–3, 107, 167, 195–96, 275, 283
Pentateuch 3, 7–9, 13
Pentecost 13
Perez 134, 148–49, 151–52
Persepolis 266
perseverance 197, 215, 255

Subject Index

Persia/Persian 16, 182, 221, 223, 225, 231, 234, 237, 242, 248–49, 251–52, 254, 260–63, 265–66, 268, 274, 276, 279, 296

persistence 23–24, 283, 285, 298

personification 25, 85–86, 95–96, 113, 210, 214

Pharaoh 206, 226, 230–31, 236, 255, 265, 279, 281

Philistines 80

Pirkei Avot 78, 206

pleasure 94, 179, 183, 188, 193–96, 201

poetry 6, 15, 24, 28–35, 40, 43, 47, 52, 55, 57, 68–69, 103, 154, 156, 158, 163, 166–67, 179, 181, 201, 208–9, 211–13, 219, 242, 297

pogrom 220, 226

polyamory 165, 177

polygamy 27, 177

polytheism 72, 263, 282–83

pompousness 79

poor 42, 63, 92–94, 97, 116, 118, 138–39, 144, 146, 200, 218, 238, 277, 279, 281

pornography 116, 167

possessions 42, 188, 193

post-exilic 5, 16, 20–21, 229, 247, 260, 286–88, 291, 296

poverty 22, 26, 71, 92–94

Prager, Dennis 76–77, 180, 190, 235

praise/praise hymns/praising God 23, 27, 37, 41–42, 45, 47–48, 50–51, 57–60, 65–68, 98, 102, 127, 189, 258, 258–59, 267, 277, 278, 288, 291, 294

prayer 22–23, 42–44, 47, 50, 52–53, 60, 65, 152, 175, 177, 192, 196, 216, 218, 235, 242, 249, 257, 260, 275, 284–85, 288, 290, 294–98

pre-exilic 229, 288

Pride 79, 81, 83–84, 119, 131, 134, 236–37, 259

priests 100, 206, 210, 222, 216, 230, 244, 253, 267, 277, 287–89, 291–93

promiscuity 174

Protestant 4, 45, 282
    Iain Provan 179, 185–86

prudishness 174, 177, 188

Psalm Forms 36–38

Ptolemy 253

Purim 13, 15, 224, 231, 238–39, 257

Rachel 148–49, 151

Rachmaninoff 20

racism 84

racist 145, 152, 158

redaction 283, 287, 292

redemption 11, 24, 149, 238, 295

Rehoboam 5, 182, 188, 289

rejoicing 23, 34, 58–59, 89, 104, 107, 157, 193–96, 235, 237, 239, 275, 277

repentance 130, 11, 120, 125, 131, 242, 287, 289–90

reproof 78, 86, 109–10

restoration 5, 16, 21–22, 219, 266, 271, 277, 296

resurrection 192, 249

retribution 45, 47–49, 77, 110, 114–15, 127, 131–32, 152, 207–8

Revelation (book) 67, 101, 252

salvation 14, 50–51, 56, 59, 214–15, 235, 277

Samaritans 268

Samwise Gamgee 146–47

Sanballat 283–85

Sanhedrin 178

Sarna, Nahum 9, 42

satan 100–101

Saul 143, 152, 224, 287, 289

scapegoating 208

Segal, Benjamin 34, 38–39, 43–44, 54, 58, 154–56, 159, 161, 163–65, 168, 170, 172, 174, 177, 183–84, 192–93, 197, 203

Seleucid 253–54

self-centered 82

self-destructive 74, 88, 259

self-pity 127, 133–34

self-righteous 118–20, 125, 127

self-worth 180

selfish 102, 235

Semitic 226, 242

Sennacherib 205, 268

sensuality 157

Septuagint (see also LXX) 4, 38, 221, 272

sex 134, 143–44, 151, 157, 173, 176–77, 180, 188, 190, 223, 286

sexual 22, 45, 84, 140, 163, 167, 168–69, 176, 179

sexualized 143

Shabbat 272

Shakespeare 26, 28–29, 75, 99

Shavuot 13–14

sheol 50, 58, 85, 89, 113, 194

Sheshbazzar 265

shofar 266

Shulammite 172

Sifrei Emet 13

Sinai 3, 5, 14, 28, 186, 206

slandering 70, 91, 279–80

Smith, F. LaGard 70

Snodgrass, Klyne 27, 121

Solomon 5–6, 27, 39, 69, 71–72, 74–75, 80–81, 84, 94, 151, 154–55, 157, 172, 176–77, 182–83, 186, 202, 259, 277, 282–83, 287, 289–90, 292

Subject Index

sovereignty (God's) 217, 255, 257–58, 278–79
Sternberg, Meir 29
suffering 6, 11, 20, 22–25, 27, 42, 49, 51–53, 64,
    75, 102–3, 125–27, 129, 131–32, 134, 152,
    175–76, 189, 192–93, 196, 204, 206–9,
    211, 214, 216, 219–20, 234–35, 239, 283,
    285, 293–94, 298
superciliousness 79
supersessionism 2
synagogue 2, 60, 207, 224, 272, 275
Syro-Ephraimite Conflict 207

Tabernacles (Holiday) 267
Tamar (Genesis) 134, 144, 148–49, 151, 286
Targum 274
Telushkin, Joseph 78
temple 14, 16, 21, 39, 57, 60, 64, 72, 80–81, 151,
    177, 182–83, 215–17, 239, 241–42, 248,
    253, 257, 262–70, 276, 285, 287–88,
    290–94, 296
temptress 25, 156
terrorism 220
thanksgiving 37, 41, 53, 56, 59–60, 217, 219,
    277–78, 291
theodicy 114
theology 36, 51, 61, 107, 112, 113, 119, 130, 144,
    152, 178, 192, 195–97, 291
Tisha B'av 13–14, 205, 207, 220
Tishrei 266, 271–72
Tolkien, JRR 24, 136–37, 140

Torah (see also "law") 4, 8–11, 14, 18–20, 26, 37,
    41, 43–47, 63, 57, 74, 90, 97, 132, 138–39,
    148, 177, 194–95, 203, 225, 266, 270–76,
    282–83, 295–96, 298
transgression 44, 110, 112, 119, 211
Trei Asar 9, 19

unfaithfulness 293–94
Unleavened Bread (Holiday) 13, 269
Uriah 143, 272
Uzziah 287–88

vanity 184–88, 194–95, 197, 201–2
Vashti 222–34, 233
vengeance 208, 215, 253
violence 71–72, 115, 169, 175, 238

Walton, John 100, 123–24, 126, 129
Wiesel, Eli 115
wisdom 1, 6, 15, 23–25, 377, 45, 47–48, 69,
    71–79, 81, 83–89, 91–92, 95–98, 192,
    194–95, 197–200, 202, 210, 219, 240–31,
    235–37, 259, 270, 275, 292, 297–98, 301
worship 23, 24, 45, 60, 64, 68, 110, 246, 253, 256,
    261, 263, 268–69, 292, 294, 296, 298

Yom Kippur 266, 292
Yazony, Yoram 18, 77, 235, 281

Zion 25, 37, 41, 60–65, 155, 207, 209–12, 214–
    15, 218–19, 277–78, 293

Ancient Document Index

OLD TESTAMENT

Genesis

1:3	101, 104
1:4	104
1:26–28	65
2:7	68, 198n34
2:24	176–77
3:16	27, 174
4:1	148
4:7	174
6:3	48
12:3	230
15:1	49
18:27	126
32:28	26
37:2	229
37:24–25	227n14
37:28	229, 255
37–50	18n37
38	134, 144
39:2	255
39:3–4	229
39:6	229, 255
39:14–17	255
39:21–23	229
40:8	255
40–41	255
41:16	255
41:29	230
41:37–41	229
41:37–44	255
41:38	230
41:38–39	256
41:45	229, 255
41:51	230
41:52	230
42:8	230
43:32	255
44:18–34	230
45:4–13	229
47:20–21	281
50:20	229, 232

Exodus

2:10	231
2:19	231
2:22	231
19:1	14
19–24	2
20:17	46
31:18	8
34:1	8n19
34:27–28	8n19

Leviticus

11	245
18:24–28	207
19:9	92
23:15–16	14
23:22	92
23:23–25	266
23:39–43	14
25:24–25	138
25:47–50	138

Numbers

5:5–8	138
29:1–6	266

Deuteronomy

6:2	76
6:5	76
9:10	8
14	245
16:13–15	14
17:18	5
19:6–13	138
22:6–7	90
23:3	133
23:3–6	27, 152
25:4	90

317

Ancient Document Index

Deuteronomy (cont.)

25:5–10	138
25:7–10	147–48
30:11–20	88
30:16–18	110
34:10	271

Joshua

1:7–8	41

Judges

2:10	132
3:24	143
19	140
21:25	117, 132

1 Samuel

10:2	148
15	224
16:11	54
16:21	286
17:34–35	54
17:37	235
22:3–4	152n23
24:3	143
24:8	224
25:23–35	80

2 Samuel

6:16	39
7	52, 61, 287
8:2	152n23
11:8	143
11–12	39n9
12	35
12:1–13	80
14:4–21	80
14:25	25n8
19:4–8	80
22	39
23:1	39
24	292

1 Kings

1:16	224
1–2	71
3	71–72
3:3	80
3:5	71
3:6–9	71
3:16–28	72

3:28	72
4:21	80
4:26	81
4:29	72
4:30	72
4:32	72
4:33–34	74
4:34	72
5:7	80
8	182n5, 288
8:24	80
9:4–5	80
10:6	72
10:14–22	81
11	72
11:3	27, 94, 155
11:4–6	80
11:40	80
12	188
18–20	293
19:2	135

2 Kings

1:8	21n2
6:24–31	216
8:10–11	268
17:7–23	72
18:5	69
22:11	274
23	294

Isaiah

5:21	118
7	207
7:6	207
9	207
11	207
22:13	195
27:1	124
40:1–2	218
41:2–4	264
41:25	264
44	264
44:24	264
44:28	264
45	264
45:1–4	264–65
45:15	232
49:14	218
49:15	218
50:6	214
51:3	219
52:9	219

Ancient Document Index

52:13—53:12	214
53	214
53:7	214
54:11	219

Jeremiah

20:14–18	214
20:15	103
25:11–12	263n4
26:18	16n34
29:10	263n4
31:15	148
31:31–34	2

Amos

5:14	111

Haggai

2:3–9	268

Zechariah

1:12	263n4
3	101n6

Malachi

4:4 [3:22]	41
4:5 [3:25]	21
4:6 [3:26]	21

Psalms

1	46–47, 52, 63, 85, 110, 113, 206, 296
1:1	41–43
1:1–2	194
1:2	43
1:3	45
1:6	45
2	52, 60, 207
2:12	42
3	30
3:5 [6]	49
3:8 [9]	49
5	39
6	37n2, 56
6:1–2 [2–3]	49
6:3 [4]	49
6:6 [7]	50
8	65
8:1 [2]	65
8:9 [1]	65
8:3–4 [4–5]	66

8:4 [5]	112
9	38, 208
10	38, 208
10:1	50
12:1	31–32
13	53
13:1–2	49
14:1	77
18	39
18:27	32
19	43–45
19:10 [11]	45
22	50, 55
22:1 [2]	50, 117
23	34n9, 38, 40, 50, 53–56, 156, 205
23:2	158
23:3	149, 210
23:4	235
24:1–2	66
26:7	59
27	38, 55–56
27:1	56, 235
27:2	56
27:4	56
27:6	56
27:7–10	56
29:11	299
30	56–59, 150
30:9 [10]	57
30:11 [12]	150, 217, 238
30:11–12	57
31:1–5 [2–6]	33
31:3 [4]	34n9
32	37n2
32:1 [2]	42
33:8–9	66
36:5–6 [6–7]	66
36:7 [8]	141
38	37n2
39	48–49
39:4–5 [5–6]	185
39:4–6 [5–7]	48
39:5 [6]	185
41	63
41:1 [2]	42
44:11 [12]	214
44:22 [23]	214
45	60
46	61, 63
46:1–3 [2–4]	61
46:4 [5]	61
46:5–7 [6–8]	61
46:4–8 [5–9]	62

319

Ancient Document Index

Psalms (cont.)

46:10 [11]	61
46–48	61, 63, 207
50:2	171
50:23	59
51	37n2, 39n9, 40
51:18–20 [20–21]	39n9
53:1	77
57:1 [2]	141
58:6–9 [7–10]	64
61:4 [5]	141
68:30 [31]	59
72	60, 69n1
73	45–37, 267
73:1	45
73:2–3	45
73:4	47
73:11	47
73:16	46–47
73:19	47
74:13–15	124
82	226
84:4 [5]	42
88	50–52, 56
88:1 [2]	50
88:3–5 [4–6]	50
88:6–8 [7–9]	51
88:9 [10]	52
88:10–12 [11–13]	51, 57
88:13 [14]	52
88:14–18 [15–19]	51–52
89	52, 207
90	47–49
90:1	47
90:2	47
90:4	48
90:7	48
90:10	48
90:11	48
90:12	75
90:13	115
90:15	115
91:4	141
95:2	59
93–99	61
96	291
96:7	32
100	59–60, 278
102	37n2
104	66, 87
104:26	125
104:27–28	66
105	291
106	291
106:1	267
107:1	267
107:22	59
109:10	63
111:10	76
116:17	59
118:1	267
118:29	267
119	45, 208–9
119:99	78
119:103	45
120–34	64
121:1–2	64
122:1	64
122:6	64
125	64
126:1–3	277
126:1–6	65
127	69n1
130	37n2
132:13–14	65
132:13–16	277
133:1–3	278
134:1–3	278
136	267, 278
137	62
137:2	217
142	39
143	37n2
145	42
145:15	32
145:15–16	66
146–50	67
147:3	110
147:7	59
149:3	39
150	67–68, 278

Proverbs

1:2–6	72–73
1:7	73
1:8	84
1:10–19	85
1:20–33	86
1:29	76
1–9	67–68
2:5	76
2:6	73
2:10	73
2:16	84
3:7	76
3:13	95–96
3:15	95

320

4:5–9 74–75
4:7 75
5 84
5 84
6:6–11 93
6:20 84
7 84
8:1–21 86
8:15–21 87
8:22–31 87
8:32–36 88
9:4–6 88
9:13–18 88–89
9:8 78
9:10 73
10:1—22:16 69
10:4 93
10:12 75
10:27 76
11:2 81
11:24–26 92
11:28 92
12:10 90
12:15 77
12:16 91
12:25 90
13:14 75
13:23 92
14:6 73
14:12 79
14:23 93
14:27 76
14:30 83
14:31 92
15:1 90
15:3 77
15:16 92
15:33 76
16:5 81
16:16 75
16:25 79
18:12 81
18:17 91
19:2 75
19:21 77
20:1 91
20:4 93
20:6 95
22:4 81
22:7 93
22:12 77
22:17—24:22 69
22:24–25 91
24:13–14 75
24:17–18 89
25:2 74
25:17 90
25:21–22 90
25–29 69
28:6 92
28:11 92
29:3 85
29:23 81
30 69
30:7–9 93
31 69, 85, 93–94
31:1 85
31:2–9 93–94
31:10 94–96
31:10–31 93

Job

1:1 100, 109, 120
1:2–3 100
1:3 100, 130
1:7 131
1:8 101, 120
1:16 114
1:21 101, 189
1:22 101
1–2 99
2 127
2:3 102, 109, 120
2:4 121
2:4–5 102
2:7 102
2:8 102, 126
2:9 102, 239
2:10 102, 127
2:12 103
2:13 103
3 99, 127
3:1 103
3:1–26 214
3:3 103
3:4 104, 128
3:5–6 104
3:7–8 104
3:8 124, 128
3:9 105, 128
3:10 105, 128
3:11 128
3:11–19 105
3:20 128, 150
3:20–21 128
3:20–26 106
3:26 106

Ancient Document Index

Job (cont.)

4:2	109
4:4	109
4:5	109
4:5	109
4:6	109
4:7–11	109
4–27	99
5:17	110
5:17–27	109–10
5:18	110
6:10	111
6:28–30	111
7:1	112
7:5–6	112
7:17–18	112
7:19–21	112
8:3–7	110–11
8:5–6	131
8:20–22	111
9:15	113
9:22	112
9:23	112
11:13–20	111
13:4	127
19:25	113
29:13	115
29:15–16	116
24:19–25	113
28	99
28:20–28	126
29–31	99, 120
30:1	116
30:9	116
30:10	116
30:11–15	116
30:19	126
30:19–23	117
31:1	116
31:9–12	116
31:22	116
31:35–40	117
32:1	117–18
32:2–5	118
32–35	120
32–37	99
33:9–18	119
33:26	120
33:30	120
34:7–9	120
35:16	120
37:24	120
38	127
38:2	128

38:2–3	121
38:3	128
38:4–7	122
38:7	128
38:8	122
38:12	128
38:16–18	122
38:17	128
38:19	128
38:24	128
38:29	128
38:40	128
38–41	99
39:1	122
39:9	122
39:13–18	128–29
39:19–20	123
39:19–24	129
39:26	123
39:30	128
40:1	123
40:4–5	123
40:7	123
40:7–4	123
40:15–18	124
40:24	124
41:1 [40:25]	124, 128
41:2 [40:26]	125
41:3 [40:27]	125
41:4 [40:28]	125
41:5 [40:29]	125
41:33–34 [25–26]	125
42	99
42:2–6	126
42:6	126, 130
42:7	127, 130
42:10	130
42:11	115
42:12	130
42:15	139
42:16–17	130

Ruth

1	139
1:1	132–33
1:3	133
1:8	142
1:8–9	133
1:10	134
1:11–13	134
1:14	135
1:15	135
1:16–17	135, 144

Ancient Document Index

1:18	137	2:2	160
1:19	137	2:3	160
1:20–21	137	2:3–6	160
1:22	14, 138	2:5	169
2	139, 143–44	2:7	160
2:1	145	2:8–9	161
2:2	139, 141	2:10–15	161–62
2:4	139	2:11	14
2:5	139	2:16	171
2:7	139	2:16–17	162
2:8–9	140, 142	3	172
2:10	140–41	3:1–2	162
2:11–12	141	3:3	163, 168
2:12	144	3:4	163
2:13	141	3:5	163
2:15–16	142	3:7	155, 172
2:19	142	4	163, 170
2:20	142	4:1	163–64
2:21	142	4:2	164
2:22	142	4:3	156, 164
3	143	4:4	164
3:1–4	143	4:5	165
3:5	144	4:6	165, 168
3:7	144	4:9–11	165
3:9	144	4:10	176
3:10–13	144	4:12	166
3:11	145, 145n15	4:12–15	166
3:18	146	4:14	168
4	146	4:16	166
4:1	146	5	163, 172
4:3–4	146	5:1	167–68
4:5	147	5:2	167–68
4:7	147	5:3	168
4:11–12	148	5:4	168
4:14–17	149	5:5	168
4:15	210–11	5:7	168, 175, 210
		5:8	169
		5:9	169

The Song of Songs

		5:10–16	169–70
1:2	157, 176	5:14	173
1:2–4	156	6:1	170
1:3	161	6:2	170
1:4	154–55, 157, 161, 163	6:3	171
1:5	25, 155, 158, 164	6:4	171
1:5–6	157	6:5	171
1:6	177	6:8–10	171–72
1:7	155, 158–59	6:13 [7:1]	172
1:8	169	7:1 [2]	172
1:9	164	7:2 [3]	172
1:12	155	7:4 [5]	173
1:13	168	7:5 [6]	173
1:15	159	7:6–9 [7–10]	173
1:16	159	7:8 [9]	156
2:1	160	7:9 [10]	173

Ancient Document Index

The Song of Songs (cont.)

7:10 [11]	27, 174
8:1–4	174
8:6–7	175
8:8–9	158
8:10	175
8:11	155
8:11–12	176–77
8:12	155

Ecclesiastes

1:1	181
1:2	183–84, 186
1:3	185
1:4	186
1:4–11	189–90
1:5–7	185
1:9	181n2
1:12	182
1:13	187
1:15	186
1:18	188, 199
2	195
2:1	194
2:1–11	188
2:13	187
2:16	188
2:17	22, 189
2:24–25	193
3:1	191
3:2–8	186, 191
3:9	185
3:11	192
3:12–13	193
3:17	203
3:19	187
3:20	187
3:21	195, 198
3:22	193
4:1–3	189
4:2–3	197
4:9–12	137
5:7	203
5:10	188
5:15–16	189
5:18–20	193
6:1–2	188
6:3	197
7	198
7:2–4	199
7:15–17	199
7:26–28	26
7:26–29	198

8:1	200
8:5	203
8:15	193
8:16–17	192
9:4	197
9:7–10	194
9:9	198
9:11–12	200
9:13–18	200
10:18	199
10:19	200
11:1	200, 201n35
11:6	200
11:8–10	194
11:10	185–86
12:1	196
12:1–7	201
12:7	198
12:8	182, 202
12:9	202
12:9–10	203
12:9–12	182
12:10	202
12:11–12	202
12:12	183
12:13–14	187, 203

Lamentations

1	209
1:1	209
1:2	210
1:4	210
1:8–9	210
1:9	210–11
1:10	210
1:11	210–11
1:12	211
1:14	211
1:16	210
1:17	211
1:18	211
1:20	210–11
1:21	210–11
1:22	210
1–5	208
2	209
2:1–3	211
2:3–5	212
2:6	212
2:7	212
2:8	212
2:10	212
2:11	212

Ancient Document Index

2:13	212	3:12	256
2:14	212	3:13	227
2:15–16	212	3:15	227
2:19	212	4:1–3	227
2:20	212	4:13–14	228
3	206, 209	4:14	232
3:1–26	214	4:15	224n5
3:21	214	4:16	233
3:25–27	214	4:17	233
3:28–30	215	5:1	233
3:31	215	5:2	234
3:40–42	215	5:9	236
3:45	215	5:12–13	236
3:48	215	5:14	232, 239
3:66	215	6:1	232
4	209	6:2	232
4:1	215	6:6–11	232
4:4	215	6:7–9	236
4:10	216	6:12	239
4:11	216	6:13	240, 256–57
4:13	216	7:3–4	234
4:14	216	7:6	234
4:17	216	7:9–10	232
4:20	216	8:1–2	236
4:21–22	216	8:7–8	229
4:22	216	8:11	238
5	209	8:15–17	237
5:1	216, 219	8:17	285
5:15	216, 238	9:10	238
5:19	217	9:15–16	238
5:20	217–18	9:16–19	238
5:21	217–18	9:20–32	13
5:22	217–18	9:22	238
		10:1–3	229–30
		10:3	256

Esther

1:1	222
1:8	222
1:11	222
1:19	251
1:22	222
2:5	223–24
2:7	139, 223, 229, 256
2:8	229
2:9	229
2:10	223–24
2:15	224, 224n5, 229
2:17	229, 256
2:19–23	224
2:20	224
3:4	225
3:6	225, 231
3:8	256, 280
3:8–9	225

Daniel

1:1	244
1:2	244, 257
1:3	255
1:3–4	244
1:4	255–56, 259
1:5	245
1:6	244
1:7	244, 255–56
1:8	245
1:9	257, 259
1:17	257
1:20	259
1–6	242–43
2	249–50
2:4	242
2:12–14	256

325

Ancient Document Index

Daniel (cont.)

2:18	256
2:19	257
2:20–23	259
2:24	256
2:25	255
2:27–28	255
2:30	259
2:32–33	249
2:34–35	249
2:37–44	250
2:46	256
2:48	256
2:48–49	245
3:8	255
3:16–18	246, 257
3:26	257
3:27	246
3:28–29	258
3:30	246
4	247, 258
4:2	257
4:6	256
4:9	256
4:15–16	247
4:18	256
4:34–35	258
4:37	259
5:1	247
5:5	248
5:7–8	256
5:11	259
5:13	247
5:14	259
5:15	256
5:18	247, 257
5:21	257
5:22	247
5:24–28	248
5:25–28	273n22
5:28	251
5:29	246, 255
6:3	248
6:4	257
6:5	248–49, 255–56
6:8	251
6:12	251
6:13	249
6:16	249
6:18	251
6:26–27	258
6:28	246, 249
7	249–50, 254
7:1	257
7:3–8	250
7:11–12	250
7:13	252
7:13–14	251–52
7:17	254
7:17–18	250, 254
7:21–22	254
7–12	242–43, 253
8	252
8:1	242
9	257, 260, 290, 295
9:2	16
9:5	290
9:25–26	253–54
9:27	252
11:31	252
12:1	258
12:11	252

Ezra

1:1	261, 263n4
1:2–4	262
1:7	265
1:8	265, 265,n8
1:11	265n8
1–6	266, 280
2	266
2:41	267
3	272
3:1	271
3:2	266
3:3	266
3:4	266, 274–75
3:10	267
3:11	267
3:12–13	267
4	280
4:3	268–69
4:5	269
4:6	280
4:7	274, 280
4:10–16	280
4:21–22	280
5:14	265n8
5:16	265n8
6:3–5	262
6:11–12	269
6:22	269
7	269
7:6	270
7:10	270, 273n21, 296
7:11	270
7:12	270

Ancient Document Index

7:14	270
7:21	270
7:25-26	720
7-10	266
8:22	276
9	290
9:3	282
9:6	290
10:1	281
10:10-11	281-82

Nehemiah

1	280, 290
1:3	276
1:6	290
1-7	266
2:6	284
2:8	284
2:9	276, 284
2:10	283
2:19	284
2:20	284
3:3	276
3:6	276
3:13	276
3:14	276
4:1-3 [3:33-35]	284
4:10-13 [4-7]	284
4:14 [8]	284
5:7-11	281
5:15	281
6:2	284
6:5-7	285
6:8	285
6:12-13	285
6:12-13	285
6:16	285
8	271
8:1	271
8:1-3	271
8:4	272
8:4-8	272
8:7-8	273
8:8	274
8:9	276
8:9-12	274
8:13	296
8:17-18	275
8-10	266
9	290
11-12	266
12:40-43	277
12:45-46	277

13	266
13:1-3	282
13:24	273-74
13:25	282
13:26	282
13:31	276

1 Chronicles

2:4	152
4:10	288
6:32	290
10:13-14	289
13:3	289
15:13	289
16	291
16:4-7	291
16:34	291
16:41	291
21	292
22	287
22-29	292
22:1	292
22:2-19	292
22:19	289
23	291
23:1	292
23:2-32	292
24:1-19	292
24:20—26:32	292
25	291
27:1-34	292
28:1—29:30	292
28:8	289
28:9	289
29	287
29:10-13	288
29:25	291

2 Chronicles

5	287
5:13	291
5:13-14	291
6	288
6:36-39	290
7	287
7:3	291
7:6	291, 294
7:14	288
11	287
11:16	289
12:14	289
14:4	289
15:2-7	293

327

Ancient Document Index

2 Chronicles (cont.)

15:12–13	289
16:12	289
17	287
17:3–4	289
19	287
20:3–4	289
20:5–12	289
20:18	294
20:21	291
24	287
25:35	16
26:18	288
26:21	288
29:5–11	293
29:25	291
29:28–30	294
30	287
30:18–19	294
30:20	294
30:27	294
31:21	289
34:3	289
33:1–9	289
33:12–13	289–90
35	294
36:22–23	296

INTERTESTAMENTAL WRITINGS

1 Maccabees

6:7	253

Sirach

Prologue	1, 10

NEW TESTAMENT

Matthew

5:44	37, 90
11:14	21n2
24	252
24:15	241, 252
27:46	50

Mark

1:6	21n2

13	252
13:14	252
15:34	50

Luke

1:17	21n2
18:9	118
18:13	118
18:14	118
22:20	2
23:46	33

John

1:21	21n2
1:23	21n2
19:37	254

Acts

4:23–31	60
20:35	92

Romans

1:21–22	122
5:3	107
8:18	107
12:15	103
15:27	275

1 Corinthians

7:4	167
7:12–16	283
15:3	3
15:32	195

2 Corinthians

3:14	3
4:18	107
6:14	283

Philippians

1:23	107
2:14	107

1 Thessalonians

4:18	107

2 Timothy

3:16	8

Ancient Document Index

Hebrews

1:8–9	60
8:7	3
9:1	3
9:15	3
9:18	3

James

1:2	108
5:11	108

Revelation

1:7	254
12:9	101
17	252

RABBINIC WRITINGS

Talmud

Baba Batra 14b—15a	10

Megillah

14a	214n2

Pirkei Avot

4:1	78

Printed in the USA
CPSIA information can be obtained
at www.ICGtesting.com
LVHW080838211023
761653LV00004B/161